Can This Marriage Be Saved?

Can This Marriage Be Saved?

Real-Life Cases from the
Most Popular, Most Enduring Women's
Magazine Feature in the World

By the Editors of
LADIES' HOME JOURNAL®
with Margery D. Rosen

WORKMAN PUBLISHING, NEW YORK

Library of Congress Cataloging-in-Publication Data

Can this marriage be saved? : real life cases from the most popular,
enduring women's magazine feature in the world / from the editors
of Ladies' home journal.

p. cm.
ISBN 1-56305-628-3 (pbk.)
1. Marriage—United States.   2. Married couples—United
States-Psychology.   3. Man-woman relationships—United States.
I. Ladies home journal.

HQ536.C344 1944   94-4541
306.81'0973—dc20   CIP

Front cover photos courtesy of Comstock

Workman books are available at special discount when purchased
in bulk for special sales promotions as well as fundraising or educational use. Special book excerpts or editions can also be created to
specification. For details, contact the Special Sales Director at the
address below.

Workman Publishing Company, Inc.
708 Broadway
New York, NY 10003

First printing
Manufactured in the United States

Contents

Part 5

Part 6

Part 7

FOREWORD

——✦——

When Myrna Blyth, the editor-in-chief and publishing director of *Ladies' Home Journal,* asked me to write a foreword to this wonderful book, I was honored. The column "Can This Marriage Be Saved?" not only is the most popular women's magazine column of all time, but it has also served to legitimize marital counseling in this country.

There is no getting around the fact that every marriage faces problems. Over the years, in my private practice of clinical psychology as well as in listening to people's discussions on radio and television, I have been stunned by how often the theme of marital conflict recurs. However, many couples can prevent their problems from reaching destructive proportions by learning to be honest about what they are feeling, thereby avoiding years of resentment that eventually can spill over into scalding words and deeds. Besides telling your partner what you feel, it is essential that you listen to what he or she says without shutting out what you would rather not hear—a difficult task, it is true, but well worth the effort.

There is something about the institution of marriage that propels us to give up the caring self of courtship to become a serious role-taking husband or wife, too often putting the most creative, playful parts of ourselves elsewhere. It is as if the top of the wedding cake, the layer with the miniature bride and groom, truly represents the couple. Put under a glass dome at the moment of marriage, they stiffly stand there with air removed and no way to breathe and grow.

Soon love is felt to be an obligation, something we're supposed to do, as opposed to the voluntary offering it once was. It is this change, unconscious though it may be, that begins to take the life force away from the individuals making up the couple and tries to meld them into an amorphous "we." The "we" stands for a person, not yet defined, but becomes the center of a boxing ring where the partners battle for whom the "we" more closely represents.

Although we would all probably agree that discussions about who does what after marriage and how decisions will be made should occur before the wedding, couples rarely deal with all these issues before a conflict arises. Many of us naively assume that things will naturally work themselves out.

And so the battles start. At first they may be small, ending with a kiss and lovemaking. But if guidelines for solutions are not in place, a distancing occurs. At first so small as not to be noticed, the rift grows larger and the lover begins to be seen as someone who cannot be told all, for fear of judgment and other consequences. Finding fault and blame becomes the purpose of an argument—a device that only guarantees the maintenance of the status quo.

CAN THIS MARRIAGE BE SAVED? offers an opportunity to do something else. Not only does this book offer a reflection of the problems any of us might face in a marriage, but it also give us an opportunity to see the problem from our partner's point of view, providing a much-needed insight into his or her world. When we are defending ourselves to our spouse, we are too often incapable of stepping back and seeing that we are limited in our understanding of the issues because of our own personal agenda. Most of us would choose not to admit it, but in truth, we tend to bend things so that we're seen in a good light.

This book allows you to see both sides of an issue without being personally involved. Exercises allow couples to examine marital problems through role-playing, even taking the "other side" to see how it feels. The more you are able to put yourself into these roles, the better your chance to experience the conflict without any of the resultant pain and destructiveness to the relationship. Playing out the parts with your loved one will give you both great insight into how similar events might be played out in your own relationship.

Research suggests that the first argument a couple has contains the seeds of all their succeeding arguments. Wouldn't it be wonderful if we could learn the techniques of communication by practicing them while using the real-life situations of others? This book helps you do that.

CAN THIS MARRIAGE BE SAVED? has the potential to lead you along the path of marital enlightenment. As I have learned from my clients, so too can you learn from the people who have shared with you the most intimate details of their lives. They offer you a great gift: the ability to love wisely. Accept it.

Sonya Friedman, Ph.D.
Author of *Secret Loves: Women with Two Lives*

CAN THIS MARRIAGE BE SAVED?

—◆—

WHEN "CAN THIS MARRIAGE BE SAVED?" debuted in the January 1953 issue of *Ladies' Home Journal,* it immediately captured the attention of millions of readers. Forty years later, that fascination endures—and the reason is simple: This column is about real people in real-life dramas.

It zeroes in on the problems every one of us faces in marriage—and offers practical ways to solve them.

Over the years, "Can This Marriage Be Saved?" has provided a window into other people's lives: We have seen good relationships strengthened, bad ones healed. In fact, a close study shows how accurately the column has reflected social revolutions—and evolutions.

Back in the love-honor-and-obey fifties, most wives stayed home. Their husbands were the undisputed breadwinners—and the fact that they controlled the purse strings also meant that they wielded most of the decision-making power in the family, too.

1

As women moved into the work force in increasing numbers, couples chronicled in "Can This Marriage Be Saved?" also wrestled with the difficulties inherent in sustaining a marriage and raising a family when both parents' paychecks were needed to stay afloat financially, or when stressed-to-the-limit wives realized they couldn't be all things to all people. Couples argued, some loudly and bitterly, others with icy silences, each locked in a cycle of blame that made them feel like adversaries in a never-ending war.

Certainly a large part of the column's appeal lies in the vicarious thrill we get from reading the sometimes Byzantine sagas of other people's intimate lives. We're all a bit curious to find out what's really happening behind someone else's bedroom door. And we're compelled to keep on reading because of the drama of the unfolding story and of how this shattered marriage can possibly be made whole again.

Another reason "Can This Marriage Be Saved?" is as popular and vital today as it was forty years ago is that millions of readers see themselves and their marriages reflected in its pages. The column's format—first her turn, then his—shows readers, simply and dramatically, that there are two sides to an issue, two ways of observing a problem; and the counselor's section shows that both may be valid—but a couple must learn to compromise.

Each story told here is true. Each husband and wife is interviewed by the *Journal,* and the words we read are the words they used. Readers can't help getting caught up in the drama: "How could he do that to her?" they think as they read the wife's tale. "No wonder," they say after hearing the husband's version. Rarely do readers have an opportunity to feel someone else's anxiety, frustration, and pain so keenly. And as they discover how the counselor guided troubled couples toward peaceful solutions, they find clues to resolving their own domestic dilemmas.

But perhaps the most astonishing lesson to be learned from this column is that while the specifics change from month to month and from decade to decade, the underlying issues that can shake the foundation of a marriage remain fundamentally the same. Particularly intriguing are the ways in which these problems repeat, time and again, from one generation to the next. Therapists know that couples often replay—unconsciously—the experiences, attitudes, and patterns of behavior they witnessed in childhood. And that means the model for our marriage is our parents' marriage. Troubled though it may be, it is really our only model. We only see as much of all other marriages as polite society permits.

Because of their early experiences, couples also bring to marriage a hidden agenda—expectations they are hardly aware of—for how a spouse should think, speak, and act. And when a spouse doesn't follow that script, when his or her expectations are different from your own, it can trigger a host of problems. In fact, *Can This Marriage Be Saved?* shows us seven basic areas of conflict that can doom a relationship.

The first, *trust,* is the cornerstone of a marriage. Many couples mistakenly believe that a trusting relationship refers only to sexual fidelity, but that's just a small part of it. Certainly a spouse's unfaithfulness is deeply wounding and many feel so betrayed when they discover a partner's affair that they are unable to forgive, forget, and move on.

But as *Can This Marriage Be Saved?* shows us, the concept of trust actually goes far beyond the bedroom. The simple, basic belief that a partner is true, honest, and reliable is fundamental to a healthy relationship. Where there is trust, partners feel nourished and comforted. Self-esteem and confidence is high and the ability to weather adversity strong. Indeed, over the lifetime of a marriage, trust will be the single most important marker of deep and lasting satisfaction. Can you trust your partner to support and encourage your dreams and goals? Can you count on him not to humiliate or embarrass you, or reveal your weaknesses and fears in front of others? In a trusting marriage, you feel safe enough to admit and face your vulnerabilities, because you know your partner will always be there for you.

If trust is the cornerstone of marriage, then *communication* is the cement that binds it in place. Couples must be able to express feelings, clearly and specifically. That means sharing hopes, dreams, successes, and failures—as well as discussing how to discipline the children or whose turn it is to walk the dog. It also means banishing the mind-reader syndrome, to which many couples, newlywed or long married, unwittingly fall victim. The belief that "if he [she] really loved me, he [she] would know what I feel and what I need" is bound to lead to misinterpretation and misread signals—and myriad problems. But just because a couple are talking doesn't mean they're communicating; the way something is said, the tone of voice as well as body language, speaks volumes, too.

While disagreements and conflict are unavoidable in marriage, how spouses deal with and manage *anger*—their own as well as their partner's—is another minefield. Some people don't even realize they are angry. Others know they are, but are unaware of what they are really fighting about. The wife who finds herself enraged at the fortune her husband spent on a new stereo may not be upset about money; she may unconsciously feel hurt and resentful that he has time for his friends but none for her. The husband who complains that his wife's new job is causing her to neglect the children may fear that he will be ignored. Locked in a cycle of anger and blame, some couples are unable to relate to each other in any other way.

The key to managing anger lies in unearthing buried hurts and resentments and dealing with them calmly instead of denying them, silently acquiescing, blaming a partner, or distancing oneself emotionally.

Of course, fueling many a battle is the unspoken *struggle for power* and control in a relationship. A marriage is supposed to be a partnership. Husbands and wives should feel accepted and loved, not judged, criticized, or belittled. If decision making is always lopsided, if one voice is always heard and one partner forever lives in the shadow of the other, resentment brews and spills over into other aspects of married life. Life becomes a constant competition. The outcome of each match is duly noted and the stakes are high. Through *Can This Marriage Be Saved?*, we witness how couples break the power stalemate, how they learn to recognize and reward each other's stengths instead of feeling threatened by them.

Perhaps the most obvious battle for power is over *money* matters. Rare is the couple that doesn't fight about finances. Yet, while they may be arguing over whether to put their savings in a joint or separate account, or why money was spent on things they don't really need, money is a symbol—for power as well as for love. Since money means different things to different people, we each have our own ideas about saving and spending it. A husband may insist on controlling the family finances because that's the only way he can feel like a man. A wife may splurge on a designer suit to get back at a domineering or neglectful husband. *Can This Marriage Be Saved?* shows how couples can reconcile the underlying issues that money matters represent.

Battles over *sex* are as charged as battles over money. Whether it's how often, how sensitively, who initiates, and who backs away, a couple's sex life is invariably affected by what else is going on in the marriage. When husbands and wives complain that sexual intimacy is less than satisfying, it invariably signals that some essential need somewhere in the marriage is not being met. Where once there was passion, now there is routine—or nothing at all. Or perhaps sex has become the weapon with which one partner punishes the other—only to ultimately destroy the marriage.

And last, conflicts can of course be triggered by *others*—in-laws, children, ex-spouses, stepchildren—if that relationship is not firmly grounded. Couples can work as a team to deal with insidious outside influences before they tear the marriage apart.

Of course, understanding where the potential for marital problems lies is not the same as knowing how to solve them. Couples also need both practical advice and skills to defuse hostility and resolve differences. This book highlights the best of forty years of insights, techniques, and practical advice to make sure husbands and wives don't behave in old, predictable, destructive ways and that they begin, instead, to build a healthy, loving relationship.

The one thing each of the couples in the stories you are about to read have in common is their willingness to try. They made a commitment—to themselves and to each other—to make their marriage a priority. It takes courage to face problems in a marriage head on, and deciding that it's time to consult a professional therapist is a scary step.

But what makes working on a marriage much less frightening is the realization that although people cannot and never will have the power to change their mates, they do have the power to change themselves. *Can This Marriage Be Saved?* proves that each partner in a marriage can transform his or her own actions and reactions. They can make their own choices. And that brings them a giant step closer to where they both want to be.

PART 1

TRUST: THE CORNERSTONE OF MARRIAGE

—⁘—

TRUST IS THE CORNERSTONE OF A HEALTHY, deeply satisfying marriage. In a trusting relationship, partners are, quite simply, honest with each other. Their words and actions are not shadowed by deceit; they don't sacrifice a partner's needs for their own, or pursue their own goals at the expense of a mate's. Most important, they make a total commitment to each other, a commitment that helps each feel emotionally nourished, comforted, and supported. In fact, over the lifetime of a marriage, couples consistently report that trust is the single most important marker of lasting happiness.

Often, couples become stuck on the most obvious violation of trust—infidelity—and that error in itself can cause them to overlook or fail to recognize other problems in their marriage. However, as painful as it is, a marital affair, as we shall see in a later chapter, is usually a symptom of other serious problems, often unconscious or unacknowledged, in a marriage. The concept of trust, however, actually goes far beyond the sexual fidelity into every aspect of a couple's day-to-day life.

In a trusting relationship, husbands and wives make the marriage a priority. Despite the demands and pressures from children, work, community, or other family responsibilities, the relationship comes first. And that means carving out specific times to do things together, to finish a conversation uninterrupted—even scheduling sex. It also means being able to count on your partner to work through problems, in spite of the difficulties or disappointments that are inevitable in every relationship.

In a trusting marriage, partners are also empathic. Empathy means being able to put yourself in another's shoes, to see a situation from your mate's point of view. It's not easy to be empathic, but it is essential to sustaining trust. A trusting partner encourages and supports a mate's goals and dreams; she shows genuine happiness for his joys and successes, concern for his sorrows or setbacks. He respects and accepts a spouse's anxiety, anger, or fear—without judgment, condemnation, or disparagement—even if he doesn't agree. The partner who always dismisses or ignores a spouse's feelings, needs, or ideas—or who fails to validate her perceptions—is betraying marital trust.

Seemingly unimportant violations of trust can trigger intense uncertainty and ambivalence in marriage as well, a factor that many people fail to realize. In a trusting marriage, you can depend on a mate in ways large and small. It's one thing to rage at infidelity's flagrant breach of trust. It is much harder to justify anger or resentment when a partner repeatedly fails to make key decisions about family finances . . . to discipline the children responsibly and consistently . . . to follow through with promises . . . to keep secret a mate's confidences and insecurities. Yet each of these failures is a violation of trust. What's more, when partners breach the privacy inherent in marriage by parading grievances or embarrassing a mate in front of others, they also violate trust.

Can This Marriage Be Saved? reveals how lack of trust can slip at first unnoticed into an already strained relationship. We hear couples complain bitterly, often publicly, about important dates or anniversaries forgotten; about a partner's constant tardinesss for events that are important to a mate; about key messages that are never given. Slowly but steadily, mistrust chips away at the foundation of a marriage. Unwitting couples wonder what went wrong.

The long-term effects of living with someone you cannot trust are devastating to your sense of self. When a partner doubts a mate's integrity, he or she becomes unsure, insecure, anxious, perhaps even fearful for her physical safety. The person feels trapped, guarded, vulnerable, and may act in unkind ways, which only serves to further push a loved one away.

Nevertheless, time and again in *Can This Marriage Be Saved?* we have watched as couples, reeling from the pain of betrayal, pick up the pieces of their marriage. Restoring trust takes time—perhaps because it is the bedrock of a relationship, it is the most difficult piece to repair. Many fear they won't succeed. But, as the following stories poignantly reveal, it is through weathering the crises that couples, given time to heal wounds and share intimacies, often build an even stronger foundation for their relationship.

"I WAS UNFAITHFUL"

***K**itty had had a brief affair with a coworker, but Mike couldn't forgive or forget. How can a couple let go of past hurts and build a happier future?*

KITTY'S TURN

"**I** made a bad mistake, but it's in the past and I can't keep paying for it forever," said Kitty, thirty-five. "I've begged Mike to forgive me, but he can't get beyond the affair.

"It happened two years ago, but from that moment on nothing else has mattered to Michael. He makes me take our daughters with me everywhere I go, like little chaperones. He won't even drive down the street of the hotel where it happened. I probably shouldn't have told him the details he demanded to know, but I wanted to be completely truthful after the way I hurt him.

"I'm the last person on earth that anyone—including myself—would expect to have an affair. We've been married for thirteen years and Michael was my first lover. I met him when I was walking home from religion classes one night. A friend in a car stopped to chat and Michael happened to be with him. I saw him again at a dance the following weekend and I was thrilled when he pulled me onto the dance floor . . . he literally swept me off my feet.

"I suppose I was looking for someone to take charge. Mike had his life planned out. He told me he had just leased space for a lumberyard he intended to own one day. We started dating and got married within a year. He was solid and dependable and I loved him very much.

"But Mike has always been insensitive to my feelings. The first several years of our marriage we never had any time together. I was working full-time in an office and

11

Mike was working night and day getting his business started.

"I felt terribly neglected, but I never mentioned it. When Mike would ask me if I was happy, I'd say yes. My father owned his own business in our town and was never home either, so I thought this is what marriage was like. My mother never complained—if she ever felt lonely or her feelings were hurt, nobody knew about it.

"By the time our first two daughters were born, I thought I had adjusted to married life. I was still working full-time while my mom, who lives just a few miles away, kept the girls. I was going to secretarial school at night because Mike said we needed more money. When I'd ask if there were problems with the business, he'd brush me off. He never discussed anything important with me.

"Mike took me to the hospital the night our third daughter was born, but he didn't come back the next day. No flowers, nothing. Can you imagine? I have never been so hurt in my life. He said he had work to do. I think the real reason was he was disappointed it wasn't a boy; he couldn't bring himself to see the new baby.

"My job was a lifesaver for me. For the first time in a long time, people were telling me, 'Kitty, you're smart . . . you're nice . . . you're doing good work.' I was suddenly feeling good about myself.

Mike resented my job because I was getting raises and promotions and because I had friends of my own. Everything he said to me now was a put-down, even if he pretended it was a compliment, like 'You look pretty in that new suit, Kitty. You sure fit in there with all those corporate executives, don't you?'

"Mike thinks I had the affair because I had never slept with anyone except him. Actually, sex never meant all that much to me. At home, I was nothing but a maid and bed partner, and not even our lovemaking seemed to please him.

"Gradually, we started bickering. Now we're always fighting. One night I blurted out that I wasn't sure if I loved him anymore. Mike was stunned.

"About the same time, Kevin, a man at work, was giving me the big rush, asking me to lunch and calling me night and day. He'd hang up if Mike answered, and I'd call him back once Mike had gone to work. Then I started meeting him. I thought I was in love with him.

"It was a very short affair. I ended it when I found out from other people in the office that this guy had given the same lines to other women. I felt like such a fool, and I realized how much I loved Mike and our home and family. But then Kevin's wife called and told Mike, and when Mike confronted me, I couldn't lie anymore.

"At first, I blamed myself. What

kind of person was I? But a few months ago, Mike's anger really got out of control and he started hitting me. He'd grab me by the hair and tell me what a witch I was, or pin me down on the couch so I couldn't get away from him while he called me vile names. I lived in terror of his rages. One night our eldest daughter found me in the bathroom crying after Mike had hit me. I decided I couldn't let the girls live in such an environment, so I packed them up and we moved to my mother's house.

"It's been two months now, and although Mike has begged me to come back, I'm afraid too much damage has been done. I'm convinced he'll never really forgive me."

MIKE'S TURN

"Kitty's wrong," said Mike, thirty-six, a well-built man with a tense manner. "I can forgive her, but I can't forget it, ever. What man could?

"If I want to punish anybody, it's the man who used Kitty. I want to strike out, to hurt someone, to make him pay for the pain that was tearing my life apart. But the bottom line was that Kitty chose to go to bed with this guy—no one made her do it.

"When she left, I checked into a psychiatric hospital. I knew I needed help. I was there for four weeks and I learned a lot in the individual and group-therapy sessions about how wrong it is to use physical force to express anger. I was a scrapper when I was a kid and the way I dealt with problems was with my fists. When I couldn't hurt Kitty enough with my words, I started to push her around, but hurting her made me feel worse, not better.

"Something reminds me of the affair every single day. I despise being lied to, and even though she has stopped seeing this guy, I can't help wondering if she's telling me the truth. I feel safe only when the girls are with her.

"Kitty says I'm insensitive? I'm not a mind-reader, that's for sure. I never realized I was neglecting her and the girls. I thought our marriage was fine. It seemed to be pretty much like my own parents' marriage and they've been together a long time. I had been breaking my back to make a go of this lumber business, and in all the years we've been together I never heard her complain.

"I've loved Kitty from the first moment I saw her. I couldn't believe my good luck when she agreed to marry me. I could never understand why Kitty loved me anyway. I don't consider myself that nice looking, and Kitty is so pretty and sweet. Her dad was also better off financially than mine. I've always felt he thought I wasn't good enough for his daughter.

"I guess you could say I'm a

workaholic—but my dad was, too. I'm trying to do what's right for my family. Kitty says I'm never satisfied, but the truth is I'm worried. I had $350,000 invested in this yard—and everyone knows the building business is way off. I didn't want to worry Kitty, but I guess that was a mistake, too.

"I've never been a romantic person—I don't remember sending flowers after the first two girls were born either—but I do feel terrible about not coming back to the hospital after our last baby was born. I honestly had work to do, but I'll admit I was crushed not to have had a boy.

"Kitty doesn't think she changed after she took the job in the city, but I saw it happening. She was all wrapped up in the business world; my opinions meant nothing to her. One morning I told her how pretty she looked in a new business suit and she bit my head off. She never introduced me to the people at work and she treated me as if I was in a completely different social group.

"Kitty is not the only one who was neglected; the wall between us started in the bedroom. She had never shut me out before the new job, but now, she says, she doesn't have the energy. I know Kitty never really enjoyed sex, so it gave me the feeling that I wasn't very good.

"When the phone calls started, I didn't suspect anything, but one day this guy's wife called and told me

the whole story. It was over by then, according to Kitty, but I can't describe the shock and pain I felt when she admitted it. To think she'd been calling him from our house.

"I trusted Kitty; she was an angel with no dirty thoughts. I never dreamed she could do this, but I know now that she doesn't excuse the way I treated her in the last two years. If you're lucky, there's one real love in your life, and Kitty is mine. If she never comes back, I'll still love her forever. But there are three girls who won't grow up in a broken home if I can prevent it."

THE COUNSELOR'S TURN

"Kitty and Mike's immediate problem was to stop focusing on the pain they had suffered," said the counselor. "But their underlying problem, which had been present long before Kitty's affair and Mike's abusive behavior, was that their perception of marriage was based on a fantasy.

"In observing their parents' marriages, they had placed themselves in stereotypical roles where Mike was the breadwinner and Kitty was the dutiful wife. They concluded that marriage meant leading separate lives, shielding each other from problems and emotions. This couple assumed that things would go on like this forever. They were unable to cope when things didn't work.

"Real commitment had been nonexistent in their relationship. In trying to imitate her mother's passive role, Kitty never complained or argued with her husband, thus ignoring her own needs and feelings to keep her husband happy and her family harmonious. But she was denying the reality that their relationship left her feeling empty and neglected.

"Mike, also following his father's model, believed a husband's job was to work hard to provide a successful living for his family. Mike had Kitty on a pedestal as a paragon of virtue and serenity. He was honestly amazed to learn of her early unhappiness when she confessed to doubting her love for him. Kitty accused Mike of being insensitive, when in fact she had intentionally and successfully concealed her real feelings for years. For his part, Mike had also shielded his wife from any concerns he had about his business. Although he thought he was protecting her, he actually intensified her loneliness.

"When Kitty's new job gave her self-esteem a much-needed boost that unfortunately led to the affair, Mike's old feelings of inferiority resurfaced and they began communicating with sarcasm, accusations, and hostility. Kitty did not have the affair out of curiosity or desire for sexual excitement, as Mike assumed, but rather from her need for warmth and appreciation. Mike's knowledge of her unfaithfulness caused him to resort to the physical methods of retaliation that he had used successfully when he was younger.

"In spite of everything, Kitty and Mike loved each other and wanted to rebuild their marriage. Mike's counseling in the hospital had helped him stop his abusive behavior, so Kitty agreed to return home with her daughters while she and Mike sought counseling together. The girls, now ten, seven, and five, had been confused and heartbroken by the two-month separation and were overjoyed at their parents' reconciliation, which further motivated Mike and Kitty.

"At their first session, I told them that their marriage would never be the same again, but it could be better. I explained that as a therapist I could give them tools and encouragement, but they would have to do the work of rebuilding. I also insisted that they evaluate their reaction to me after our first meeting and that if we didn't click, I would help them find the right person. People do not hesitate to get a second opinion on a medical problem, and they should have the same standards for assessing a marriage counselor.

"By understanding their false picture of marriage, of each other, and of themselves, Kitty and Mike began patching together their marriage by asking, 'Who am I . . . Who is she . . . What can we as husband and wife be together?' The first thing Mike did was to hire a manager to help him with the lumberyard, leaving him more time to spend with his wife and daughters. This convinced Kitty that Mike was sincerely determined to change and she no longer felt neglected when he had to be away.

"We worked extensively on changing their old communication patterns, where Mike had accused while Kitty had defended and apologized. This is a common and dangerous cycle in abusive relationships. The person who feels worthless strikes out at the other; since Kitty felt guilty, she unconsciously signaled permission to continue the abuse. Kitty and Mike realized how destructive these patterns had been. It was an important breakthrough when they stopped blaming themselves and each other, enabling them to focus on the future instead of the past.

"I told Kitty and Mike that they would never forget the affair or the abuse and they expressed tremendous relief to learn that forgetting the past is neither possible nor healthy. I told them that these events were so painful because they kept piling more hurts on top of the old ones. I assured them that the hurts would lose their present significance once they began putting positive things into their marriage.

"To find these positive things, we scheduled what I call 'Sweeps Week,' just as TV networks do when they show their best efforts. I told Mike and Kitty to do one thing each week that said 'I care about you,' and then, in the evening, each had to guess what the other's act had been. This enabled them to focus on the positives instead of taking each other for granted, and it also expanded their language of caring. Kitty and Mike delighted in this exercise. 'Mike counted taking out the trash one day, even though he has always done that,' Kitty told me, laughing, but with obvious affection, and Mike, looking straight in her eyes, replied, 'That's because I've always cared about you.'

"Next I gave them a formula for approaching touchy subjects, like Mike's running into reminders of the affair. Step one was to start any such discussion with a positive remark, because the other person responds much better if the most negative feeling doesn't come first. Mike would say, 'Please remember how much I love you and want to make our marriage work, but I really get upset when I drive by that hotel.' Step two was to accept the other person's feelings without trying to fix them. Kitty especially had difficulty with this, but she learned that listening to Mike was the most helpful step she could take. Kitty and Mike began to open up to each other. It was a real turnaround for Kitty to say she was angry or unhappy when she had grown up believing that she shouldn't; it was the same for Mike, who had learned from childhood that the only acceptable way to express feelings of vulnerability and disappointment was through anger.

"I also gave this couple some safety valves to use at home. I advised a forty-five minute limit on their volatile discussions, telling them to either write out the rest of their feelings and exchange them later, or postpone discussing the problem until our next session. They agreed to stop any conversation if they began to lose control, with each one taking responsibility by saying, 'I am getting too angry talking about this' rather than 'You're making me angry.' Kitty and Mike found that this strategy kept them from falling back into their pattern of arguing.

"Next, we explored their sexual relationship, which in the past had pleased neither of them. I discovered that Kitty and Mike believed that both partners had to reach orgasm for lovemaking to be satisfying. I told them that while this is important, it should not be their sole goal. Feeling good about what they are doing, and who they were doing it with, was just as important. I also encouraged Mike to ask Kitty what pleased her since she was the only expert on this. Kitty learned to say, 'I love it when you touch me here . . .' and Mike began to understand that her response was just a statement of her preference, not a criticism of his past performance.

"With their new communication skills and their goal for lovemaking being simply to please one another, this couple discovered that there was a huge middle ground between 'Yes, I want to make love' and 'No, I don't want to.' Saying no is not taken as a rejection when partners use a three-part formula I told them about. Saying 'I don't want to now' indicates that this is a temporary preference; 'I don't want to, but how about doing this instead' shows acceptance of the person and provides a pleasurable alternative.

"For example, Kitty felt free to say, 'I don't want to right now because I'm too stressed out from dealing with the kids, but how about if we cuddle on the couch?' In the past, Mike would avoid hugging, which had been their unspoken signal for wanting to making love, if he felt too exhausted from a twelve-hour day. Now he realized it didn't have to be an all-or-nothing proposition. When he said, 'What I'd really like is a back rub,' he began to feel warmed by a new kind of intimacy.

"Mike and Kitty both had a lot of forgiving to do, but they are a bright couple who discarded their rose-colored glasses. After two months of weekly sessions, I stretched them to three-week intervals, then to six-week intervals. Mike courageously agreed that Kitty should keep her job because the satisfaction from her work meant so much to her. 'I know now that she comes home to me because she wants to, not because she has to,' he said. After a year, they began to schedule appointments only when they felt in need of a booster shot. 'I can't believe it, but you were right,' Mike told me during their last visit. 'In spite of everything, our marriage is better than it was before.'"

WHAT IS TRUST?

Trust is the expectation, often unspoken, that someone will be there for us. When trust is broken, we no longer feel safe—emotionally, physically, or spiritually. Rebuilding feelings of self-worth can take a long time. Before Mike can trust Kitty again, he must be convinced not only that she takes responsibility for the pain she has caused him, but also that she is sincere in her promise to change her behavior. Most important for this couple, as well as others whose relationship is shattered by infidelity, is that they learn to view an affair not as a catastrophe precipitating the end of their marriage, but rather as a red flag that underlying issues need to be addressed.

"My Husband Is Having an Affair"

Eileen's husband met the other woman at church. Why do even the nicest men stray?

"Until last week, if you'd told me that my husband—the Cub Scout leader, the perfect Southern gentleman who doesn't have a mean bone in his body, the man who sings in a church choir—was having an affair, I would have laughed in your face," said Eileen, forty-two, her eyes swollen from days of crying.

"We've been married for eight years—this is the second marriage for both of us—and in all that time, I swear there's never been one single problem. Marrying Russell was the most wonderful thing that had ever happened to me.

"I was raised in a small coal mining town in Virginia. My father was killed in a train accident when I was in the sixth grade and life was a struggle for my mother. We were poor, but we all had enough to manage. My family is extremely loving, warm, and deeply religious.

"I was nearly eight years older than my brother and sister and I took on a lot of the mothering roles. I was always the good girl, really responsible, the kind of kid who wouldn't go out to play on Saturday until the wash was done.

"After high school, I went to the state university, and when I was twenty, I married my high school sweetheart. Eric was the best-looking guy in the class and brilliant. He's a lawyer now. We were married for thirteen years and he was physically and psychologically abusive to me and to our two boys—not every day, but six or seven times a year he'd beat the daylights out of us.

"I filed for divorce three times. Although I knew that staying together for the kids was a bad idea, I couldn't leave. The way I was brought up, when you get married it's till death do you part. I kept thinking I was doing something that made him behave that way.

"Russell and I were good friends for years before we became involved. I knew his first wife had divorced him after seven years and that they had a very amicable split. Anyway, as the years went by, I realized I was deluding myself about my first marriage. The day after I filed for divorce for the last time, I was feeling really down; I needed someone to talk to, so I gave Russell a call and told him everything. He was shocked; he had no idea that things weren't perfect in my marriage.

"We started seeing each other and our relationship grew intense pretty quickly. My kids adored him. After years of being terrified of their father, Russell was a miracle. We had a big wedding—on Valentine's Day, in fact—and it was beautiful.

"By this time, Russell was getting serious about his music. He wanted to be an opera singer, so a few weeks after the wedding we quit our jobs and moved closer to where this teacher whom he studied with lived. We bought a gorgeous three-bedroom house on a corner lot. Within a few weeks we both found jobs—Russell sold insurance during the day and took classes at night; I got a job at the local library.

"Everything was fine, although Russell had some problems at work. He quit his job because he was dis-gusted with it; then he got another selling job, but that didn't work out either. He kept changing jobs— once or twice more, I can't remember. He told me there was no growth at either place.

"After a while, he also gave up the idea of being a professional singer. Russell is so gifted, but he didn't think we could manage financially. I was actually making a lot more money than Russell, so I kept my job, although I desperately wanted to spend more time with my boys. I also started going to school a few nights a week. It was tough, but I got straight A's.

"Like I said, things were great. You can count on one hand the number of arguments Russell and I have had in the last eight years. You can't even call them arguments; we just have disagreements, usually over stupid things. Maybe I'll be upset that Russell spends so much time with his fishing club or in his workroom downstairs cleaning the rods or whatever.

"Since Russell also sings in the choir on Sunday morning, we can never get away for a weekend, which I would dearly love to do. But he works so hard and he needs to relax. I don't begrudge him that, although I'm pretty exhausted after working and cleaning the house. It would just be nice to go out to dinner or a movie. No, I've never said anything to Russell about helping out. Well, okay, maybe once in a while I'll slip and say something sarcastic like, 'Russell, is there something bothering you?' And he'd say, 'No, nothing's wrong.'

"You have to understand, my husband is the most honest human being you will ever meet. He will not lie. So if he said everything was fine, it never entered my mind to question him.

"But in my heart, I figured it was something I was doing wrong. I started reading all these books and asking myself what I could do to improve. Keep the house cleaner? Cook more?

"Then, just last week, I sifted through the mail, and for some reason I looked at the phone bill. I don't know what possessed me to open that bill, because usually I put it aside and let Russell deal with it. I noticed there were a lot of calls to this one number in the next town. I knew Russell didn't have any customers there. I stared at the bill for a long time and realized that a lot of the calls were made when Russell was out of town on business. Was he really having an affair? I wondered. I went into the house to look at the old phone bills we keep in the back of Russell's drawer. Sure enough, each showed several calls to the same number, going back over a year.

"I had the operator check the number and she gave me the name and address of a woman I recognized as someone in our church. Oh, my God, I thought, it's been in front of

me all this time and I couldn't see it.

"I drove to the church because I knew Russell was going to choir practice that evening. I waited in the car in the parking lot until I saw him. I could tell by the look on Russell's face he knew that I knew. I asked him if he was having an affair and he said yes. I said, 'Do you love her?' And he said, 'Yes.' I said, 'Do you want to marry her?' and he said, 'I don't know.'

"I wanted to die. A lot of that night is a blur, but I know that I started taking every pill in the house—of course, all I had was aspirin and a few diet pills.

"What did I do wrong now? I know it's hard to understand this, but I love this man so much; I can't let this relationship go. How can I help him?"

RUSSELL'S TURN

"I love my wife and I know I need help," said Russell, forty-one, as he sank wearily into his chair. "How could I mess up my life so badly? How could I cause this woman, whom I love so deeply, so much pain? She deserves someone better than me.

"Eileen is special. Things just seem to come easy for her. She's a terrific mother, terrific at her job. She gets straight A's in her courses—I was always a poor student. And she has a zillion friends. I still have trouble getting close to people.

"I've always been a real loner. I was born in Alabama and when I was eight my family moved to Ohio. My mother was a housewife, very religious, very soft-spoken, and very subservient to my father, who was a truck driver, so he wasn't home much. When he was, Dad ruled the house as if he were king and everyone else was his servant. He drank a lot and ran around with other women, but my mother would never leave him.

"Mother was very strict with my two younger sisters, but anything I did was fine with her. I was the center of her world. She pampered me and watched over me like a hawk.

"I loved the outdoors and spent much of my childhood roaming the woods by myself. Music was my other love. I sang in the choir and was a member of all the student theater productions. My voice teacher in high school tried to convince me to make music my career—he told me I had a great tenor voice and as good a chance as anyone of making it. But I didn't want to work that hard, and I didn't believe I had the ability.

"I married my high school sweetheart and enrolled in the state university, but I flunked out after freshman year. Failure number one.

"Then I was drafted. It was during Vietnam, so I joined the Navy, but my blood pressure went skyhigh and I was discharged after thirty days for hypertension. Failure

number two. Soon after that, my marriage broke up. Failure number three.

"I didn't know what I was going to do with my life, but since everyone always told me I'd make a great salesman, I figured I'd try it. I found a job selling life insurance; three months later, I almost went broke. Failure number four. I bounced from one selling job to another, but I kept getting fired because I couldn't keep up with my paperwork. I had so many black marks on my record, no one would hire me. I did construction work to make ends meet, but when I was almost thirty, I thought: You enjoy music so much, let's see if you can make a living out of it. I started taking classes at a music school and got a job in the library. That's when I met Eileen.

"After her marriage broke up, we started to see each other and I knew it was the best thing that had ever happened to me. Three months later, I begged her to marry me.

"Everything was going along just fine. Believe me, until this mess, I'd been true-blue to Eileen. And I love her kids as if they were my own. But I was floundering, so I quit school again, found another sales job, and settled for singing in a small opera company and the choir. I thought about how I was turning forty, and I guess all the failures in my life finally just wore me down.

"Then one day while I was singing in the choir I noticed this gorgeous woman in the congregation staring at me. I was flattered by her attention, so I went up to her afterward and started a conversation.

"It turned out that we were on the same fund-raising committee at church; no one else signed up, so it was just the two of us. One afternoon we were meeting at her house and before I knew it we were in bed.

"I felt terrible, but, like an addict, I kept going back for more. I started reminding myself of the things that were wrong with my marriage. How Eileen would always nag me to help out around the house. How our sex life was great, but with this woman, well, it was fantastic. I'd see her maybe twice a week at a motel or at her house before her kids got home from school. She was a bookkeeper and she worked only in the morning; her husband was a workaholic, so he was never home.

"I'll tell you this, though. While Valerie was no match for Eileen, I could talk to her in a way I could never talk to my wife. I'd tell her about my problems at work and how I always messed up my life. How could I tell these things to Eileen? I'm married to Superwoman. Hell, she even makes more money than I do.

"But seeing Eileen try to kill herself . . . I'm so confused. I can't believe I'm saying this, but I'm torn between the two."

THE COUNSELOR'S TURN

"In my experience," said the counselor, "there are usually three reasons for marital infidelity. It can be a symptom of something wrong in the marriage—not just sex. It can be the result of two people growing and changing so much they are no longer in love or compatible. Or, as in this case, it can be the self-indulgent act of one partner who feels he or she is entitled.

"Initially, I was most concerned about Eileen. Although I did not believe she was suicidal, she was devastated by Russell's betrayal. A conservative, religious woman, she considered her marriage vows sacred, and when her world was shattered, so was she.

"Since childhood, Eileen was the good little girl who tried so hard to please that she lost all sense of self-esteem and self-confidence. She became a doormat for her abusive first husband, then for Russell.

"Russell was the selfish, pampered son who grew up in a household built on religious platitudes but lacking in real moral teaching. He never developed a sense of responsibility and he stumbled through life with the attitude that nothing really mattered.

"Even as an adult, Russell found it difficult to connect with people except on a superficial level. Unassertive and not particularly ambitious, he continued to take the easy way out. For instance, he did the fun part of his job—schmoozing with customers—but he pushed his paperwork aside.

"Russell's lifelong string of failures came to a head as he approached forty, a birthday when many people take stock of their lives. Russell found himself wanting, and it was at this point that he was particularly vulnerable to an extramarital affair. He simply couldn't say no.

"My first goal in counseling was to convince Eileen that she had done nothing to provoke the abuse in her first marriage or the infidelity in her second. The latter had far more to do with problems Russell refused to deal with. However, she certainly didn't have to stand for it anymore.

"One of my first questions to Eileen was, Where's your anger? Despite her husband's infidelity, she was still wondering, How can I help him? Such continuous self-sacrifice was unhealthy. Instead, I told her to tell Russell exactly how she felt and what she expected of him: He was to end his affair immediately. He was to start helping her around the house. He was to stop spending so much time in his workshop or going fishing, and instead take her antique shopping or out to dinner or whatever else she wanted to do.

"This was very difficult for Eileen, not only because she had spent a lifetime caring for others, but also because she truly believed that 'a good wife doesn't ask.' I ex-

plained that many people aren't as perceptive as she is and that Russell especially had to be told something point-blank before it would occur to him to do it.

"Eileen forced herself to think of her own needs more. When a savings bond came due, she used the money to buy herself a new car—a red Firebird. She had always wanted to cut back her working hours; this time Russell was supportive, although it thrust financial responsibility squarely on his shoulders. He rose to the challenge.

"For the first time in his life, Russell started to look at himself candidly. He truly loved Eileen and he realized how special their relationship was and how close he had come to destroying it. I agreed with him that while extramarital sex could be exciting, the thrill was more akin to the 'forbidden fruit' and was not as satisfying in the long run as the deep and lasting love he and Eileen shared. In fact, I told Eileen and Russell that one reason I felt they could repair the damage was that their marriage was built on a firm foundation.

"Russell promised to take some drastic steps of his own. He broke off the affair and started working diligently at his job, doing the paperwork on weekends if necessary. As the orders started coming in and his boss acknowledged his success, his self-confidence rose. He started helping around the house. He stopped comparing himself to his wife and instead started really talking to her—and that communication has bonded them further.

"This couple was in counseling for a year and a half. By the end of our last session, Eileen told me, 'I know Russell truly loves me as much as I love him; I know he grieved with me through this ordeal.' Do the memories still hurt? I asked her. 'Time has made it easier,' she admitted. 'Although I've forgiven him, there will probably always be a lot of pain. But I do trust him. Believe me, I couldn't live with him if I didn't.'

"I believed her."

AFTERMATH OF AN AFFAIR: WHEN TRUST IS SHATTERED

When trust is so irrevocably broken, how can you go on? Two-thirds of the couples who seek counseling after an affair do get their marriage back on track. To help reestablish trust that's been broken or to save the marriage, keep the following in mind.

1. First, end the affair. Couples can't begin to rebuild unless they are both motivated to save the marriage.

2. Give the wounded person time to feel angry, vengeful, and hurt after he or she discovers the affair. Their belief system and, along with it, their self-confidence, will be shattered. It can take as long as a year or more to process the pain.

3. Seek professional counseling, preferably together, but if a mate resists, it's imperative to go alone. A skilled therapist can guide patients past self-righteous anger and help them take a microscopic look at the underlying problems in the marriage. What's more, counselors—as well as husbands and wives who have been in therapy—report that once one partner makes a significant change, the relationship is bound to change, too. In time, the wounded party may see the affair as a signal that something was wrong and needed to be fixed.

4. The persons betrayed must let their partners know that they need to hear some recognition of the pain and hurt they have caused. Time and again, this simple acknowledgment was the turning point for marriage recovery, one that allowed the partner to forgive and move on. Too often, one spouse will say: "It didn't mean anything." "I didn't care about her. It was just sex." That's not true. Infidelity is a profound betrayal of trust; continuing to deny it will only stall healing.

5. Don't rush into any major decisions. It's difficult, if not impossible, for anyone to think clearly at a time like this.

6. Partners who have been betrayed must remind themselves that an act of infidelity does not mean that they personally have failed. There is nothing wrong with them—they are not unworthy, unlovable, inadequate. Rather, they have relationship problems that must, and can, be dealt with.

"My Husband Is a Compulsive Gambler"

N*ick had lied to Kim for twenty years. Although he swore he'd changed, can she ever learn to trust him again?*

"Six months ago, I kicked my husband out of the house," said Kim, thirty-seven, her voice shaky. "Nick is a compulsive gambler and, although I've adored him for twenty years, I can no longer continue to be married.

"Except to discuss our kids, Nick and I have barely spoken—he's living in an apartment across town. Then last week, he called to tell me he'd gone to Gamblers Anonymous. He promises he's going to stick with it this time and he begged me to let

him move back in. I don't know what to do. How can I ever trust him? I thought asking Nick to leave was the hardest thing I'd ever have to do, but healing our marriage seems impossible.

"I met Nick when I was sixteen. My family—I was the youngest of four girls, all far prettier and smarter than I was—had just moved to New England from Milwaukee, and I was finding it hard to make friends. Nick was a senior. Handsome and charming, he was clearly the smartest, most popular boy in high school. It was love at first sight for me and I was astounded that a guy like him was actually interested in a girl like me.

"After one date, we were inseparable. Although my parents wanted me to go to college, I couldn't wait to marry Nick, settle down, and raise a family. We were married two months after I finished high school.

By then, Nick had a job working for a shipping and packaging company and I was a secretary for a businessman in town. I thought my dreams had come true.

"For a while, they had. Nick's family welcomed me with open arms. We moved into a small house down the street from his folks and his mother treated me like the daughter she never had. She was always there to help out and when the kids came along—Kelly will be eighteen next spring and Sean is thirteen—she volunteered to babysit so I could go back to my old secretarial job. She was generous with her money, too, popping over regularly with shopping bags filled with new clothes for the kids.

"Nick put in long hours on the job. His shifts changed every few months. He took lots of overtime and, since the company is a round-the-clock operation, he could conceivably be working all hours of the day or night. When he told me he had to work late, there was no reason not to believe him.

"But I started to get increasingly anxious about money. We never seemed to have any, even though Nick was working all the time. If I dared ask about it, he'd fly into a rage. 'That's my job,' he would shout, 'the home is yours. That's the way my father did it, and that's the way I do it. The bills are getting paid, aren't they? You have food on the table, right? So leave me alone.'

I was never allowed to see his paychecks. Whenever we were low on cash, Nick had a ready explanation. I learned not to ask too many questions or I'd unleash the Irish temper.

"For years, I convinced myself that things were really all right. After all, my husband wasn't a goof-off, or an alcoholic like my father was. My sisters and I adored him, in spite of his outbursts. Mother always made excuses for him, anyway. She always forgave him: 'Oh, Daddy didn't mean that,' she'd tell us. She insisted we all love each other, never fight or argue.

"So, like my mother, I whitewashed my life, literally. I became a cleanliness fanatic. The kids were immaculate, the house was immaculate. I could calm myself that way for a while, and then I'd feel anxious again and start yelling at my kids. Of course, Nick was the good guy. He'd come home and say, 'Guess where we're going? Disney World!' My stomach would churn. Where, I wondered, did the money for this trip come from?

"Then, one night, my worst fears came true. Nick came home and told me he had gambled too much at the racetrack. He explained that it was near the office and he had stopped off with the guys now and then—to try his luck. I asked how much he lost, but I never got a straight answer. It was enough, he said, that we had to take out a second mortgage on our house.

"I was hysterical, but Nick was so remorseful and promised it would never happen again. So we took out a second mortgage and I tried to forget it ever happened.

"This became a pattern. Things would be fine for a while, then I'd notice that money I was sure I'd deposited in our joint account was gone. When I asked Nick about it, he always had a ready answer. And, as I said, if I even hinted that I thought he was gambling, he'd deny it vehemently. My daughter told me—just recently, in fact—that Nick used to borrow money she'd earned from baby-sitting. She was covering up for him, too.

"I never thought of Nick's gambling as an illness. I just thought there must be something wrong with me, something I wasn't doing or giving him. I fooled myself into believing that each time was really the last time. If I ever mentioned anything about gambling, he'd accuse me of blaming him for one mistake for the rest of our lives.

"But I found a bank statement stuffed in the drawer that proved he'd squandered the money we had gotten from a personal loan—money earmarked for Kelly's college education. I told him he had to go to Gamblers Anonymous to get some help. He refused, but the children and I started going once a week to Gam-Anon, a support group for families of compulsive gamblers.

"Those meetings opened my eyes. I can't describe how relieved I felt to hear the stories of all those other people whose problems were so much like mine. I realized that compulsive gamblers always have a ready answer or excuse for what they do. And I realized I was actually encouraging his addiction by ignoring it. These people gave me the strength to do what I should have done a long time ago: Give Nick an ultimatum—get some help or leave.

"It hasn't been easy, but I've managed okay. At this point, I don't know how I feel. How can I be sure this won't happen again? I told him the only way I'd ever consider getting back together was if we first went for marriage counseling so we could at least learn to speak to each other. I love him, but I don't know if I can live with him."

NICK'S TURN

"I've been living a lie for years," said Nick, thirty-nine. "But I've learned my lesson. I've changed, and I want Kim and me to be together again.

"To me, gambling was always second nature. I grew up in a small town and as far back as I can remember, I rarely told the truth. It was a knee-jerk reaction, a way to protect myself, I guess. I remember my father whacking me and my younger brother if we did or said anything that displeased him—even something as minor as being late to dinner. He was an iron worker, a real physical guy, and he'd hit us with his hand or a wooden paddle. I felt so protective toward my brother that I'd race home from school or bring him with me when I hung out with my friends just to get him out of the house in case Dad came home in one of his bad moods.

"Dad was an alcoholic, and a violent one, too. My mother didn't do much to help him, either. Theirs was a pretty traditional relationship. Dad gave my mother a certain amount of money to run the house, and that was it. I wasn't close to either of them. I can never remember talking to my father about anything of any substance. He wasn't around a lot and was private with his own time. I know he had a regular card game and, although he made a good salary, from time to time, money would be tight. At one point, when my father lost his job, we had to move in with relatives for a few months. I assumed he gambled—but no one ever talked about it. Neither one of my parents ever shared their feelings and I certainly didn't think they cared much about mine. Although I was captain of the football team, neither one ever attended a game. But I had a close group of friends—guys I'd grown up with. They were a second family.

"When I was a freshman in high school, I took a job as a stock boy in a department store. I worked after school and on weekends so I could have the things my friends had—clothes, a new baseball glove, money for the movies. After high school I wanted to be a teacher, but my father wanted me to be an engineer and he refused to help with tuition unless I went to the college he wanted me to go to. I felt I had no choice, but my heart wasn't in my studies and I dropped out my junior year. I found a job with this international packaging company; the salary was good and the benefits excellent. Since Kim and I planned to get married, I thought it was a good move.

"The first few years, I did well. I moved up fast and, by the time I was twenty-five, I was in charge of a department of one hundred and fifty people. I'm not sure what happened to me then. Maybe I can't handle success. I started to feel overwhelmed. I had a hard time delegating and yet there was too much work for me to do. I hated to reprimand people, and having to fire someone—forget it. I couldn't do it. I developed an ulcer.

"I started to get anxious about money when Sean was born. I felt tremendous pressure to give my children a better life than I had had. I also lost touch with my old friends. When I worked the two to ten P.M. shift, I fell into the habit of stopping off at the track on the way home.

"At first it was a lark, something to do. I felt less lonely at the track. I would catch the last two or three races. The first couple of times I won decent money—two nights in a row, I came home with over five thousand dollars in my pocket. The next night, I gambled it all away.

"That became a pattern. Winning, losing, winning, losing. All the time I was betting, I was trying to pay off the bills, too. When I was short, I'd get cash advances on my credit cards to use at the track. Or I'd borrow from my mother, even my daughter once or twice. I didn't want Kim to know. I was secretive and defensive, and when she confronted me or asked about money, I'd clam up or lash out at her. And I adamantly denied I was gambling.

"As time went on, I got deeper and deeper in debt. I lied through my teeth and told her I'd never do it again, but all I was waiting for was another chance at the track.

"I did attend one meeting of Gamblers Anonymous, but I didn't even stay till the end. I thought the program was ridiculous. 'I'm not as sick as these people,' I told myself. When Kim laid down the law and kicked me out, I was indignant at first. But I knew she was right. I started going to GA after work in the evening and vowed to stick with it—and I have. But I can't make Kim believe that I've changed for good. She keeps throwing my past mistakes back in my face. She blames me for everything. When she does, I can't help getting mad. I'm afraid it might be too late to save our marriage, but I want to try.

THE COUNSELOR'S TURN

"As in any relationship where trust has been broken, Nick and Kim had to rebuild their marriage from the foundation up," said the counselor. "At Gam-Anon meetings, Kim realized how badly she had been hurt by Nick's addiction. She had been burned too often to freely trust her husband again.

"Although Nick insisted he'd changed—if he hadn't already been going to GA meetings, I would have insisted he begin—it was going to take a long time, and require a lot of effort on both their parts, for Kim to feel that he had.

"As I do with all couples—even those who are living apart—I asked Nick and Kim to make a commitment of at least three months of weekly counseling. By that time, couples have usually hit upon at least one issue that makes them both want to call it quits. If they can get past this point, however, they usually have enough confidence as well as the essential tools to cope with problems as they arise.

"Once they made a commitment, I wanted to make sure they understood about addictions in general and how they destroy a relationship. Anyone growing up in a family with addictions, especially if the addiction is not addressed, is also at high risk for developing an addiction. It's not uncommon for the children of addicted parents to avoid feelings and instead tap into a quick feel-good mechanism, anything to help them make sense of an unpredictable world. The child of an alcoholic may become an alcoholic, too. Or he may become addicted to gambling, sex, or even to work. Rather than learn the skills needed to deal with stress, Nick used gambling to camouflage his inadequacies and give him a false sense of power and control. Understanding this helped Kim be more compassionate about the obstacles Nick had to overcome.

"It was also important for Nick and Kim to understand themselves and their own feelings better. Kim, especially, had little sense of herself. She grew up to be a replica of her mother, an uncomplaining woman who never felt entitled to express her feelings, opinions, or needs. Kim was a pleaser. Despite the obstacles thrown in her path, she was determined to make everything work, and for many years she did.

"It's not surprising that Nick and Kim were attracted to each other. Kim saw her charming, handsome father in Nick. And in Kim, Nick found all the love, acceptance, and appreciation for his accomplishments that had been missing from his childhood. Because of their childhood experiences, however, any show of anger—be it their own or their partner's—was frightening and to be avoided at all costs. One of our early goals was to help them both recognize when they were angry, and then learn to deal with that anger in a constructive way.

"I told them both, 'Tune into your own body; when you're upset, what happens?' Kim realized that anger made her anxious: Her stomach would churn, her heart race, and she'd squirm in her seat. Assuming she was to blame for their troubles, she'd either keep quiet or give in. Nick tended to pull away emotionally and physically when angry. He'd cross his arms, get a distant, glassy look in his eyes, and when pushed to his limit, he'd explode in rage.

"Once they could recognize the early signs of their anger, they set about learning to deal with anger that arose in the middle of their often incendiary discussions. 'Conflict in marriage is not the problem,' I told them, 'It's how you deal with conflict that makes the difference.' I also told them not to get hung up on who's right and who's wrong. 'You don't have to debate each other or try to have the last word in every conversation. But you do have to listen and try to empathize with what your partner is feeling,' I advised.

"To do this, I taught them a structured speaking and listening technique called The Dialogue, developed by Harville Hendrix, Ph.D., a psychotherapist and director of the Institute for Relationship Therapy in New York City. The technique can be especially helpful for couples dealing with addiction problems. In such cases, partners' needs may be very different, yet they must talk calmly to each other. For example, Nick was told at GA—quite correctly—that, once he recognized his problem and made amends to those he had hurt, he must forget about the past and live in the present. Kim couldn't do that. She had been so damaged by his deceit that she needed to talk, over and over again, about her pain. Nick had to be able to listen, empathize, but not react defensively or angrily. Although it sounds simple, it's not. Few people really know how to listen to another person and feel what they are feeling, without jumping in with their own ideas, opinions, or hidden agendas. Couples like Kim and Nick, who have been fighting for years, are so locked into their adversarial roles that fighting becomes the only way they can relate to each other. They don't know how to handle differing opinions about even the most elementary things—which restaurant to go to, which TV show to watch.

"I told this couple, 'This process will prevent every interaction from becoming a 'you' versus 'him' battle. It will allow you to experience angry feelings and understand them, instead of running away or ignoring them.'

"This technique was especially useful when Nick and Kim had to talk about volatile money matters—buying a car, renting a new apartment (their home was foreclosed due to Nick's gambling debts and Kim had to move out), making a budget. Kim found this very painful, but with my coaching she was able to say, 'I feel threatened. I was so naive, and you took advantage of me over and over again.' Nick listened, repeated verbatim what she had said, and empathized with her anxiety and frustration without reacting defensively. 'I can imagine you felt really scared and alone,' he said. Kim melted. For the first time, she felt he understood. Nick, too, learned to express his feelings to Kim whenever he felt he was being unjustly accused or if he was under a lot of stress and overwhelmed by responsibilities. 'Instead of running to the track, I talk with Kim,' he told me at one of our last sessions.

"Learning to share feelings and experiences helped Kim and Nick develop an intimacy long lacking in their marriage. After four months, Kim invited Nick to move back home.

"I still see Nick and Kim periodically, and they are both continuing to attend meetings of their recovery groups. 'Just like an alcoholic can never have one drink, I know I can never place one bet,' said Nick. 'It's too easy to slip back. But you know, I have more confidence now. I don't have the urge to gamble anymore. I don't need it.'"

A TRUST CHECKUP

The first step in understanding and overcoming an addiction is to seek professional help. Kim and Nick found it at Gamblers Anonymous and its allied group for the families of compulsive gamblers, Gam-Anon. But as this case makes clear, trust is not an isolated phenomenon. When trust is broken in one area of a marriage, it puts other areas in jeopardy, too.

Trust means being able to count on someone to be there for you at all times. How much can you and your mate really trust each other? On the line next to each situation, rate whether it is A) easy, B) somewhat difficult, or C) difficult for you to get help, support, or encouragement from your partner when:

1. ____you feel indecisive.

2. ____you're depressed.

3. ____you feel exhausted.

4. ____you feel guilty.

5. ____you need encouragement.

6. ____you need advice.

7. ____you feel like a failure.

8. ____you're in physical pain.

9. ____you're in a money crisis.

10. ____you feel humiliated.

Talk with each other about your responses. Then try this exercise as a first step in boosting the trust between you: Tell each other about one family or social situation when your partner has not been as helpful or supportive as he or she might have been. Maybe Thanksgiving dinner at your critical in-laws is tough for you to sit through. Or perhaps your husband has difficulty socializing at school functions since he doesn't really know the other people all that well. Once you each identify the situation in which you would like support, work out a way to signal to your partner during that time. Your personal signal could be a light touch on the elbow or a raised eyebrow—any way that sends a personal SOS so your partner can respond. Once you do this—and see positive results—you strengthen the bonds of trust.

"I CAN'T FACE ANOTHER CHRISTMAS WITH THIS MAN"

Alan had a secret bank account for years. How can Jane ever believe what he tells her?

JANE'S TURN

"Alan and I have the shell of a marriage; inside, there's nothing," said Jane, forty-two, a slim, dark-haired woman who spoke so fast it was hard to follow her. "I'm sure everyone thinks things have always been just fine. We go out with friends and have a good time; we're always there for our kids and their activities. On the surface, we function like every other couple. 'Function' is a good word because it is more like a business relationship than a marriage— and a lousy one at that.

"Once we get home, there is no communication or love—only bitterness and resentment. Other than talking about practical things—like who will pick up Tommy, who's ten, at basketball practice or take Eric, eight, to his friend's house—we hardly say two words to each other. I even have to push and prod Alan to do that.

"For a long time, we played 'let's pretend,' but in the past few years I don't think either of us had the energy to do even that. I'm furious and think I have every right to be.

"Until very recently, Alan was out of work again. This is the sixth time in twenty years—wouldn't you wonder? In the beginning, I didn't think too much about it, to tell you the truth. But then I noticed a pattern. Every two or three years there would be some insurmountable problem at work and Alan, who's an accountant, would leave on his own or be fired. It was always something different. The boss doesn't appreciate him . . . the work isn't challenging enough . . . whatever. Alan is the kind of guy who gets into a job two hundred percent. He's a workaholic—that's one of the problems, which he never seems to realize. He wears this beeper on his belt, and as soon as that thing goes off, he rushes to the phone and then to the office. I can't tell you how many times he's left in the middle of a basketball game or even on a Sunday night. Nobody is that indispensable.

"At first, I accepted his explanations. But what was okay when we were in our twenties, with no kids and no mortgage to worry about, is not okay when we're in our forties and I'm trying to figure out how we can stay afloat, never mind send the kids to college.

"I cannot keep supporting us on my teacher's salary. I've already taken on more extra consulting projects for the superintendent than I can manage. I'm burned out—and sick and tired of it all. I'm tired of explaining to the boys why Daddy and I aren't talking, and I'm tired of stalling bill collectors. Alan's long periods of unemployment have put a terrible emotional and financial strain on our marriage. We were severely in debt, and if I hadn't been working, I don't know what would have happened. It's a miracle we squeaked by.

"You know, I try to talk about this to Alan, but I get this feeling he never really listens. He argues with me, all right, but he doesn't hear what I'm saying. I get so mad that I lose it sometimes. He's a master at nodding at the appropriate times, but I can tell when he's tuning me out. We replay the same old battles over and over again; I can hear the script in my head.

"I feel as shut out as I did as a kid. I've never gotten along particularly well with my parents. Mother especially was critical and judgmental. My dad was more loving, and there were times when I thought that maybe he understood me. But when push came to shove, guess whose side he always took?

"Dad worked for the town government and never made very much money, which meant that Mother had to work six days a week at a dry-cleaning store. She resented it, but I was thrilled—I got to spend a lot of time by myself. I was one of the original latchkey kids, but I loved it. I'd come home from school and watch TV or do my homework and read. When Mother and Dad were around, there was just so much stress that I'd often go into the bathroom, turn the shower on, and sit there reading magazines just to escape from them.

"I didn't feel good about myself until college. That's when I met Alan. We were best friends for two years . . . Alan was funny and charming. But what I liked most about him was that we would have these monumental talks. He was always there to listen, which is a far cry from the way I feel now. We eloped during my senior year—I couldn't handle making wedding plans with my mother.

"After we graduated, I started teaching and Alan worked as an accountant for a small clothing business. I suppose we felt the real financial pressure once we had children. Our sex life was surprisingly good for a while, but now, we never make love.

"Who knows, maybe we would have gone on like this for twenty more years, but last week, something happened that propelled me right over the edge. I was clearing out my desk drawer and found an unfamiliar bank statement. Apparently, Alan had opened an account years ago in his name—and he had twelve thousand dollars in it! I felt as betrayed as if he had had an affair. Here I am worrying and struggling, and he has all this money in this bank. I find this unforgivable. What else is he hiding? How much can I trust him?

"I thought about how the holidays are coming up and I can't make it through another charade of another "merry" Christmas. This is a time of endings and beginnings, and I want this New Year to be a fresh start. This is my last-ditch effort to make this marriage work."

ALAN'S TURN

"I'm not surprised that Jane has neglected to tell you what a witch she can be," said Alan, forty-two, whose quiet voice and demeanor belied the anger in his words. "She can be so hurtful, dripping with sarcasm, accusing me of being a failure when I've been working my tail off. She says I'm never there for her and the kids—well that's a lot of bunk. The jobs I've had were all important, pivotal positions. I have a responsibility to my boss and the people who work under me. She should understand that. Plenty of men work longer hours than I do. I feel *she's* never there for *me*.

"Do you know what it's like to live with a person whom you know, just know, is convinced you're a screw-up? I feel like there's no support for me at all.

"I've tried for years to talk to Jane if I had a problem at work, just like we used to. I've always valued her advice; she has a better feel for people and how to get along than I do. But whenever I did, Jane would immediately act as if what I was saying would lead to some awful catastrophe. She never heard what I was saying; she was too busy panicking and obsessing. So maybe I built this wall up around myself, to protect myself from her. What else could I do?

"Jane was the first person who

made me feel like I had something genuine to offer. I'd been a loner growing up. When I was ten, I had a bad accident playing baseball—I broke my leg in several places. It never healed properly, and I was in pain for years. There were all sorts of complications that I can't even remember and, as a result, my left leg is still shorter than my right by about two inches.

"Anyway, for two years I had to stay at home, mostly in bed, while it healed. I remember kids coming to talk to me at my bedroom window and I'd beg my mother to let me go out, but she always said no. She was afraid I'd hurt myself. Mother always told me how terrific I was, but I knew better; I knew what she was saying wasn't true. I was a total disappointment to my dad. He worked as a truck driver and he was this real macho kind of guy. Although he was rarely home, I know he was embarrassed to have a son who was such a wimp. By the time I did go back to school, I found it hard to make friends.

"When I met Jane, all that changed. I felt like I had a best friend, and it was a terrific friendship that grew into much more. It's hard to say when the problems started for us—all I know is that I've been unhappy for a long time. I don't understand why I do some of the things I do, either. Take that bank account. I don't know why I kept it from her. I didn't mean to be

hurtful. It made me feel good to know that money was there, that I could amount to something after all. I don't know why I've made so many job changes either; most of the time, I left on my own. See, I throw myself into work, but after a while my interest fizzles. I hit a plateau and then get bored. I think that's the way you grow, but Jane thinks it's irresponsible.

"You know, occasionally, when we're out with people, I catch glimpses of the old Jane, the funny, energetic woman I fell in love with. But once we get home, that woman becomes a shrew. Maybe I work so much because I hate to come home."

THE COUNSELOR'S TURN

"Alan and Jane were engaged in a dance of anger, blame, and abandonment that had gone on for so long it was difficult to break," said the counselor. "In fact, for the first few weeks, I wasn't sure this marriage could be saved. They had lost the friendship that had been the foundation of their marriage and now were so intent on proving their individual points, and placing the blame squarely on each other, that I was little more than a referee in their cold war.

"Finally, I told them: It's time to decide if you want to make this marriage work. If you do, you each have to take responsibility for having created the problems in your relationship and start acting like allies instead of adversaries.

"My first goal was to help them recognize that many of the patterns in their behavior stemmed from experiences they had as children.

"For instance, Jane's childhood world was not a safe and happy place. She grew up with deep-seated feelings of insecurity and a lack of self-confidence, not surprising considering that her overcontrolling mother rarely showed her any affection. Although Jane's father occasionally was nurturing and gave her the feeling that he understood her, she never knew when he would abandon her and rush to take Mom's side. He made it clear that her mother's feelings and needs, not Jane's, were paramount.

"In a similar way, Jane looked to her husband to rescue her in marriage, and when he created problems rather than saving her from them, her resentment grew deep. To protect herself, Jane withdrew. Like the little girl who used to hide in the shower, she pulled back from Alan, and though she honestly felt she was telling him how she felt, she kept most of her real thoughts to herself. Many of these angry feelings triggered her anxieties and chronic worrying as well as her harsh, sarcastic attacks against Alan. In counseling, Jane said that unless she made her point as strongly as she did, Alan wouldn't hear her. Alan was a master of emotional withdrawal and, when

he pulled back, Jane felt he was abandoning her the way her father used to. Jane promised to hold back the angry words if Alan would promise not to shut her out.

"Many of Alan's problems also stemmed from his childhood. His injury was the first blow to his self-confidence. Because he spent so much time alone with a mother so overprotective that she never placed any demands on him or let him try anything for himself, Alan grew up feeling like an outsider—different, and not as good as others. To him, his mother's constant praise was hollow: He hadn't done anything, so how could he deserve praise? As a result, he never felt challenged and never developed the feelings of self-reliance children need to make their own way in the world. His father's obvious disappointment further reinforced the message that even if he tried, he'd probably fail.

"But in the beginning, this couple's strong and solid friendship served them both. The job now is to reach back to that friendship and relearn how to work together as a team.

"Before we could tackle many of the material problems, however, we needed to shore up Jane's and Alan's self-confidence. I saw them both individually for several sessions to do this. I wanted Jane to see how she was using her anxieties in a controlling way. 'There's a lot of strength in you, Jane,' I told her. 'You don't have to worry at the first hint of a problem.' Because Jane would automatically go into panic mode, I told her to try to concentrate on her abilities and remind herself that she always manages to work through her problems. As she became more confident, her anxieties lessened and Alan felt more comfortable being there for her.

"The focus of Alan's individual session was his lack of confidence in relationships at work. While Jane and Alan both used the term 'workaholic' to describe Alan, I believe he was actually overcompensating for his own feelings of inadequacy. He would pour himself into his job, over and above what is called for, as a way of proving 'See, I am good after all. I am needed. I'm a man.' Then, too, when people at work didn't respond to him or weren't as totally accepting of him as his mother had been, it triggered those old childhood hurts of feeling defeated and rejected. I believe Alan's secret bank account was his way of exerting some control over his life.

"Once they were able to recognize these patterns, Jane and Alan felt more accepting and less hostile toward each other. I told them that the only way that they could continue to make progress was to act this way even when I wasn't there to intervene. They agreed to take the time each day to talk about issues that bothered them, and as soon as the discussion began to disintegrate, one of them had to call time out. At that point, they both wrote down what they were feeling so they could remember it and talk about it with me at their next session.

"While these two had long argued about Alan's job situation, they had never talked about it in a way that allowed them both to express their feelings honestly and figure out what to do. But now that Alan had heard the hurt in Jane's voice instead of the sarcasm, he vowed to put boundaries on his workload. In time, he understood that he didn't need to work all hours of the day and night, that he could delegate many of his responsibilities, freeing himself to spend more time with Jane and the boys. When Jane saw this, she began to like him better and trust him more. Her anxieties about financial problems lessened. 'She still gets the crazies sometimes,' Alan said at one of our last sessions, 'but I don't take it personally anymore.'

"Such fundamental changes in the way we behave take time. After I had seen this couple for a year and a half, they had stopped trying to compete with each other in their who's-right-who's-wrong game and had begun to feel like friends for the first time in years. Says Jane: 'I realize now that though our problems may not go away, our attitude toward solving them can make all the difference.'"

LEARNING TO WORK TOGETHER TO RESTORE TRUST

Jane and Alan had been trying to one-up each other for so long that they lost sight of the importance of acting like a team—a key principle for any healthy marriage. The following rules—good advice for every couple—helped them refocus their priorities:

1. Remind yourselves that there are no bosses in a marriage.

2. Mutual respect is essential: Respect your partner's way of thinking and getting things done as well as his or her opinions.

3. Keep a tight reign on your tendency to judge and find fault with your partner's thoughts or ideas when they're different from yours. You're not required to think and feel the same, merely to compromise.

4. Avoid making unilateral decisions. Teamwork means consensus, and consensus is based on sharing.

5. Make sure your common goals and objectives are clear. Repeat them often if necessary.

6. Be on the lookout for competition between you. Marital teamwork is not a contest and you aren't adversaries. Neither has the edge or is better than the other.

7. Teamwork means mutual support and encouragement. For instance, instead of negating your spouse's ideas, acknowledge the truth or positive aspects of what he or she is saying. Then you can add your own suggestions to the mix.

"My Husband Was an Alcoholic"

T*ucker has stopped drinking, but Katie still feels she can't trust him. Can a couple ever truly recover from one partner's addiction?*

"They say you have to be crazy to marry an alcoholic," said Katie, thirty-three, a tall, slender redhead in neatly pressed jeans and a pink shirt. "I wasn't crazy, I was just naive. I met Tucker at an airline Christmas party. I was a stewardess; he was a junior executive—and so charming and handsome that I was a goner. I did notice that he drank a great deal, but I thought, 'Well, so what? He likes to have a good time.'

"He took me to dinner and it was very romantic. As we saw more of each other, I knew Tucker was the man for me. The drinking bothered me, but I was in love and thought, 'Oh, when we're married everything will be better.' He told me he was going on the wagon—and he did for several months, during which time we were married.

"But one day he started drinking again, worse than ever. Then he began staying out until nine o'clock every night. I'd be waiting home with dinner ready, but he'd come in and pass out. I'd cover him up so he wouldn't catch cold, wrap his dinner in waxed paper—and cry my heart out. I'd be torn between pity for him and shame at myself for whatever I was doing to make him this way. You see, I didn't blame him for the drinking, I blamed *myself*. I felt I was letting him down, not giving him all he needed emotionally.

"Tucker's mother, Constance, added to my insecurity—always talking about how prominent their family was and making it clear I didn't belong. It was true that our backgrounds *were* different. Tucker's

41

father, who died when Tucker was sixteen, had been the head of an important bank, and the family had lived in a big house with two maids. Constance had always assumed that Tucker would marry one of her wealthy friends' daughters.

"Instead, he picked me, a poor girl from a factory town in Scotland. My parents were good honest people, but they were dour and stern. They both worked long shifts in the factory and didn't have any time or affection for me. My dream had been to get away from that grim little town and travel the world. So I left home when I finished school—and started working for the airline.

"Constance looked down on my background. Once, at her home, a well-to-do friend of hers asked whether my mother or father was a cousin of the Duchess of Argyll. I thought, 'Wow, my mother-in-law is really ashamed of me.'

"When Tucker and I had been married a year, I got pregnant. Tucker brought home a bottle of champagne—and ended up drinking it himself. I had problems with the pregnancy and had to stop working. Not long after I quit, however, Tucker lost *his* job. It seemed he'd been coming back from lunch too drunk to work or not coming back at all. Since we now had no money, we had to move in with Constance. I was more humiliated than ever.

"A couple of months ago, I gave birth to Melissa. But the day after I got out of the hospital, Tucker went on a three-day bender. When he came home smashed, Constance wouldn't let him in. I remember I was screaming that I wanted him with me. She finally let him in, but on her terms: Stop drinking and get a job. He agreed. Over the next few months, however, he'd say he was looking for work, but he never showed any sign of it. Constance would give him money and he'd be off. He never drank at home, he'd just take off.

"It pained me no end that Tucker's first priority was liquor. It was like a replay of my childhood. I was not getting enough affection. One night I even packed a bag and threatened to leave. Tucker didn't notice the bag until I said good-bye. Then he broke down and begged me to give him one more chance. I loved him, so I said yes. Besides he wasn't physically abusing me.

"I guess I was just hoping that he would straighten out. Every so often he would stop drinking—proof, he said, that he could cure himself. My hopes were really buoyed when Tucker got a job. With money coming in, we were able to move into our own place. Maybe now we were finally on the right track.

"That hopeful feeling ended abruptly the night Tucker didn't come home. It was nine o'clock and the office closed at six. Maybe he was just working late. I started dialing Tucker's old haunts. When I reached a seedy tavern by the docks, the bartender said, 'He's not here,' but I could hear Tucker in the background. So I hung up and called a cab and grabbed my daughter out of her bed. I carried Melissa in and there was Tucker, slumped over the bar.

"He looked disgusting. But what made me really furious was that he had all this money beside him and we had been eating hot dogs all week. I grabbed the four drinks that were lined up in front of him and poured them all over him. Then I scooped up the money and marched out to the cab.

"The next night it snowed and Tucker came home. He staggered in, smashed to the gills—and crying. He handed me a five-dollar bill and told me he couldn't handle the responsibilities of being a husband and a father. He was going to Florida, he said, to be a beach bum.

"I was too upset to cry. I stayed up all night pacing. He's gone for good, I thought. Melissa will grow up not knowing her father.

"The next morning, I got a phone call: Tucker had hitchhiked as far as some mall in New Jersey, where he'd been mugged by teenagers who stole his coat and pants and belt and beat him up. The police found him in the morning, covered with dried blood, and he was in the hospital, recovering from pneumonia and a broken nose. Apparently he had hit rock bottom and was now asking for help. He would

enter a rehab clinic for one month, and during that time he would be introduced to Alcoholics Anonymous. I was thrilled to hear that he wanted help! Now we'd *finally* pull our marriage together.

"With Tucker away, I got a part-time job in a bakery to pay the bills. But we were always behind on our rent and the landlord evicted us and I had to move in with Constance again.

"A woman at the bakery told me about Al-Anon, a support group for families of problem drinkers. That evening—still several weeks before Tucker was due to return—I attended a meeting. I was shocked when they said that drinking was never a spouse's fault. I had always felt sure that I was to blame. They also told me that Al-Anon would always be there for *me*—just as AA would be there for Tucker.

"It's been a year now since Tucker completed his treatment and he hasn't touched a drop of liquor—his longest dry spell since I've known him. He seems determined to stay sober and religiously goes to his AA meetings.

"So you'd think everything would be perfect now, but it isn't. I'm still afraid to really trust Tucker. Last week, for example, he was late getting home from his new job with an air freight company—and I began to cry. He walked in and saw the tears and said, 'Katie, you have to stop assuming the worst about me.'

"My Al-Anon friends tell me my

fears are natural, after all those ups and downs and broken promises. I'm terribly scared that Tucker will get upset, so I walk on eggs around him and pamper him. For instance, I still take care of the family finances, something I think he resents although he never mentions it. I even try to keep Melissa from bothering him when he comes home.

"When Melissa does act up around Tucker, he indulges her, giving her whatever she wants. And then he smiles smugly, like the big expert on children, and says I should be more flexible. I feel like bopping him. I often think, 'Where were you when we needed you all those years?' but I don't say anything.

"We're still living in Constance's house although we now have enough money to get our own place. But last time we moved out, Tucker fell apart. So I don't push.

"There were years I would have given anything to see Tucker sober. But now? I feel let down and tired of pretending everything's great. That's why I wanted to come to counseling. I can't go on the way we are."

TUCKER'S TURN

"I knew I wasn't ready for marriage," mused Tucker, a tall, handsome man with warm blue eyes and thick brown hair. "I had always been a goof-off. I could count on getting by in school because teachers always liked me. And my mother doted on her little black sheep. Frankly, I couldn't wait to go to college and escape. My mother was smothering me.

"College was where I began my heavy drinking. Going out with the guys was a lot more fun than studying, and the booze kept me from facing myself. Still, I got by. I told myself I could quit anytime.

"Katie and I didn't know each other at all when we were married. The reason I asked her to marry me was to feel like a grown-up and get away from my mother. But my heart wasn't in it. The night I proposed, I couldn't wait to drop her off so I could go get drunk. *That* was how bad my problem had become.

"Those early years must have been brutal for Katie. I never blamed her for my drinking, although I sensed that she blamed herself—and I let her. I did, however, resent her interfering with my drinking, like demanding money to buy food or something.

"Although I never abused Katie physically, I certainly did emotionally by disappearing for extended periods. When she and Melissa came home from the hospital, I took off for a couple of nights. I don't know what I did; I often had black-outs that chill me just to think about. Probably in the back of my mind, I thought if I disappeared enough, she'd leave me. In a way, I was trying to goad her. But she never did leave.

"Being robbed and left to die in

44

a gutter was probably the best thing that could have happened to me. It forced me to see how low I'd sunk and to drop the charade that I could cure myself.

"When I finished drying out, I was too embarrassed to tell Katie how scared I was and how much understanding I'd need. I felt she'd already given me more support than I deserved. Luckily, I could talk about my fears with my AA group. I don't think we'd have made it this far if I didn't have AA.

"Actually, I sometimes think my AA friends believe in me more than my wife does. For instance, she won't let me take over the family finances. I guess she expects me to slip off the wagon and spend all the money on a drunken spree. I try to help with Melissa, but Katie seems to resent it—as if she doesn't trust me there, either.

"On the one hand, I really want to assume responsibilities, like being a good father and husband. But on the other, I'm scared. I look at our angelic daughter and feel this need to make her proud of me. I've never tried to make it as a grown-up before. What if I can't?

"I don't know how to tell Katie that I need for her to believe in me, that she can lean on me. She doesn't tell me about her doubts or suffering, but I'm sure that they're there. She doesn't even complain that we're still living with my mother. I guess Katie doesn't want to rock the boat.

As a result, we're sort of stagnating. I've heard from my friends in AA that a lot of marriages fall apart once the drinker becomes sober and a lot grow closer together. Ours isn't growing anywhere. It's just there."

THE COUNSELOR'S TURN

"The empty feeling that Katie and Tucker described," said the counselor, "is not at all unusual for a couple recovering from alcoholism. Both were disappointed that Tucker's new sobriety wasn't able to solve all problems. They also felt a lot of fear—fear of bringing up toxic issues of blame and self-doubt and fear that Tucker would drink again.

"There was reason, however, to be optimistic about Tucker's continued sobriety. He had already been dry for a year. And an informal survey of AA members shows that alcoholics who have been sober for one to five years have an eighty-six percent chance of getting through the next year without drinking, and after five years that chance goes up to ninety-two percent. Another good sign was how devoted Tucker was to his AA meetings. Katie, too, had kept up with Al-Anon, even while they were in therapy. Marital counseling, I must point out, is not a substitute for these programs.

"In counseling, however, there were areas for us to work on, especially the hard feelings that had built

45

up between them. Katie was walking on eggs, as she put it, and Tucker was also keeping things in. I coached them: 'Tucker, tell Katie how that makes you feel,' or 'Katie, are you sure you are not angry at him now?' I wanted them to understand that once you can verbalize feelings, you don't have to resort to alcohol or packing a bag to make your point.

"One big challenge we had in therapy was to help Katie, who had a take-charge personality, hold herself back from some of Tucker's problems. At one point, she allowed Tucker to take care of the finances, but she became so anxious about the bills that she actually went behind his back and paid some of them. Tucker was understandably furious.

"In counseling, Katie recognized that by growing up with reserved parents who had little time to spare for her, she had learned not to rely on anyone. I suggested that she try to monitor her feelings to see why she had trouble allowing Tucker to struggle. In a matter of months, Katie found that she was able to stop mothering Tucker most of the time and they both felt better.

"We dealt with another issue between them: Melissa. Tucker would waltz in from work, pacify the child by indulging her, give Katie a lecture on child-rearing, and go off to his AA meeting. This quite rightly made Katie mad. But what she didn't realize was that Tucker's unsolicited advice covered

up his deep uncertainty.

"The remedy was for Katie to stop undermining Tucker's parenting skills. I told Katie that when Melissa came to her with a problem, she should occasionally say, 'Gee, honey, why don't you see what your Dad thinks about that.' I also recommended that she do a little selective complaining to Tucker, as in 'I can't cope with Melissa today; will you try?' With that, Tucker has proved to be an affectionate parent.

"All these tensions in the marriage had been heightened for Katie by the fact that she was stuck with Constance, a critical mother-in-law who never stopped harping on her. But Tucker also had problems with Constance: Although he had always acted as if he wanted to get away from his mother, he had in fact only prolonged his dependence upon her through his drinking and bouts of joblessness. In counseling, he began to understand his complex love-hate relationship with his mother and to recognize his need to get away from her in order to be a true grown-up. Recently, Katie and Tucker took a big step in solving their problems with Constance by signing a lease on an apartment of their own.

"This couple now have the commitment and ability to know their own vulnerabilities—and to respect one another's needs. The last time I saw them they were selecting wallpaper patterns together. Nobody looking at them would have guessed that their happiness comes not from the absence of problems, but from the courage and determination to conquer them."

HOW MUCH IS TOO MUCH?

Trust is an issue that comes up over and over again for those who have lived with or known someone suffering from an addiction—be it to alcohol, drugs, or gambling. Time and again they wonder: Can we count on him to be there, emotionally and physically? What's more, as Katie and Tucker's case shows, once trust is shattered, it can take a long time to rebuild the relationship.

Although Tucker did finally conquer his drinking problem, countless other couples are forced to deal with the difficult task of getting an addicted person to face his problem in the first place. Many of these victims deny their problems, to themselves as well as to their loved ones. Could you or your spouse be one of them? How can you judge how much is too much? The following questions can serve as a guide. Ask yourself honestly:

1. Are you drinking more, and stronger, drinks now than you used to?

2. Do you feel sorry or guilty about your drinking?

3. Do you find yourself unable to do something difficult unless you have a few drinks first? Does alcohol give you the boost of courage or energy you need to get going?

4. Do you insist to everyone, including yourself, that you are in control of your drinking?

The hardest step in overcoming an addiction is breaking through the denial. Once you can face the problem, you can reach out for help. You can talk to a clergyman, a doctor, or a therapist who is specially trained and knowledgeable about substance abuse or other addictions. You can also join one of the many self-help programs, such as Alcoholics Anonymous, or investigate in-patient treatment programs at a hospital or, if you can afford it, a private clinic.

For more information, contact: Alcoholics Anonymous, PO Box 459, Grand Central Station, New York, NY 10163 (212-870-3400); Al-Anon Family Group Services, PO Box 862, Midtown Station, New York, NY 10018-0862 (212-302-7240); National Council on Alcoholism and Drug Dependence, 12 West 21st Street, New York, NY 10010 (212-206-6770); or consult your phone directory.

"I Can't Stand to Have My Husband Touch Me"

Sarah gave her love to Jim in every way but one. Yet how can a couple stay close if a wife won't let her husband near her?

SARAH'S TURN

"I can't stand to have my husband make love to me," said Sarah, twenty-two, a lovely brunette with a childlike face and worried eyes. "Jim tries to be patient, but I know he's miserable. And who can blame him? One day he's going to get so fed up he'll leave me. I can't bear the thought of that happening and, still, I go into a panic and jerk away every time he touches me.

"The ironic thing is that I love Jim with all my heart. We've been married two years and he's everything I could ever want in a husband—warm, kind, honest, gentle, yet very masculine. I've never been able to figure out how I came to rate such a man, and now here I am, shoving him away from me. Something must be terribly wrong.

"I don't want a marriage like my parents'. I was conceived on their wedding night and they ended the sexual part of their relationship a short time later. My father was forty-six when I was born and my mother was eighteen years his junior. This was Dad's first marriage

48

and my mother's second; she had a small son, Tom, whom my father adopted. Mom was—and is—a magnetic, sensual woman and a sexless marriage must have been a great trial for her. I remember as a child asking if I'd ever have a baby brother or sister. There was bitterness in her voice when she told me, 'Not unless a miracle happens.' When I was older she explained that my father found lovemaking distasteful.

"I'm sure in his own way Dad loves Mom very much, for he gives her anything she wants. Mom, for her part, has provided him with a peaceful, unpressured life and a well-run home. Whenever there were problems in raising Tom and me, it was our mother who always took care of them. While I never saw my parents demonstrate physical affection, they took great pains to spare each other's feelings.

"My teen years weren't particularly happy ones. I was shy and withdrawn and my social life came through my more outgoing half-brother. Our home was a gathering place for his friends and Mom was an adored den mother. She and Tom included me in whatever the group was doing.

"I became sexually active early. Maybe it was my own special sort of rebellion. I went with two boys during my high school years. Both were much older than I, and both were disasters. The first and only man I ever loved was Jim. Jim was newly discharged from the Navy, grieving over his mother's recent death, and in need of someone to care for him. He was a friend of my brother's and, when he looked at me, I knew right then that I was never going to feel lonely again.

"I was nineteen to Jim's twenty-three, and one year into college. My parents wanted us to wait until I graduated to marry, but we were too much in love.

"Jim and I married with stars in our eyes and a belief that the future would take care of itself as long as we could be together. We decided we wanted a rural life away from the pressures of society. Mom had inherited some property out in the country and gave us six acres. We bought a portable storage shed to camp in, twelve feet by twenty-four feet, and set out to build a real home. For financing we had the money Jim had saved in the Navy.

"That small amount of money has lasted us almost two years, which should tell you something about the way we've been living. This whole time Jim has been working on our dream house. He's hauled in rock from the river bank, mixed concrete under the blazing summer sun, pulled lumber out of salvage yards, and found carved French doors in a garbage dump.

"During the first months I tried to participate, but soon I began to realize I was more of a handicap than a helpmate. I'm not a carpenter and the hard physical work is more than I can handle. I've lived through the house construction vicariously, listening as he described every nail he'd driven in. And, in bed at night, he read me to sleep from his builder's handbook.

"Jim is so good and works so hard. He deserves a warm, responsive wife. Why can't I be one? We enjoyed a good sexual relationship during our courtship days, but from our honeymoon on it's been downhill. At first, I chalked it up to the fact that the novelty had worn off and I put on a pretense of responding for Jim's sake. That's no longer possible. Now, the mere thought of lovemaking fills me with revulsion. When I do force myself to attempt it, I tighten up inside and am in agony.

"I don't know what has happened to me. If I can't do something about myself fast, I'm going to lose the person I love most in the world."

JIM'S TURN

"I don't know what I've done to ruin things between Sarah and me," began twenty-six-year-old Jim, a tall, soft-spoken man. Whatever it was, I'd like to redeem myself. There isn't anything I wouldn't do for Sarah if she asked me, but she keeps insisting there's nothing to discuss.

"Maybe this is to be the story of my life, failing the people who de-

pend on me. That's what I did to my mother. She was a high-strung woman who, in her later years, became an alcoholic. She used to holler and rave at my easygoing, fun-loving father, accusing him of all sorts of things, until I was ready to throttle her. I'd come straight home from school to keep her calmed down as well as to give her some company. I was scared that one day she'd just take off on us.

"During my senior year, Mama had a stroke, which left her partially paralyzed. I couldn't take it any longer. Immediately after graduation, I joined the Navy. While I was in the Navy, Mama had a second stroke and went into a coma. I rushed home, but not in time. Soon after her death, I discovered that everything she had accused my father of was true. He had been sleeping around for years and had a full-time mistress. As soon as the funeral was over, he married her.

"I think back now and wonder how I could have been so blind to Mama's suffering. What I should have done was get her away from my father before the pressure in her life became too much for her. The only thing that got me through the time of Mama's death was meeting Sarah. I dated very little in high school— how could I when I had to be home with Mama every evening? For me to fall into a relationship as wonderful as this one seemed like a miracle. Maybe I shouldn't have proposed. I didn't know what I was going to do with my life. But I did know that I wanted Sarah to share it.

"Moving out to the country, building a house together, and being free of outside pressures seemed like heaven to me, and Sarah said she felt the same way. I'd never done much with my hands before, and the challenge of trying to build a house from the foundation up seemed staggering at first. But the more I've gotten into it, the more excited I've become, and I discovered I had abilities I never knew about. It would be great if Sarah wanted to work alongside me as we had originally planned, but she doesn't have to. It's enough to have her nearby, giving me emotional support.

"We don't have much money, but so what? Our needs are few; we've got a place to sleep, enough food to eat, and each other. At least, I thought we had each other until Sarah began turning off sexually. It happened gradually. In the beginning she used to be as eager to make love as I was. Then she began to be 'too tired' and 'not in the right mood.' Now she's crying before I can even put my arms around her. I feel like some sort of monster, inflicting torture upon this poor, quivering creature who can't stand for me to touch her but keeps insisting she loves me.

"It's obvious that Sarah wants more than I am able to give her to be happy. If I can't make her that way, she should find someone who can."

THE COUNSELOR'S TURN

"Sarah and Jim entered counseling for a sexual problem," said the counselor. "Soon, however, it became clear that this was a symptom of an even more serious and potentially destructive problem. Jim and Sarah were not able to let go and trust each other enough to share their feelings. Each was so terrified of losing the other that neither would risk expressing emotional demands.

"The fear of abandonment was a longtime nightmare for both of them. Jim had spent his childhood and teen years trying to protect himself from this by appeasing his unhappy mother. When he released his grip on her by joining the service, his worst fear was realized. She did desert him—by dying. He then discovered that his father had emotionally abandoned both of them many years before.

"Sarah, for her part, had been raised in a home in which the woman's primary duty had been defined as protecting her husband from inconvenience and conflict. 'Keep everything smooth and peaceful, or you will drive your man away,' was her mother's motto. By the time she married Jim, Sarah had already made the unconscious decision never to ask for anything. But she resented the fact that Jim did not adequately provide for her emotional needs. Small irritations piled one on top of the other until the inevitable explosion occurred—silently, within Sarah herself—surfacing in the marriage bed.

"My first step in counseling this couple was to help them establish open communication about their inner feelings. One of the exercises we used to accomplish this was to have them hold hands, look into each other's eyes, and express their devotion. 'I love you,' each told the other. 'No matter what you reveal to me, I will not leave you. Whatever our problems are, I want to work them through with you and stay with you and remain married to you.' As they became more secure about the permanence of the relationship, it became easier for them to articulate what was bothering them.

"Sarah, in particular, was dissatisfied with the way their life was going. As a bride, she had been enchanted by the romantic picture of roughing it in the wilderness, but two years of loneliness and boredom had taken their toll.

"'I want us to develop a social life—eat dinner in a restaurant once in a while, have friends, go to an occasional movie—spend some time together doing something other than house building,' she told Jim in a burst of vehemence.

"'Well, sure,' he said obligingly.

'Why haven't you ever said so?'

"As Jim and Sarah became more comfortable with each other on other levels, we were able to tackle their sexual difficulties. Sarah's parents' unhappy marriage had provided the backdrop for her own distorted feelings about marital sex. With her mother as a role model, she held the unconscious view that a responsive, sexual woman was a threat to her husband. This feeling had become so ingrained that logic could not conquer it. Jim too had developed some warped views about what constituted 'good sex.' Neither understood that physical contact doesn't have to end in intercourse.

"During counseling, I invited this couple to experiment with other ways of enjoying sexual intimacy. They were guided through a series of exercises originated by sex researchers Masters and Johnson to reduce the fears about sexual performance that couples commonly experience. Jim and Sarah's deep affection united them in their efforts to make the sexual part of their relationship satisfying, although their progress was not always smooth.

"After nineteen sessions, eleven taken together and seven individually, Sarah and Jim reported that they felt much more secure not only about their overall relationship, but also about their sexual one. The last time they came to see me was to report that Sarah was four months pregnant."

LEARNING TO BE CLOSE AGAIN

Trust in marriage means many things. To trust someone fully means to reveal yourself—your insecurities, weaknesses, and failures—to another. It can be frightening, as it was to Sarah, to be vulnerable; and when such fear arises, it's not uncommon to find it manifested in the bedroom.

Couples who haven't made love for a long time have to rediscover how to be intimate. To do this, it helps, paradoxically, to pledge to abstain from intercourse for one week. A couple may kiss, hug, take a shower together, or even give each other a massage (excluding the genitals), but refrain from anything more. They should also talk about what feels good and what doesn't, what their fantasies are and what they don't like. This way they can both focus on their individual sensations, as well as the joy of being together, without worrying about performance. And they will also realize that closeness and touching don't have to lead to intercourse.

PART 2

WHY HUSBANDS AND WIVES STILL CAN'T COMMUNICATE

O VER AND OVER AGAIN, COMMUNICATION problems are targeted as the number-one cause of marital strife. "We're just not communicating," is a common lament—every column since the inception of "Can This Marriage Be Saved?" describes at least one way (though usually more) in which husbands and wives either misread, or miss entirely, what their partner was saying. As a result, minor problems escalate into profound misunderstandings, layered with hostility, frustration, and blame.

In many cases, couples think they're communicating, but the messages aren't getting through. *Can This Marriage Be Saved?* shows us that if husbands and wives can pinpoint why they're having trouble, they can sharpen their communication skills. In fact, in this conflict area more than any other, there are specific techniques and strategies for sharing ideas and feelings that couples can learn and practice— often initiating dramatic changes in the way they relate.

In many other cases, communication problems stem from differences in conversational styles between men and women, styles that can be traced right back to the playground, where little girls place a premium on talking and sharing secrets in order to make friends and be close, while little boys rely on displays of athletic prowess.

Early on, girls are schooled in the intricacies of intimate relationships. *Can This Marriage Be Saved?* shows that when women grow up, they still put a premium on talking and sharing. Wives tend to be the emotional caretakers of the marriage. More attuned to their own feelings as well the shifting tides of their relationship, they notice and bring up problems more often than men do.

In fact, in column after column, we meet women who yearn for their husbands to be a sounding board or to lend a sympathetic ear—someone with whom they can discuss their feelings and hash over problems. But men want action: Almost invariably, they'll interrupt a wife's recitation of a problem at work or with the children to jump in with a quick-fix solution. What's more, once a man suggests an idea, he often considers the case closed. Given such disparate styles of communication, it's common to hear wives complain: "He doesn't care . . . he doesn't love me . . . he always tunes me out." Or for husbands to announce in frustration: "You want to know why I tune her out? Because she talks everything to death!"

Another common reason for communication foul-ups is what we call the mind-reader syndrome. Many couples—newlywed as well as long-married—fall victim. "If he really loved me, he would know what I want" is a typical complaint. So is: "She's not saying anything; she must be mad at me." Men are also much less likely than women to ask questions of a personal nature. They frequently think: "If she wants me to know, she'll tell me." Unfortunately, this clinging to misconceptions about the way a partner ought to act often prevents couples from saying, honestly and directly, what they really feel and need.

Communication problems also occur when couples fail to state specifically what they really mean or want and, instead, couch those feelings in criticism of each other. Often, couples forget to use what marriage experts call "I" messages, which help each partner focus on his or her own feelings and take responsibility for them. Instead, they tend to launch conversations with "you" messages, which are hostile and blaming; unconsciously and almost automatically, they put a partner on the defensive.

How can a couple make sure they're communicating instead of criticizing? By beginning their conversations this way: "I feel hurt when . . . I worry that . . . I'm puzzled about . . ." instead of with "you" messages, such as "You're always late . . . You're just like your mother . . . You never call . . ." Of course, not every conversation that begins with "I" is appropriate or helpful in opening up blocked communication channels. When a partner says, "I'm sick of talking to you about this," or "I think you're a jerk," they're using what is called a "false I" message—one that's guaranteed to inflame rather than improve communication.

Timing can be equally crucial in getting your message across. The husband who wants to discuss a problem about the office when his exhausted wife yearns for sleep, or the wife who bombards a work-weary husband with a crisis the moment he walks in the door, fails to appreciate how important it is to pick the right time and place to get a message across.

Also important is the need to discuss one issue at a time—especially if it's a volatile topic. Many couples "kitchen-sink" their conversations: They start out talking about one problem and wind up arguing about another. Or one partner responds to a spouse's complaint by lobbing a nasty retort of his or her own, and the arguments escalate until neither can remember what they were talking about in the first place.

Couples chronicled in *Can This Marriage Be Saved?* also discover that there are other ways we communicate besides talking. Most of us don't realize that how we say something—our body language, facial expressions, and tone of voice—is as important as what we say. A curl of the lip, a roll of the eyes, arms tightly folded across the chest, or a false smile says contempt loud and clear. A glazed look or monosyllabic answers to a spouse's question says, "I'm fed up . . . I don't care about what's important to you."

Communication problems also occur at the listening as well as the speaking end—and once again, some of them may be linked to gender differences. Linguistics studies reveal that men tend to listen silently. They rarely nod in agreement or give their partner a verbal signal ("mm-hmm") that they've heard. On the other hand, women punctuate their listening by nodding their heads or saying mm-hmm at regular intervals. Because of this, wives may feel their husband is ignoring them. Husbands may interpret a wife's nodding to mean, Sure, I agree with you—only to be dumbfounded when she tells him later that she doesn't.

Couples who communicate well are empathic listeners. That means they listen for intent, not just content, and try to hear the feelings behind their partner's words: Is she or he tense? Worried? Happy? Listening empathically is hard work and doesn't come nearly as naturally as most people assume, even if they love each other very much. To be empathic listeners, people must put their own egos, feelings, comments, and judgments on hold. And they must look at each other when they talk, not at the newspaper, a cookbook, or out the window. One point *Can This Marriage Be Saved?* makes clear is that many people think they're listening, but what they're really doing is trying to figure out their own response. They lie in wait for the conversation to slow down so they can jump in with their own observations, opinions, or arguments.

As the following case histories illustrate, many people don't realize they aren't saying what they mean—or meaning what they say. Recognizing how each partner contributes to communication problems is the first step in changing old patterns and reconnecting in new, more loving, more empathic ways.

"HE CRITICIZES EVERYTHING I DO"

When "Can This Marriage Be Saved?" debuted in January 1953, couples were facing many of the same problems they are today. In this, the very first column, newlyweds Diana and Guy had no idea how to talk to each other and resolve their differences. Under the constant barrage of criticism, trivial skirmishes soon escalated into all-out war.

DIANA'S TURN

"I have no home, no children and no peace," said pretty twenty-two-year-old Diana. "I have no husband and no love as I think of it. Guy never kisses me except when I'm frantically busy at some household task, and then his kisses are rough and hurt me. For six years my husband has made love to me as a matter of routine, like taking in a bottle of milk—something to be done in a hurry. And he picks the time; I don't.

"My secretarial job is as hard as Guy's job, but Guy refuses to so much as dry a dish. He throws a newspaper on the floor for me to pick up, and then complains our apartment looks like a pigsty. When dinner is five minutes late, he flies into a fury, but he won't even help me with the marketing. We own an automobile, but Guy won't allow me to drive it. When we drive anywhere, it's where he wants to go.

"My savings are supposed to be set aside so we can buy a house, but in fact they're always being frittered away on his car. Guy says that we're too young to own a house and I wouldn't know how to keep it anyway. I want my babies while I'm young, but my husband seems determined to postpone having a family until he's an old man. He says I'd make a rotten mother.

"Guy criticizes everything about me. My tastes in clothes, my hairdo, even my Saturday art classes—one of my few pleasures. Other people— my boss, the girls and young men I work with—find things to admire about me, but from Guy I receive only nasty comments, never a word of affection or praise.

"I knew Guy just six weeks when we eloped. I was barely sixteen and had just begun dating and dancing and having fun. I thought marriage would be wonderful. I think I fell in love with Guy because he was nineteen and seemed like an older man to me. And he was so gentle and kind. . .

"My family was really poor, but one place we lived, just a shack really, had a backyard with a big tree and a swing. There were nine of us kids and it was hard to be alone, but often at night I would slip out of bed and go to the tree. I would swing and swing—higher and higher—to see if I could reach a star with my toe. The night I married Guy— this may sound crazy and corny, but it's true—I felt as though I'd touched a star. Something in me wished and believed the lovely, peaceful feeling would last forever.

"The feeling didn't last. Even our honeymoon was awful. We ran off to Las Vegas in a car Guy borrowed from a friend; the car broke down and the repairs took all his money

and mine, too. I had a job, of course; I've always worked. When we got back here to Los Angeles, with only ten cents between us, we had to go and stay with Guy's family. His mother was furious over the marriage—she hated to lose Guy's earnings and didn't mind saying so— and she was dreadful to me. His father wasn't so bad, but he drinks too much and doesn't work half the time and is forever cadging loans from Guy.

"After I took all the abuse I could stand from his mother, we moved in with my family. Two of my sisters doubled up with my little brothers so we had a room to ourselves, but Guy criticized my whole family.

"Finally, we took our own apartment; in six years we lived in seven different places—the landlady asked us to move out of the last one because we quarreled so much—but none of our places has been a home. Clearly, we're unsuited to each other in every way.

"My back isn't strong, and sometimes it pains so much I can hardly bear it. The doctor says the pain is caused by worry and nerves. Sometimes I cry for hours; I have horrible nightmares and even cry in my sleep. I'm trying so hard to please Guy and I'm always and forever failing. For six years, I've been a failure in everything.

"The lawyer I went to for the divorce suggested I come to you for advice and that's why I'm here. I want a divorce, a new life, a new start. I'm young. Surely I'm entitled to a home and children and a husband who loves me. I don't see how you can help me and Guy make anything of our marriage, but if you can, I suppose I'm willing to try."

GUY'S TURN

"Sometimes when Diana is crying the way she does," said the twenty-five-year-old Guy, "I think I'll go crazy. I'm back listening to my mother crying over imaginary aches and ills and making me take care of the twins and put supper on the stove, while she lies on the bed jawing about my dad being no good. Diana thinks her back and her nerves are all my fault, like everything else that goes wrong. She's just like my mother, always whining and complaining and crying for sympathy or compliments.

"My wife wears tight sweaters and skirts to the office, and then comes home and tells me how cute her boss says she is. Then she has another crying spell unless I tell her she's beautiful, when her boss—that big shot—has already said it, and said it better, as she doesn't hesitate to tell me. I'm just a dumb mechanic, and these days my wife is too high-toned to be interested in machinery.

"Maybe she should have married a big shot like her boss, or an art professor like the one whose classes she goes to on Saturday mornings, or some movie star like Clark Gable who'd hand her a line of mush all the time. She'd probably condescend to dress up and primp for Gable the way she primps for the office. You ought to see what she wears at home for me! Any old thing will do.

"I've done everything on earth to please my wife, but Diana is a girl you can't please. We've moved seven times in six years to find an apartment she likes, and now she's insisting that we buy a house we can't afford. Sure I'd like my own home someday, and some children, too, but what's the hurry? Why can't we wait?

"Diana thinks I'm a dope, but I think she's the one who's completely childish, thinking of nobody except herself. Our meals are always two hours late and then the food isn't fit to eat. You can hardly get in our kitchen for the dirty dishes. One thing I always wanted when I married was a clean, peaceful place to go to when I finished my day's work, the kind of place my dad never had with my mother. Living with Diana, I sure haven't gotten it.

"When I was a boy and would think about finding a wife, I'd picture someone docile and pretty and sweet, not necessarily brainy and with a lot of ideas, but someone who would keep a nice clean house and look after me the way nobody ever had. Diana at first seemed that way to me—shy and sweet and kind of scared, not a know-it-all like most girls. You should have heard her say how wonderful I was to be so smart about mechanical things. Boy, did she change in a hurry! Now, she's forever nagging to drive our car, and she doesn't know beans about how to treat a car. She wrecked the one I borrowed for our honeymoon and ruined our trip, so we had to go to my home to stay. My mother kicked up one of her rows and Diana couldn't handle what I'd been taking all my life. She'd have left me then if I hadn't agreed to stay with her family. Let me tell you, my family is no bargain, but hers is worse.

"Diana and I haven't had a peaceful day since we married. If she wants to go ahead and get a divorce, it's all right with me. A new shake might be better for both of us. I'm sick of things the way they are. But if you can help change things and improve Diana, I'll do my part."

THE COUNSELOR'S TURN

"Diana and Guy got off to a wretched start," said the counselor. "Both were unready for marriage, both were selfish and immature, ignorant of themselves and of each other and of the differing family backgrounds and experience that had shaped their personalities. In short, they knew nothing of the meaning of marriage.

"For instance, their sexual rela-

tions were disappointing. Diana was a romantic, chronically resentful that marriage didn't provide the thrills and fun she missed in her teens. On the other hand, Guy was contemptuous of tender lovemaking in marriage, which he considered 'unmanly.' During our sessions it became clear that his contempt and the 'roughness' during lovemaking of which Diana complained were based on ignorance: This young husband was actually unaware that sexual satisfaction for women existed. Several good books on the subject enlightened him, and once he learned to show tenderness and consideration for Diana, this couple's sexual maladjustment was solved.

"When Diana stopped reporting office compliments to her husband and bought a few pretty dresses for home use exclusively, she soon received from Guy the compliments and praise she had been tactlessly demanding. By the same token, Guy's vanity was soothed by the extra attention, and his jealous belief that Diana was forever comparing him disadvantageously with other men was changed into pride that he had such a beautiful wife.

"Diana and Guy saved their marriage not only by changing their attitudes and behavior, but also by applying thought instead of emotions to their problems. A new marriage would have solved nothing for either of them, since their basic trouble lay within themselves. For six wasted years, both honestly believed they were trying to please and understand each other, when in truth, they were merely indulging in harmful criticism. They promised instead to eliminate mutual criticism as far as was humanly possible; and they endeavored to understand themselves and each other and to communicate their needs honestly. As a logical result of this gradual reeducation, they began to give each other that loving help and attention that is marriage.

"Diana's poor housekeeping stemmed from a weak, inefficient mother and a slovenly girlhood home. Similarly, Guy's unrealistic dream of perfect meals served in a clean well-run home, with himself doing nothing to assist, represented a rebellion against a dominating mother who overloaded him with housework when he was young and made him the butt of jokes by male friends. Once this couple realized the origin of their combative attitudes, they became more tolerant of each other and found their own solution: Guy, a better cook than Diana, began helping her plan the menus and, thus, was painlessly led into carrying his fair share. He enjoyed teaching Diana to cook and she enjoyed learning. Incidentally, shortly after the meals prepared by both started reaching the table on time, Guy voluntarily offered to teach Diana how to drive a car and they began sharing the use of the troublemaking automobile.

"The questions of home ownership and children, both legitimate desires of Diana's, were tougher to solve. Guy shrank from assuming additional financial responsibility and, again after several sessions, the reason for his reluctance became apparent: Guy had seen his amiable but weak father, to whom he was devoted, crushed by the excessive demands of his dominating mother. Diana, insistently clamoring for a home and children as her right, had given no thought to her husband's desires and fear of running into debt.

"When the two started driving around on Sunday to inspect housing developments, they told themselves they were merely looking. But here again, Diana discovered a fact about her husband she hadn't learned in six years of quarreling. Indifferent to home ownership, Guy was extremely interested in rare California plants and flowers, which dated to the time when he worked as a yard boy on a big estate. In the end, they purchased a small house with a big backyard and Guy has a garden. Diana and Guy now garden enthusiastically together, their first common interest. As an outgrowth of Diana's genuine interest in his gardening, Guy became interested in her love of painting and joined the weekend class he had previously jeered at. Two pictures hang in their living room—a landscape by Diana, a seascape by Guy. She considers his painting far better than hers, and is quick to call it to the attention of visitors. The two have changed the pattern of destructive criticism into constructive mutual praise and approval. Their in-law problems have also been solved: since they now understand the 'why' of their elders' failings and virtues, they can calmly discuss their shortcomings.

"A year ago Diana gave up her job—'little Guy' was wanted by both. Diana is now awaiting the birth of a second child. She no longer needs to demand assistance from Guy because he gives it freely, anticipating her wants because of his pride and joy in his wife, child, and home. The two frequently inform us they are supremely happy—since they've realized they have to work at marriage, they have earned a good successful union."

STANDING UP TO PUT-DOWNS

Many husbands and wives feel unfairly criticized by their spouses, yet find themselves powerless to defend themselves. If you have a similar problem, these steps can help you rebuild your self-esteem and regain your footing:

1. Remind yourself that you are entitled to your feelings and have every right to speak up and say: "I feel offended by what you just said," or "That was inconsiderate." If the insulting behavior continues, try to control yourself and not lash out wildly in defense. Instead, walk away. You'll be sending a far more powerful message.

2. Choose your words with care to avoid fanning the flames. Speak firmly, but in a way that doesn't demean your partner.

3. Try not to respond to criticism by hurling criticism of your own. This escalates the argument and deepens the power struggle. If you think you can't respond reasonably, say so: "I'm too angry to talk about this right now. After I've had a chance to calm down, we'll continue."

4. Ask yourself if there might be even a shred of truth in what your partner is saying. If there is, can you negotiate a compromise? Sometimes your partner really does have a point, but he's blowing it way out of proportion. Think about what he says and decide if there are changes you can make that might ease the tension.

"MY PERFECT HUSBAND WANTS OUT"

oward and Gail had a model marriage—until the day Howard suddenly packed his bags. Why would a man run from the family he's loved for twenty years?

"This is a nightmare, and soon I'm going to wake up," said Gail, a trim forty-year-old with perfectly coiffed blond hair, classic clothes, and tears in her eyes. "Night before last, we finished dinner, the boys went up to their rooms, and Howard and I sat down in the family room to have our coffee. Nothing out of the ordinary. But instead of bringing up something about the office or the church, Howard said in this calm voice, 'Gail, I'm leaving you.' Like a bolt out of the blue. I couldn't speak. My friends always told me my marriage was too good to be true; I'm beginning to think they were right.

"Howard and I met when I was in junior high and he was a senior in high school. He worked after school at Friendly's, and my girlfriends and I used to go there, order sodas, and flirt with him. I couldn't believe it when he asked me out. My parents said I was too young to date, but finally, when I was in the tenth grade, they invited him for dinner, and after that they let me go out with him.

"By then, Howard was a sophomore at MIT, and they were so impressed with him. I mean, Howard's incredible—sensitive, hardworking, brilliant, and good-looking, too.

"Anyway, we got married when I was nineteen and a sophomore at Tufts. Howard already had a good job at an engineering firm, the first step to owning his own company.

"My parents gave us a beautiful wedding, although Howard's parents weren't exactly thrilled that it was a Methodist ceremony. They're

65

an old Boston family, High Church Episcopalians. He wanted to do whatever made me happy, and since I had always been involved in my church, Howard agreed to become a Methodist and raise our children as Methodists. This does not qualify as an interfaith marriage in my opinion, but his mother was really uppity about it.

"This never bothered Howard, though; he doesn't have a warm relationship with his mother at all. It's cordial but cool. She's what I would call an alcoholic, but Howard calls her a lady drunk. She never takes a drink until after dinner, and then she goes upstairs and drinks herself to sleep every night. As far as I can tell, she's always been too hung over to do much real mothering. Howard and his two brothers brought themselves up with the help of a sweet old housekeeper whom they adore.

"Howard's father is a nice enough man, but aside from earning a lot of money—he's a corporate executive—he was indifferent. I'm the oldest of five, three girls and two boys, and my mother has devoted her life to us. My father spent a lot of time at his job with an electronics firm, but he was always home for dinner, and he helped us with our homework, took us on camping trips, things like that.

"I told Howard right from the start, I wanted my own kids to have the same kind of childhood. Howard never objected, and he was making

enough so we could afford a four-bedroom house in a good school district. Our first son, Scott, was born while I was still in college and the second, David, just after my graduation. My mom helped with Scott so I could stay in school, but I couldn't wait to graduate and become a full-time mother.

"I did want Howard to be a very involved father and he certainly went along—happily, it seemed—with everything I suggested, starting with being my labor coach and moving right along with being on the board of directors at the nursery school, being a member of the Booster Club, coaching the soccer team, even chairing the board for the Methodist summer camp where the boys and I go every summer. I work as a counselor there and Howard comes up on weekends. He likes the time alone during the week to read and go to plays and things. It all worked out.

"At least I thought it did. Oh, I suppose there were signs of trouble over the last few years, now that I look back. For one thing, our sex life is, well, pretty nonexistent. I figured it was some kind of mid-life thing and maybe he just lost interest, so I never said anything to Howard; I didn't want to embarrass him. To be honest, the last time we made love was a year ago. I'm sure there isn't another woman, though.

"What's wrong? The boys' behavior for starters. Scott and David are now sixteen and fifteen and the teenage years have been hard on Howard. He hates rock music, the needless phone calls, and the general state of chaos the house is always in. Howard is a neatness nut and has always done his share of the housework. Now that I have a part-time administrative job at a boarding school nearby, plus all my usual volunteer work, I've fallen down on my end of the job at home. The boys' clothes and things are all over the place. But is this such a big deal? Look, they don't do drugs, and they get pretty good grades. What Howard sees as problems are just normal growing pains, if you ask me.

"So all right, Howard has complained about the boys and the house, and we haven't been making love. But was that supposed to prepare me for his announcement? He only agreed to come here on the grounds that we consider it divorce counseling. Howard has no intention of trying to save our marriage, but I can't imagine life without him. How can I change his mind?"

HOWARD'S TURN

"**D**o you know what it's like to wake up one day and realize that all the time and energy you've devoted to your family has been a complete waste?" asked Howard, a distinguished-looking forty-four-year-old with graying temples.

"When I married Gail, she said her dream was to bring up kids in the same good family atmosphere she had enjoyed as a child. That appealed to me. From what I could tell, her parents had done a great job. My mother is very proper and reserved and she spends her evenings drinking alone in her room. My father is a pleasant guy, but he never had much time for us, either.

"I never minded all this, really. I'm naturally self-sufficient and don't remember having any particular highs or lows as a kid. I was good in school and I knew I wanted to get into a good college and have a career. Actually, I guess I'm kind of a loner. But Gail—she's the joiner. I pretty much had to get on this board or that committee or I never would have seen her. But I also believed she knew what she was doing. She said we had to be involved parents, she pushed religion, and I went along with everything—even the church camp, which was a great experience for Gail and the boys, but it made a summer bachelor out of me.

"Of course, even if they'd all been home during those months, I still wouldn't have had any time with Gail. From the minute Scott was born, motherhood has been Gail's priority. Certainly our sex life took a backseat, though I don't think Gail ever noticed. Or cared. And she has let me know in no uncertain terms that as the father of two boys I have a responsibility to be a role model. I was also supposed to be a modern husband and do housework and cooking.

"In case you think I never complained, I did. Not very often and not in an angry way, but I did tell her how I felt. Gail just never paid any attention.

"The funny thing is, if I thought the boys were turning out okay, I would have continued to live her way. But frankly, none of this attention has had any effect on my sons. Don't get me wrong—I love them, but I don't believe that boys who wear earrings are normal teenagers. They have girlfriends, so I assume they're okay in that area, but why a healthy American male would want to spike his hair with green gel and wear an earring is beyond me. They do their homework, but they're not getting top grades, and they have no ambition that I can ascertain. They talk back, they throw their stuff all over the place—I've had it.

"Look. I'm a conservative New Englander. I had a job after school from the eighth grade on. I think they're spoiled rotten.

"But what does it matter what I think? Gail is always right. Well, fine. She can listen to that blaring music, watch them squander the most important years of their lives. I don't want any part of it. I don't care if I live in a furnished room somewhere, as long as there's peace and quiet. I'm not worried about being lonely. I'm alone for all intents and

purposes anyway. And no, there is no other woman. I don't think I'll trust myself to get involved again.

"Don't try to talk me out of leaving. Just give us some advice about how to have a civilized divorce. For once in my life, I'm not going to say yes when I know I should say no."

THE COUNSELOR'S TURN

"This is one of the most difficult cases I've ever handled," said the counselor. "Howard had spent a lifetime keeping the peace, first by steering clear of his alcoholic mother, who was never emotionally available for him, then by complying with Gail's every wish and command to create a storybook family. As he pointed out, he was a yes-man, and when he admitted that nothing was working out the way he had imagined, it was as if a dam had burst. In his mind, he had rejected marriage and family life, and by the time he had told Gail, his decision seemed irrevocable.

"At first, I went along with Howard's phrase, 'divorce counseling,' humoring him to gain his confidence. I saw the two of them separately for some time until I felt a joint visit would be fruitful. I would have lost Howard early if he thought I was forcing him to participate in a reconciliation.

"During her first session, Gail was frightened and puzzled, and one could certainly sympathize with her.

Still, as we worked together, she started to see how she had taken advantage of Howard's compliance, a coping style he had learned as a child. She also admitted that Howard, in his own polite way, had indeed given her warning of his dissatisfaction—warnings she had ignored. Finally, Gail learned to face the fact that there had been too much focus on the children and that some measure of discipline was in order.

"Meanwhile, in separate sessions with Howard, I gently encouraged him to consider what his life would be like in that furnished room, or for that matter, to consider if he really wanted to be alone for the rest of his life. Gradually, he realized it might be worth trying to save the marriage.

"The first joint session was not very successful, since Gail dominated the conversation and Howard sat stone-faced, saying only that he had known this would be useless. However, subsequent sessions went much better; Howard began to exercise a newfound ability to express negative feelings, and Gail, in the therapeutic setting of my office, found it easier to listen. I advised them to make a point of taking turns talking every evening at home. In preparation, I saw Howard privately again, to help him get in touch with his physical response—such as a knot in the stomach—whenever Gail said something to which he objected, and then express his opposition.

"It was during this time that a great many changes were decided upon: Howard dropped several boards and committees that didn't interest him; the boys were given house rules and chores; Gail cut back on her volunteer work to have more time with Howard and more time to do her share of the housework. And most important, Gail and the boys agreed not to attend the church camp that summer. Instead, the boys found summer jobs, and at one point, Gail's mother came for two weeks while Gail and Howard took a trip to the Bahamas.

"Those weeks alone proved to be just what this couple needed. With none of the distractions of work, community, home, and children, Howard and Gail focused on each other for the first time in years—fell in love all over again.

"In the year since they finished counseling, I've been in touch several times. The oldest boy, Scott, is now eighteen and a freshman at Boston University, with plans to go to law school. He has adopted a much more conservative look and has a steady girlfriend whom Howard and Gail approve of. David, while still into punk styles, will enter Juilliard next fall, where he plans to major in music. Howard and David will never be close, but at least they coexist peacefully.

"Howard in particular looks forward to the empty-nest years, which are closer than he had realized.

Gail still has her part-time job and some of her volunteer work, but she now accompanies Howard to the theater, and they have joined a literary discussion group. Clearly, what had looked to all the world like a perfect marriage was certainly not—but the marriage that Howard and Gail now have, though not perfect, is loving and certain to endure."

LEARNING TO TALK—AND REALLY LISTEN

Throughout most of their marriage, Gail and Howard had been running on parallel tracks. Like many couples, they communicated about the mundane, superficial aspects of their lives—Who is going to drive the boys to soccer practice? What time is the school board meeting?—but forgot about sharing their hopes and dreams, failures and uncertainties. Gail, in fact, was so caught up in her daily activities she never heard many of the things her soft-spoken husband had been trying to tell her.

Do you, like Howard, feel that your partner either doesn't listen or misinterprets what you're saying? The counselor who helped this couple communicate on a deeper level coached them in a technique called reflective listening. Here's how it works:

Set aside at least half an hour (perhaps after the children are asleep). Take turns being the sharer of information or the listener. The sharer has ten minutes to speak freely about anything that's on his or her mind (initially, it's best to avoid potentially volatile subjects). The listener must look directly at the sharer and refrain from interrupting, judging, or rushing in with a comment. After ten minutes—use a kitchen timer if you like—the listener must recap not only what the sharer said, but also the feeling behind those words. The sharer then says "Yes, that's right" or "No, that's not what I meant" and, if necessary, repeats the comments. This way, the sharer knows his or her feelings and thoughts are truly being heard and valued. Although at first Howard and Gail felt that this exercise was awkward and artificial, it soon became much easier for them. For the first time in many years, they began to really communicate.

"HE'S SO IRRESPONSIBLE"

———

*F*rustrated, frantic, and furious, Maggie can no longer live with a man who promises to do things but never follows through. What happens when one partner's anxiety overwhelms a marriage?

"**I** love Tim more than I've ever loved anyone, but I can't live with him one more day," sobbed Maggie, twenty-eight, her blue eyes red from crying. "We've been married four years and we've been on an emotional roller coaster almost all that time.

"Tim and I both grew up as Navy brats. I come from a family of five kids and Tim has two brothers. We left the States when I was five and lived all over the world until my last year in high school, when we moved to Norfolk, Virginia.

"My parents have been married for thirty-five years, and they have a solid marriage. They've always been very affectionate, but it couldn't have been easy for Mom, raising all of us and moving so many times. Sometimes Dad would drink too much and I know that bothered her.

"Mom was the practical parent; Dad was impulsive, emotional, and indulgent. He's a great entertainer and everyone loves him. When we were little, we were very poor. Dad owned a small string of grocery stores before he joined the Navy, but each one failed. Every time my father got a new posting, the move would be wrenching, but I landed on my feet. I made friends easily, and I was a model child and a good student. I was constantly worried about how Mom was feeling though. I was the family peacemaker. Mom knew she could count on me.

"So did the girls in my freshman dorm. I went to a small women's

71

college two hours from home, and there, too, everyone came to me for advice—they put a sign on my door that said 'mental-health clinic.'

"After college, I shared an apartment with my brother Matt and started working for a Head Start program. Matt introduced me to Tim. They'd been childhood friends.

"One night Matt and I went to a political rally, which was absolutely uneventful, but we ran into Tim and ended up arguing politics until one in the morning.

"I thought Tim was adorable and very smart. The following week, he called and asked me to dinner. We had a lovely meal—but when the check came, he didn't have enough money. I told him not to worry, but he was so embarrassed. And that, I must say, foreshadowed a lot of the problems we're having now.

"After a week of seeing each other practically day and night, Tim was telling me how much he loved me. After less than a year, we had a huge wedding with a terrific jazz band, and we all danced through the night. But things just haven't been right since. We can't get in sync. I'm detail-oriented; he's the opposite. Tim says I'm crazy to get worked up about things, but he doesn't understand that he never does anything that he promises to do. Bills have to be paid, but I don't trust him for a second to pay them on time. He borrows library books and never returns them. We have

seventy dollars worth of library fines right now. And parking tickets! I can't think about how many he has!

"Even more embarrassing—we'll meet friends for dinner, and he never has enough money to pay the check. Now, that was cute on our first date, but it's not cute anymore. Unless I nag, nothing changes. I hate having to remind him that he's going to miss an exit on the expressway, but if I don't, he'll drive right past it.

"But it's more than his being irresponsible about little things. Tim never wants to be with me anymore. Maybe some of it's my fault. I have a wonderful but demanding job as director of community educational programs for underpriviledged kids, and until a few months ago I was going to night school. For two years, we hardly saw each other.

"Now there's no fun or romance left. I try to kiss Tim or reach for his hand and he pulls away. When I ask what's wrong, he either says 'Nothing' or marches into his office.

"I know Tim's work is very important to him. Last year, he finally quit his radio job and decided to try free-lance writing. We figured in six months we'd know if he could make it. He worked at home and did well.

"Unfortunately, he's become this incredible workaholic. And since his office is in a corner of the bedroom, he never seems to be able to distance himself from work. I'll be in the kitchen, telling him about something that's really upsetting me at work, and he'll just tune out. He even takes work-related phone calls at any time of the day or night.

"I hate the fact that he never listens to me anymore. He pretends to, but I can see his eyes glaze over.

"Lately, we've been having terrible fights. Out of the blue, he'll start kicking a chair for no apparent reason. Often he's upset about things that happened ages ago. So I cry my eyes out and try to drag out of him what's wrong.

"These battles are so draining that last week I told Tim I have to move out for a while. I'm just so furious and frustrated, and I need some space to think about things."

TIM'S TURN

"I can't believe she wants to leave," said Tim, twenty-nine, a handsome man in cutoff jeans and a T-shirt. "But Maggie's right; I hate the way things are between us, too, and I don't know what to do about it. I've tried to be the kind of husband she wants, but half the time I have no idea what's bothering her. She gets so emotional it scares me.

"I'm not used to this kind of constant crying. No one in my family ever acted this way. Like Maggie said, my father was also in the military and we moved a lot when I was younger. But my parents never seemed to fight. Everything in my family was kept on an even level.

"My parents were affectionate, although nowhere near as touchy-feely as Maggie's family. I had a temper and I'd pop off about a lot of things; part of it was typical teenage rebelliousness, but there were other things, too. I'd felt established in junior high school, then we moved abroad. Those were unhappy years for me. I hated the Vietnam War, I was very cynical about my parents' generation and didn't know what I wanted to accomplish in life—but I never felt comfortable talking to my parents about anything remotely personal. My father died of a heart attack when he was fifty. Oh, he was drinking and smoking far too much, but I also think he was miserable about his work and he held it all in.

"In college, I decided to become a journalist. I snagged a job on a small paper in Oklahoma and was back visiting my family for Easter when I met Maggie. I purposely took a job back home so we could be together.

"As Maggie said, I hated that job and finally quit to free-lance. That was scary. I worked like a demon, but since Maggie was at school most nights that was fine.

"So here I am, working my tail off, and Maggie's on my case about how I don't love her and I'm not connected enough. She hangs all over me and wants to make love all the time. I don't know how to react when she climbs into my lap when I want a quiet minute to sit and read the newspaper. I feel smothered.

"She also accuses me of not listening to her. Believe me, I pay attention, but when you hear something twenty times, you can't digest it anymore. Maggie always beats a problem to death.

"But I should also say I love my work and it's hard for me to break away from it. I'm finally doing something I love and people are recognizing that I'm good at it. Why can't my wife see that?

"Anyway, she's right about how we go in cycles. Things are better for a while, then before I know it she's berating me for being irresponsible. I'm fed up. She's not my mother, and I don't want to be henpecked about paying the bills, going to the bank, returning library books. I don't want her keeping schedules for me and reminding me to buy a present for my brother, whose birthday is three months away. And Maggie is the worst backseat driver you ever met. If the light turns green and I don't go that second, she jumps all over me.

"Most of the time I never bother to tell her how I feel. Why should I? I rarely win arguments. She's much better at expressing herself and I wind up looking like the bad guy.

"So maybe I'm just not able to have an emotional relationship. I feel inadequate and I know you're going to come down like a ton of bricks on me. But I can't deal with Maggie any more than she can deal with me."

"When this couple came to see me, Maggie was sobbing and desperate," said the counselor. "She was afraid of her husband's waning sexual interest and frustrated by his irresponsible attitude.

"Tim was confused. On one hand, he felt helpless in the face of his wife's outbursts and genuinely puzzled as to why she perceived him as disconnected when he thought he was a loving husband. But Tim also felt smothered by Maggie's demands for attention and affection and besieged by her constant nagging.

"After listening to Maggie for a while, I told her gently but firmly to stop crying and speak slowly so we could sort out what was troubling her.

"As Maggie began to tell me about her family history, it became clear that while there was undoubtedly a tremendous amount of love, affection, and devotion in her family, there was also a history of alcoholism and depression. While Maggie hadn't experienced her father's alcoholism as anything terrible—he was not an abusive alcoholic who disappeared for days at a time but rather the drinker whom everyone indulged—his illness affected her nonetheless. Highly sensitive, Maggie's role model was her mother, herself a super-responsible woman who tried to do everything for everybody.

"Even as an adult, Maggie never felt she could stop worrying and relax for a minute. She continued her do-everything-for-everybody role in college, at work, and in her marriage. Maggie took Tim on, much as she would any project—she agonized about him constantly, trying to prevent or forstall any problems.

"Tim was passively aggressive in response to Maggie's pressuring. He was angry at his wife for smothering him, but since he came from a family where no one ever said how they really felt or what they needed, he wasn't used to expressing his anger. Instead, his irritation took the form of forgetfulness, distractedness, and lack of interest in sex. The more Maggie pushed for attention, the more Tim would pull away, which, of course, made her even more anxious.

"Tim, like his father, was congenial and outgoing, but he'd picked up the family trait of not recognizing his own needs as well as tuning out those of other people, especially to avoid conflict. In the process of numbing himself to Maggie's demands, he numbed himself to responsibility—hence the parking tickets and overdue books. My work with Tim was to get him in touch with his feelings and then to prompt him to speak up.

"One of my recommendations to Maggie was that she see a colleague of mine, a psychiatrist trained in psychopharmacology—the use of medication to help in the therapy process. I felt strongly that there was a biochemical basis for Maggie's difficulty in focusing on her worries without feeling overwhelmed. My colleague confirmed my opinion, but Maggie didn't want to take an antidepressant. So, with the psychiatrist, she worked out a program to strictly monitor her diet, sleep, and exercise habits to see if there was a connection between her lifestyle and her mood swings.

"By keeping a meticulous daily log of her activities we saw that as little as one half hour of sleep each night could affect the way Maggie acted at her job as well as with her husband. Whether she exercised or drank coffee also influenced her, as did her menstrual cycle. The link was so clear that Maggie resolved to take an aerobics class three times a week and aim for eight hours' sleep at night. She switched to herbal tea at work instead of coffee and now rarely drinks alcohol.

"These simple changes showed Maggie she was capable of self-control, and once she became conscious of this, she was able to stop smothering Tim with demands for affection. Simply backing off for a little bit got immediate results, which, in turn, was strong positive reinforcement for her. 'It's like magic,' Maggie reported. 'If I give him space, he reaches out to me.'

"Maggie also learned not to get

furious if she sensed that Tim wasn't listening to her. 'If I see his eyes glaze over, it's a signal to me to stop and ask myself if I've said this a hundred times already,' said Maggie.

"Tim was tremendously relieved when he realized I wasn't going to put the full responsibility for change on his shoulders. I did suggest, however, that he join one of my weekly therapy groups, and this proved a real catalyst for him. In the beginning, Tim was characteristically late for the group sessions or would forget about them completely. Yet each week, several other people challenged his forgetfulness, often echoing what Maggie had been telling him all along. This finally helped him realize that he, too, had changes to make.

"To help Tim separate himself from his work, they decided to rent a small office for him downtown. 'So now I really can leave my work at the office,' Tim said. He also takes the initiative in planning activities for them to do together on a regular basis.

"I suggested that Maggie let Tim see the consequences of his inactions. Maggie had reached the point where she was assuming her husband wouldn't do something before the situation even arose, and she had to stop running interference for him.

"'If he has no money the next time you go to dinner, what could you do?' I asked. 'Well, I could go to the ladies' room and let him figure it out, instead of handing him the money,' she replied. Having a reasonable option made her feel better. Since bill paying was also a big issue, Tim made a commitment to pay them every month and Maggie vowed not to nag him. While he didn't pay them as quickly as Maggie would have liked, they did get paid, and the couple's credit rating remained strong. Similarly, Maggie stopped nagging about the parking tickets, and Tim found he was unable to renew his license unless he went downtown to the motor vehicle bureau and settled his fines in person.

"But most important for Tim, instead of withdrawing, he has learned to tell Maggie how he feels in a straightforward way and not store up hurts only to explode in anger later. Since Tim has been so sincere in his efforts to change in other ways, Maggie can accept his criticism without feeling threatened.

"Maggie and Tim ended couples counseling after a year, but both continued in groups—Tim for two years and Maggie for three. 'I realized there was more about me that I wanted to change,' she explained. 'And since we'd made so much progress in such a short time, I was inspired to continue on my own.'"

GETTING TO THE BOTTOM OF A COMMUNICATION LOGJAM

Sometimes what appears to be a marital issue really has its source in a problem that "belongs" to one spouse. Real marital difficulties develop around it, but these cannot be dealt with, let alone resolved, until the root problem is uncovered. After all, you can't end an argument with your spouse if you're not talking to each other. That's what happened to Maggie and Tim.

Couples will benefit if they can recognize the behavioral clues that often mask depression and indicate the need for professional help. Do you or your spouse exhibit or is one of you troubled by:

1. Changes in sleeping and eating patterns.

2. Withdrawal from family and friends.

3. Lack of interest in activities or events that once gave pleasure.

4. Reduction in sexual activity or intimacy between the two of you.

5. Talk of a despairing nature: "It's no use," or "Things will never get better."

6. Inability to derive pleasure from any aspect of life.

7. General irritability.

"We Have Nothing in Common Anymore"

After twenty-five years of marriage, George and Marge were convinced that their differences far outweighed their similarities. What happens when two people who love each other drift apart?

MARGE'S TURN

"Who is this man I'm married to?" demanded Marge, fifty, a tall, slender woman with a tense, unhappy face. "George and I have just celebrated our silver wedding anniversary and I still feel as if I don't know him. I am equally certain he doesn't know me.

"On the one hand, my husband can be jovial and happy-go-lucky, always out for laughs and a good time. He has a million friends and every one of them thinks I'm so fortunate to be married to such a fun-loving guy. But let George have a few drinks and a different side of him emerges. He will turn on me in a rage and pour out a hate-filled diatribe of cruel and vicious insults.

"I don't mean to imply that George is an alcoholic. He doesn't drink often, but when he does take a drink or two, usually at a party, I brace myself for what will follow. The moment we've left the group, Mr. Nice Guy disappears. George goes into a tirade, accusing me of being frigid, penny-pinching, nagging, bitchy—every hideous adjective he can come up with. When we get home, I bury my face in my pillow and cry my eyes out. I feel so worthless. But in the morning, George reverts to his sunny self, spilling over with apologies for having had a few too many. When I try to discuss the previous night he refuses to acknowledge that any scene occurred.

"I fell in love with George because of his exuberant approach to life. I had been raised in a family that put duty before pleasure. My father, a German immigrant who never went to high school, had educated himself by taking correspondence courses. He worked as a self-employed building contractor and supported us so well that Mother never had to work outside the home. Dad doled out money to her to run the house and I don't think she ever knew what they had in the bank. Both my parents were strict disciplinarians and my sister and I were always on our best behavior.

"I don't know much about my parents' personal relationship. I now think there may have been some problems, but they didn't let it show. They lived apart for three years while I was a teenager, but that was supposedly because my father had to be away on business. Dad and Mama never argued. I can remember only one fight, during dinner one night, when Mother got up, walked around the table, and slapped my father. I will never forget the shock of seeing her do something so incredibly out of character.

"My high school years were pleasant. I made good grades and enjoyed sports, although I didn't date much. After I graduated I went to college, but soon dropped out to take an office job. I had no particular career goal. All I really wanted was to be a housewife and mother.

"When I was nineteen, I married Frank, my girlfriend's brother. It was a foolish thing to do—I was in love with love, not with Frank. Although I soon realized I had made a mistake, I hoped that once we had children life would be better. When three years passed and I still had not become pregnant, my mother-in-law casually mentioned that Frank was sterile. He had known all along and had never told me. After that, there just didn't seem to be any reason to stay married.

"George came into my life two years after my divorce. He was a salesman for the company I worked for and I was immediately attracted to him. But George was married, and although he and his wife were separated, I still didn't feel we should go out together. I encouraged him to give their relationship one final chance, but the effort was not successful. Once George was legally free, we were married.

"I can't put into words what I actually expected from the marriage. I know I hoped it would be more than it is. When I look back over the past twenty-five years, I feel as though we have been treading water. Except for having raised two children, now on their own, we have nothing to show for all our time together.

"Not that I ever expected to be rich. I knew George had an obligation to the three children from his former marriage, and I never quarreled over the portion of his income that went to them. What I have resented is his inability to adjust his lifestyle to compensate for that expense.

"Although George won't admit it, we live hand-to-mouth. He works on commission and his earnings have never been consistent. It's true that many of his career problems have not been his fault. He started a promising business and that didn't work; his partner was unreliable. I don't blame him, but his stubborn refusal to accept our situation makes me furious. How can he take afternoons off to play golf when we need every penny? How can he expect us to eat out with friends several nights a week when I'm going crazy figuring out how to put food on the table?

"I went back to work several years ago to help make ends meet. My job consists of dull, boring, unrewarding office work, but that's all I feel qualified to handle. George uses my earnings to subsidize his membership in the country club. He's the only one who uses the facilities—I'm too tired after work and housekeeping to even think of going there. But George shows no appreciation of my efforts. Many nights he doesn't show up for the dinner I've fixed, and he doesn't even call to tell

me he's not coming home. Hours later, when he finally walks in, he can't understand why I'm not in the mood to make love.

"I don't feel that our relationship has any meaning for George. I'd like us to spend time alone together to discuss what matters to each of us. But every evening, George wants to be out socializing. When I attempt to talk to him about the problems in our marriage, he acts as though I'm speaking a foreign language.

"I don't want a divorce. George and I have invested too much of our lives in each other to split up now. But the thought of going on as we have been for another twenty-five years is more than I can face. It was different when the kids were home. I felt confident and secure in the role of mother. Now that it's just George and me, I feel so unfulfilled and empty. Our relationship is all I have left—and it isn't enough."

GEORGE'S TURN

"I don't know what I'm doing at a counseling service," said George, fifty-six, a handsome, white-haired man with an affable grin. "I'm a fun-loving guy who takes life as it comes. The last thing I want is for some cockeyed therapist to change me.

"My dad was the same sort of person. All the youngsters in the neighborhood loved him. He'd take us all fishing, build a bonfire, tell us scary stories—he was like one of the kids. My mother was the one who always played the heavy.

"My father was a dredge operator who worked at dam construction and every six to eight months he'd be transferred to a new location. I had attended twenty-four schools by the time Mom finally put her foot down and announced she was sick of moving. From then on, my brothers and I saw Dad only on weekends and our mother took over control of the family.

"As a kid, I had one big dream— to become a doctor. When I graduated from high school I was drafted into the Navy, where I trained to become an operating-room technician. I served as a surgical assistant during the Korean War and was more competent than a lot of the doctors. After my discharge I entered college on the GI Bill, fully intending to go to medical school. That plan fell through and I have no one to blame but myself.

"I got married—which was crazy for a young man in my position— and then my wife, Sheila, immediately became pregnant and had to stop working. I held all sorts of odd jobs in the evenings and on weekends, and we borrowed money from our parents, but the bills kept mounting. Sheila nagged me to leave school and get a full-time job.

"My grades kept dropping. I blamed that on financial pressure, but to tell the truth, that was only part of the problem. During my years in the service, I'd forgotten how to study. When I flunked out of college in my junior year, I was actually relieved. Finally, I could go to work and support my family.

"I found a job selling office supplies, and I was good at it. Our finances improved, but our marriage didn't. Sheila was on my back constantly and I could hardly bear to come home at night. Two more babies arrived, which added to the chaos. We were both miserable and decided on a trial separation.

"That's when I met Marge. She was tall and stately, lovely to look at and as soothing to be with as Sheila was overbearing. At Marge's urging, I returned to Sheila to give our relationship one last chance. The reconciliation was a farce; my heart and mind were totally focused on Marge. Although the divorce was at my request, it was painful. I have always felt guilty about leaving Sheila with three children.

"Marge insists that we have nothing to show for our twenty-five years together. What does she want, a twenty-room mansion? We have two fine kids, lots of friends, fun times to remember, and good health.

"Having been through eight hellish years of bickering with my first wife, I resolved that things would be different this time. I'm proud of the fact that I've kept my oath. Marge isn't the easiest person to live with, but I've tried to ignore the negative and focus on the positive. When she gives me the cold shoulder sexually, I grin and bear it. If she doesn't want to go out partying, I go without her. Marge is a martyr. When she starts pulling her 'poor me' act, I just close my ears.

"Marge's big complaint is that I sometimes get rowdy after partying and pop out with things that might have been better left unsaid. I occasionally do that—but I always apologize. A guy can't be held accountable for every remark he makes when he's had one beer too many, now, can he?"

THE COUNSELOR'S TURN

"When this couple walked into my office, my initial reaction was an echo of George's," said the counselor. "What in the world, I asked myself, are these two people doing here?

"Within a few minutes, however, it became obvious that there was a tremendous difference in their personalities. He was a ride on a roller coaster that had no end, while she was a gentle canoe trip on a rippleless lake. Despite the fact that they had shared their lives for twenty-five years, neither had developed any tolerance for the other's individuality. Marge felt George's social behavior was extravagant; he felt she was cold and a party pooper. Although there

were certain areas in which they were compatible (they had no friction, for instance, over raising their children), they were in total disagreement about the the use of their money and leisure time.

"Most important, and hardest to deal with, was that each had perfected a facade that prevented sharing and self-exposure. In George's case, the facade was a clown mask, fashioned after the personality of his genial but weak-natured father. 'Keep laughing and you won't notice what hurts you' was his motto. George was really filled with bottled-up emotions—hostility toward his nagging first wife and resentment toward Marge when she exhibited any of her annoying traits. He also felt guilty about what he saw as his life's failures—his unsuccessful first marriage, his aborted dream of becoming a doctor, and his ineffectual business ventures. Because his Mr. Nice Guy image was so important to him, he successfully repressed these feelings most of the time. When his control was loosened by alcohol, however, they came bursting to the surface. George did not have a drinking problem per se; he drank very occasionally and then in moderation. But he did use liquor as a scapegoat when his frustration level became too high.

"Marge played the role of martyr. Her father had been the sole provider and authority figure and she viewed George's easygoing approach to life as a sign of irresponsibility. Sensing that his extravagances were his subtle way of spiting her, she retaliated by denying herself any pleasures.

"Their behavior was so deeply ingrained that for a while I was afraid counseling would not be productive. Each wanted the other one to be fixed up, but was resistant to any idea of changing themselves. The turning point came when Marge admitted she was partially responsible for their problems. George was then able to face up to his own contribution to Marge's unhappiness.

"As Marge recognized, this couple's problems were compounded by a breakdown in communication. George bottled things up and Marge spoke in generalities. 'George does not understand my needs,' she would say accusingly, defying her husband to figure out what these needs were. George, understandably frustrated by this game-playing, shrugged off the challenge and went his own way. In counseling, Marge learned to be more specific about what she wanted. One assignment I gave her was to come up with a list of things that would give her pleasure. Amazingly, she was unable to do this. She had sunk so far into her martyr role that she could not be the least bit self-indulgent. Finally, with reluctance, she revealed that she would like to be able to soak in a hot bath for an hour after work. The idea that she had been depriving herself of such a simple luxury was so ludicrous that even Marge laughed.

"Soon George and Marge began to air their feelings and to develop an appreciation for each other as individuals. By sharing the details of his past with his wife, George was able to confront his negative emotions and understand where they came from. He learned to express his feelings on a daily basis, instead of letting them build.

"Marge and George have learned to make compromises and now spend leisure time in activities they both enjoy. Marge joins George for tennis and golf on weekends and is more open to home entertaining. George, though still gregarious, spends many more evenings at home, and if he does decide to have dinner at the country club, he phones Marge to ask her to join him.

"Now that she, too, is enjoying the club facilities, Marge no longer complains about the cost of membership. A contributing reason for this is an increase in family income. Marge recently received a surprise promotion at work: She was made office manager—a direct result, I believe, of her new, positive approach to life.

"Three months after this couple terminated counseling, I phoned Marge. 'There's not much news,' she told me, then added, 'except that I've fallen in love with my husband.'"

LEARNING TO ACCEPT—AND APPRECIATE—YOUR DIFFERENCES

Despite the fact that these two have shared their lives for twenty-five years, neither has developed a tolerance for the other's individuality. Like George and Marge, many couples mistakenly believe that partners must think and feel exactly the same way in a good marriage. In any close relationship, differences in opinions and priorities, as well as in the way each partner handles anxiety and stress, are bound to develop. Although Marge and George didn't notice these differences when they were caught up in childrearing, once the nest was empty the disparity appeared glaring. Unwittingly, this couple has created a communication gap that affects every aspect of their relationship.

If you and your partner are struggling with similar issues, break the stalemate by keeping the following points in mind:

- **Acknowledge the part you both play in any problems you may be having.** Marge and George automatically assumed the fault lay with their partner.

- **State your needs and feelings as specifically as you can without being accusatory.**

- **Be willing to compromise.** If Marge stops playing the martyr and joins George on the tennis court once in a while, she will realize how much fun she can have and he will be more open to quiet evenings at home.

- **Develop an appreciation for each other's individuality and perspective.** Stop trying to be right. Instead, adopt the motto "I could be wrong."

"HE ALWAYS TUNES ME OUT"

—◆—

Barb can't understand what happened to the caring, thoughtful man she married. Howie can't understand why his wife is so upset. Instead of trying to find out, she screams and he withdraws, preferring not to listen to what he doesn't want to hear.

BARBARA'S TURN

"I don't even know where to begin," said Barbara, thirty-four, a short, dark-haired woman in a pink jogging suit. "Howie has things worked out just the way he wants them, with no thought to my wants or my needs.

"I thought we were going to have the perfect marriage. Howie and I were best friends for two years before we became lovers.

"But we've been married four years now and Howie has taken a 180-degree turn. There are no more jogs in the park or breakfasts out. No romantic dinners. Howie used to take the initiative. Now all he does is stay home and watch a baseball game or read some esoteric German philosopher.

"So we lead separate lives. We have no family life—and he doesn't seem to care. The more I explain that he's just not there for me and our daughter—Callie is thirteen months old—the more he withdraws.

"Some days I can't bear to get up in the morning. I go to the office—I'm a personnel director at a computer company, but I've worked only three days a week since Callie was born. I race home from the office to watch Callie so Howie can work. We both decided when I got pregnant that we didn't want to hire a baby-sitter, so he's been Mr. Mom for the past year. Since Howie works at home—he also has a carpentry business and does fine cabinetry—we thought that would work.

"When I get home, I barely have time to change my clothes before I'm on duty until Callie goes to bed. By then, I'm catatonic. I have no energy left to talk to my friends anymore.

"Another reason I've lost touch is that no one seems to be good enough for Howie. He used to be gracious about doing things with my friends and family. But now he calls my friends boring airheads.

"Weekends are worse. I feel like a single mom. Howie says this is the only time he can get any work done, so I'm in the park all by myself, pushing Callie on the swings. I see all these moms and dads together and my heart breaks. What kind of life is this? We never make love anymore either. Howie literally pushes me away.

"And he feels totally put upon if I ask him to do anything. Everything with him is a big deal. My mother was coming for a visit last month and I asked him to install a simple window fan in the bedroom so she'd be comfortable. He never did.

"Then he gets on me about spending money. Howie's needs are maybe four new T-shirts every year, so compared with that, naturally my needs seem excessive. Well, I'm the one who's working. Don't I have a right to buy my daughter something if I want to? I don't buy any-

thing for myself. I buy toys, for heaven's sake, or something for the house. Recently we had a huge fight because I bought a lamp for the bedroom. I'm tired of living with hand-me-downs from our parents. But when I explain that, he gives me a dirty look, arches one eyebrow, and walks out of the room. Or he explodes, just like my father. I could never deal with Dad's out-bursts—they seemed so illogical, just like Howie's.

"I'm the youngest of three. My dad was a manager at a paper-processing plant and my mother was a stay-at-home mom until I was in college, when she went back to work at a gift shop.

"Everyone in my house was sort of closed off. I remember having dinner at a friend's house when I was in junior high and it was a revelation to discover that people actually talked to each other at the dinner table.

"I thought that if I did well in school, Mom and Dad would be pleased, but even though I got good grades, they didn't seem to notice. I'd often spend the night at a friend's house; I loved chatting with someone else's mother.

"I couldn't wait to go to college to get away. I attended a small Midwestern church-affiliated school that had offered me a scholarship. After graduation, I lived at home until I found an entry-level job as a secretary. Finally, I had enough money to rent an apartment—which brings me to how I met Howie.

"Howie's parents, who are wealthy, bought this small, run-down apartment house for Howie to fix up, manage, and live in rent-free. That was very generous, but I think they did it because they were afraid their son would never be able to support himself. Anyway, I rented an apartment in Howie's building and we quickly became friends. After about two years, we realized that our relationship was shifting. We were married a few months later.

"At first, Howie was really tuned in to what I needed. Now he's living on another planet. Recently, I'd been out shopping all day with Callie. I came in loaded down with bags. I desperately wanted Howie to take the baby, give her a snack, and help me put away the groceries. Anybody could see I was wiped out. But not my husband. He strolls into the kitchen, says hi, gets a soda, and goes back to his workshop.

"On top of that, when I get home from the office, so excited to see my daughter, she runs to her daddy. I think Howie encourages that, too. We've been having rip-roaring fights all the time. Both of us have terrible tempers and we dig in our heels. In the past, if a relationship didn't work out, I always thought it was my fault. This time, I know it's not."

HOWIE'S TURN

"I married my mother," said Howie,. thirty-five, a sandy-haired man in a work shirt and frayed jeans. "We used to call my mother 'the little general.' Well, Barbara has turned into such a critical, overbearing person, I often get this déjà-vu feeling: I'm twelve years old again and my mother is shouting orders. My philosophy then was—and still is—to keep out of sight.

"I'm from St. Louis. My family still lives there and they can't understand why I don't. Mother always complained that my father wasn't involved enough in the family; she wanted him to be the boss, to help her manage all of us. My father would give anything for me to come home and join him in his real estate firm; both of my younger brothers are now full partners. They all have these huge homes and fancy cars. That's not who I am.

"My parents always seemed to find time for the things they wanted me to do, but never for what I wanted. I'd spend hours reading in my room or puttering in my workshop—my father did buy me some equipment most kids would kill for. Throughout high school, I had a sense that nothing I did got a response from my parents—positive or negative.

"As soon as I graduated from college, I headed for New York. I didn't know anyone there or what I wanted to do; I just had to get as far away from Missouri as I could. I did odd jobs, tending bar, working in a hardware store. When my father realized I was never going to come home, he bought this building for me to manage.

"I wanted to go out with Barb the minute I saw her, but she can close off and look very aloof, so I figured she was involved with someone. Barbara thinks the relationsip has changed dramatically from the way it was when we were dating. I don't think it's all that different. Maybe I do want to stay home. What's the point of going out for the sake of going out?

"As far as socializing with her friends, well, unless I can really feel I'm learning something from people, I see no point in having a relationship. I'm not interested in neurotic, superficial people.

"Okay, so maybe I don't have an official job like Barb does, but I resent her implicaton that I'm a freeloader in this relationship. I manage the building where we live, renovate all the apartments, paint them when necessary, collect the rents, and do whatever maintenance work a superintendent in an apartment building does. I don't think Barb has the slightest idea how much effort that takes.

"Plus, I'm trying to establish myself as a master carpenter. I love the creative effort involved in choosing the woods, designing a piece that is aesthetically beautiful yet functional, too. Right now, my work is my focus. Finally, it all seems to be coming together. Yet I sacrifice three workdays a week to care for Callie. The problem is, I need structured time to finish a piece of furniture. I need more than just a half hour here or there.

"Barb doesn't appreciate what I do or what I need to do it. She'll barge into the workshop and say a fan needs to be installed or the air conditioners have to be cleaned. If I don't drop everything right that minute, I'm screwing up.

"Then there are the times when I'm supposed to have these supernatural powers to read her mind. The other day with the groceries is typical. I didn't realize she wanted me to help. I came in to say hi and I got my head blown off.

"I also don't like being told that I'm rejecting her in bed. She's the one who doesn't want to make love. You can tell when someone is just going through the motions.

"But I adore my daughter; I'm a terrific father, and Callie and I have a special relationship. Barb is jealous. When she comes home, if Callie doesn't rush into her arms, Barb thinks she's being rejected. Of course Callie loves her. But she's only thirteen months old. It's only natural that since she's spent the day with me, she'd take a little time to warm up to Barb.

"As far as the weekends go, what can I say? I don't love going to the playground. I go there with the baby during the week and weekends are two days when I can grab some uninterrupted work time.

"Money is a real issue for us. The furniture we have is just fine. In fact, I think Barbara spends entirely too much on things we don't need. Callie's playroom looks like Toys 'R Us.

"Look I'm here because Barbara insisted. And although I know you're not supposed to take sides, I'm sure you're going to label me the bad guy in all this."

THE COUNSELOR'S TURN

"I've never seen a client as angry as Barbara was," said the counselor. "At our first session, she shouted nonstop, berating Howie for not caring and not being involved. She believed that Howie had set up their life exactly the way he wanted it and that she was the drone who shouldered most of the financial and household responsibilities. As she saw it, her options were few.

"Howie couldn't figure out what was going on. From his point of view, he was giving much to the relationship. It was essential for Barbara and Howie to understand why the other reacted the way they did. I believed that once Barbara understood that Howie withdrew because he was frustrated and not because he didn't love her, she'd feel less alone and more eager to find constructive ways of working together. In turn, if Howie could become aware of when and why he was ignoring her, he'd be able to change. For this marriage to work, both of them needed to negotiate solutions instead of ignoring the other person or screaming.

"One of the most important things I did for Barbara and Howie was to provide them with an impartial sounding board. They are both intelligent people who really do love each other, but they were so burdened by the responsibilities of parenthood that they were unable to think clearly.

"A vivacious, strong-willed woman, Barbara grew up in a home where nothing she did seemed to have much impact. Her mother was emotionally needy and her father was a passive man who had little interaction with the family except when he blew up in fits of anger for no apparent reason.

"Howie came from a traditional, wealthy Midwestern family. His father was undemonstrative and wrapped up in his business dealings. His mother was domineering and critical. Everyone in the family learned that the only way to get along with her was to tune her out. Neither parent bothered to take Howie's interests into account. To cope with disappointments, Howie learned to turn a switch in his head, to withdraw and disengage. He also learned that the only way he was going to do what he wanted was to pursue it single-mindedly. Howie never knew what it meant to be in a reciprocal relationship; nor did he believe there was any point in cooperating or talking things over.

"Compounding the problem for this couple were their different social styles. Howie was a loner who prided himself on his offbeat ways. Barbara was sociable and liked to go out.

"Before we could get any work done, however, I had to help Barbara calm down. This wasn't easy. I told her that although she did have the right to get upset with Howie, the intensity of her anger was out of proportion to the 'crime.' In time, she began to ease up.

"Barbara's number-one complaint was that Howie had arranged their lives the way he wanted and that she had no options. Since I wanted her to be more self-determining, I said, 'Forget about Howie; let's talk about you. What in your world would you like to change?' Barbara was able to see there were many things she was pleased with. She was making a good salary working three days a week—most women do not have that option. Furthermore, she enjoyed her work.

"At this point I said, 'So what can you do to change the things you're not happy with?' While their decision not to hire a sitter seemed like a good one at first, it was not working. I suggested that hiring someone to care for Callie would give Barbara time for herself after work, and Howie time to work during the day, freeing both of them to enjoy family time.

"I wanted to make sure Barbara understood that Howie's contribution to the family was as important and valid as hers was. Giving him an established, uninterrupted time to work and telling him she appreciated his efforts allowed Howie to be more responsive to some of the other things she was saying.

"Together, we settled on a plan: Barbara agreed to make a list of the things she'd like Howie to do each week. This way, they could discuss the timetable and Howie could say, 'Yes, I can put the fan in this afternoon, but I won't get to the air conditioners until Wednesday.' Although Barbara might want the job done sooner, she felt better knowing it would at least get done.

"Barbara also had to learn that she could not expect Howie to read her mind. If she needed help putting away groceries, she had to say so. She has become better at voicing her needs simply and clearly and Howie has been more willing to help her. Barbara also admitted that perhaps she was so jealous of Howie's closeness to Callie that she bought her all those toys to try to make up for her time away. Now that she feels better about herself and her daughter, Barbara has stopped spending so much on toys. In turn, Howie has agreed to spend a little to fix up the house.

"Reaching a compromise when it came to their social life was trickier. As Callie gets older, I told them, they will most likely make new friends through her whom they both like. Already, since they've been spending much more time together, they have become friends with two other families they see in the park.

"In the past, Barbara and Howie were so angry that neither had felt very loving. As the tension eased, their sex life improved, too. Barbara and Howie ended therapy after a year, pleased with the progress they had made and confident that they could negotiate solutions as problems arose."

CURING THE MIND-READER SYNDROME

Although they don't realize it, many couples are victims of the mind-reader syndrome. This can happen if one person has difficulty getting in touch with his or her own feelings, much less communicating them to a spouse. Such people believe that their partner will magically know how they feel. A wife may assume that, because her husband loves her, he'll automatically know she needs transition time after grocery shopping or work to unwind. That's just too much to expect from any person.

Could this be happening in your marriage? Perhaps you are not explaining your needs or expressing your thoughts as clearly as you think you are. Use this short personal checklist to focus your feelings and specify what you'd like to change instead of complaining or criticizing.

When a disagreement surfaces, ask yourself:

• **What exactly am I thinking and feeling right now?**

• **What do I want my spouse to know right now that he or she may not realize?**

• **What is my partner thinking I mean?**

• **What am I assuming he knows that he may not have thought of?**

• **Am I acting in childish or petty ways that I thought I had outgrown? Are my tone of voice or my actions telling my partner something that I'm not saying directly? Could he be misinterpreting what I really mean?**

• **Is there one thing I could do differently to make my spouse understand?**

Taking the time to do this will help you clarify your own needs so you lessen or avoid problems entirely.

"WE CAN'T AGREE ON DISCIPLINE"

Like many parents, Annie and Tom found their constant bickering about handling the children was pushing them farther and farther apart. How can a couple learn to discuss their different opinions so they present a united front?

ANNIE'S TURN

"We've only been married five and a half years, but it seems as if we've already faced a lifetime of problems," said Annie, thirty-eight, a tall, thin woman with wavy brown hair. "In that short time, we had two children—Janie is five and Tommy Jr. is four; I lost my parents; my husband, who's an accountant, lost his job three times, and I had to support us while we lived for a year with Tom's parents. In fact, he's out of work right now.

"At least we're back in our own home, but life is total chaos. I still work full-time, so Tommy Jr. is in preschool all day and Janie is in all-day kindergarten. I dash out of the office at five to pick them up on my way home. Tom spends his day going on interviews or sending out résumés. As soon as I walk in, he disappears, and I'm left in charge of everything.

"And I'm doing a lousy job. The children are out of control. They fight with each other, they fight with me. I often wonder if it would be different if I stayed home; we'd have more time, so maybe things wouldn't be so crazy. Anyway, a few weeks ago Tommy Jr.'s teacher called to say he was disrupting the group. It's difficult for me to talk about this; you see, Tommy masturbates constantly. I've read enough childcare books to know that if a child does that excessively, it's abnormal.

"Tommy started doing this the year my mother was dying. Mother was an alcoholic and by last year couldn't take care of herself anymore. I had moved her in with us and hired a visiting nurse, but it was still very difficult for the kids.

"The fact that Tom and I can't agree on how to handle Tommy's problem is a perfect example of how we can't agree on anything anymore. My husband thinks we should slap him, but I don't believe in spanking. I try to talk things out with my children and explain why I want them to do things.

"Whenever I ask my husband for help with the kids, all he does is criticize me. He says I spoil them, that I give them too many choices. I shouldn't let Janie decide what she wants to wear to school, I should tell her what to wear. I shouldn't ask what kind of cereal they want, I should just put it on the table. He tells me that bedtime is a nightmare because I drag out the bath time and the stories. The kids are so hard to calm down that I swing between frustration and tears. But his methods sound like boot camp.

"We both also get very upset when our kids act up in front of other people, and we argue about that, too. Last Christmas at my sister's house was horrendous. Our kids were all over the place. Tom was mortified. My sister was angry. And I felt it was all my fault.

"I've been taking care of people my whole life. I'm the oldest of five and we grew up in a suburb of Chicago. My father ran his own company and he was pretty successful. I adored him, but he worked all the time and we hardly ever saw him. I suppose that's how he dealt with Mother's alcoholism.

"My brothers and sisters and I had our own ways of coping. We were all very extroverted, did well in school, and were involved in every activity. We dreaded going home.

"Still, I think we were a close family, although from time to time we'd get into rip-roaring fights. We would get things off our chest and then be done with it.

"After college, I decided to go for my M.B.A. I found a job at a large insurance company and I've worked my way up to head of the human resources department. That's where I met Tom. We'd been acquaintances for about two years, started dating, and friendship grew into passion. Tom was quiet, smart, and funny. After seeing each other nonstop for one month, we got engaged. We were married six months later.

"Actually, I got pregnant three months after we got engaged. While we'd planned on getting married in November, we moved everything up to September. It was a huge country club wedding, but it was not fun for me because at the last moment, Mother started drinking and barely made it through the ceremony.

"We went to Mexico for a honeymoon, then moved into a new house. I worked until I had Janie, then took a six-week maternity leave.

"Three weeks after Janie was born, my father died. I was devastated, but I think that my new family kept me going. Tommy Jr. was born a year later, but three weeks after I brought him home from the hospital, Tom lost his job for the first time. Corporate reshuffling. We couldn't afford the house, so we moved in with my in-laws. That was a depressing time. My mother-in-law thought she knew everything about raising children and didn't hesitate to tell me my way was wrong.

"That's when Tom decided to help my brothers manage my father's company. Since he was working, we were able to buy another house down the street. But after a few months, the company was in trouble, so once again, Tom was out of work. He found a new spot fairly quickly, but then that firm went bankrupt.

"I guess it's not surprising that there's no laughter in our house, no closeness. Tom and I rarely make love anymore. And I'm so tired of hearing him tell me that the solution to all my problems is for me to be more organized. By the time I get everyone in bed, I'm wound up like a corkscrew. I can feel the tension right here in my throat. This is not a marriage. At least it's not the kind I want to have."

TOM'S TURN

"Well, this is not the kind of marriage I want to have either," said Tom, thirty-nine, in a quiet, deliberate voice. "We love each other, but we can't stop arguing."

"The fact that I'm unemployed at the moment doesn't help. I've been sending out hundreds of résumés, and I'm trying to be optimistic, but it's not easy.

"Annie and I are like robots. The tension is terrible. The reason we haven't made love is that she's either exhausted or too tense.

"As soon as we had kids, it was clear that Annie and I have different opinions on how they should be raised. I think I noticed it when we first took Janie out of the crib. Annie would lie down next to her on the bed to get her to go to sleep. I thought that was the wrong thing to do, and now, four years later, she's still doing it. And she's still reading six stories a night. She complains that bedtime is horrendous, but she brings it on herself. When the kids drive her crazy, she comes to me, crying, 'What should I do?' Well, I've already told her. After a while, I washed my hands of the whole mess.

"I guess it boils down to the fact that Annie's idea of treating inappropriate behavior—whether it's Tommy's masturbation, Janie's tantrums, or fights they have with each other in a restaurant—is to discuss everything. She reads many childcare books, but, hey, you don't reason with a four-year-old!

"Of course, how we're going to discipline is never really up for discussion. Oh, she may ask my advice, but it's clear she fully intends to handle it her way; it's not negotiable. I think mothers do have a more intuitive sense of what little kids need. Maybe I'll get more involved when the children are older.

"Sometimes, rather than argue, I walk back into my den and read the newspaper. It's not like me to get into a fight. Annie's the emotional one. I think that's probably one of the reasons I fell in love with her.

"I'm an only child and I was born in Germany. My parents moved here when I was five. Father was a quality-control expert in a meat factory and Mother worked as a bookkeeper—I was an original latchkey kid. I don't remember a lot about my childhood except that my parents were strict. If I did something wrong, out came that wooden spoon. My parents didn't discuss much.

"I always dreamed of being a pilot or an architect, but my parents wanted me to become an accountant. So I enrolled at the University of Illinois and from day one, I was an accounting major. After college, I was offered a good job at the company where Annie still works. We really did have a fast courtship, but a few weeks after the wedding, I lost my job. It's been a roller-coaster pe-

riod for me—trying to support my family and to settle arguments between Annie and my mother. I know she's a difficult woman, but Annie should let those comments roll off her back. Annie ignores me—as she does the many reasonable suggestions I've made to help her get more organized. For instance, I suggested that when she cooks, she should clean up as she goes along. I told her not to let the wash pile up in the laundry room but to bring it right up after she's done. Why don't I help her more, she wants to know? Because she never lets me! Annie thinks she has to do it all—and better than anyone else."

THE COUNSELOR'S TURN

"How to reconcile different styles of discipline is a common problem for many couples," said the counselor. "But for Annie and Tom, their inability to resolve their differences was proving painfully divisive.

"The oldest of five, bright, articulate Annie couldn't stop proving to herself and everybody else that she was in control: Of course she could handle a full-time job, two kids, and still keep a clean house. So what if her husband was out of work? Annie had a lot invested in this image of herself, since she had always received praise for her ability to coordinate everything so smoothly.

"Reluctant to admit it, Tom was

frustrated that his wife was the sole breadwinner and had been several times in the past. Tom had a strict upbringing, which he continued with his own children. His mother was outspoken and controlling, and although Tom often ignored her and encouraged Annie to do the same, he had internalized many of his parents' beliefs about raising children. Annie needed to be able to take charge and tell her mother-in-law to mind her own business.

"While Tom was initially attracted to Annie's drama and emotion, he hated to fight and was easily frustrated by his wife's obsessing about problems. As far as he was concerned, you discuss a problem once, present a solution, and move on.

"After listening to Tom and Annie, I suggested they bring Tommy Jr. to see me, too, and I spoke with his teacher to get her perspective. I explained to Annie and Tom that for a young child, masturbation is one way of relieving stress and calming down. All children masturbate, but by the age of four, they usually have learned that it is something you do in private. Tommy, however, was under so much stress, he was unable to control himself.

"One key element in easing Tommy's stress was to ease the tension at home. Annie knew she needed to calm down, but she didn't know how.

"I explained to Annie that often children of alcoholic parents grow up in an environment so unpredictable that they develop a compulsive need to control everything. As a child, Annie felt responsible for her brothers and sisters, much as she feels responsible for every aspect of her children's behavior now.

"Although Annie and Tom thought they were communicating, there was little meaningful dialogue between them. As soon as Annie walked in the door, Tom checked out. She was exhausted and frustrated and, although she was unaware of it, angry—angry at Tom for not working (and guilty about feeling that way) . . . angry at her mother-in-law for intruding in her life . . . and angry at herself for feeling conflicted about working. Like many working mothers, she enjoyed her job, but she longed to be at home with her children.

"About four months after I started seeing them, Tom found another job. By this time, Annie felt strong enough to speak to her supervisor about taking a three-day-a-week position. 'If I'm not department head, I can spend more time with my kids. There'll be time for more responsibility later,' she said. While this decision is not one that every woman can—or should—make, it was the right one for Annie.

"Having his mother more available eased Tommy's stress. She continues to remind Tommy that masturbation is a private activity and that he can't do it at school or in the family room, and the problem has decreased.

"Next, we addressed discipline problems in general. I told Tom I did not believe in spanking; nor did I think Annie was spoiling the children by giving them choices or reasons for behaving a certain way. However, I did feel she was inconsistent in her approach. Tom agreed to listen to other ideas, and as he saw that these discipline strategies worked, he stopped automatically resorting to spanking and criticizing.

"My first suggestion was that they put routine back into their children's lives, since children need to know what to expect and what is expected of them. Tom and Annie determined to stick to a regular schedule for meals, baths, and bedtime. Annie found that when she let go a little, Tom was capable of picking up the slack: He cleaned up the kitchen after dinner while she got the kids ready for their baths.

"I also suggested they try to give their children incentives for behaving well. For example, using a kitchen timer has been an effective tool. At bedtime, the timer goes on, and if Janie and Tommy are in their pajamas when it rings, they can have storytime; if not, they forfeit it. Annie has agreed to a limit of two stories. And she no longer lies on the bed with them when they go to sleep. 'I thought they'd make a big fuss when I stopped,' she said, 'but

now that the whole evening is calmer, they really don't mind.' The payoff has been more time for Annie and Tom to talk at the end of the day. They make a point of going out every Wednesday night—kid-free time. And now that they are more relaxed and comfortable with each other, their sex life has improved, too.

"I also suggested they help their kids understand that all behavior has consequences. Annie set aside a time-out corner, filled with pillows and books, where the kids can go when they need to calm down.

"Janie and Tommy's sibling rivalry was classic, but Tom and Annie had interfered in their fights instead of teaching them how to resolve their conflicts. Since children love games and humor, I suggested creating their own People's Court—like the TV show. Now, if either child has a problem, they come to a parent, who plays Judge Wapner, and present their sides. Before long, everyone's laughing.

"Morning battles lessened when Annie helped Janie pick out her clothes the night before. As for getting the last word with her daughter, Annie has learned to just let go. 'I realized how silly it was to stand there arguing with a five-year-old,' she said. Also, when they go somewhere special as a family, they give the kids clear, positive instructions. Telling them 'We know you're excited about the Christmas party and you'll be able to help decorate the tree and open two presents' works better than giving them a list of things they aren't allowed to do. And since they feel closer as a couple, Annie has found the confidence to stand up to her mother-in-law.

"Tom and Annie stopped coming to see me together after nine months, although I am still in touch with Annie. 'I feel like we're a team,' she says. 'When a problem comes up, Tom is by my side.'"

WHEN YOU FIGHT IN FRONT OF THE KIDS

Before couples like Annie and Tom can calmly negotiate compromises and discuss consistent discipline strategies, they must first get a handle on their fighting. It helps to remind yourselves that no two people are carbon copies of each other; the way you raise your kids has a lot to do with the way you were raised. Disagreements are bound to arise and, when they do, it's crucial to remember that it's not whether you fight but how you handle the fight that's important. In fact it can teach your children a valuable lesson about expressing feelings and resolving differences. If arguing in front of your children seems to be getting out of hand, keep the following rules in mind:

1. Promise each other you will not resort to name-calling, insults, or sarcasm.

2. Try, too, not to lapse into angry silences. Emotional distances can be scarier for kids than outright fighting because they just don't understand why Mom and Dad aren't talking. They assume it must be something they've done. It's better to say directly: "Mommy and Daddy are having an argument right now. Sometimes parents fight, just like kids fight. But we're trying to work it out."

3. When you're really furious, agree to disagree. Call a time-out period if tempers get too hot.

4. Don't threaten to leave or get a divorce. In the heat of anger, we often say things we don't mean. Kids don't know that and are confused and frightened by unfulfilled threats.

5. When you're calm enough to discuss strategies, remember that there isn't one way to handle discipline problems with children. Respect the fact that you are each entitled to your opinion. Does one of you feel more strongly than the other about an issue? Implement that person's suggestion first. If it fails to work, try another idea.

6. Work on your marriage. Get a baby-sitter so you can regularly spend time alone together. If you remember to keep your relationship healthy and nurturing, it will be easier to resolve any disagreements you have.

"WE CAN'T DEAL WITH OUR DAUGHTER'S ILLNESS"

Devastated by the diagnosis that their four-year-old daughter had leukemia, Janey and Greg failed to understand that their inability to communicate made the crisis even harder to bear. Can a couple torn apart by tragedy ever be close?

JANEY'S TURN

"Last December, when the doctor told Greg and me that our four-year-old Mary would die before morning, Greg mumbled something about an important business appointment and left me praying alone by her bedside all night," said Janey, twenty-six, the mother of three. "A miracle occurred and God granted us another remission—Mary's third since she was diagnosed with leukemia at the age of nineteen months.

"During the December crisis, she was in the hospital for six weeks of extremely painful chemotherapy. During those terrible weeks I saw practically nothing of Greg. He visited the hospital regularly to check on Mary's condition, but he never stayed.

"Two years later, he was named western sales manager for a large pharmaceutical company, and the day he landed the promotion, he resigned from our family. Every time I've even hinted that we deserve a few crumbs of companionship, Greg flies into a crazy, uncontrollable rage.

"My mother had a dreadful temper; the least trifle turned her into a madwoman and I would run for cover. When Greg explodes, I try to slip out of sight inconspicuously or at least I try not to provoke him further.

"When I fell in love with Greg—I was seventeen and he was twenty-one—I was thrilled by his ambition. But I didn't dream that it would ruin him as a human being. When we began dating, my mother tried everything to break us up. She might have succeeded, but I loved Greg so much that I started sleeping with him—he's the only man I've ever slept with—and having sex with him was so wonderful that I had the courage to go against Mom and my religion.

"Well, I got pregnant and Greg proposed to me like a shot, although he hadn't planned to marry until he finished his undergraduate work and got an M.A. in business administration. As it turned out, our marriage and our first son's birth didn't slow Greg down a bit. I quit college and took a secretarial course so he could concentrate on his studies. He graduated with top honors, came in first in his class, and landed a sales position with the pharmaceutical company.

"By then our second boy was on the way, but I was able to continue to work even after we were the parents of two children. My best friend, Jan, lived next door with her husband, Artie, and their kids, and she was always glad to sit for us.

"Greg and I were perpetually tired, and that was when Greg's temper explosions started. At first, I blamed his awful scenes on exhaustion and the strain of having two crying babies in a small apartment. For a while I actually encouraged Greg to stay late at his work to spare him the uproar and chaos. But when he took advantage and stayed later and later, my feelings were terribly hurt.

"Many nights he crawled into bed at two or three in the morning and woke me out of a dead sleep, wanting sex. I cooperated in the lovemaking as well as possible, but he could sense my lack of enthusiasm and it made him furious.

"But there are other times when Greg blows his stack that leave me totally baffled. Not long ago, he brought home some theater tickets as a rare, unexpected treat. I was very pleased, but apparently I must have said or did the wrong thing to show my pleasure. He suddenly yelled that he could see I had no interest in the theater—or in him, either. He tore up the tickets and rushed out the door.

"It's especially hard for me to believe that Greg loves our daughter Mary in spite of his protestations of devotion. Unless new medical discoveries are made, Mary will never be strong and healthy. The doctors say she may not live to grow up. Greg admires health, strength, and success—and nothing else."

GREG'S TURN

"If you saw Mary today, you would think she was a cute, normal four-year-old—until you noticed the lacy cap she wears to cover a bald patch on her head," said thirty-year old Greg, a somber-faced six-footer. "Mary is extremely small for her age, but recently she has begun to grow a little, which would seem to indicate that the pituitary, which the doctors describe as seriously damaged, hasn't been destroyed.

"Janey won't admit that Mary may never grow up. Last December, when they predicted that Mary wouldn't live through the night, Janey waited and prayed all night, confident of a miracle. She was granted her miracle—indeed we have been blessed with three remissions. But some day our luck is bound to run out. When I was sixteen, I watched my father die of leukemia. I watched a grown man fighting to survive long enough to educate four sons. Then, I watched him lose the battle.

"I used to think that I had inherited Dad's strength of character, but when Mary's illness was diagnosed, I learned that my strength and confidence had limits. I do okay handling everyday business affairs, but in a real crunch, Janey is stronger than I am. She not only stuck it out that night last December, but she has stuck through the whole damned siege. On that worst night of all, Mary was in a coma—unconscious and uncaring whether I was there or not. Her face was swollen and distorted from the drugs they gave her and she had lost her long, beautiful blond hair.

"I left her in the hospital room with Janey and drove back to my office bawling like a baby. I was able to work once I got to the office, but that night I found myself praying. My father was an agnostic and I thought my philosophy similar. Everything about a dying kid is different. Your mind spins in endless circles—why did it have to happen to our beloved Mary? Why did it happen to us?

"Sometimes I am haunted by the notion that I might have passed along my father's genes to my daughter. There's no medical evidence, of course, but I do brood. I've never dared discuss this with Janey. There are too many important things we don't discuss. She evades or refuses to answer my most urgent questions and her silence drives me nuts. I realize I should be more patient, but I can't. I've inherited my Dad's horrible temper, but I season it with caution—a twist aimed at self-preservation. Dad was a good guy at home, but he wrecked his career by popping off on the job. At work, I hold myself under iron control. But at home, where it's safe, I explode. I know it's hard on my family, but at times Janey provokes me

101

almost to madness. Without some measure of release, I would burst.

"In the third week of our daughter's December ordeal, Janey was about to collapse from the nursing strain, but she refused to leave the hospital unless I took her place. I arrived just as they were preparing for a bone marrow puncture. The doctor punched a long, fat needle into Mary's arm. The local anesthetic did no good at all and Mary screamed with pain and jerked the needle loose.

"I drove home and found Janey asleep. I ached to get in bed beside her, but I knew better than to try. It was unlikely that Janey would reject me—she would cooperate in her distant way.

"I lay down on her chaise longue and quite soon she awoke. She didn't ask why I had left the hospital and I didn't say. She told me Jan and Artie had taken the boys for the weekend, and I said 'Great, just great,' words I didn't mean.

"Janey got up and put on her clothes in the bathroom behind a closed door. As she left for the hospital she asked if I would be at the office in case of emergency. I said 'Probably,' and she said 'Fine, that's fine,' words she didn't mean.

"Janey and I can't communicate anymore. We began losing touch even before Mary's illness. During our courtship we were very close. We discussed everything. She encouraged me in my plans, she praised my ambition, and I thought she was impressed by my early triumphs. In the beginning, she took a job to help out financially and I was grateful. But then she began telling people—particularly Jan and Artie—how she was assisting in my advancement. Maybe she didn't intend to, but she made it sound as if she was the power behind the throne.

"When our boys were still in diapers, I began to notice that Janey never asked or seemed to listen when I talked to her about my work. It hurt to feel her pull away from me, and when I'm hurt I get mad. I can't help it. The madder I got the more Janey withdrew. I found more satisfaction at work.

"Shortly before I was promoted, my immediate superior stopped at my desk and gave me four theater tickets he couldn't use. He said he would see me at a big conference the next day. I jumped out of my skin— it was the first I'd heard that I was invited to the conference and it was evidence that I had a good chance for the promotion.

"I hurried home to tell Janey; we hadn't gone out in a long while. I pulled out the tickets and asked if she would like to see the most popular show in town. Janey never conceded to having a preference of any kind and as usual, she searched my face for a possible clue to my wishes.

"I got the promotion," Greg said heavily, "but soon afterward there was a flare-up in Mary's illness and my big job looked like small potatoes. No one who hasn't gone through the experience can know what it's like to live with a leukemic child. But I hope that counseling will help us come back together so we can operate once again as a team. We need all the help we can get to brace ourselves for Mary's fate."

THE COUNSELOR'S TURN

"The burden of their daughter's tragic illness was made heavier by Janey and Greg's lack of communication," said the counselor. "This lack was evident in the first of the six joint sessions we had. The two sat as far apart as possible and when I requested that they bring their chairs closer together, their body language spoke of two sharply dissimilar personalities. These dissimilarities accounted for some of their difficulties in facing their grief together and drawing strength and courage from each other.

"Janey's expression was remote and her smile was forced and unconvincing. It seemed clear that she needed some understanding of her deep inner reserve and almost equally clear that Greg would be unable to supply it. Where she was passive, Greg was outgoing and aggressive. He watched me in a challenging, show-me way and he jittered with the nerves he denied.

"Janey thought Greg lacked any feeling except anger and a drive for power and sex. In counseling, she learned that Greg's fits of rage cloaked his insecurity and fear. Greg boasted to me of an almost ideal boyhood but, as the truth emerged, it developed that he grew up believing himself to be dumber than his three older brothers and determined to prove otherwise.

"This enlightened Janey on the subject of Greg's bad temper and made her more compassionate. She learned that Greg possessed compassion when he told her of his hidden anquish that his heredity might be responsible for Mary's illness. This shared knowledge relieved Greg's guilt and demonstrated to Janey that he did love Mary, but he showed his love for her and his other children by being successful in his career.

"Greg desperately needed the praise that Janey had found easy to give in courtship. She tried to free her suppressed feelings, driven deep inside by the rages of her mother. Janey's mother pried and pried to discover what her daughter most desired—and then deprived her of it as a punishment. Small wonder Janey hesitated to express her preferences on just about anything. With difficulty, she in time began to make known her desires. She taught herself, also with difficulty, to initiate sex with Greg in moments when she truly felt affectionate. They began to compromise and respect each other's differences, and Greg has cut down on his working hours to spend time with his family.

"The problem of Mary's illness is still with them, of course, but recently I received a note saying Mary was still in remission. Greg and Janey now feel that their marriage is strong enough to face the trial that might come in the future."

TEN QUESTIONS TO HELP YOU ZERO IN ON THE REAL PROBLEM

When we expect our partner to think or behave a certain way, rather than communicate our feelings directly and honestly, we are often following old scripts without even realizing it. Many times, these hidden expectations—the unconscious, unspoken needs for ourselves or our partners that we bring to a marriage—can prove divisive if they are long unacknowledged.

However, understanding the needs a couple bring to the relationship is the first step in learning how to deal with problems. Couples must learn to talk not only about what is bothering them, but also about what they expect from themselves and each other. Use the following short questionnaire as a catalyst for conversation and a means to fine-tune your relationship.

On separate sheets of paper, write your answers to the following questions. Then, share your lists.

1. How do I describe myself? My mate?

2. What messages did my parents send me about who I am? Did they make me feel confident in my abilities or fearful?

3. What are the traits that bother me most about myself? About my mate?

4. What beliefs or opinions do I hold about human nature in general? How do these beliefs affect my marriage?

5. When I was little, could I talk easily with both parents, or only one?

6. When my parents were angry, how did they display that anger? Did they shout or were they cold and silent?

7. Who made the important family decisions? Who makes them now?

8. How were household responsibilities divided when I was growing up?

9. When things don't go my way, how do I feel? What do I do about those feelings?

10. Is it important for me to always be right?

FIGHTING FAIR:
THE FINE ART OF
MANAGING ANGER

—

A NGER IS INEVITABLE IN MARRIAGE. IF TWO people are living together, they are bound to disagree about small, seemingly petty things ("Whose turn is it to walk the dog?" "Why am I always doing the laundry?") as well as larger, more significant issues ("How should we handle our two-year-old's tantrums?" "Why don't you ever back me up me when your mother criticizes me?"). Yet anger itself is not the real problem. It's how couples handle and deal with anger that separates a healthy relationship from one at risk.

People manage their anger in different ways. Some deny it: In the short run, it's easier and less painful than admitting the anger and dealing with the potential repercussions. Such people bury their resentments, legitimate though they may be, deep inside. And in the heat of an argument, they crumble as soon as a spouse gets defensive, or worse, counterattacks.

Women in particular have a difficult time dealing with anger because they are often made to feel guilty about feeling anger in the first place—witness the countless wives interviewed for *Can This Marriage Be Saved?* who wonder "Do I have a right to be angry?" or "Besides, what good will it do?" Our culture teaches that men who speak their minds are assertive and strong. Women who do so are bitchy and shrill.

The problem is, unexpressed anger doesn't just disappear. Years of denial can eat away at self-esteem, as well as trigger migraines, ulcers, and a host of other stress-related ailments. It also saps energy—physically and emotionally—and as recent medical studies report, may be a leading culprit in heart disease. Anger that is not dealt with appropriately seethes beneath the surface, only to erupt in a volcano of rage (often toward the wrong person) over a seemingly innocuous comment or action. The woman who is furious at her boss or her mother-in-law, but who doesn't dare to express her anger, may lash out at her children or her spouse.

While many husbands and wives deny that they're angry, others nurse their anger. Holding on to grudges and hurts gives them a sense of power they wouldn't otherwise possess. Since they may believe they're incapable of coping with any type of open confrontation, keeping their anger simmering on a low flame provides a protective shield that makes them feel less vulnerable. Those who nurse their grudges are often mistrustful and mad at the world. It's hard to knock that chip off their shoulders.

Still other people vent their anger, often in the mistaken belief that "getting it off my chest" is healthy and clears the air. Sadly, explosive tirades only push a partner further away—and give them more reasons to continue doing exactly what provoked their spouse in the first place.

Yet the most pernicious way of handling anger in marriage is not to handle it at all. This is when anger becomes self-perpetuating, locking husbands and wives in a vicious cycle of blame and hostility. Stuck in repetitive arguments that go nowhere, some couples dig in their heels in a vain attempt to prove themselves right and their partners wrong. Every conversation becomes a confrontation and the slightest provocation sends tempers flaring as each person falls into old, hurtful patterns. It's not uncommon for these warriors to drag a third party—usually a child—into the arguments to bolster their respective positions. In time, the only way such couples relate is through their anger and bickering.

Interestingly, some couples are actually aware of the uselessness of their self-perpetuating fights, yet neither partner can figure out how to break the stalemate. *Can This Marriage Be Saved?* shows that it's possible to direct anger to improve a marriage rather than destroy it. A key step is for each person to recognize the part he or she plays in provoking and sustaining the anger. Another is to learn to recognize the feeling of anger immediately—not an easy task if a couple have been suppressing negative feelings for a long time.

In *Can This Marriage Be Saved?* we also watch as each spouse learns to tune in to the body's individual reaction to anger. These anger signals—when the stomach churns, the heart races, the muscles tighten in the temples, neck, or back—are too often dismissed. When heeded, however, they can serve as warning signs that buried anger and resentment need to be addressed and resolved. Once husbands and wives learn to express their needs effectively, they can disagree constructively—brainstorming, negotiating, and when appropriate, compromising. In this way, both partners maintain self-esteem— and their marriage, too.

"All He Does Is Scream"

Married barely one month, Diane was ready to call it quits. How could she live with a man whose temper raged out of control?"

Diane's turn

"I couldn't believe it. He was yelling so loud, his face was purple and he was sputtering with rage," said twenty-six-year-old Diane, in tears as she pulled off her oversized black sunglasses and settled into the couch.

"This is not the man I married. Kirk used to be so sweet, so kind. Actually, he reminded me of my father. But we've been married barely one month now, and I keep asking myself, 'What on earth did I ever think I had in common with this man?' Just the other night Kirk took a handful of plates and smashed them on the kitchen floor because he said I had left such a mess. Okay, I should have wiped the counter down a little more carefully. And maybe I should have hung up my clothes after I got out of the shower. Kirk's first wife was a great housekeeper and a gourmet cook, and I can't compete with that. Still, I don't think it's necessary to start breaking china.

"As far as Kirk is concerned, I can't do anything right. Last week he was on me about my talking on the telephone. I know I spend a lot of time on the phone with friends and with my mother, whom I talk to every day. What can I say—I'm a telephone person.

"I'm sure he'll also tell you I never want to make love. Well, what does he expect? When he carries on the way he does, I don't feel like holding his hand, let alone making love.

"We probably fight the most, though, about money. He thinks I spend too much. 'This house looks like the U.S. Customs Office,' he'll scream. I do spend a lot on clothes. But I work, and at this stage in my life I think I deserve it.

"I admit I'm obsessed with money. My whole life my mother would get all the hand-me-downs from our relatives and make me wear them. Look, I know this must sound terrible, but I want to have a nice apartment and nice clothes without worrying about whether we'll have enough money to pay our bills.

"I thought Kirk felt the same way, but clearly I was wrong. His latest business scheme—managing a chain of dry-cleaning stores—recently fell apart. And he really doesn't seem to care all that much. But I'm trying to figure out how to stop panicking about money.

"Maybe my mother was right. Maybe I did marry beneath me. You know, I have never really gotten along with my mother, and I'm so glad I'm not like her. Always, Mother would compare me to my friends, telling me how I wasn't as pretty as Phyllis or wondering why Linda got an A on a project and I didn't.

"I graduated from high school with a C-plus average, good enough to get into a local college. A lot of my friends were going away to school, but I didn't want to do that. In fact, until I got married, I lived at home. And, though my heart wasn't in it, I got my bachelor's de-gree in education. My parents want-ed me to be a teacher.

"Well, I absolutely hated teach-ing, and after two miserable years I quit. A friend of mine was starting her own interior-design business and she asked me to work with her. That intrigued me, so I started helping her out. But Mother still thought it wasn't good enough, be-cause I wasn't a professional. 'My children should have done better,' she'll moan. Part of me gets furious when she says things like that, but the other part wonders if I jumped too quickly into this marriage.

"I met Kirk about a month after I broke up with someone I had dated for a long time. I was twenty-five and really wanted to settle down. A friend fixed us up and I was attracted to him right away, but since he had just separated from his wife, I was more than a little leery. Kirk kept calling me, though, and finally, after a year, I said yes.

"The relationship became very intense very fast. After a few weeks, Kirk asked me to move in with him, but he didn't want to get mar-ried again. I understood that, but I refused to live with him unless he married me. 'I don't want to lose you,' he told me, so we set the date.

"Well, as I said, it didn't take long for things to go to hell in a handbasket. I never thought I'd be seeing a marriage counselor when I've barely unwrapped my wedding presents. But I want this mariage to work, and I think Kirk does, too. I know how much he wants to have an Ozzie and Harriet family life. But Ozzie didn't scream at Harriet and throw things on the floor. Kirk has got to change, and that's all there is to it."

KIRK'S TURN

"Diane may think I was out of control, but I was really trying to calm her down," said Kirk, twenty-seven, in a soft voice. "She is just like her mother. She gets nuts sometimes, and I don't know what to do.

"Look, I know this is all my fault, and I think I know why. I come from a broken home myself. My parents split up when I was four. In those days, divorce was a terrible stigma. When the kids would ask where my father was, I'd lie and say he was working late at the office.

"I guess I wanted to please my father, although he's a very difficult man. I hate to admit it, but I have his temperament. I have a short fuse. I loved my mother, but I think I blamed her for my father's leaving. My mother died when I was eighteen—she had a brain tumor and was very sick for about a year. Somehow I managed to graduate from high school, but I had no idea what I was going to do.

"I'd been dating this girl for two years, and after my mother died, we decided to get married. I was nineteen, she was seventeen. She wanted to get away from her mother, and I had nobody, so I married her. We were divorced after four years.

"All this time, I drifted from job to job. I like people, so at one point I tried selling cars. But I didn't have a glib tongue. There are some guys I worked with who could sell you the Brooklyn Bridge twice. Not me. I don't have a head for business.

"I really thought this dry-cleaning company was going to work out, but I guess Diane is right. Maybe I'll never amount to anything.

"I still get furious though when she gets on me. Despite what Diane says, she's not the most open person in the world. When I try to tell her how upset I get when she's messy, she doesn't talk about it like she says she does. Either she screams that I'm a jerk, or she gives me the silent treatment.

"I swore I would never marry a second time; I didn't want to go through all the hurt again. But when I met Diane, I fell head over heels. She was gorgeous. And she had a lot of class.

"I don't know why things went so wrong. I guess I'm very difficult and hard to please, but some of the things she does would make anyone go crazy. Like when she's on the phone all evening! Why can't she say, 'Look, Kirk's home now, I've really gotta go'?

"Diane gets mad when I don't want to go out with her friends, but I don't have anything in common with those people. They're all college graduates.

"And one more thing: Does Diane think she married a millionaire? I want her to have nice things. But let's face facts, we don't have that kind of money.

"It's not my style to talk to a stranger about personal things, but damn it, I've never loved anyone like I love Diane."

THE COUNSELOR'S TURN

"To be honest, when I first met Diane and Kirk, I doubted their marriage would last," said the counselor.

"Diane was furious, and it took quite a while to stop her from interrupting whenever her husband spoke. Her aggressiveness, however, was a mask for a deep sense of insecurity and low self-esteem—not surprising, considering her mother's barrage of criticism.

"Nevertheless, as far as Diane was concerned, all their problems were due to Kirk. And she never tired of telling him so. Unfortunately, Kirk shared her view. A kind and sensitive man, Kirk had been devastated by his parents' hostile divorce. Torn by guilt that he somehow had caused the breakup, he was so anxious and emotionally needy that he leapt into an early first marriage. When that relationship fell apart, when he was subsequently unable to hold on to any job, he saw it as further proof of his failure. His anger and his explosive episodes were the only way he knew of defending himself.

"My first step in counseling was to help Diane and Kirk understand clearly that they were both responsible for the problems they faced in their marriage. I also pointed out that they had in common a real yearning for a warm, close, mutually dependent relationship. And they were both highly motivated to achieve it.

"Although she resented the way her mother treated her, Diane had failed to shift her allegiance to her husband and to separate herself from her parents' expectations. As a result, there wasn't enough emotional glue in their relationship to help them overcome the normal marital difficulties.

"In fact, despite her claims to the contrary, Diane had in many ways grown up to be just like her mother, losing her temper and belittling Kirk as her mother belittled her father. Also, like many couples, Diane and Kirk both expected the other to be the 'parent.' While Diane expected Kirk to be a good provider, Kirk expected his wife to run an orderly household. When she turned out to be as messy as a teenager, when she stayed on the phone with her friends all night, he felt shortchanged. But he had to realize that losing his temper didn't work.

"After several weeks of counseling, Diane finally began to see how she contributed to the difficulties they were having. It helped when I pointed out that much of her anger at Kirk was irrational: Kirk wanted her to have nice things; he simply wasn't earning enough to buy them for her.

"This led to an intense discussion about Diane's own career. I told Diane that if she wanted the trappings of a better lifestyle, she'd have to provide them herself. With her usual initiative, she scanned the help-wanted ads and decided to pursue a real career in interior design. She applied for a training program at a major department store and her acceptance into the program was a much-needed boost to her self-confidence. As she started to feel better about herself, she felt better about Kirk, too. Much of the tension between them eased.

"I must say, Kirk really surprised me. A man like Kirk is usually very resistant to treatment, yet he blossomed as we focused on his many fine qualities, particularly his sensitivity and his compassion. As he gained more confidence, he felt more capable of standing up to Diane. He learned, too, that instead of exploding, he should simply walk out of the room until the heat of his anger subsided. Then they could continue whatever conversation they were having.

"Most important, Kirk started looking for work and was offered a position at the post office. Though it's not a high-level job, the benefits are excellent and his future looks bright.

"During one session, Kirk and Diane ironed out a division of labor; Diane agreed to handle the finances. Before long, she had placed some of their earnings into an IRA account and used some for a down payment on a small house that they could rent out for extra income. As a result, she felt less anxious about money.

"For his part, Kirk willingly agreed to take on the household duties, as long as Diane promised not to be such a slob. And if Diane agreed not to talk on the phone when he was home (she did), then he agreed to go out with her friends once in a while (he did and had a wonderful time).

"Diane and Kirk ended counseling after fourteen months. Although all their problems are not resolved—Diane will probably always be the kind of person who occasionally thinks the grass is greener on the other side of the fence—at least she has learned to count her blessings. Most important, they both learned to share the responsibility for problems that do come up and to work together to solve them."

DEALING WITH A SPOUSE'S ANGER

While Kirk needs help in dealing with his anger, it's essential for Diane to know what to do in the face of her husband's outbursts.

It's not easy for anyone to deal with a partner's anger. Therapists recommend the following ideas to help partners remain strong when a spouse loses control. See which ones work for you.

1. **Learn to really listen to a partner's anger.** It's not easy to do that, let alone empathize when faced with a barrage of insults or threats; most of us react quickly and heatedly with angry accusations of our own. This is especially true when a mate pushes our "hot buttons," such as bringing up old issues or comparing you to your mother. However, when you take a deep breath and hear your partner out rather than cutting him off, anger de-escalates.

2. **If your partner insists you don't understand, assure him you're trying to.** Ask for specific examples to make the situation clearer to you: Questions such as, "What exactly do you mean?" or "What about my tone of voice is so hurtful?" will move the discussion in a positive direction.

3. **Validate his angry feelings.** Telling someone he has no right to be angry, or that he "shouldn't feel that way," fuels anger. You can't pass judgment on how someone feels.

4. **Take responsibility for your behavior in triggering the anger.** You may be provoking (albeit unconsciously) a spouse's fury. What steps can you take to change your behavior?

5. **Think of a way to short-circuit a spouse's anger.** You might agree on a code word that one of you can say when tempers seem to be getting out of control. One couple purposely chose a comical word—rutabaga—as their anger signal. Whenever they say it, they usually laugh—and that breaks the cycle of tension and shouting.

6. **Call a time-out if a partner is losing control,** just as you do when a child throws a tantrum. Tell him you refuse to be spoken to in such an angry, humiliating, or abusive way. Leave the room, but make it clear you'll be available to talk once he calms down.

"He Says I'm Pushing Him Away"

Laura and Stewart were having a hard time adjusting to parenthood. What happens when every discussion snowballs into a long, ugly battle?

LAURA'S TURN

"This is supposed to be the happiest time of my life," said Laura, thirty-eight, a pretty, petite woman who barely took a breath between thoughts, "but I'm miserable.

"I have a beautiful child—Max will be two next week—and a wonderful job, but my marriage is falling apart. Stewart and I fight constantly, usually about stupid things at first, which soon escalate into all-out war.

"One of our biggest fights is about sex. Or, rather, the lack of it. Before Max, our sex life was great. But to be honest, the thought of sex rarely enters my mind these days. Either I'm thinking about the baby or I'm too exhausted. I'd like to have another child, but Stewart complains I'm just using him as a baby manufacturer.

"Stewart was different from anyone I'd ever dated. We met through friends and married nine months after our first date. It was a fabulous wedding at a very elegant restaurant in the city, then we went to Bermuda for ten days. I went back to work—I'm vice-president in charge of planning and development for a large hospital—but since I was thirty-five, we wanted to start a family.

"Finally, I got pregnant. That was a fabulous time for us. I felt terrific, and even though I gained forty-six pounds, I remember this as the most idyllic time of my life. We traveled, made plans, had great sex.

"I worked up until a week before I was due, then planned to take a two-month maternity leave. But my delivery was horrendous. After

115

seventeen hours, the doctor decided to do a C-section.

"My recovery was awful, too. All that maternal bonding . . . well, it wasn't happening. I felt none of that instant love—only out of control and panicky.

"Most of all, I was, and still am, scared that my child will grow up to dislike me the way I dislike my own mother. But while I was a basket case, my husband turned out to be a natural father.

"I don't know when we started bickering; we both have tempers. I'm a yeller—my mother is, too—and Stewart can be as sarcastic as she is. But what really gets me is when he starts to tell me something, then clams up and walks out of the room.

"Ignoring me is the worst thing you can do; it was another of Mother's tactics. Mother and I had a very acrimonious relationship—she clearly favored my sister, Judy, whom I'm still not close to. Judy did everything Mother told her to. I was bratty, 'the selfish one,' and jealous of the attention Mother paid her.

"I was Daddy's girl, though now my father practically worships Stewart. They're best buddies. Like my father, Stewart works in his family's business—they manufacture handbags and small leather goods. Frankly, I've never liked my in-laws. Stewart's father is a tyrant. I know Stewart is unhappy and stressed out, but he idolizes his dad and keeps trying to prove himself.

"The problem is, I'm always left doing everything—the grocery shopping, making Max's appointments with the pediatrician, checking to see if he needs new sneakers . . . Must I also remind Stewart to do the few things he promises he'll do?

"Sometimes, I don't know why I bother. When Stewart tries to help, he gets everything wrong. He takes Max to the park but forgets to take his hat or bottle of milk. He offers to watch him so I can lie down, but if Max cries, Stewart gives him juice even though it's right before dinner. Then he's not hungry when he's scheduled to eat. I keep telling him that kids like routine, but he doesn't get it. I clip articles on child care, but he never reads them.

"Then, last month, he announced that he wanted to start his own company. Let's be realistic. This is the kind of thing you do when you're younger; it will take years to turn a profit. Am I supposed to support all three of us?"

STEWART'S TURN

"When will she ever shut up?" asked Stewart, thirty-nine, an athletic-looking man whose voice was heavy with resignation.

"Laura's constant anxiety, her panic over the littlest thing . . . I can't stand it. Life according to Laura is so hard, you'd think this was *The Grapes of Wrath.* She never stops reminding me how much she does and how little I do. If I forget to call the plumber within the time frame she deems acceptable, she hits the ceiling: 'Did you call? Why didn't you call? You know, Stewart, I do this and I do that. . . .'

"I was treated like that growing up—in fact, my parents still treat me like a twelve-year-old. Both my parents were first-generation immigrants, very Old World. I was never close to them or to my sister, Marcy.

"Despite all that I achieved—I was the first kid in my family to graduate from high school, not to mention an Ivy League college—I know my parents thought of me as the black sheep of the family; Marcy was the good kid, I was the bad kid.

"No one ever laughed in our house, or rarely. That's one of the things that attracted me to my wife: She had spunk. I idolized my father and dreamed about working with him. Growing up, I expected to take over the business after he retired. During vacations and over the summer, I would work in the factories and warehouses . . . I traveled with him to the Far East, learned four languages—I loved it.

"But things aren't working out. I know I have to leave. I'm not enjoying my work anymore, but I'm confused and, I guess, scared. And I'm not a kid anymore. I have a family to think about. It would be nice if my wife could support me a little. I

can't talk about it with Laura, though. She gets panic-stricken.

"Laura is a perfectionist. There's no room for anyone else's opinion, and certainly not mine. I try to help, but with Laura I can never win. Well, guess what? I'm not going to try anymore. Period. I don't need to read an article from some magazine about how to give my kid a bath. Listen, I've gone to every single pediatrician's appointment Max has had, so don't tell me I'm not a full partner. She takes me for granted, and I'm sick of it. So I forgot Max's hat. Big deal. The kid has a hood on his sweatshirt. He'll live. So I give him a little juice. If he eats at seven o'clock instead of six, Laura has a fit.

"And you wouldn't believe the things that come out of her mouth. To be blunt, she's a bitch, hurling four-letter words, telling me she hates me.

"I agree that we fight about stupid things. The other night, I got so mad, I put my fist through a door. Then she demands that I tell her I'm sorry. When someone says that to me, I see red. That is something my parents always said. Sorry for what?

"She used to be my best friend. But now she doesn't have the slightest idea what's really bugging me. We never make love; I try to be affectionate, but she brushes me off, so lately I've stopped trying. I expected this right after the baby. But it's been going on too long now. She's pushing me away. You know, one day I really am going to leave, and when I do I won't come back."

"What happened to Laura and Stewart happens to many couples when the pattern of their relationship is disrupted," says the counselor. "Neither one really wanted to admit how much their lives had changed after they'd had a child.

"However, these two brought a higher than usual degree of competition and resistance to change in marriage. Instead of recognizing what they were doing and learning to compromise, each refused to bend until the other did first. Such competition is common, particularly in couples who are still dealing with unresolved sibling issues or who have come from homes where parents favored, or appeared to favor, one child over another. Laura and Stewart often tried to one-up each other: Who's the better parent? The better lover? Who initiated sex last time? Who will apologize first?

"My goal was not to make the problems go away, but rather to help Laura and Stewart lessen their duration and better deal with them. While the intensity of their conflicts was great, I sensed that, deep down, these two really loved each other.

"High-strung Laura was a perfectionist who thrived on organization and control. She had always been a success, yet motherhood presented her with a host of unpredictable situations over which she had little control. Her new-mother anxiety was fueled by her desperation not to make the same mistakes her mother had made.

"When she became anxious, Laura fell into a pattern of thinking solely of herself. When I first met her, she was angry and jealous that her husband was so comfortable with Max, while she felt so unsteady and unsure. She had convinced herself that she wasn't a good mother, and although Stewart tried to reassure her, she couldn't hear him.

"Compounding their communication problem was the fact that Laura presented her worries in such a way that Stewart perceived it as nagging and frequently responded to her with a patronizing, 'It's so easy; if you can't do it, I will' attitude. This invalidated her concerns and made her feel out of control.

"I told Laura she had to change the way she communicated her fears to Stewart. In time, she was able to speak in a nonanxious way so he didn't automatically tune her out. He, in turn, had to listen to the feelings behind her words. To do that, he had to promise to set aside everything that he wanted to say, all his defenses and comments, and simply hear her out. This technique is called reflective listening, and in many cases the therapy process in general can serve as a model of behavior for each partner. During a session, I listen empathetically to each person in turn. By hearing me encourage Laura to talk about her feelings, Stewart learned how to do the same at home.

"But more than speaking in a less anxious way, Laura had to develop confidence in herself as a mother. I pointed out that because of her perfectionism, Laura had a list of 'shoulds' that few people would ever attain. 'Take a look at your son,' I told her. 'He's thriving, he's happy. You must be doing something right!'

"Another factor dividing this couple was Laura's desire for her husband to help with the baby, although she was unwilling to relinquish any decision-making. I explained that while Stewart's way of handling Max was different from hers, it was no less correct. If Stewart is going to take Max to the shopping center, let him decide if he wants to take along a bottle of milk. 'Cross that off your list, Laura,' I told her. 'You don't have to worry about everything all the time.'

"As Laura's anxiety about her mothering began to lessen, I pointed out that the distance between her and Stewart had grown because they each had different ways of dealing with problems, ways that were often in conflict. Laura obsessed; Stewart denied. As a result, everything became a power struggle.

"When I first met Stewart, he was depressed. He needed to talk about the possibility of his leaving the family business. This would ease his fears about making the break and not being able to support his family. But rather than talk with Laura, Stewart's inclination was to tell her one or two things, then cut short the conversation. 'That's not a discussion,' I told him. 'Share your anxieties with Laura and engage her in listening to you.'

"At the same time, however, Laura had to overcome her resentment about being the breadwinner if Stewart went off on his own. Laura had an I-want-to-have-my-cake-and-eat-it-too attitude toward Stewart's plans. For a long time, she was unwilling to admit that one of the reasons she was so upset at the thought of Stewart's going off on his own was the fact that this was in some way an abrogation of the contract they had made with each other when they got married. Yes, of course she would work, but her salary would be gravy. 'Many women are like this,' I told her, 'but things change. You made a commitment to each other, and if it means you have to shoulder most of the financial responsibility until his business gets going, so be it.'

"'When Stewart starts a discussion about his work and plans for the future,' I continued, 'you must listen carefully to what he is saying and not pepper him with questions and let your own fears silence him.'

'You're right,' Laura said. 'It doesn't matter who makes the money. It's our money.' Stewart did leave his father's business at the end of last year and started a competing firm.

"As the tension eased between them, as they learned to control their hair-trigger tempers, they started to laugh again and enjoy being together. Since each was waiting for the other to make the first move sexually, I also gave them the assignment of taking turns seducing each other. This wasn't as easy as it sounded, since the power struggles between these two were long-standing, and they were both too proud to say, 'I need you; I want you.' Once they did, Laura realized how much she enjoyed sex with Stewart and how much she had missed it.

"As Laura gained more confidence in her mothering abilities, she became less rigid about schedules and stopped insisting things be done only her way. 'I was trying so hard to surround us with perfection,' she said when we ended counseling after a year and a half. 'I've learned that if I just ease up on myself and everyone else, things have a way of working out.'"

HOW TO END AN ARGUMENT— SO YOU'RE BOTH HAPPY

1. **Stop trying to win.** In most arguments, each person is a little right and a little wrong.

2. **Schedule a time and place to resolve conflict.** Timing is everything. Don't bring up important issues when you are too tired or too rushed to resolve them.

3. **Be clear and specific.** Discuss one issue at a time and stay focused on the point you are trying to make. Try to be as neutral as you can in presenting your point of view.

4. **Make suggestions for resolutions,** brainstorm ideas, and pick one to try that seems to satisfy both of you the most. If that doesn't work, don't despair. Pick another.

5. **Call a time-out** when either of you is so white-hot you will soon say or do something you regret. Remove yourself, temporarily, from the situation. You can say "I'm feeling very angry and I'm beginning to lose it now. I want to take a time-out." Or "I see you're very angry right now. Let's discuss this tonight, after the kids are in bed." Make a definite time and place to continue the conversation. Then, leave the room and do something physical—walk, jog, clean the garage—anything to defuse angry energy. When you're calm, ask your partner if he's ready to resume the conversation. (If he says he's still too angry, respect his feelings and wait.)

6. **Promise each other you won't be nasty, sarcastic, or personally critical.**

7. **Don't insist on the last word.** You may win the battle but lose the war by building resentment.

"I Don't Want to Be a Battered Wife"

Craig was affectionate with Lisa—until something set him off. What happens when an abused wife refuses to go on pretending?

"I don't want you to think that Craig is a terrible person," said Lisa, a pretty, intense-looking woman of twenty-eight, with thick dark curls and pale skin. "Maybe there's something I do or fail to do that really triggers his anger.

"I guess I've always let people down. Even as a child I remember so clearly trying to make my parents happy, but I always seemed to mess up, even when it came to little things like having good table manners or cleaning up my room. If one toy was out of place in my room, my father would pick it up, throw it against the wall, and scream at me. Sometimes Mom and I would have to lock ourselves in the bathroom until his temper subsided. Mother was always crying. My father finally left when I was twelve, but even then, life was grim. Mother was so depressed, all she could do was lie in bed, watch TV, and drink. I shouldered most of the household chores, and became something of a recluse. I had little time for friends. I dated a few boys in high school and after graduation, but nobody special.

"That's why I was very ripe—if not starved—for affection by the time I met Craig. He was a research analyst who'd come for a meeting at the Board of Health office where I worked as a receptionist. We

121

chatted awhile, and when he asked me out, of course I said yes.

"Craig was very affectionate. We went out every night and fell so crazily in love that we decided to get married just three weeks later. I can't even describe how wonderful it was to be Craig's wife. We spent every spare moment snuggled up together, very, very close. Not that there wasn't a dark side . . . like the time he was on his way to work and I ruffled up his hair when I hugged him. Craig smacked me—hard. I was shocked. But he quickly put his arm around me and kissed me. 'Look, I'm sorry,' he said. 'But don't do that again. Don't fool with my hair.' I felt terrible for making him angry, but I tried to forget about it.

"Craig wanted to have a family right away, which made me very happy. How tenderly he held me when I told him I was pregnant! Life seemed perfect then. And it was, except when I did some little thing that provoked him. He would give me a shove or a smack on the back. Craig never stayed angry, and I wasn't supposed to, either. I had to pretend to recover faster than I did or he'd get upset all over again.

"By the time our little girl, Betsy, was four months old and sleeping through the night, I became pregnant with Jamie—we wanted the children to be close in age so they could play together. Craig adored kids. But as our life grew more complicated, the hitting

incidents became more frequent. By the time I was six months pregnant with Randy, Craig would strike me every few days. The harder I worked at trying to figure out and eliminate whatever was irritating Craig, the worse it seemed to get.

"Lately I spend a lot of time wondering: Am I falling down on the job or is Craig being unrealistic? I do my best, but still he finds fault with me or the children. If they are shy, fearful, or frustrated— as all kids are at times—he worries that they won't be popular.

"Yet those worries are nothing compared with his totally mis-placed jealousy. Craig has absolute-ly no reason to be jealous, but one night he arrived home just when the new pastor dropped by to intro-duce himself. Craig walked in and his face contorted with anger. What now? I wondered. As soon as the young pastor left, Craig grabbed me by the hair and said, 'In another sec-ond, you'd have been on his lap.' Then he slapped me and sent me spinning across the room. Did he really think I was flirting with the minister?

"That night I slept in the extra bed in Betsy's room. Craig kept pounding on the door, begging me to forgive him, but I stayed where I was. My little Betsy actually climbed out of her bed and gave me her stuffed bunny to help me fall asleep.

"The next morning, Craig was

sitting at the kitchen table with his clothes all rumpled. I guess he had fallen asleep in his suit. He tried to be nice. I was seething inside, but I still knew better than to make an issue of his behavior.

"In truth, though, I'm worn out physically and emotionally. I know I should be more forgiving, but it's gotten harder for me to turn around and say, 'Oh, it was nothing, honey.' At this point, there is so much tension between us that when we make love, I just lie there like a zombie.

"I probably wouldn't even have come for help if Betsy hadn't been playing with my makeup last week. She took some dark gray eyeshadow and put it all over her cheeks. When I asked her why, she said, 'I'm the mommy after the daddy's hit me.' I thought then about all the pain I suffered during my own childhood, and I realized I had to stop covering up—for everybody's sake."

CRAIG'S TURN

"I know I have a short fuse," said Craig, a tall, thin, freckled man of thirty-four, with sad gray eyes. "But Lisa should remember how much I truly love her.

"I wouldn't hit her, though, if she didn't provoke me. And I do think she should learn to forgive me, be done with it, and not hold a grudge for as long as she does. Am I that bad a guy? My father used to hit my mother—and me—sometimes. He was a very loving man, but that's what he did when he was sore about something. It really wasn't such a big deal. I mean—it wasn't as if I thought there were those who love and those who hit. In my life, those who loved did hit when the situation called for it.

"I fell in love with Lisa the day I first saw her. There was something about her—something so womanly. I never thought she could love a lonesome misfit like me.

"Lisa and I went out that same night, and it was a very passionate evening. We clung to each other, and I think by the end of our second date we were naming our children. Though it must have seemed presumptuous, I was ready to make a commitment to her. I had always been a lonely kid. My mom died when I was ten. After that I was always the outsider at school. I wanted to make close friends, but I didn't know how. But with Lisa, I began to feel wanted and important.

"Within weeks we were married and so in love. Did I hit her back then? Only after real provocation. I guess there was a time or two, but she's the first to admit that she deserved it . . . after she'd messed up my hair, for example. She knew I had a meeting with my supervisor that morning and I was already late.

"We wanted a family right away. Betsy, our first baby, was an angel. And we knew we wanted more. Each birth was more special than the previous one.

"But the problem was, too often, I'd see the reality of our life and feel swamped. It was—is—chaotic: kids ripping apart the house, making a constant racket. I could see what a strain it was for Lisa, what with all the runny noses, coughs, and dirty diapers. Then, as the kids grew older, I became very anxious—and a little frightened. The problems and the possibilities for disaster are so real. I worry about things going wrong.

"I know Lisa does a good job with the children. But if I see she's tense or tired or annoyed, I feel guilty that I'm messing up her life. It drives me nuts to see her unhappy. That's when I might give her a shove. I figure, if she's unhappy, if she's going to leave me, then I'll give her reason to. Once I came home and saw this guy in the living room—a real handsome guy—and I felt as if someone had punched me in the stomach. Lisa introduced him as the new minister, but minister or not, I saw the way he looked at her legs. Had she been coming on to him?

"Lisa's my whole life. I don't know why she can't be more understanding. I don't want my kids to be the sad little oddballs that nobody plays with. And I don't want my wife to be dissatisfied. I want everybody to be happy. Is that so bad?"

"It was clear," said the counselor, "that both Lisa and Craig felt desperately responsible for each other's happiness, and inadequate for not being able to maintain it. Given their backgrounds, it is not surprising that Craig resorted to physical abuse to express his panic at the thought of losing Lisa . . . and not surprising that Lisa felt she had to take it. Nevertheless, I told them firmly that there was to be no more violence. They could be annoyed with each other and they could argue, but there was nothing Lisa could ever say or do that would justify Craig's hitting, slapping, or shoving her.

"This was actually news to Craig, who in fact said, 'Well, when *is* it okay to hit your wife?' Because his otherwise kind father had hit his mother regularly and without remorse, he honestly believed that some physical force was acceptable and not uncommon in marriage.

"For her part, Lisa had so little self-esteem that she allowed herself to be abused—physically and emotionally—to please her husband. Although it made her increasingly depressed to do so, she would hide her true feelings simply to placate Craig. They had merged so wholeheartedly at the outset of their marriage that they had almost forgotten they were separate people. One of my first goals was to show both

Craig and Lisa that they needed to step back and allow each other to experience his or her own pain, fatigue, and worry without feeling pressed to correct it. I told Lisa emphatically that she had a right to her anger and her sadness—even if that made life temporarily uncomfortable for Craig.

"During one session, Lisa remembered in a rush of tears how deeply responsible she had felt for cheering up her depressed mother. This realization was cathartic and very constructive. It was essential for Lisa to recognize that this was a fairly easy trap for her to fall into, too, with her own daughter.

"I suggested instead that she begin to recognize her inner signals and cultivate her own interests. This was an entirely new concept for Lisa, but she took it to heart. One afternoon she arrived exhilarated with the news that she had enrolled in a modern-dance course—something she had always yearned to try.

"Craig, so long haunted by the fantasy that his mother, in dying, had rejected him, projected this fear of abandonment onto Lisa. He grew unrealistically concerned that she, too, would leave him.

"After a few sessions, Craig was able to see that in many instances his own insecurities triggered anxieties that were totally unrelated to the situation. His violent reaction to the incident with the young minister, for instance, was a response that was quite inappropriate. I suggested that he try to monitor his anxiety when it came up, and to consciously calm himself down, either with deep-breathing techniques or, if necessary, by leaving the room until he felt much calmer.

"Craig and Lisa's relationship had begun in a very physical way—cuddling and clinging interspersed with violence—but there had never been much honest communication between them, except in seeking and giving I'll-always-love-you reassurances. As their life became more complicated, the tension and the abuse increased. When Craig hit Lisa in front of the children, he was trying to tell her, in a very inappropriate way, that he needed her and could never give her up. In therapy, this couple learned to ask each other 'How was your day?' in an interested, receptive fashion instead of in a defensive or nervous tell-me-you're-happy-or-I'll-panic-and-feel-like-a-failure way.

"Craig also came to realize that he was projecting his own fear of failure onto his children. Once he could acknowledge that his worrying about their sociability came from his own sense of inadequacy during a lonely childhood, he began to short-circuit his erroneous belief that Betsy, Jamie, and Randy had to be perfect. When he finally relaxed and stopped constantly judging his children, the tension at home began to ease.

"Many months have passed since

Craig hit Lisa, and this has rekindled Lisa's sexual feelings for her husband.

"They have worked very hard in therapy and still come to see me if either one feels the need to talk. They have, however, succeeded in ridding themselves and their marriage of the desperation that allows one partner to resort to violence and the other to accept it silently."

FINDING THE STRENGTH TO FIGHT BACK

Too many battered women blame themselves for the emotional or physical abuse they endure. They may think: "I deserve it." "I'm just not good enough for him." "It must be something I'm doing wrong." Or, lacking self-esteem and confidence, they believe that the abuse is simply something they must shoulder, their sorry lot in life. These women don't know what to do to break out of the cycle, or even what's really wrong in their relationships.

Unlike Lisa, a woman may not be able to change her partner, but she can make changes in her own life. The first step is to seek help. There are shelters and self-help programs across the country for abused women. If a shelter or recovery program tells you they cannot help you, ask for a referral. Call these numbers for additional information and guidance:

The National Domestic Violence toll-free hotline, 1-800-621-4673; The National Coalition Against Domestic Violence, 202-638-6388; The National Clearinghouse for the Defense of Battered Women, 215-351-0010. Many states also have toll-free hotlines for domestic violence. Check your telephone directory.

If you are a victim of abuse, it's critical to speak to someone who will believe your story, support you in your desire for protection, and respect your privacy. Confiding in the wrong person, someone who reinforces your belief that you are to blame for the violence or minimizes the offending behavior, can be harmful. Seek out professional counselors, legal advisers, medical doctors, or community groups that have experience in dealing with abused women and can explain your legal rights, especially related to child support and custody.

Build a support system. Controlling partners often try to isolate a spouse from friends and family—all the more reason to keep those relationships intact. Stay in touch with friends, other mothers, coworkers, and people you meet in self-help groups.

"ANGER WAS TEARING US APART"

red was furious and Ginny didn't know how to get through to him. What happens when resentment rages out of control?

"There's no one I can talk to about what's happening," said Ginny, thirty-six, a slim woman with long blond hair. "If I tried to discuss it with my friends, they'd undoubtedly advise me to leave Fred. I don't want to do that. We've been married for two years and I love him very much. But I'm honestly afraid our family life will be destroyed if Fred can't learn to control his violent temper and if we can't resolve our conflicts over Peter, who is my seventeen-year-old son from my first marriage.

"These days Fred is like a ticking time bomb, ready to explode at any moment. He's always had a temper, but over the past few months it has gotten much worse. Usually, Fred's outbursts take the form of shouting and verbal threats, but twice he has slapped me—hard—and he has also come close to hitting Peter.

"Yesterday, for instance, I returned home from the supermarket to find Fred shouting at Peter because he had neglected to rake the leaves as he had been told to do. Thankfully, he managed to regain his composure. But I'm sure that one of these days he won't be able to. Lately, it seems I'm reliving a childhood nightmare. My father used to hit my mother and I remember lying in bed, listening to them argue in the next room.

"Dad was an electrician, a very dour man whom I could never feel close to. Mom was a housewife who did whatever Dad told her to do. Although I was much closer to her, they were both incredibly strict with me. I was an A student and never even got into trouble, but they would often scream at me and

127

berate me for small things. I lived in a constant state of panic, never sure what I should or shouldn't be doing.

"The summer after my high school graduation, I met Carl, my first husband. We started to date regularly and I convinced myself I was in love. Carl worked for an oil company and for the first year of our marriage we were sent to Alaska, a heavenly distance from my dominating parents. That was where Peter was born. Then Carl was transferred to Texas. Dutifully, I went along, although by this time it was clear that our marriage wasn't bringing either of us any happiness. We had almost nothing in common, and he spent so little time at home that he was more like a visitor than a husband.

"Soon, we were fighting constantly, and so despite my guilt over hurting Peter, I asked Carl for a divorce and began looking for a job to support myself and my son. I wasn't qualified for anything except a low-paying clerical job; I was overjoyed to find a spot at a large manufacturing company headquartered in town. Although the work was tedious and my heart ached when I dropped Peter off at the day-care center, I was able to buy food and pay the bills every month.

"Being a single mother was hard and for several years I didn't date often. But when a friend said she had a special guy she wanted me to meet, I agreed to a blind date.

"Fred and I were strongly attracted to each other right away. Back then, Fred really seemed to love Peter, and I have happy memories of the three of us going for bike rides and picnicking by the lake. It was a year and a half before Fred proposed marriage. During much of that time we lived together in my apartment, but until we married, Fred kept his own place.

"To be honest, the arrangement bothered me a lot. It seemed ridiculous to be paying two rents, and the fact that Fred had a home to run off to whenever we argued made me very insecure. Fred seemed to be standing with a foot in each camp: He was one half of a couple, but he also had all the freedom of a single guy. Although he said he needed the apartment so he could have time alone, I didn't believe him—but since we weren't married, I didn't feel I had the right to complain about the situation.

"Unfortunately, I can't discuss anything with Fred. When he's angry, he stalks out the door and I'm terrified he'll leave me. Fred and Peter are my whole life now—after we married I quit my job because the long hours and tedious work depressed me, and fortunately Fred earns enough to support us comfortably.

"Yet despite my fears, there are times when Fred is thoughtful and attentive. He never forgets a birthday or anniversary. Sometimes he even brings me one rose just to say I love you.

"The problem is, we can't stop fighting about Peter. The first year we were married, Fred worked at night—he manages a newspaper printing plant—and since Peter was at school during the day, they rarely saw each other. But now Fred works during the day and the two are constantly at each other's throats.

"I know it isn't all Fred's fault; Peter can be extremely difficult. When I divorced Carl, Peter sided with his father, and he resents the fact that another man is in control of the household. But Fred doesn't understand how sensitive Peter is and how much he suffered as a result of the breakup. I believe Peter should be reasoned with gently; certainly the poor boy shouldn't be threatened with violence.

"The first time Fred hit me, I couldn't believe it had happened. After one of his explosions at Peter, during which he threatened to knock some manners into him, Fred stomped toward the door. I ran to block his way, hoping we could all sit down together and talk the problem out. Fred tried to shove me aside, and when I clung to his arm, he slapped my hand. The second time he hit me was after an almost identical episode—except that then he smacked me hard across the mouth.

"The tension in our home increases with every day and I'm worn out from acting as a buffer between my husband and my son. I'm at a loss about what to do. I love Fred and don't want to leave him, but if he can't control these rages, I think divorce will be my only way out."

FRED'S TURN

"Ginny's worried about my temper, and she has reason to be," said Fred, thirty-eight, a short, well-built man with a tense manner. "The truth is, I'm worried myself. If the situation at home doesn't change soon, I'm afraid I'm going to lose all control and knock my stepson through the wall.

"Peter hates the fact that I've replaced his father, and he's doing everything he can to drive me crazy. He taunts me to the breaking point and Ginny stands behind Peter, no matter how he acts.

"I give Peter far more, materially and emotionally, then I ever dreamed of receiving when I was a teenager, yet all I get in return is disrespect and rudeness. My own parents separated before I was born and I never knew my natural father. The man I was raised to call Dad worked as a truck driver. He resented me deeply and refused to adopt me. My half-brother, who is eighteen months younger, was praised and worshiped, while I was ignored.

"So I channeled all my energy into my schoolwork and I excelled—at least until I got to high school. After all those years of having my triumphs pass unacknowledged, I just said to heck with it and stopped trying. If my mother ever stood up for me, my stepfather blew up at her, and on several such occasions he hit her. By the time I reached high school, I was a scrapper, too; I'd punch instead of argue. It just seemed natural to swing out at people when I got angry.

"After I graduated, I went into the Air Force and was sent to Vietnam as a helicopter mechanic. When I returned, I took a job at a printing plant. I also made a hasty marriage. Our divorce, after six years, was painful, but frankly I was relieved to escape from all the hassle. I thoroughly enjoyed having my own place to unwind when I needed to. When Ginny and I decided to live together, I kept my place because it gave me the opportunity for that occasional solitude. Some evenings I'd go there and watch TV—although I know Ginny didn't believe me when I told her that.

"Frankly, living with Ginny as her husband is nothing like living with her as her lover. Before we were married, she was gentle and undemanding, but the moment the knot was tied, she started nagging and crying. She sits home all day, waiting for me to come and be with her. I've suggested she take a part-time job, but she maintains she's not qualified for anything except clerical work.

"At this point I feel as though I'm going to crack. Ginny won't even allow me to go off by myself and cool down the way I used to. She has some crazy idea that if I'm not nailed to the living room, I'm out womanizing. Despite her suspicions, there's no other woman in my life.

"I love my wife, and I want to love my stepson. But they gang up on me; I'm an ogre to Ginny, a meal ticket to Peter. And when the tension mounts, I lose control. God knows, I don't want my wife to be afraid of me. I think, though, that she's the one who needs to make changes."

THE COUNSELOR'S TURN

"This couple were in counseling for six months before anything truly constructive happened," the counselor said. "By the time a breakthrough did occur, I had developed strong doubts that the marriage would survive. Although both Fred and Ginny paid lip service to the necessity of establishing real communication, each was holding back honest feelings and waiting for the other to do a complete turnaround.

"Then, after six months of unproductive sessions, a battle to end all battles took place between Fred and Peter about the boy's refusal to lower the volume on the television. Ginny, as usual, sided with her son and Fred hauled back and hit her. Peter, terrified, phoned the police.

The officers advised Ginny to press charges or to have Fred placed under a peace bond so that if he struck her again he would receive an automatic fine. She chose to do the latter.

"Shocked, Fred took a firm stand also. 'I am totally frustrated,' he told Ginny. 'As far as you're concerned, I'm the bad guy in the marriage and you're the innocent victim.'

"At this point, the couple made a conscious decision to stop blaming each other and to at last let me help them work together to reconstruct their shattered relationship.

"Both Ginny and Fred came from backgrounds that had programmed their reactions to life's pressures. Beneath Fred's polite facade was a backlog of seething fury that had been building for years. His wife's siding with her son instead of with him triggered the old feeling of family rejection he had experienced in childhood. When he struck out at Ginny, he was, in effect, striking back at all the people in his life who had caused him pain.

"Ginny was equally insecure in intimate relationships and had a deep-seated distrust of men. As a child, she had been emotionally abandoned by her father, and this had bred in her such a feeling of worthlessness that she found it impossible to be calmly assertive. She either let everyone—Fred, Peter, her parents—walk all over her, or she reversed gears and overreacted by weeping and nagging.

"Ginny also suffered from guilt over having disrupted Peter's life by divorcing his father. Because of this, she felt obligated to be unconditionally supportive during his conflicts with Fred, despite the fact that having to take sides during their battles was unbearable.

"As Fred and Ginny came to realize how the pain they had experienced growing up was affecting their present relationship, they became much more accepting and understanding of each other. Ginny's greatest problem was a lack of self-esteem. A major step for her during counseling was to accept Fred's offer to cosign a student loan so she could attend a two-year business school. And Fred joined a national support organization for abusers who have problems controlling their anger. In the nonjudgmental atmosphere of this group, he learned how to dissipate his anger before it exploded.

"Encumbered by emotional baggage from their respective childhoods, this couple had found it hard to pull together as a parenting team. Ginny, in particular, had so resented the unreasonable restrictions placed upon her when she was growing up that she had been reluctant to set any limits at all for Peter. But, as old wounds healed, she was able to examine her attitude toward her son and see that he did indeed need some discipline.

"When Ginny and Fred began to present a united front, Peter's initial response was resentment, but gradually it gave way to grudging respect. Today, enrolled at the state university, he phones home frequently and confesses to feelings of homesickness for both mother and stepfather.

"Fred and Ginny have been in counseling for almost two years. Fred continues to attend meetings of his abusers group and physical violence is no longer an issue in their marriage. Ginny is now working as a personnel director for a medium-sized company. Secure in her own self-worth, she does not need to depend upon Fred for a sense of identity, but she does take great pleasure in his openly expressed pride in her accomplishments.

"Given the many problems they have had to work through, this couple have naturally experienced occasional setbacks; however, Fred and Ginny are convinced that the improvement in their relationship has been enormous and that their marriage is steadily growing stronger and happier."

GETTING A HANDLE ON ANGER

You can learn to manage your anger even if you haven't had much control in the past. It won't be easy and it won't be quick—but by carefully monitoring your feelings and responses to different people and situations, you can better understand your reactions and change them. Here's what you can do:

1. First, give yourself permission to be angry. Not all the time, and not for any reason, but feeling anger is a normal, expected, and acceptable emotion. You are not a bad person for getting angry, so don't drown yourself in guilt.

2. Monitor your behavior for one week. Who did you get angry at and why? Can you determine any "hot buttons," guaranteed to set your temper flaring? What results did your anger produce?

3. Recognize your body's reactions to anger and don't ignore these messages. When your hot buttons are pressed, does your stomach churn or your heart race?

Do you feel a tightening in your temples, neck, or back? Tuning in to the messages your body is sending can help you handle anger. Many times we are unaware that we are being hostile to our mates. Getting in touch with your anger responses will help defuse arguments before they rage out of control.

4. Learn to state what you feel when you feel it. Without being hostile, demeaning, or blaming, talk to your partner so he not only hears you, but is motivated to change. Be as specific as you can about what is upsetting you as well as what your partner can do to make the situation better.

"MY HUSBAND IS SO MOODY"

Life with Rob was an emotional roller coaster. How could Andrea stay with a man who was so out of control?

ANDREA'S TURN

"I can't believe this is happening again," said Andrea, thirty-two, a soft-spoken woman in a gray knit tunic and matching skirt. "Everything was going so well, but then Robert's cycles of depression and anger reappeared. He won't talk to me. He snaps at Jimmy, our two-year-old son, and whenever I ask what's wrong, he gets furious and shuts me out.

"Robert's mood swings have been happening on and off since we were married, six years ago. On top of all this, he doesn't lift a finger around the house and I'm getting tired of doing all the work.

"My own parents fought constantly, mostly over money. They're still fighting over the same things to this day, so I assure you, I have no illusions about living happily ever after. But I swore I would never have a marriage like theirs, and look what's happened: This is my second, and now it's falling apart.

"Soon after I married my first husband, I realized I didn't really love him; I had just been desperate to get out of the house. I was also so afraid of arguments that I let him make all the decisions. Finally we were divorced and I moved back to my parents' house, but nothing had changed there. That's when I decided to make a clean break, so I packed up and moved to California.

133

"About five years after I moved here, I met Robert. I was working at a large hotel downtown and he came in to reserve a banquet room. We started talking, and when he asked for my phone number I was really excited.

"We hit it off right from the start. Robert was a social worker counseling kids at a local juvenile center; we had so much in common. Like me, Robert had been married once before and was determined to make his next relationship work.

"A month after we met, Robert moved into my apartment, and four months later we were married. Almost as soon as we were married, our relationship seemed to change. For one thing, I was fired from my job because my boss didn't want anyone who wasn't willing to be on call twenty-four hours a day, and now that I had Robert I certainly wasn't. For six months I looked for a new job, and by the time I found a spot in an insurance office, we were pretty broke.

"Just about this time, Robert decided that working at the juvenile center was too emotionally draining. He was burned out, he said, and he was going to try working as a salesman for a computer software company. He worked on commission and he was quite good at selling, but in the beginning money was tight.

"Still, there were blessings: We had fallen in love with a little house and scraped together every penny we could for a down payment. And we decided to start a family. Life was stressful, but we thought that once we bought our house everything would fall into place.

"Unfortunately, it didn't. For one thing, we'd been buying everything on credit so we could save all our cash. After we moved into the house, we realized how financially strapped we were and how much we owed. On top of that, I had to have surgery for infertility—there was scar tissue on my fallopian tubes, and if I had an operation, perhaps then I could conceive. Of course, I had the operation, but I was out of work for six weeks, and though my medical bills were covered, I didn't get a paycheck.

"Well, that just about put us under. I was upset, but Robert became terribly depressed. That was the first time I witnessed one of his moods. But it certainly wasn't the last—they occurred frequently after that. Sometimes they lasted ten minutes, sometimes ten days. He'd withdraw from me completely, refusing to talk and refusing to make love. He'd mope around, expecting me to wait on him hand and foot. The more I asked what was wrong, what I could do to help, the angrier he became. I didn't know what was happening and I started to think I was to blame.

"The worst part was when Robert's depression turned to rage. Just like his father, the least thing would set him off. You see, although his family always pretended nothing was wrong, Robert's father, who died ten years ago, was an alcoholic. Whenever he drank, he would be especially hard on Robert, his only child, criticizing him about everything. If Robert ever tried to talk to his father about it, he was either yelled at or ignored. His mother, a shy, quiet woman, was apparently unwilling or unable to stand up to her husband, and Robert had to handle all of it himself. Robert doesn't drink, but he's like his father in other ways.

"Usually Robert calmed down after these explosions. In fact, for almost two years things did seem better and we became very close again. I even became pregnant! It was a difficult nine months, and then I had to have a cesarean, but Robert couldn't have been more supportive. I thought our dark days were over.

"Needless to say, I was wrong. A few months ago, Robert started having problems at work. He and his boss can't seem to get along and it looks as if Robert will have to change jobs. I've tried to get him to talk, but he ignores me. Once again he's moping around the house. Just last week we got into a huge fight because it takes him four days to carry the trash cans from the curb to the backyard. I'm not a slave, for heaven's sake. I'm a nervous wreck again; I eat to calm myself down, so my weight is zooming up. And our sex life? It's nonexistent.

"I love Robert, but his anger and depression are leaving no room for our marriage. I've been thinking about a divorce. If he doesn't change soon, I don't see that I have a choice."

ROBERT'S TURN

"Andrea is fed up and I don't blame her," said Robert, thirty-four, a pleasant-looking man in a tan business suit. "I know my moods can be scary, but I would never hurt her or Jimmy.

"I don't mean to yell, but Andrea has a way of pushing my buttons. Whenever I feel low, she nags me constantly. And when Andrea tries to get under my skin like that, it really makes me mad.

"I wasn't very happy growing up. My relationship with my father was lousy. He would call me stupid whether I came home with a low grade on a test or accidentally burned the toast. He humiliated me in front of my friends.

"I think my father was a very unhappy man, so he sought relief in the bottle. I first remember him drinking heavily when I was thirteen. I hated his drinking, but any discussion on my part was impossible.

"By the time I went away to college, the drinking was so bad we never knew if he'd be coming home that night. And he was always a belligerent drunk, going out of his way to irritate people and to humiliate me in particular. I guess I learned early on to put up a wall so he couldn't get to me. Andrea thinks these moods are new and her fault, but she's wrong; I remember getting depressed like this back in junior high.

"Anyway, I thought going away to school would help, and it did—for a while. I met my first wife during my senior year. The marriage lasted only three years and probably worked for less than two.

"About a year after my divorce was final I met Andrea, and I was immediately struck by her independence and strength. Our relationship progressed quickly; before I knew it we were planning a wedding. The problem was, I didn't think I was ready to be married again. I wanted to postpone the wedding until I had worked out my problems, but I didn't have the guts to tell her. I was afraid I'd lose her.

"Shortly after we were married, I decided to quit the counseling center and start my sales career. My father had always told me I could never be a salesman—he didn't think I had the personality or the wherewithal to do it—but that only made me more determined.

"I really liked selling, and I was doing well, although I see now that Andrea and I bit off more than we could chew by buying the house. We were also trying to have a baby,

but we couldn't. It was all too much and my moods began again.

"Now, when I get depressed I just want to be left alone. It's not that I don't want to help out; I simply can't. But no matter how bad I feel, eventually I get over it. Although I have tried to explain this to Andrea, she either starts to cry or insists on bugging me. That makes me angrier, and before I realize what's happening, I'm yelling and knocking over chairs.

"Lately it seems my depressions are more frequent. The pressure at work is mounting—I have a new supervisor and he and I don't see eye to eye. I want very much to quit, maybe even start my own small firm, but I have a family to support; I'm too old to start over.

"I love Andrea, and I give her a lot of credit for hanging in there. Maybe I'm not cut out to be anyone's husband. I'll take the blame for our problems, but can't she understand that there are times when I need to be alone?"

THE COUNSELOR'S TURN

"At first, this couple's problem seemed to be one-sided," said the counselor. "But although it was true that Robert's periods of depression and rage were a major source of conflict, Andrea, too, shared responsibility for the trouble this marriage was in. One key issue for this couple was their inability to communicate what they wanted and needed from each other.

"Like many children of alcoholic parents, Robert came to this relationship carrying some heavy emotional baggage from the past. When a child is growing up, he needs to be able to trust his parents. But an alcoholic parent can't always be trusted. Robert never knew when his father would lash out out at him, much less come home at all. He never learned the importance of sharing his feelings with others and was left instead with a great deal of unexpressed rage.

"As an adult, whenever anything bothered him, Robert coped by withdrawing, and he viewed any attempts to help him as an invasion of privacy. He reasoned that telling Andrea how he was feeling would make him vulnerable, as he had been as a child.

"Robert continued this pattern over the years; as soon as something shook his self-confidence—financial problems or a crisis at work—he reacted by internalizing the problem and blaming himself. Ironically, Robert's perception of his own problem was not off the mark. He simply needed help marshaling his many good qualities to overcome his negative behavioral patterns.

"Andrea's childhood experiences, although not nearly as difficult as her husband's, had also failed to teach her how to communicate effec-tively. Since her parents fought constantly over the same problems, she never learned how a couple can work through problems and solve them. Desperate for a 'nice' marriage, she deferred to her first husband's every wish, which made her unhappy.

"In her relationship with Robert, she shifted gears and became all-controlling. When Robert was depressed, she probed relentlessly for the cause of his mood. When she was unable to find out what was wrong—when, in fact, Robert pushed her away—she dealt with her frustration by overeating and then blaming her husband.

"In our first session, I outlined three goals for this couple. The first was for them to make a firm commitment to make this marriage work. I pointed out that because of their inability to connect on an emotional level, much of their marriage was based not on intimacy but on accomplishments—saving for a house, trying to have a child, and so on. I also referred Robert to a colleague of mine, a psychiatrist, to see if medication—perhaps an antidepressant—would be helpful. For the time being, we've decided to see if other avenues prove fruitful.

"The second goal was for each to take a share of the responsibility for their problems. For a long time, only Robert was willing to do this. Andrea persisted in seeing herself as the blameless victim of Robert's moods. It was essential, then, for them to decide who was responsible for what.

"We began with the practical aspects of their life—deciding, for instance, which chores were appropriate for each partner to do. Once Andrea saw that these basics were being taken care of she began to relax and soften her adamant stance against Robert.

"At the same time, I urged Robert to take at least twenty minutes a day to relax, either by practicing deep-breathing techniques or by meditating or doing yoga. Although many people dismiss such simple measures, recent studies have proved that depressed people like Robert show remarkable progress when they implement relaxation techniques to combat stress. And although Robert agreed that he could not always withdraw from the family—that is, have the luxury of being the 'sick' one—I instructed Andrea that when he wanted to be alone, she must respect his wishes.

"The third and most difficult goal was for them to learn to share their feelings. We worked on a simple exercise: Each was to pick one upsetting incident and say, 'When you do this, I feel this way.' Just learning to recognize a feeling and expressing it in a nonthreatening way was a big step.

"When I discovered that Andrea and Robert had spent virtually no time away from home together since their marriage, I suggested that they arrange for a baby-sitter on a regular basis so they could get out of the house and into a neutral environment away from chores that needed to be done. The time alone reinforced their deep feelings for each other and gave them more practice in communicating.

"And the more they communicated, the more they realized how good their marriage really was. Robert has learned that he needn't be afraid to express his fears to Andrea, and this trust has given him a renewed sense of confidence. Rather than become immobilized over a possible job change, he has been setting up interviews with executive placement firms.

"Robert's openness has had a positive effect on Andrea. Although she will probably always worry about problems until they are solved, Andrea has learned to keep her anxieties at a manageable level, and she has acknowledged that overeating is the way she copes with stress and not something that is Robert's fault.

"Although this couple terminated joint counseling two months ago, we agreed that Robert would continue to see me for a while longer; he still feels the need to talk about ways to handle his moods when they do shift. However, as the couple find out more about themselves, they know that any problems that crop up will be ones they can tackle together."

THE BLAME GAME

While Robert acknowledged his problems, Andrea acted like a martyr and refused to believe that she played a part either in triggering or exacerbating their difficulties. This happens in many marriages. Couples break out of such a blaming impasse only when each partner stops insisting that their ideas and opinions are infallible, takes responsibility for his or her own behavior, and makes healing the relationship the top priority. This exercise will help those trapped in a cycle of righteous blaming to take constructive steps to work on the real issues dividing them:

1. Think of an issue that's currently causing pain in your relationship.

2. In three sentences, write down your position on that issue.

3. Pretend to be your partner and describe how he or she sees that issue. Be fair.

4. Now ask yourself: What would have to change inside for me to see the issue from my spouse's point of view? Again, be as honest as you can. Are these changes ones I'm comfortable with? If so, why am I not making them? Why are they difficult for me?

"WE CAN'T STOP THE CONSTANT FIGHTING"

Although Ronny and Ted loved each other very much, their heated arguments were unabating. Could they ever stop battling and start loving again?

RONNY'S TURN

"This is crazy. We can't stop fighting," said Ronny, twenty-six, her long dark hair falling in soft curls around her face. "We love each other, we really do. But lately, whenever we are together, all we do is scream.

"Look, I know how dedicated Ted is to his work. All his life he's loved music and wanted to be a recording engineer. He's very, very talented. He told me that in the beginning the hours were going to be crazy. But now he's been at the studio for a long time. Ted never went to college and he started working right after high school. But I ask you—how long do you have to pay your dues?

"You know, I never, ever see him. I work at an advertising agency—I'm assistant to the art director—and I love it. But Ted's day starts when I'm coming home. And if they need him, he can be there for two or three days on end.

"I can't understand why Ted doesn't put his foot down. He's talented, and they know it. Why can't he say, once in a while, 'I'm leaving at six-thirty or seven?' Or, 'No, I won't work all night.'

"I miss him so much. We met through a friend of mine at work, and before we were lovers, we were such good friends. That meant a lot to me. Until Ted, I kept getting involved with guys who were all wrong for me. They were selfish. They were chauvinistic pigs who were so abusive—not physically, but mentally. They'd say they loved me, then I'd find out they were sleeping around.

"With Ted, that all changed. We used to talk about absolutely everything. But now he's never there for me. I feel so lonely and I'm getting very depressed. Even when Ted is home, he doesn't want to do anything but sleep. I'll say, 'Do you want to see a movie?' And he'll shrug his shoulders. 'Do you want to go to the art museum?' 'Whatever,' he'll say.

"I'm also tired of feeling like a drill sergeant around here. I don't like having to order Ted around, reminding him a hundred times to take out the garbage. I don't want to be that kind of wife. I'll give you a perfect example: Last month, my younger brother came to visit. I'd asked Ted if he could please fix the shower and he had said he would. I gave him plenty of notice. I kept reminding him to do it, but he never did it. I admit, I lost it. But it was the straw that broke the camel's back. If he's not going to follow through, then he should tell me instead of yessing me to death and then doing zero. I'm not his maid; I have a full-time job, too.

"Sometimes I get this real déjà vu feeling. My mother used to wait on my father hand and foot. She was the perfect little homemaker, and she kowtowed to my father on every front. Well, I refuse to do that.

"Actually, until I was about thirteen, I was Daddy's little girl. Then the fighting started, and as far as my father was concerned, I couldn't do anything right. My grades weren't high enough, I dressed like a tramp, I hung out with the wrong kids. I think I was just a normal teenager, but my father was so strict that my memories of my adolescence are of constant fighting.

"I left home as soon as I graduated from high school and came to live in the city with my older cousin. Soon after that, I met Ted.

"With all the other men in my life, no matter how terrible things got, I'd always stick it out. That's the way I am. And I'll fight to make this work, too. But I can't help thinking, what's the point?"

TED'S TURN

"Believe me, Ronny just doesn't understand how things work in my field," said Ted, twenty-two, a tall, thin man with long blond hair. "I'm an engineer in a recording studio. You have to pay your dues. And when you do, it pays off. People are beginning to recognize my talents. Clients ask for me. That makes me feel terrific.

"But most of the time, I feel like I'm on a treadmill. No matter how hard I work, how hard I try, I'm hit from all sides with demands.

"Ronny is an incredible nag. 'Take the garbage out.' 'Pick up your clothes.' 'Fix the bathroom.' I wish she'd just get off my back. Look, I work terrible hours. When I get home, my head is splitting. All I want to do is go to bed.

"Ronny won't give an inch, and I can't believe how much she reminds me of my mother. I wasn't very happy as a kid. My parents were always fighting—they finally divorced when I was eleven and my sister and I went to live with my father and his girlfriend. No one paid much attention to me.

"I didn't do well in school—I got into trouble a lot. But I loved music, although my mother was freaked out because I wanted to play drums. For years she kept harping on how she really wanted me to play the saxophone.

"You know what makes me nuts? Ronny calls me at work all the time. Look, I'm surrounded by a million guys there. What am I supposed to say when she calls and harangues me about something? Should I air the dirty linen in front of everyone?

"You know, when Ronny fights, she can be so nasty. I tell her something in a quiet moment—like how I get real nervous when one of my bosses walks into the studio—and then when we're fighting, she throws it up to me. I think that's really below the belt.

"Other times, she's cold. I don't get it. Is she purposely trying to end this relationship? Doesn't she know I love her? Maybe you can help."

THE COUNSELOR'S TURN

"Ronny and Ted were two intense, passionate people whose lives were totally out of sync," said the counselor. "They were very much in love, but each was in a different phase of life when they met. As a result, they had strikingly different expectations about marriage.

"Ted was a mensch—a kind, sensitive man totally unlike the other men in Ronny's life. When his parents divorced, he was left to his own devices. He grew up alone and lonely, watching TV, getting lost in his music, and trying to distance himself from his intense, controlling mother. In his father, he saw a man who didn't want to get emotionally involved with his family, who let others make decisions for him. Still, emboldened by his music, Ted developed his own work ethic, and at an age when most kids are still in college or dancing at disco clubs, he started working.

"Now, at twenty-two, Ted was working long hours trying to get ahead in his career. Although he loved his wife, he was unable to devote the time and energy necessary to build an intimate relationship. Ronny represented a mother figure who would love him, care for him—and, frankly, clean up after him. He certainly didn't want or expect her to be like his demanding, nagging mother.

"Ronny, at twenty-six, had already been working in her chosen field for six years and she was ready to settle down. Ronny grew up in a middle-class household where Mom was Betty Crocker and Dad was king. A strict authoritarian, Ronny's father was unable to accept his daughter's typical rebelliousness during her adolescence and constantly took to criticizing her. As a result, Ronny grew up with low self-esteem and a tremendous need to prove to herself that she could make a man love her—no matter how horrible he was.

"Ted was the first truly kind, decent man Ronny had met. Although she appreciated his many fine qualities, she wished he was more of a go-getter who could provide the lifestyle she wanted.

"When they first came to see me, Ronny was furious. She was hurt and disappointed that Ted didn't want to devote more time to their marriage. While she supported Ted's career, she had also expected that the years of round-the-clock working would be over by now.

"Compounding the problem was the fact that Ronny also felt guilty for feeling the way she did. After all, her husband wasn't gambling or running around with other women. He was working. How could she complain about that? Ronny's depression was triggered by the fact that she didn't feel justified in expressing her anger.

"One of the first things I did was to point out that Ronny had a right to expect that her husband think about her needs and desires as well as his own. But I also made it clear that some of Ronny's other expectations were unrealistic for now, considering her husband's age and career. Unless she accepted this and adjusted her timetable accordingly, their marriage would not make it. Ted was devastated when I said this and at first he did not want to return to counseling. However, I explained that the only way they were going to resolve their differences was if they both took off their rose-colored glasses and viewed their relationship honestly.

"In a short time, Ronny really did change. She loved Ted and had a lot of faith in his ability. Once she was able to tell herself that in time Ted would move ahead in his career and they would be able to have a more normal existence, we were able to focus on other problems.

"The most immediate one was their constant fighting. Not only did their expectations clash, but there was no time to talk through differences. The fact that Ted avoided confrontation exacerbated the situation.

"To defuse the fights and help Ronny and Ted refocus their energies, I established some rules: no name-calling, cursing, screaming, or walking out of the room. Also, neither was to use something the other had revealed in confidence as a weapon.

"Another aspect of fighting fair is learning to acknowledge each other's feelings without judgment or criticism. That meant they had to clarify daily what their expectations and needs were. For instance: Instead of expecting her husband to read her mind and pick up the dry cleaning, and then berating him when he didn't, Ronny had to say: 'Ted, could you please pick up the dry cleaning tomorrow?'

"At the same time, Ted had to stop seeing himself as the poor henpecked husband. Until they came for counseling, Ted didn't understand the role he played in their problems. He saw himself as the victim of a nagging wife.

"There was also an issue of control: Ronny admitted that, like her father, she wanted to be in charge

of every situation. Ted resented that, but since he preferred to avoid confrontation, he tried to control the situation another way—by purposely, or unconsciously, not doing what she asked. This is what therapists call passive-aggressive behavior.

"However, I told Ted that if he didn't want to be nagged, then he had to be more responsible and follow through with his promises. He understood and made an effort to change.

"I also told Ted that the fact that his time was so limited was all the more reason for him to let Ronny know in other ways, however small, that he was thinking of her. That could take the form of talking to her when she called him at work (Ronny promised to curtail the calls, and Ted acknowledged there was no excuse for not returning a call when he was free), buying her flowers, or making suggestions of things to do on his weekends off.

"As time went by and his talents at work were recognized, Ted gained the confidence to ask his superiors for more money as well as a more reasonable work schedule. Much to Ronny and Ted's delight, his boss agreed.

"This couple ended therapy after fifteen months, comfortable with themselves and each other and better able to put their priorities in order."

RULES FOR FIGHTING FAIR

Before any couple can even begin to solve their problems, they have to learn how to fight fair. While Ronny and Ted had a right to expect certain things from each other, the means they were using to achieve their goals were hurtful and divisive.

Have you and your spouse been fighting a lot lately? Do arguments escalate until you're both shouting things you later regret? The following ground rules for fighting fair helped this couple take the fire out of their fights so they could refocus their energies on practical strategies for resolving their differences. Make a promise to:

1. Give each other permission to be angry and not feel guilty about having those angry feelings.

2. Understand that, although you disagree, you are not enemies and will not attack each other—physically or verbally. Avoid name-calling, cursing, or screaming.

3. Never use something that has been previously told to you in confidence as a weapon in an argument.

4. Never walk out of the room until you both agree that an argument is over—or you have both agreed to table the problem and have chosen a specific time to bring it up again.

5. Acknowledge each other's feelings and perceptions without judgment or criticism. There's no 'right' way to feel.

These rules will help put boundaries around your arguments. Once the hostility is curtailed, you'll be able to talk, reason, and negotiate compromises.

PART 4

WHO'S THE BOSS? THE BATTLE FOR POWER AND CONTROL

MARRIAGE SHOULD BE A PARTNERSHIP OF equals—but all too often, that's not the case. Power struggles—some obvious, others subtle—permeate every relationship. And while we most often think of power in terms of who controls the checkbook or who's the boss in the bedroom, the battle for control is fought in many other arenas. Whether the issue is which movie to see on Saturday night, how to discipline the children, where to spend Christmas, or which friends to socialize with, countless husbands and wives are jockeying for power and control.

Traditionally, the scales of power were tipped in favor of the financial heavyweight. Whoever made the most money controlled the purse-strings—and the marriage. Roles, tasks, and responsibilities were clearly defined and divided according to gender.

But as women entered the work force in increasing numbers, the power pendulum swung in the opposite direction. In fact, the women's movement in general has changed the expectations of stay-at-home wives as well as those who work outside the home. In the last two decades, women interviewed for *Ladies Home Journal's* column "Can This Marriage Be Saved?" have consistently demanded a larger role in family decision-making, no matter the size of their paycheck or whether they received one at all. While many husbands clearly respect a wife who wants an equal voice in marital decisions, some are threatened by this change. In fact, one of the most wrenching marital dilemmas facing couples in recent years has been learning how to renegotiate roles and expectations without triggering a power dispute.

There are many ways to wield power in a marriage. Some are blatant: The partner who barks orders, insists on having things a certain way, or even resorts to violence is clearly pushing for control. Frequent criticism and fault-finding—as well as being disrespectful, sarcastic, or humiliating to a spouse in front of others—are also ways of exerting power and proving who's the boss.

But no less controlling is the quiet manipulator who sulks, cries, plays the martyr—or dismisses a partner's actions, ideas, or opinions as unimportant or ridiculous: "How would you know? I'm the one who understands kids," a wife may insist when arguing with her husband about how to discipline the children. Instead of discussing the situation, explaining her views and listening to his, she asserts her power and implies that his way is the wrong way. Similarly, the husband who tunes out and pretends to listen to his wife's problems—while reading a newspaper or watching a football game—registers high on the power/control scale, too.

Another type of power struggle is set in motion when one person insists on his or her version of the truth: Whether recalling an incident, describing a family vacation, or even voicing an opinion about a new movie, these people are convinced that the way they think is the way everyone should think. Does a mate view the situation differently? She must be wrong.

Perhaps the most common, though frequently unrecognized, power struggle is when partners treat each other in what marital therapists term a passive-aggressive manner. This occurs when partners undermine each other by pretending to cooperate; instead, they then either ignore what a partner has said, or promise to do something with no intention of actually following through. The result: a cycle of nagging and ignoring that frustrates everyone and triggers frequent skirmishes in the ongoing battle for control.

Being able to recognize marital power struggles is a key step in defusing them, but equally important is understanding why a partner is so desperate for total control. Some spouses unwittingly set up a power struggle out of a deep-seated need to protect themselves emotionally. Perhaps they grew up in a home punctuated with bickering, fighting or uncertainty—we see this often when a father or mother was an alcoholic. To feel safe, calmer, more in control, they want to make every decision themselves.

Other people control out of fear. They think: "If I trust someone else to be in charge, if I put down my guard for an instant, I'll leave myself wide open to pain and hurt. I'll be vulnerable." Still others have such low self-esteem that the only way they can feel good about themselves is by belittling others—and those closest to them are the most likely targets. Sadly, while the ego boost is only temporary, the damage to the marriage is often long-term.

Whenever one partner feels powerless, manipulated, threatened or demeaned, resentment brews. Instead of acting together as a team, each interaction becomes a competition, a game of one-upmanship. Who's winning? Who's giving in? In such marriages, any criticism or disagreement is taken as a personal rejection. Slights and aggravations are duly noted—and the stakes are high.

Ultimately, the only lasting way to defuse a power struggle is to learn to accept each other fully. Acceptance is the opposite of being competitive, critical, or blaming. It doesn't mean being, thinking, or feeling the same as your partner. In any close relationship, differences in opinions, priorities, habits—even in the way stress, anxiety, disappointment, and anger are handled—are bound to develop. Yet, time and again, we meet couples in *Can This Marriage Be Saved?* who, instead of being empathic, attempt to coerce their partner into doing or feeling exactly the way they do. Instead of being encouraging of a partner's goals and interests, they feel threatened and so disparage them. Inevitably, intimacy withers.

Can This Marriage Be Saved? makes it clear that in order to avoid power struggles, couples must learn to express feelings and ideas clearly in the face of criticism or disagreement—without resorting to accusations or criticisms of their own. They listen empathically to a partner's ideas and feelings, acknowledging his or her strengths and supporting his or her weaknesses. As we shall see in the next two chapters, "Love and Money" and "In the Bedroom," they are flexible enough—even in areas where power struggles are the most destructive—to negotiate changes and cooperate. In that way they are free to concentrate on what they share, rather than on what divides them.

"MY HUSBAND WANTS A PERFECT HOUSEWIFE"

Steve said he supported Hannah's career, but he still wanted her to be the model corporate wife. What happens when one partner expects too much?

HANNAH'S TURN

"Okay, so there were dog hairs all over the seat of the car," said Hannah, thirty-five, sinking her lean, nearly six-foot frame into a chair. "Is that enough to trigger a rampage?

"I am not kidding. When Steve pulled into the garage the night before last, he purposely looked inside my car and then stormed into the house, raving like a madman about dog hairs. Look, I'm not a world-class housekeeper, but I also do not have time to run a household the way Steve's mother did.

"On the day of the dog-hair incident, I had driven our daughter, Sharon, to school so her science project wouldn't get wrecked on the bus. This made me late for work—I have a three-day-a-week job as music editor of a regional magazine—so I was rushing all morning to catch up. Then I used my lunch hour to take the dog to the vet. And, as usual, I dashed home so Sharon, who's ten, wouldn't be alone after school. I picked up around the house a little, did some work on a book I'm writing about music appreciation for kids, and started making dinner. The idea of vacuuming the car never entered my mind.

"So in comes Steve, carrying on about how he knew I'd leave the car a mess after the vet appointment. I have never been one to engage in shouting matches, so I just stood there. Before long, he was on a roll, bringing up everything that bothered him . . . like, I'm not tough enough on Sharon, who is going to become a slob like me . . . I don't go to the functions that wives of his colleagues go to . . . I waste time and money on yoga classes and writing my book. He hit me with a whole litany of offenses, then marched out of the room. I stood there crying, unable to think of a single word to say back.

"Now, this isn't the first time Steve has criticized me so vehemently. He's been treating me like this for years, but I guess this last time pushed me over the edge. I insisted we find professional help.

"Actually, I think it's already hopeless, even with your help. Maybe we're just too different to stay married. Steve comes from a large, boisterous, upper-middle-class family. He grew up in an exclusive Chicago suburb; his mother was your typical clubwoman, his father a very successful businessman.

"My family is the opposite. Both my parents are artists and I'm their only child. We never had a lot of money, but I had a childhood filled with trips to museums and the ballet. We lived in a loft in Greenwich Village, and you could never tell where the studio ended and the living quarters began.

"I never had much of a social life, though. I was always so tall, and the kids at school weren't into the arts, so I was a loner. Even when I was a scholarship student at Juilliard, I never found my niche socially. Steve was the first person besides my parents who ever made me feel loved. And I do still love him—that's what's so terrible about this.

"Our first meeting was so romantic. I was a member of a string quartet, and when we played in Chicago in December, Steve came to the stage door with a dozen roses for me. He said he had been in the audience the night before and that I was the most beautiful woman he had ever seen. Do you believe that? I could tell he meant it, and the fact that I was three inches taller than him didn't seem to matter.

"We had a whirlwind courtship because I went back to New York and he went back to Philadelphia, to finish his M.B.A. at Wharton. Still, he did the most romantic things, like surprise me with a visit on Valentine's Day. Steve still does romantic things every now and then, although I know it's just because he feels guilty for being so hard on me.

"We were married in May of that year, eleven years ago, and moved to Virginia. Steve had landed a good job with a manufacturing firm and he had to begin right away. It seems our trouble started the minute he carried me over the threshold. All of a sudden, my romantic suitor turned into a neatness fanatic.

"Although I was very busy working full-time at the magazine plus playing with the local orchestra during the season, I was expected to do all the housework, too. Steve helped, but he always implied that he was doing it because I hadn't done a good enough job.

"When I got pregnant, Steve felt it was important for me to cut back on my activities and be home more. I knew I would have to drop out of the orchestra, but I was able to arrange a part-time job at the magazine.

"I've tried hard to keep up all my interests, but Steve has never supported me. Would it have killed him to stay with Sharon some nights so I could continue to play my cello?

"No, I never said anything to him. It was clear Steve just didn't care. So I tried to work on myself a bit. I signed up for a yoga class at night. Steve agreed grudgingly to stay home with Sharon, but I could tell he didn't approve.

"Then something happened that made me wonder about this marriage. I called after yoga to say that a few of us and the instructor were going for coffee so I'd be a little late. Steve blew up. He accused me of having a crush on the instructor!

"On the one hand, I should have just laughed it off. But on the other, it proved that our relationship has dissolved into a lack of trust."

STEVE'S TURN

"I do love Hannah," said Steve, thirty-seven, a sandy-haired man with a vibrant manner. "The trouble is, the things that drew me to her are the things that cause problems.

"Hannah is a dreamer. That's great, but there are times you have to discipline yourself to get on with the business at hand, especially when you have a family.

"Take this book she's writing. She could have had it finished months ago if she had only worked at it systematically. But no, she dawdles, she leaves manuscript pages all over the house, she wastes time staring out the window. Meanwhile, the house is filthy and she's ordering in pizza.

"I am not exaggerating. I will concede that my standards for housekeeping are pretty high, but Hannah is truly impossible. When she goes into her creative mode, she's in another world. She doesn't see dirt. She leaves dishes in the sink and uses paper plates.

"Okay, I probably got a little carried away the other night, but that business with the dog was the straw that broke the camel's back.

"Still, it's not just the housework. Hannah is simply not there for me. Oh, I don't expect her to attend every company dinner. But I would like her to participate a little bit in my company's social plans. All the wives do. What gets me is that she not only won't join me, she's smug about it. She says she's not that kind of wife.

"So what kind is she, then? Certainly not a very demonstrative one. I'm not referring to our sex life, which has always been fine. She doesn't make me feel like she loves me, I guess.

"Listen, I like to think of myself as a bit of a romantic. And when I do something romantic, I'd like her to reciprocate once in a while or be appreciative. I've slacked off with the corny gestures since they're not getting me anywhere, but every now and then, I look at her and I have to go splurge on flowers. Since I first laid eyes on her, I thought of her as a Modigliani painting, with that mesmerizing beauty, so pensive and ethereal. She still affects me that way. I give her the flowers and—nothing. Just a cold thank-you.

"I wish I knew when and where things went wrong. We didn't spend much time together before we were married, but we did talk about the future. And we both decided she would drop out of the orchestra when the baby was born. So why am I the bad guy?

"Okay, this yoga business does drive me nuts. I'm home alone with Sharon, and Hannah's off doing some Eastern thing and going out afterward with cute young guys. Couldn't she spend that time with me?

"I don't think Hannah wants this marriage to work. I think she's deliberately or subconsciously provoking me. My heart would break to lose her and Sharon, but what can I do?"

THE COUNSELOR'S TURN

"After only one session with this couple, I knew that the first step had to be the hiring of a cleaning woman. No amount of counseling would do as much for them.

"Naturally, they protested, since they were paying my fee, plus a baby-sitter in the afternoon, but I made them realize that in their case, household help was not a luxury but a necessity: It was needed to defuse the present tension. Hannah found someone who could come every other week, and as I predicted, the level of tension between them dropped dramatically.

"Now we were free to move on to the problem of Steve's constant criticism of Hannah. Because of his resentment over her messiness, Steve had unconsciously gotten into the habit of belittling his wife. When I pointed this out, Steve vowed that he would change. He made a conscious effort to focus on the ways Hannah was a wonderful mother and to compliment her in that regard. She's very involved in her daughter's life and takes her to numerous cultural events. She also treats her daughter with deep respect. These are all qualities that Steve had always admired but never mentioned before.

"Of course, Hannah's housekeeping standards are not the same as Steve's, but our third task was to get her to realize that even her laissez-faire upbringing did not excuse total disregard for order in the house. During one session, Hannah admitted to being provocative on this issue.

"'I guess I'm just angry,' she said at one point, 'angry that Steve doesn't appreciate what I do, angry that he made me give up things I really love, like playing the cello.

"That's when Steve spoke up. 'Look,' he said, 'until now, you never mentioned all this. I can't read your mind.' Steve explained that he thought he had been communicative and that they had reached a mutually acceptable decision about Hannah's leaving the orchestra.

"At this point, I reminded them of Steve's comment that Hannah had distanced herself from him. As she had said, she was not the type to engage in shouting matches, but in fact, she had long had a problem responding to Steve on any level. Shy and insecure with her peers as a child, she still found it difficult to open up, which Steve, understandably, interpreted as coldness.

"I gave Steve and Hannah a simple assignment. They were to concentrate on the little things they could do to show tenderness and love, whether it was a good-bye hug in the morning or a quick phone call during the day to say I love you. Long-married people, I noted, often forget that the simple romantic gesture can help cement a relationship.

"I also instructed Steve to curtail his verbal barrages and to make sure he gave Hannah time to respond. If he was upset about the dog hairs in the car, he was to mention it, then wait for her to say something instead of marching out of the room. When we play-acted this scenario in my office, Hannah said, 'The next time I feel as if I have too much to do, can I ask you to take Sharon to school or take the dog to the vet?' This was a breakthrough for Hannah and Steve saw her point, congratulated her for speaking up, and agreed to take on more chores around the house.

"This was the beginning of a pattern of compromises for this couple that helped steer their marriage back on course. Hannah has gotten more involved in functions having to do with Steve's work, and now that she's met more of the other wives, she is not as uncomfortable with them as she thought she would be. She's learned to respond appreciatively to Rob's romantic gestures, and they've made an effort to go out more just for fun.

"When Hannah finished her book, she decided not to embark on another project for a while but rather to resume playing the cello with a local string quartet. Now that Hannah gives so much more of herself to him, Steve is not troubled by the fact that she wants to take an occasional yoga class. He has begun to truly appreciate this time alone with his daughter. 'And it's become a family joke that Daddy takes the dog to the vet,' he told me during one of our last sessions.

"Steve and Hannah ended counseling several months ago, confident that they had overcome their major problems and had the tools to solve any others that come up in the course of their relationship."

UNMASKING THE REAL ISSUES

These two aren't really fighting about dog hairs or dishes. For Steve and Hannah, battles over housework are often red herrings, as they are for many couples. Unwittingly, they have fallen into a power struggle that gets played and replayed.

If you and your partner often argue about the same, seemingly trivial issues, that may be a warning signal: Perhaps the surface arguments are masking another deeper, more troubling, problem you need to discuss. It's helpful if you can take a step back and try to observe your interactions with an impartial eye and ask yourselves: What are we really fighting about here?

In this case, Steve's resentment of his wife's messiness blinded him to her many wonderful qualities. He fell into the habit of belittling her. Hiring a housekeeper to come in twice a week was a turning point. Now that the housework was no longer a kindling point, they could focus on the real issues—for instance, Hannah's anger that Steve doesn't appreciate her interests, as well as her inability to express her feelings in the face of frequent criticism. Once she expressed herself, Steve made an effort to get out of his attack mode and, if he did have something to say, to at least wait for her to respond before marching out of the room in a huff.

They were then able to negotiate compromises and eliminate their constant bickering. For her part, Hannah is much more willing to join Steve for his business obligations—happily, in fact.

"He's a Child, Not a Husband"

Sally tried to be the good wife, but Gary still expected more and more. What happens when your best is never enough?

SALLY'S TURN

"What does he want from me?" asked Sally, thirty-three, as she dropped her briefcase on the floor and settled into a chair. "I'm trying to be a good wife, but as far as Gary is concerned, it's not enough. 'You don't care...You don't love me as much as I love you...You never listen.' I'm worn out from his litany of complaints!

"I have a full-time job—I'm in computer sales and it's a tough, competitive job. Even though I leave the office at seven, sometimes seven-thirty, at night, I still cook dinner for my husband. I'm so exhausted some nights I can't even see straight. Yet he'll burst through the door and launch immediately into some heavy discussion, telling me about his problems at work or wanting to know everything that happened to me that day. I feel ambushed. But if I don't give him my undivided attention, he goes berserk.

"I know, I know. You're thinking I'm horrible and ungrateful, but please hear me out. Gary is devoted, kind, loving, generous to the point of extravagance. Most women would give their right arm for a man like this, but sometimes he's just too much for me. He tells me how much he needs me and I feel as if I'm going to jump out of my skin.

"With Gary, every conversation has to be deep and involved. Do I have to listen to him analyze every action from every angle? Last month he called me at work; I had four people in my office and I couldn't talk. I could tell he was hurt, but I wasn't about to sweet-talk him out of it with all those people listening. He

157

didn't speak to me the whole night.

"That is typical. If I'm short with him, or I say something he takes the wrong way—usually something so minor I'm totally unaware he's offended—he'll remember it for days and get back at me, either by not talking or by refusing to make love. Most times, our love life is fabulous—except when he feels slighted and punishes me by depriving me of sex.

"Other times Gary gets furious, just as my father used to. I'm drained by his outbursts. I never knew how to calm my father down either. I grew up in a traditional home; we were the only professional family in our blue-collar suburb. My father was a commercial banker, my mother a housewife. I was Daddy's girl and he was my role model—since there was no son in the family, I was brought up to be the tough super-achiever. Thinking back, I realize my father was interested only in how well I did in school. If I told him I got ninety-five on a math test, he'd ask why I didn't get one hundred. Every once in a while, when he was angry, he'd explode, kicking over a wastebasket or slamming doors. There would be days when he didn't speak to me or look at me.

"I was a goody-goody. I studied hard and I'm proud that I always had a job after school and paid for all my own clothes and gifts. I had lots of friends and tons of boyfriends, but never anyone serious. I was deter-mined to be successful in my career before I got married. I didn't want to be dependent on anyone.

"When I was a freshman in college, my parents' marriage fell apart. Mother discovered that Dad had had a mistress for ten years. She tried to kill herself by swallowing barbiturates and we had to put her in a hospital for four months. I transferred to a school near home so I could nurse my mother and talk some sense into my father, but it finally dawned on me that I couldn't fix things. Dad is now married to that woman and my mother is very bitter. She calls me all the time, weepy or despondent.

"Of course, that explains the distance I sensed but couldn't figure out as a child. You see, outwardly we were the happy family, but behind the facade, there was little emotion.

"This is the total opposite of my life now. Gary is all emotion. We met at work. Gary had been with the company for ten years; five months after I started, he was promoted to head my department.

"My first impression: He was gorgeous—I mean movie-star gorgeous. Every woman in the office had a crush on Gary, but I honestly didn't consider him a dating prospect. First of all, I had a strict rule about not dating anyone from work, let alone my boss. It was more than unprofessional; it was stupid. Besides, Gary was fourteen years older than I; he'd been married before and had a son, who's now in college.

"We were just real good buddies for about eight years. In fact, he was more like a confidant. If I had a problem with the guy I was dating, Gary would help me work it out. There was always a lot of energy and special chemistry between us. Our relationship changed the night a colleague got married. We were both invited to the wedding, but since neither of us was dating anyone at the time, we decided to go together. It was a magical evening—and Gary ended up sleeping over.

"That blew my mind. I told myself this had better work out, because if it didn't, we were in big trouble. I was so nervous when I saw Gary at work the next day that I spilled coffee on my new suit. When he stopped by my apartment that evening, we had a long talk and decided it wasn't going to work. We desperately tried to avoid each other. It sounds so corny to say that passion got the better of us, but it did. I was torn; I knew I wanted to be with Gary more than I'd ever wanted another man in my life, and I knew the feeling was mutual.

"For over a year, we lived this crazy life, bending over backward to avoid any evidence of impropriety. After about six months, Gary decided to quit his job and start his own consulting business. That meant we could finally make our relationship public. We were married at a small hotel on Long Island—and, as it turned out, people had known about us all along but didn't care.

"But things haven't gone smoothly. I'm nervous about Gary's career change. Right now, I'm pretty much supporting us, since it takes a long time to build up a profitable business. Gary wanted to fly to L.A. to make a presentation to a possible client. I pointed out that it was an expensive trip, and since there were perhaps twenty other people making a pitch for this client, maybe it wasn't worth it. He hit the ceiling and said I had no confidence in him. Also, we had talked about having a baby—I'm going to be thirty-four in May and Gary is forty-eight. I wanted to take time off after the baby, but how can I do that if his income is so low?

"Look, I'm embarrassed about being in counseling, but Gary insisted I come. He wants me to change, but I am what I am. Why can't he accept that?"

GARY'S TURN

"She doesn't get it. She just doesn't get it," said Gary, forty-eight, a tall, handsome man in jeans and a sweater. "What's the matter with her? Most women would die for a husband to treat them the way I treat her. You see how she's rolling her eyes now? That's the way she acts with me most of the time. I try to get her to talk, to tell me about her day and how she's feeling, but she interrupts me.

"And she doesn't listen when I talk either. She's totally closed off, even in bed. We'll be making love and I can sense that her body may be there but her mind is a million miles away. She's a cold fish; I know she's thinking about everything but what she should be thinking about. I tell this woman how much I adore her and she gets silly. Like it's a big joke. As soon as our lovemaking is over, she practically leaps out of bed. It makes me crazy. This rage just comes over me.

"I've always been an emotional kind of guy. We were very poor when I was growing up—my mother cleaned other people's houses and I slept on a roll-out cot in the living room—but I was tough. My mother and I were very close—she was president of my fan club and incredibly supportive. She never put any limits on my dreams. It wasn't that way with my father; there was always a real distance between us.

"Dad was a postal clerk, hardworking but undemonstrative. He loved me, but he never said it and never showed it. Would you believe I have no memories of him ever hugging me? He would often do what Sally does—I'd be very excited about something and he'd make fun of that enthusiasm.

"When I was about seven, my mother got very sick. I think she had some kind of nervous breakdown and she was in a sanitarium for about two years. My dad joined the Navy and I went to live with my aunt until my mother was well enough to come home. That was a terrible time. Not that my aunt wasn't kind or loving, but I was terrified that my mother was going to die. When she came back, she was never the same, and I was always worried something would happen to her.

"I knew that I'd have to pay for my own college education, so I did. I earned a four-year swimming scholarship, and then, since I wanted to work with underprivileged kids, I also went for a master's in psychology. During vacations, I found a job at a large computer company and they offered me a full-time position when I graduated. It was too much for a poor kid to turn down, so that's how I got into sales management.

"I think my psych background and my ability to make people feel comfortable and motivate them have served me well. That doesn't mean I don't need confidence-boosting myself, however. I'm more than a little scared about making this move professionally. It's not easy to head off in a new direction at my age. Many people in the business thought I was nuts to give up a prestigious job with a solid company at a time like this. But one morning I looked in the mirror and said, 'Gary, you gotta make a change.' I was dissatisfied. So I made my move.

"I thought Sally would be more supportive. When I first met her, I was completely blown away. I don't think Sally knows what a powerful sexual energy she has. I also had so much respect for her and the way she did business. She's smart and savvy. It kills me that Sally doesn't think I can make my consulting firm work. But I don't think I can tell her how frightened I am about starting a new career. She'd flip out. She's not a risk-taker.

"We had a really big disagreement about a trip I wanted to take to L.A. last month. Sure it was a gamble, but you're not going to get ahead if you're not willing to stick your neck out. Sally looks at life with a glass-is-half-empty attitude; I look at the same thing and see a glass half full. By the way, I made that trip and I won the account. However, since I spend most of my time trying to drum up new clients, I'm hit with a hell of a lot of rejection. When I get home, I don't want to be treated like a delivery man dropping off a package."

THE COUNSELOR'S TURN

"Sally and Gary were atypical of most couples I see," said the counselor. "Usually, the wife complains that the husband doesn't listen, doesn't talk, and is unemotional. In this case, the re-verse was true. I could tell immediately that in this relationship, Sally was the doer; Gary was the be-er. She intellectualized; he emoted. Unfortunately, Gary interpreted his wife's behavior to mean she didn't love or care about him.

"Serious, guarded, businesslike, and pragmatic, Sally had great difficulty getting in touch with her feelings and expressing them. The first child of unemotional, undemonstrative parents, she grew up in a home where love was conditional: If she performed well, she was praised. The message from her parents, especially her father, was, Try harder; if you push a little bit more, you'll win Daddy's love.

"Sally grew up to be ambitious and driven, a woman who was the opposite of her helpless, dependent mother. If there was, a problem, she learned to zero in on what was wrong and fix it.

"As a child, however, when she tried to soothe her moody father's unpredictable temper or win his admiration, she was confronted with icy silences and rejection. Gary's outbursts left her similarly frustrated.

"Although she refused to admit it for a long time, Sally had been devastated by her father's affair and her parents' divorce. She had adored her father, modeled herself after him, and her image of this perfect man was shattered. The experience left her with a deep lack of trust for men in general. At the same time, she felt weighted down by her mother's almost total dependence on her. When Gary demanded her total attention, it reminded her of her mother and she felt smothered.

"Bright and articulate, Gary was a passionate man who looked you right in the eye and leaned toward you as he spoke. But he was also an angry man with a chip on his shoulder, a sad look on his face, and pain in his voice. When he first came to see me, he was furious and spoke in a harsh, accusatory way. Pointing a finger at his wife, he would say over and over again, 'You don't get it, do you? You just don't get it!' When he did this, Sally would start to cry; she really didn't get it.

"Gary grew up in a poor home. When his mother took ill, she remained hospitalized for two years. His father left him in the custody of his aunt and Gary felt unloved and rejected, terrified he'd be out on the street. After his mother finally came home, Gary became highly solicitous of her every need. Although the family was reunited, Gary still felt his position was precarious. He put pressure on himself to be the perfect little boy.

"Much of Gary's rage, however, was directed toward his father, who was unable to provide for his family and was emotionally remote. Now, in his relationship with Sally, he felt he was again giving emotionally and getting little in return.

"In the most basic terms, Sally had to learn to give and Gary had to learn to pull back. But the process was a slow one. I don't think Sally understood how skittish she was about revealing herself to men as well as to me. I suggested that she come for individual counseling, and for several months she came one week alone and the next week with Gary.

"Initially, every time our conversation veered toward a discussion of how Sally felt about something, she would change the subject yet continue to deny that she was afraid to talk about her feelings. This is what she did with Gary at home and in bed. In time, my constant reassurances gave her courage to open up. Once she learned to take a risk with her emotions, she discovered that Gary didn't turn away.

"This process was helped when Gary learned to curb his angry outbursts, which he did once he understood that he was trying to see how far he could push her. When he was feeling upset, I suggested he count to ten or go out for a jog.

"At the same time, Sally had to learn to respond positively to Gary. Instead of making jokes or rolling her eyes, she owed it to him to listen and be more sensitive, although she didn't have to put up with his rages. When he acts like that, I told her, 'Don't cajole him. Clear out.' One weekend when they were visiting friends in the country, Gary again felt she wasn't paying enough attention to him and started to lose his temper. Sally told him she was going to leave if he didn't calm down—which she had in the past threatened to do. When he didn't, she got in the car and drove home. Gary took the train back to the city, and by the time he got in the door, he realized he had overreacted and apologized.

"However, Sally had to acknowledge that there were times when she wasn't listening to Gary at all. Gary had a right to feel nervous about his new business venture. 'He is facing rejection every day', I told her, 'and he needs to talk about it.'

"As Gary pulled back, Sally had more room to move toward him. However, I told Gary that while I didn't think he expected too much in general, he did expect too much of Sally. 'Perhaps another woman wouldn't feel pressured the way she does, but you chose Sally. You love her and you want to make this work. Sally has her limits, and you haven't been respectful of those limits.'

"This couple stopped coming to therapy after two years, although I still occasionally see them separately. Gary's firm is doing surprisingly well, considering the sluggish economy. Sally, who has been unable to get pregnant, is now considering artificial insemination. They just returned from a long weekend in Florida. 'I truly feel that Sally loves me,' Gary says. 'After all, who else would put up with a guy like me?'"

THE KEY TO ACCEPTANCE

To feel loved and nurtured, we must feel that our partners accept us completely. That sounds simple, but it's far more complicated than most couples believe. Although Sally and Gary insisted that they were there for each other, they both had difficulty being truly empathic. Empathy means being able to put yourself in another's place: to feel what they feel and see what they see, without losing yourself in the process. If you can empathize with your partner, you will be able to understand without words and forgive when necessary, even though you disagree.

Encouragement focuses on what's right with your partner, on his or her strengths and positive attributes, rather than on what's wrong. That way you send the message: I believe in you. You don't have to be perfect to be loved by me.

And finally, the ability to see the person as separate from the performance conveys the final message that, even though you don't agree, or you see things differently, he or she is still valued and loved.

"NOTHING I DO IS EVER GOOD ENOUGH"

Susan's marriage to an older, wealthy man seemed like a dream come true. But Christopher's constant criticism was literally making her sick.

"Christopher said we should see you, and he's usually right," said Susan, twenty-three, a strikingly beautiful young woman whose eyes were shadowed from lack of sleep. "This past year has been awful. We fight all the time about everything. Christopher says I spend too much time with the baby. He says I should know better than to allow Jason, our fourteen-month-old, to wander everywhere, getting cracker crumbs in the living room and dining room. He says I'm never there for him, that the house is a mess, dinner is terrible.

"I feel so scared. It all started about two years ago, actually. I had just found out I was pregnant and I was thrilled. Christopher wasn't dying to have kids—at the time, we'd barely been married a year—but he said he was pleased.

"Anyway, I was walking down the street one day, and all of a sudden, I felt my throat tightening and I couldn't swallow. I started gasping for breath. I almost passed out. Thankfully, a neighbor was walking by, saw me, and helped me home. After resting, I felt better.

"I assumed my symptoms were related to my pregnancy. I told the doctor, who said I was doing just fine and the baby was healthy. Still, I started to worry. Would I really be able to handle this baby? Christopher is a very busy, very important man. He came to this country from England when he was twenty-one with hardly a nickel to his name, and he's built this major business-equipment manufacturing company all by himself. His workdays are long and exhausting.

"I had a perfect delivery, but after Jason was born, my symptoms got even worse. At first, Christopher was wonderful. He took me to all the best doctors in New York. One told me I had asthma, so I walked around for a while with this inhaler. But it didn't help. I was sure I was having a heart attack, but a famous cardiologist assured us that I was healthy as a horse and should try to relax. At that point, I think Christopher just gave up on me.

"Anyway, Christopher hasn't been much help with the baby. Oh, I know he adores Jason and loves to play with him, but he never likes to do things like feed or bathe him. If I'm tired, he says, 'Go hire someone to help.' Well, I'm not comfortable doing that. Is it unreasonable to expect a father to want to spend more time with his son?

"I just feel so overwhelmed. I can't do everything around here, especially now that we're in the middle of this huge renovation. I loved our other apartment, but Christopher wanted a large place, so he bought these two apartments and we're combining them.

"Now they're doing this construction all around us. I know it will be gorgeous—Christopher is bringing in the finest marble from Italy for the bathrooms and he's hired the best decorator in the city. But he's such a perfectionist. If everything isn't exactly so, if the carpenters leave a speck of sawdust on the floor, my husband goes crazy. He'll pout for hours, or get one of his headaches and disappear into the bedroom for days.

"We probably argue the most, though, about dinner. Christopher expects a gourmet meal on the table every night. Last week, I took the baby to a friend's house—I don't know very many people, and this lovely woman I met at a Mommy and Me class invited us over. Anyway, it was a wonderful afternoon and I lost track of the time. When I got home, it was too late to start dinner, so I ordered in a barbecued chicken.

"Well, Christopher was livid. He went on and on about how I couldn't possibly love him if I was serving him take-out chicken. I couldn't believe it, but he was quite serious. And he was just as livid when he discovered that I had bought only plums and peaches at the market. He wants an array of fruit to choose from; otherwise, he says there's nothing to eat.

"Nothing pleases him. Certainly not my friends or any of the activities I suggest. And he can be unbelievably rude to people.

"Our sex life is practically nonexistent. When we first met, Christopher was into drugs and we'd go out to dinner, come back, get high, and make love. But one night I had this terrible reaction—a convulsion, really—and after that I refused to do any more drugs. I begged him to stop, too, and he finally did—that night scared him also. I think we started having sexual problems then. Of course, since we're fighting so much, who's in the mood?

"And now there's this problem with my mother. She had another fight with her landlord and she was evicted from her apartment and has absolutely no place to go. We have a zillion empty rooms, so I suggested Mother move in with us.

"Well, Christopher won't hear of it. Look, I know my mother is a kook. She's always been a little wild and nutty, but in a wonderful way. My father, whom I adored, was the solid one in the family, but he died of cancer when I was twelve. It was horrible for Mother and me to watch him die. We never spoke about it; it was much too painful and I didn't want to upset her further.

"After his death, Mother seemed to get even kookier. She'd be gone most of the day, working at one odd job or another. We had very little money and our tiny apartment was a menagerie. At one point, we had nine puppies, three cats, a few gerbils, and an alligator.

"Although she wasn't a good mother by most people's standards, I knew she loved me and wanted the best for me. Somehow, she saved enough money to buy me pretty dresses and send me to a fancy private school.

"Even so, I hated school and couldn't wait to get out. I met Christopher when I was eighteen. My friend was dating Christopher's cousin and she introduced us. Christopher was thirty-eight then, but the age difference has never been a problem for us.

"I think I fell in love with him on our first date. He was so wise and sophisticated and I adored that British accent. He had no family—both his parents died about ten years ago and he rarely speaks to his sister—and I became very important to him. We dated for a year and then got married. I did a little modeling for a while, but my heart wasn't in it. I wanted to have a baby and I finally convinced Christopher.

"So now you know it all. I love Christopher and I want us to be happy again. But it's impossible to discuss anything with him. He can argue circles around me; I never know what to say."

CHRISTOPHER'S TURN

"Of course I'm upset about Susan," snapped Christopher, forty-three, a tall man with dark hair graying at the temples. "But enough is enough. We've been to some of the finest doctors in New York. Everyone says she is fine. It's time to get on with our lives.

"Okay, if we're going to do this, let's go through it point by point. Susan is just not paying enough attention to me or the marriage. I work very hard all day. My business is extremely stressful. When I come home, I expect my wife to have taken the time to prepare a decent meal. I do not consider greasy barbecued chicken to be a decent meal. She has plenty of time all day long to be with her friends, to cater to the baby—whatever it is she does.

"Look, Susan has certain responsibilities that she is not fulfilling. My job is to support the family. Her job is to run the home smoothly and efficiently. I've also told her a hundred times that if she is so overworked, she should hire someone to care for Jason, cook meals, and clean the house. We have the money. I can't understand why she doesn't do it.

"Susan just doesn't respect the things that are important to me. How could she allow a fourteen-month-old to munch crackers and spill juice on the Aubusson carpet? I am trying to provide her with a beautiful home and she shows no respect for that either. Since I'm paying a bloody fortune for this renovation, I expect everything to be done perfectly.

"You know, I came to this country with nothing. I was raised in a small town about a half hour from London. My parents were very poor. Father was a schoolmaster, cold and autocratic. My younger sister, Diana, and I were terrified of him. My parents fought constantly and

violently. I was afraid to bring any friends home, so I was very much alone as a child. I remember one time when I was about thirteen, they were screaming at each other and I marched into the dining room and told them that Diana and I couldn't stand living with them any longer. You know what Mother did? She left. 'You give me no choice,' she told me. 'Since your father won't leave, I will have to.' She moved to a flat in London and I saw her maybe once or twice a year from then on. Both my parents died about ten years ago.

"I hated school, and when I was sixteen, I left home for good. I bounced around from one odd job to another, did a lot of drugs, had affairs with a lot of women. I had a cousin in New York, so with about two hundred dollars to my name, I came to the States and found a job in a factory. It was hard work, but it was a start. And you can see I've done quite well for myself.

"I really had no intentions of getting married, but when I met Susan I was smitten. She was so sweet and innocent and absolutely beautiful. Certainly, I was very attracted to her physically, but also, unlike the older women I had been seeing, there was a real caring, loving quality about her. I adored taking her to fine restaurants and the theater. She seemed perfectly happy. I don't understand why she is so unhappy now.

"I am not rude to her friends. I prefer to come home at the end of the day and sit quietly and read. I've never had a lot of friends, and I don't see why I should start now. Besides, unlike my wife, I don't feel particularly comfortable with people.

"Now let's discuss her mother. I feel very sorry that her mother is in distress, but her mother is always in distress. She calls up in the middle of the night, hysterical about one thing after another. I've told Susan I will do everything in my power to help her find another apartment. But moving in with us is out of the question. I've had a lot more experience than Susan has. I know people, and I know that if her mother comes to live with us, she will never leave. And we will have absolutely no privacy.

"I don't know what else to say. I suggested we come because Susan obviously needs help."

THE COUNSELOR'S TURN

"When this couple first came to see me, Susan seemed quite ill," said the counselor. "She had already been to several top physicians, and as she spoke, it was clear that her problems were psychosomatic in origin. Since Susan had always catered to Christopher, he couldn't understand what had changed. He expected to always be the center of her universe, and he was furious that she was giving so much to the baby and nothing to him.

"When Susan met Christopher, she was only eighteen. Although Susan's eccentric mother loved her and tried to provide her with the accoutrements of the good life, she was so wrapped up in her own world that she paid little attention to her daughter and provided no stability for her. Susan's father had provided that much-needed security, but when he died there was a vacuum that needed to be filled. Sadly, Susan was never able to express any negative thoughts or feelings to her mother—to say, for instance, 'I'm upset that Daddy died, that you're not paying attention to me, that the house is a mess.' She buried her unhappiness and continued to do so in her marriage.

"Susan, then, was looking for a father, a man who could rescue her and treat her like a princess. The fact that Christopher was initially into drugs, well, that was part of his world, and she joined him in it. However, as a new bride, Susan felt terribly inadequate. She had never finished her education and the fact that she didn't have any skills or career possibilities made her even more dependent on her husband. When she finally fulfilled her dream of being a mother, she at last had a sense of identity. It was understandable that she would devote herself completely to the baby's care.

"Despite his financial success,

however, Christopher was also totally lacking in self-esteem and self-confidence. His mother's desertion made him feel desperately unloved and unlovable. To compensate, he created an illusion of happiness: his own perfect world, in which no one was allowed to make a mistake. He wanted to be an English lord of the manor, complete with a lavish apartment and a beautiful wife.

"Although this couple may sound like characters in a romance novel, they were far from a happily-ever-after ending and had to overcome many common marital problems. For example, Christopher wanted intimacy but feared it so much that the only way he could have a relationship was with a much younger woman over whom he would have total control. For the same reason, he had relied on drugs to get high whenever they made love. Unless he anesthetized himself, he felt too vulnerable to get close. Indeed, Christopher was so emotionally needy that food became symbolic to him of love and nurturing. When Susan failed to cook for him, he was convinced that she didn't love him, and he would often develop a migraine headache or sulk for days. This widened the distance between them.

"Also, as a couple, Susan and Christopher had no friends and few interests. The fact that they had a child so early in their relationshp compounded these problems; they had never developed a firm enough foundation to withstand the pressures of new parenthood.

"In the beginning, Susan had been so much in awe of her husband that she catered to him the way he wanted. But soon, the pressure of denying her own feelings and submerging her anger became so great that she became physically ill. The first step was to help Susan recognize her anger instead of turning her feelings into symptoms and literally taking it out on her body. Once I pointed this out, I was able to help her develop enough self-confidence to speak up and make her needs known.

"One technique that was very helpful was imagining together a worst-case scenario. I asked her what would be the worst thing that could happen if she told her husband exactly how she felt. 'He would be very angry with me . . . my marriage would end,' she told me. 'Perhaps I'd have to move to a smaller apartment. I'd also have to learn some skills to support myself,' she added. 'I'm smart, though, I can do that.'

"As we talked, Susan began to see that the worst case was not as bad as what she was living through now. And as she found the courage to express herself, her symptoms began to subside. In time she was able to say simply, 'Christopher, I do love you very much, but I cannot make a four-course dinner for you every night.' She also told him that she wanted him to spend more time alone with Jason.

"An important step for Susan was when she decided to take driving lessons. Once she learned how to drive, she didn't feel trapped in the city and she was able to visit with friends, whether or not Christopher wanted to join her. Less dependent on her husband, Susan no longer felt so angry with him. She also hired a baby-sitter to come in during the afternoon so she could take an art class and a secretarial course.

"Christopher was less receptive to my suggestions. So sure that he was right, for weeks he pooh-poohed even the implication that his behavior could possibly be causing any problems. In time, however, as he realized how serious Susan was, he really did begin to change. One dramatic session proved to be a turning point for him: Christopher began talking about his childhood and how he felt about his mother's desertion. He broke down, sobbing. Clearly, he had never forgiven himself for having caused her to leave. Once he was able to understand that his mother's leaving was her problem and, despite what she had said, had not been his fault, he was able to see how he was substituting material possessions for real intimacy and what he was doing to push Susan away. 'You have to nurture yourself,' I told him, 'and not expect someone to always do it for you.'

"At one point, I suggested that if he wanted to have a fancy dinner at night, perhaps he should cook it himself. Christopher rose to the challenge: He made a point of leaving work early to stop by the market and come home and cook dinner. He found, too, that cooking was something creative that he really enjoyed doing and that it helped him relax after a day at work. Together, he and Susan have enjoyed selecting recipes to try.

"Once he was more receptive to change, Christopher was able to see that his expectations were totally unrealistic. If he wanted to be loved, I said, he had to be loving in return. And that meant not being so demanding, caustic, and critical. Christopher began to pay more attention to what he said and how he said it. Susan has enrolled Jason in a play group and now, once a month, Christopher takes him there. Through this group they have met other couples with children the same age as their son. Christopher forced himself to accept invitations to their homes and was surprised but pleased to find that these people seemed to like him. As the general tension eased and Susan began to feel physically better, they made love more frequently and were finally able to develop a closeness that had long escaped them.

"Regarding the problem with Susan's mother, I told Susan that Christopher was right: Having her move in would only aggravate their own problems. Instead, Christopher found an apartment for her a few blocks away.

"This couple terminated therapy after fourteen months. Although Christopher still has a tendency to boss his wife around, he has mellowed considerably. Most important, he treats her as an equal partner in the marriage—which is what Susan asks."

WHEN NOTHING YOU DO IS GOOD ENOUGH

Susan's medical problems seemed to be psychosomatic in origin—but that didn't mean they weren't real. She was so upset by Christopher's constant criticism and lack of support that she literally could not swallow what was happening in her marriage.

Many husbands and wives feel unfairly criticized by their spouses, yet find themselves powerless to defend themselves. If you have a similar problem, these steps can help you rebuild your self-esteem and regain your footing:

1. Remind yourself that you are entitled to your feelings and have every right to speak up: "I feel offended by what you just said," or "That was inconsiderate." If the insulting behavior continues, try to control yourself and not lash out wildly in defense. Instead, walk away. You'll be sending a far more powerful message.

2. Choose your words with care to avoid fanning the flames. Speak firmly, but in a way that doesn't demean your partner: Stick to what therapists call the "When you . . . I feel" model. For instance, Susan can say, "When you criticize my cooking, I feel you're not paying attention to what's really important in a marriage. I love you but I cannot cook a gourmet meal every night."

3. Try not to respond to criticism by being critical. This only escalates the argument and deepens the power struggle. If you don't think you can respond reasonably, say so: "I'm too angry to talk about this right now. After I've had a chance to calm down, we'll continue our discussion."

4. Ask yourself if there might be some validity to what your partner is saying. If there is, can you do something differently? Comments become criticism when they're exaggerated and off-base. However, many times, if we allow ourselves to admit it, there is something we can do to make our interactions with a mate smoother and happier.

"WE CAN'T EVEN SPEAK CIVILLY TO EACH OTHER"

Kathleen and Paul's eight-year marriage was a never-ending power struggle. What happens when the bedroom becomes a battlefield?

KATHLEEN'S TURN

"Please believe me—I'm not a terrible person," said Kathleen, twenty-eight, brushing her long blond hair off her face, "but I do hate the person I've become. Every day I wake up and say to myself, 'Today will be different. Today, you and Paul won't

fight, you won't say horrible things to each other.' But before I know it, the fighting starts again.

"I can't believe things have gotten so bad between us. At times, the level of tension in our house is unbearable, and I think we're both shocked at how mean we can be to each other. We've been married for eight years and it looks as if my marriage is turning out to be as awful as my parents'.

"There were nine kids in my family—six girls, three boys. I was the fourth child. It was not a happy home, although you'd never know it to look at us. I call it the white-picket-fence syndrome: All the neighbors admired our family; no one knew how unhappy we all were.

"My father was an oil-burner repairman. He was always a good provider, but every night after work, he'd walk in the door, have a beer, and fall asleep on the couch. He was unemotional and never had anything to do with his kids.

"Mother was a tyrant. She was an alcoholic, although no one ever said that back then. The only way Mother knew how to discipline was through violence. And as far as she was concerned, I could never do anything right: If the pots weren't put back the right way in the cabinet, I'd get beaten with anything handy—a hairbrush, a wooden spoon. We were never allowed to make our own decisions about anything, not about the clothes we wore or the friends we had. When I think about all the time I spend with my own kids—Timmy is seven and Jeremy is five—I don't remember ever spending time alone with my mother.

"I did terribly in school and I acted up a lot. I suppose that I really wanted attention—which I got in spades. I spent many a day sitting in the principal's office.

"No one ever thought I might be smart; they just slotted me into the basic classes—I took a lot of typing and shorthand. My parents thought that was fine. In my family, girls never went to college; they became secretaries and got married.

"Mostly, I never felt I belonged anywhere, never had any friends I could trust. After graduation, I started working as a receptionist in an insurance agency and got involved with a church group. Paul was in the group's inner circle of popular kids. I noticed him right away—he's blond, blue-eyed, and very handsome, so it's hard not to— and I was totally shocked when he asked me out.

"Paul was taking classes at the community college during the day and working as an orderly at the local hospital at night, but he dropped out of school in the middle of his second year.

"Although I'd been out with several other guys, Paul was my very first serious romance. Finally, after nearly three years of dating, we were married in a church ceremony, then had a reception in my in-laws' backyard. We paid for the whole wedding ourselves.

"We didn't have any money for a fancy honeymoon trip, so we went camping out West. That was Paul's idea. I know he thinks it was a great trip, but I had a horrible time; a camper I'm not. I couldn't bring myself to complain to him, though; he was so pleased. Afterward, we moved into a furnished apartment and I went back to my job at the insurance agency. Paul took a job selling appliances; now he manages the store.

"I really don't remember exactly when things turned sour. When we were dating, Paul was caring and romantic. But once I was his wife, he started taking me for granted.

"Whenever he was upset, he'd always blame me. I'd reach for his hand and he'd pull away. If I asked what was up, he'd deny anything was wrong. 'It's your imagination,' he'd say.

"Then there was the matter of housework. Since I was working full-time, I assumed that on Saturday we'd both pitch in and do the housework. Well, Paul thought differently. He grew up in a large family, too; his mother did the housework and his father never lifted a finger.

"Even though our situation is not at all similar to that of his parents, Paul has never been open to any possibility of change. He refuses to do the laundry, refuses to wash the dishes. And when he's upset, he refuses to come to bed with me. It's been six months since we've made love.

"For a long time I tried to make the best of it. I loved him. I wanted desperately to have children and I tried to convince myself that things would work themselves out. And for a while we had some wonderful times together.

"When our children were born, for instance, Paul was terrific. But now we argue all the time about how to handle the kids; I've read a lot of books on child rearing and I've taken many parenting courses, which Paul hasn't. I must say,

though, that he does do a lot with the children. He's a Cub Scout leader and a Little League coach, the whole bit.

"Of course, once we had the responsibility of raising a family, the fights about money and finances—always a sore point—got worse. We totally disagree about how to spend whatever money we do have. I take care of the bills, so I know money is tight, but I think I should have some voice in where the money goes. I don't think we have to pay every single bill in full every month. We can pay some of the credit-card balance, then have some money left over to buy clothes for the kids, a new dishwasher, or maybe even go out to dinner with friends for a special occasion. Paul won't hear of it.

"I think one thing that bothered Paul was the fact that I started to do better at my job than he was doing at his. Although I stopped working when Jeremy was born, the last two years I was on the job I had gotten a lot of promotions and became office manager. Paul was jealous, although he'll deny it.

"You know, I try to be the good wife, but I feel helpless. Two weeks ago I refused to do Paul's laundry. It sounds stupid and childish, but I didn't know how else to get through to him. I could use a little help with the nitty-gritty stuff.

"Paul comes home from work, heads for his office in the basement—actually, it's one half of the playroom—and goes nuts because dinner isn't ready and the children's Legos are scattered all over the floor. Is he incapable of picking them up? Can't he see I'm running around like a chicken without a head?

"The saddest part is that even things that are supposed to be enjoyable turn ugly somehow. I wanted us to plan a different kind of family vacation this summer, but all Paul wants to do is to go camping again. And naturally, we got into a fight about it.

"I'm tired of having my ideas—things that are really important to me—routinely dismissed. The anger between us boils up and eventually simmers down but never really goes away. And on top of everything else, we have sexual problems. We've moved so far apart, I'm afraid we're never going to be able to bridge the gap. I just can't go on living like this—it's terrible for me, terrible for my children."

PAUL'S TURN

"You know, I'm tired of hearing what a louse I am," said Paul, twenty-eight, a man with all-American good looks.

"Kathleen is so selfish. Instead of appreciating all that I do for her—and maybe thanking me—she only concentrates on what I don't do.

"With Kathleen, I'm never ever a priority. Why should I even try to talk to her? All she does is get defensive. She doesn't want to hear my side. She just blows up and accuses me of taking advantage of her.

"I know Kathleen had it rough growing up. I was the oldest of seven kids, so I know firsthand what it feels like to be ignored, too. My folks did the very best they could, but I guess there were many times when I had no one to talk to. That's life. You can't spend the rest of your days taking it out on other people.

"My father worked for the local lighting company. My recollection is that he wasn't home much—he tried to work as much overtime as he possibly could to pay the bills. I didn't really know my father, but I do know his philosophies. I know what's right and what's wrong and that a man should go out and provide for his wife and family. I take a lot of pride in being able to do that.

"Then Kathleen, who's supposed to be in charge of the checkbook, manages to lose bills, and I get notice after notice that the electricity is going to be turned off. What does she expect? Of course I'm going to blow up. A person is supposed to pay bills, and if that means there isn't money left over, so be it. Money is very tight and going out to dinner is a luxury that we just can't afford right now.

"Kathleen blows everything way out of proportion. I work hard—sometimes fifty or sixty hours a week. My wife is home all day. Is it really too much to expect her to pull dinner together? I don't want a five-course gourmet meal, just dinner. And since she's mentioned it, yes, I do get upset when I go downstairs to work and there are the kids' toys scattered all over the place. Doesn't she think what I do is important?

"My mother managed fine, and she had seven kids running around. Kathleen has two, and she's always frazzled. She says she's too busy. So to get back at me, she dumps my laundry on the bathroom floor. Will she ever grow up?

"Kathleen says I was jealous of her success at work. That's just not true. I do fine at my own job. Okay, so maybe it's not as exciting as I'd like it to be, but I've been there a while now; I have decent benefits and three weeks' vacation. I'm not going to jump ship just for the sake of jumping.

"Sure, I'd like to do something else, but the competition is fierce, and without a college degree, I don't have much chance. I never did well in school—let me amend that; I did well in the subjects I liked, lousy in the others. When I decided to drop out of college, my father said fine, as long as I got a job. I had dreams. I wanted to teach—I enjoy being with kids and I can see myself helping them grow up to be decent human beings. But since I didn't finish college, that's not a likely possibility.

"You want to know what makes me really furious? We have differing opinions when it comes to disciplining the kids, but if I'm telling them something, instead of respecting me and my opinions, she shouts, 'Stop that. You're wrong. That's not the way you're supposed to do it.' Well, according to whom? So what if I haven't read every book ever published on how to bring up kids. I'm their father. I have the right to an opinion.

"Kathleen says that we're also having sexual problems. Why does she boil it down to sex? I get so angry at her, I don't want to be in the same room with her, much less make love. But the crazy thing is, I know that deep down I love her very much. And we have two of the greatest kids in the world. There's got to be a way to straighten this mess out."

<hr>

THE COUNSELOR'S TURN

"While Kathleen and Paul were not having a sexual problem per se, their sexual closeness was being sacrificed to the never-ending power struggle in their marriage," said the counselor. "Their bed had become a battlefield, and neither Kathleen nor Paul was willing to be the first to reach out to the other. Both of them were too afraid of being rejected. They were in serious trouble—I saw them for three and a half years before they finally felt the tension ebbing.

"Because their marital problems were so deep-seated and long-term, I worked with them individually as well as in joint sessions. It took a long time for Kathleen and Paul to realize where their anger was actually coming from and then to implement changes in the way they acted and reacted to each other.

"This is really a story about the basic issues—such as money, parenting, and household responsibilities—that every husband and wife face. However, this couple lacked the ability to recognize the real issues separating them, as well as the emotional maturity and skills needed to close the distance quickly. Consumed by anger, they both withdrew.

"Kathleen came from a family that abused her emotionally and physically. This barren family climate, filled with lots of shoulds and don'ts but very little praise, left her feeling worthless, unlovable—and desperate for attention. Unable to recognize where her feelings of rage were coming from, always expecting to be ignored, she blamed other people for her unhappiness.

"Although straight-arrow Paul did provide Kathleen with a much-needed sense of structure, he was an emotionally guarded man, so totally out of touch with his own feelings that it was impossible for him to focus on hers.

"Paul's background was similar to his wife's, and he, too, felt neglected. He had developed such tough armor, however, that it was months before he could stop denying his problems and admit that his childhood was not ideal.

"In one sense, Paul modeled himself after his father, an uninvolved man who never encouraged his bright, articulate son to stay in college or make something of his life. When Paul had to compete for jobs with men and women who had achieved college degrees, he felt inadequate.

"Paul had a preconceived, stereotypical idea of what marriage should be like and what his role in the family should be. When things didn't proceed as he assumed they would, he became furious. Since he had never learned to talk about his feelings, he either held on to his anger and brooded and pouted silently, or he became critical. On the other hand, Kathleen gave him more than enough ammunition, flying off in a rage when she perceived that she was being ignored.

"The first goal for Kathleen was to realize she couldn't expect Paul to meet all her needs, and we talked about what she herself could do to boost her self-esteem. One option was to go to school part-time. Since the boys were now in school all day, she decided to take classes in psychology and social work at the local community college in the morning and to work in the afternoon cleaning houses, so she could bring in some money but still have a fairly flexible schedule. She's very excited about her course work and she's doing well; the extra money she's earning has helped ease the family's financial burden.

"As she began to feel better about herself, Kathleen's rage subsided and she was able to appreciate the fact that Paul's ideas about parenting were just as valid as hers. Most important, she regularly tells him so.

"Paul had to realize, however, that many of Kathleen's complaints were valid. While he had plenty of the fun part of parenting, he had been negligent in sharing the work load.

"Now that Kathleen was not yelling at him so much, he felt less besieged and was more willing to help out. In time, Paul naturally started to do his share of household chores as well as the nitty-gritty things, such as taking the boys to the pediatrician or shopping for shoes when they need them.

"When Kathleen has a paper to write for school or an exam to study for, Paul takes the boys out to McDonald's—without being asked—so she can work. She, in turn, has begun to think about Paul's needs more: She makes sure the boys keep their toys in the playroom and away from their father's computer. 'And when I'm finished with my degree,

Paul might go back to college to finish up his credits, too,' she told me. Now that Paul sees that his dream can actually become a reality after all, his self-confidence has grown as well.

"When it came to resolving the power struggles over money, vacations, and other family issues, Kathleen and Paul had to learn to talk through their differences calmly and negotiate a compromise. I first had them promise never to resort to nasty or sarcastic words if they reached a stalemate. It's better to call a halt to the discussion, I pointed out, and to bring the subject up later, at a mutually agreed-upon time, than to launch into a full-scale battle.

"This technique helped them when the subject of money came up. Kathleen promised to be more diligent about paying the bills on time and keeping track of expenses. When Paul saw that she was indeed doing this, he softened and agreed that if Kathleen needed money for something for the house or for one of the boys, they could pay a portion of, say, the Visa bill that month. Paul was relieved to find that their credit rating remained solid. They also compromised on vacations, agreeing to go camping one year but to do what Kathleen wanted to do for the next vacation.

"While their sex life is still not ideal, it has improved greatly—a natural result of the tremendous decrease in hostility between the two of them. As Kathleen said, 'When you've been so furious for as long as we have, it can sometimes be easier to stay angry than to be intimate.

Neither of us wanted to take the first step and say I'm sorry. But now that we know where the anger comes from, it's easier for us to work on the problems.'"

FOUR THINGS YOU SHOULD NEVER SAY IN THE HEAT OF AN ARGUMENT

The power struggle in this marriage was fueled by the bitter arguments Kathleen and Paul were incapable of avoiding, arguments that obscured the real problems they should have been addressing. Every couple fights, but if your battles are as heated and vicious as Paul and Kathleen's, it's time to put the brakes on. The following phrases, or ones similar to them, often serve only to inflame, not resolve, an argument. Try to avoid lashing out with:

1. "This is like the time last year when you . . ." Fighting fair means you don't get hysterical—or historical. Reeling off a list of your partner's past transgressions proves that you never forget, or forgive.

2. "My mother [or my sister or anyone else] always said you'd never amount to anything." Did he marry you or your mother? Third-party criticism is destructive and inflammatory.

3. ". . . and you're a lousy lover, too." Demeaning remarks that are totally off the point linger long after an argument winds down.

4. "I want a divorce." This is one of the most hurtful things partners can say to each other. Threatening to abandon the marriage tells your mate that you don't think he or the marriage is important. Why should he try to resolve an argument?

"HE THINKS I'M NOT GOOD ENOUGH"

Now that Tony was successful, he didn't seem to need Carla around anymore. Why couldn't things stay the way they used to be?

CARLA'S TURN

"Now that Tony has everything he ever wanted, he doesn't need or love me anymore," said Carla, a petite though chubby thirty-three-year-old with beautiful brown eyes. "When we were married, five years ago, Tony's life was a mess. He had graduated at the top of his high school class but he didn't have enough money for college, so he ended up taking a low-paying job driving an ambulance. He was living at home, fought constantly with his parents, and since his job required a lot of weekend and evening work, he had very few friends.

"Now he has a college degree and a terrific, well-paying job he loves—a lot more than he loves me. Not to mention a whole new social life with his bright coworkers and their wives, who all respect him and look down on me.

"Sometimes I wish we were poor again. Back then, it was Tony and me against the world. He depended on me for everything—not just the money from my job as a typist at the city hospital, but also for companionship, encouragement, and love.

"He certainly never got any support from his highly critical family. I always tried to make our life as comfortable as possible—whether it was figuring out new ways to fix hamburger or painting our tiny apartment in cheerful colors. I even ran all over town doing errands for his parents.

"Actually, those years represented the only real family life I have ever known. My own father walked out when I was five and my mother, sister, and I never heard from him again. Since money was scarce, I knew college was out of the question, so I took business courses in high school and went to work at the hospital as soon as I graduated.

"That's where I met Tony. Although we would meet regularly for coffee in the hospital cafeteria, it took him almost a year to ask me for a real date. We saw each other for two more years before he finally asked me to marry him.

"We had a small church wedding, then moved into an apartment not far from the hospital. At my urging, Tony applied for admission to the evening program at the local university to get his degree in business administration. In two years, even though he was still driving the ambulance during the day, he had graduated with top honors and was offered a spot in the management training program of a large bank. Again, he advanced faster than anyone else.

"The day Tony got his second raise I discovered I was pregnant with our daughter, Annie. We had not planned on having a family until we had saved up enough money to buy a house, but Tony insisted on going out and celebrating anyway—in one of the most expensive restaurants in town. He also made me go to a beauty parlor, and buy an elegant new dress.

"That was a sign of things to come—although I didn't realize it at the time. During dinner Tony announced that our lives were changing. He was right: His life got better . . . mine got worse.

"First, Tony wanted me to quit my job and go to college. That seemed foolish—with a baby coming, we needed my salary. And besides, all my friends worked at the hospital. I didn't really know what to say to him and, after a while, Tony stopped bringing up the subject.

"But then, after Annie was born, Tony received a promotion and another raise. This time he really went to work on me, pushing college and telling me I needed new friends and new interests. He also wanted me to lose weight and buy better clothes to wear to the company parties. How I hated those parties! I felt completely out of place with all those people.

"Still, Tony was forever urging me to better myself—I have no drive, he used to say—and I became more insecure and miserable every day. On top of that, he started going on these buying sprees—he bought a closetful of new suits and even a fancy new car, which we certainly didn't need.

"Then, when Annie was about a year old, I started getting anxiety attacks. I would get dizzy and sweaty, and I felt as if my heart would pound right out of my chest. At first, I didn't know what was wrong, but I went to my doctor, who told me the problem was caused by emotional tension.

"Since I was feeling so miserable, our sex life, which had been just fine, started to, well, disappear. You don't want to have sex when you feel you are about to jump out of your skin.

"Things came to a crisis when I refused to accompany Tony to the bank's big Christmas dinner dance at the country club. He had bought me a slinky, expensive evening dress that was much too tight for me and I knew I would look fatter and more out of place than ever. Tony was furious! He went without me, and he didn't come home until five in the morning.

"I was out of my mind with worry. Then, when he finally walked in, he confessed that he had taken a coworker home and ended up in her bed. His excuse was that he had been drunk, but I knew better. This was just the first step: He was going to leave me, the way my father had left my mother. It was only a matter of time.

"So I packed my things, took my daughter, and moved in with my mother, who was not very enthusiastic, even though I help her out all the time. She told me that wives belong with their husbands, that men are natural chasers, and that I had better learn to make the best of a bad situation.

"Because I couldn't think of what else to do, I moved back into our apartment, but I slept with Annie in the tiny living room. I'm still there.

"I love Tony, but at this point I feel as if I'm of no use to him at all. When I was staying with my mother he begged me to come home, and although he has promised he will never again be unfaithful, that's not enough. Tony has got to accept me as I am."

TONY'S TURN

"Carla is one of the few really good people I know. She also has a very good mind—which she refuses to use—and could look lovely if she lost some weight and stopped dressing like a bag lady," said Tony, thirty-four, a thin, red-headed man who refused to make eye contact with his wife or the counselor.

"Of course, my infidelity is inexcusable, but I've apologized so many times already that I don't really see how counseling can help us. All that is needed is for Carla to forgive me, and then for her to get to work on herself and shape up.

"Right now Carla doesn't seem interested in me at all. She refuses to sleep with me. And she spends all her time and energy running errands and doing chores for everyone. Why doesn't she ever stand up for herself? Instead of having the courage to take control of her life, she blames me for her dizziness and heart palpitations.

"When I first met Carla, my life was a mess. I had very little confidence in myself—but who would with parents like mine? If my mother wasn't picking on me for one thing or another, she was shouting at me or my father. My parents argued constantly, and my bossy mother always won because she could shout louder and longer than Dad could.

"Carla inspired me to take control of my life. Although I had no serious intentions of becoming involved with any other woman— what I had seen of my parents' marriage gave me a rather jaundiced view—I found myself drawn to her warmth.

"Carla was always interested in listening to my problems and my dreams, something she never wants to do anymore. We started dating, and after thinking it over for a fairly long time, I finally asked her to marry me.

"That was the best move I ever made. Carla put her faith in me, agreeing to live in near poverty until I finished college and helping to pay my tuition, too. Our sex life turned out to be good—again, because Carla was such a loving, giving person. She even managed to get along with my parents, mainly because she catered to them.

"Now, just when all the dreams

I thought we shared have started to come true, our marriage is on the rocks. Carla is very smart, but she has no formal education. When I tried to get her to change, for her own good, she refused. Then came those anxiety attacks, which she now uses against me to avoid our making love. And she doesn't even want to discuss my career anymore. Every time I tell her how well a project is going, she looks as if she is about to burst into tears. And she goes into hysterics when I buy some new suits or a car. Well, we have the money now, so I'll be darned if I'm going to spend my life pinching pennies.

"When Carla refused to accompany me to the company Christmas party—the most important business function of the year—I blew up. I had even bought her a new dress, which I knew was a little too tight, but I thought it would give her the incentive to lose a few pounds. It was immature of me to act the way I did that night, but I assured Carla that the woman meant nothing to me. As you know, she wouldn't even discuss it.

"Carla was such a wonderful wife when we were struggling to make it. When she made her wedding vows, did she pay attention only to the 'for worse' part—and ignore the 'for better'? I want to share my life with Carla and Annie, but I can't go back to driving an ambulance."

183

THE COUNSELOR'S TURN

"Carla and Tony were experiencing problems that often arise when the balance in marriage is upset, even by a happy turn of events," said the counselor.

"Although both had emotional problems when they married, the relationship provided the support they needed to overcome their insecurities. Carla desperately needed to be needed; it was the only way she felt worthy of being loved. Tony, demoralized by his critical, overbearing parents, required unconditional love and acceptance to bolster his sagging self-esteem.

"However, once Tony became successful, the altered balance triggered the crisis that brought them to the brink of separation. Tony had changed, but Carla hadn't. And as Tony's self-confidence grew, he needed Carla's encouragement less. That's when Carla's self-esteem plummeted.

"Tony's tactless demands that Carla improve herself added to this couple's problems. Afraid to confront her husband openly, Carla was unconsciously showing her anger by withholding physical love. Of course, this only served to turn her fear that Tony would leave her into a self-fulfilling prophecy.

"Tony's infidelity was his final attempt to get Carla to come around. However, while he had expected to frighten her into compliance, his actions boomeranged.

"Carla was much stronger than he gave her credit for. She loved him and was afraid of losing him, but she had enough integrity to refuse to change just to meet Tony's social aspirations. She moved out, and emotionally she never really moved back in.

"Counseling was rough going for the first few sessions because Tony, in spite of his intelligence, was simply unable to examine the motives behind his behavior. He agreed to become involved in the counseling process only after an emotional session during which Carla threatened to divorce him.

"Even then, it was Carla who found it much easier to sort out the problems in their relationship. She quickly recognized that her need to be needed made it possible for others to exploit her. She did favors for people because she expected to be repaid in love and respect, which she was convinced she could get no other way. Yet as soon as Carla became aware of this tendency in herself, she found she could say no to unreasonable demands. This, in turn, gave her a feeling of control, which boosted her general self-confidence.

"In many ways, Tony was more insecure than Carla. Without her encouragement he would probably have continued in jobs way below his intellectual capacity, because he

184

was afraid to put his early promise to a real test. Although it took several sessions, Tony came to realize that he was projecting his own insecurities onto Carla by insisting that she improve herself.

"I explained that if their relationship was ever going to flourish, Carla and Tony had to start sharing their feelings. At my urging, they set aside specific times each day to discuss problems when they came up. Homework assignments between sessions were designed to let them sort out one issue at a time and, if possible, to resolve it before going on to the next.

"I suggested that they first discuss Carla's reasons for refusing to quit her hospital job, something that had long been a sore point between them. With her renewed confidence, Carla found she was able to tell Tony how she truly felt. As a result, he understood for the first time that the hospital was the only social setting in which she felt completely secure. To help her overcome her insecurity and expand her social circle, they planned small dinners and other occasions, inviting only one or two of Tony's coworkers and their wives so Carla did not have to face the whole company at once. Within a short time, Carla became friendly with these people on a personal basis, and was less intimidated by them in a large group.

"At another session, we dis-cussed a problem that had long troubled Carla: her belief that Tony spent money frivolously. As Tony clearly outlined their financial situation—something he hadn't bothered to explain before—Carla was able to see that on Tony's new income they really could afford some luxuries.

"After ten sessions, Carla and Tony told me they wanted to try to work on their relationship on their own. We stayed in touch with occasional phone calls, and now, one year later, they seem to have a strong, loving marriage.

"Tony is still rising rapidly up the corporate ladder, and they are planning to buy a home soon. Carla, too, has been busy, doing exceptionally well in the evening education courses she has been taking at the local university. Next semester, she plans to enroll full-time for her degree.

"Carla's newfound confidence has brought about other changes, too. Since she is no longer under stress, her anxiety attacks have all but disappeared. She has lost weight and is able to wear with pride the more elegant clothes Tony likes.

"And although she'll always be a little shy, Carla now happily attends business and social functions with her husband. I'm confident that Tony and Carla can look forward to a happy and productive life together."

KEEPING LOVE ALIVE

Too often, people who love each other forget that simple kindness and respect are essential to keeping that love alive. Although they are thoughtful with colleagues and friends, they take their mates for granted. It's easy to fall into that trap; most of us do at one time or another. But if you're in a situation similar to Carla's, where criticism is constant and demeaning, you must take a stand. Don't try to defend your actions. Most likely that will only perpetuate your spouse's negative comments. Speak up calmly but firmly and tell your mate you are offended by his tone, his choice of words, or his manner, and you refuse to be treated with such disrespect. If he persists, leave the room.

What if you're the offending partner? Perhaps you honestly don't realize that the way you say something can be as potent as the words you use. Agree to have your partner give you a signal to let you know that what you said was inappropriate. Once you know, you can apologize and then rephrase your statements.

"MY HUSBAND IS A PERFECTIONIST"

Nothing was good enough for the super-critical Arthur and, after fifteen years, Glenda no longer cared to meet the high standards he set—for himself and for everyone else.

GLENDA'S TURN

"Unless Arthur—my husband is a brilliant architect—moves his office out of our home, and quick, he can have all ten rooms to himself," said thirty-eight-year-old Glenda, mother of four, in a voice as fiery as her bright-red hair.

"Fortunately, when I finished art school, I inherited a modest trust fund. I'm now in a position to establish a separate residence, provide my son and daughters with a little peace and quiet, and preserve my own sanity.

"Arthur complains bitterly about everything. He was upset because Ellen, who is seventeen months old, dribbled milk down her chin and dropped applesauce on the floor. That domestic sight interfered with his 'creativity.' I'm an artist myself, but I'm smart enough to realize that children and messes go together. But Ellen's soppy dress, Arthur said, was typical of my bad management as a mother.

"That evening at dinner he jumped on twelve-year-old Billy and his sisters because they hadn't greeted him with cries of delight when they came in from school (as an at-home Dad, his presence is hardly a surprise to any of us) and because they squabbled at the table. He accused all three of being undisciplined, although seven-year-old Janey is a perfect little lady and just as sensitive as Arthur himself. She burst into tears. Billy took Janey's part and sassed his father. Arthur then ordered the three children to leave the table and go outside and practice self-control; he wanted them to pick three bouquets of flowers—if you can imagine making such an idiotic proposal to hungry youngsters! I told the children to stay put and continue the meal. Arthur ate by himself in the kitchen, again.

"My husband has enormous talent and many lovable qualities. However, his sulkiness, finickiness, and procrastination have become intolerable.

"Arthur and I have been married fifteen years and have owned our present home for eleven. It is nowhere near furnished. Downstairs we have no window shades. Upstairs we have fantasically expensive draperies, woven in Andalusia to Arthur's specifications. There is no sofa in our living room. Our guests sit on a lumpy contraption concocted from two beat-up daybeds, covered with Navajo blankets that Arthur admires and I despise. I have dragged him to furniture stores but have yet to find a sofa with lines, fabric, and construction that please him.

"Arthur is the only man I have ever loved. I met him at sixteen, soon after I entered art school. He was teaching an occasional class in draftsmanship. I signed up for every class he taught, but he ignored me. Through family friends I wangled an introduction.

"We dated, off and on, for years. Arthur and I went to art shows, museums, concerts, the theater. On my twenty-third birthday, after seven years, I decided I had waited long enough and should forget about marriage. My father offered to send me abroad for a year of painting, and I accepted.

"On our next date, I explained my plans to Arthur and to my astonishment, he proposed to me that same night. Two weeks later we were married.

"For two years, we were divinely happy, even though my parents' marriage fell apart during that period. Arthur was a tower of strength to both my mother and father, to my brothers, and to me. In those days he and I had no sex problems, no money problems, no in-law problems, no design problems, no problem of his incessant meddling and bossiness. Our first home was a small rented apartment. He worked afternoons and evenings in the one tiny bedroom. In the morning he worked in the office of an older architect. He left me every day at eight A.M. and was gone until noon. I missed him badly those four hours. That now seems incredible.

"Now Arthur's office is the original maid's room in our home, which directly adjoins my kitchen. In theory his door is supposed to be closed from nine o'clock until five. In fact, he bobs in and out dozens of times a day and is always breathing down my neck. When he does receive his clients, he hollers for me to be less noisy or to bring in coffee and cake. When he steps outside for a leisurely stroll in search of inspiration, I'm under orders to take his business calls, act as his secretary, and send out his bills, because he won't hire a typist.

"When I bring in groceries, Arthur instantly rushes out of his office and criticizes my purchases. I can't keep a cleaning woman; he pushes them around until they quit. He revises my menus, alters the arrangement of my pots and pans. Nothing is ever permanent, and few things tarry long in the places where I put them. Arthur uses my kitchen as a laboratory, where he tests out every new product or material that comes on the market and catches his fancy. In eleven years, I've had five new sinks and more color schemes than I can remember. Last week, he even rearranged things in my studio.

"I can't stand it anymore. If Arthur doesn't move his office, I intend to move the rest of us out."

ARTHUR'S TURN

"It is unfair to ask me to separate my work life from my home life, my emotional life," said forty-two-year-old Arthur, a tall, blond man with dazzling blue eyes. "The genuine creators, the innovators, the men I admire and venerate—men like Frank Lloyd Wright—produced and flourished while working from their homes. My home is a means of self-expression, my card of introduction.

"Most of my work has been done with churches. Almost always the church building committees I've dealt with were inexperienced people, doubtful of their own judgment, and skeptical of me and my ability. Once they entered our house, however, they quickly responded to the cheerful informality of the living room and almost visibly relaxed. Consequently, we could concentrate on the job without wasting time. Modern commercial buildings are sterile and cold.

"Besides, creativity doesn't switch itself on at nine A.M. and off at five P.M. like an electric light bulb. Just recently an idea struck me in the middle of the night. I rushed downstairs to my drawing board and in fifteen minutes had the solution to a nagging problem that had perplexed me for a week. It would surely have escaped my mind by morning.

"Glenda has been sleeping on the living-room couch, despite the lumpiness she incessantly complains of, to punish me for differences aired earlier in the day. At lunch, she cooked hamburger and beans for the fourth time that week. She allowed Ellen to smear her high chair and face with applesauce, rather than locate a bib for her. Glenda is hopelessly disorganized and lets our kids get away with murder. It is futile for me to enforce decent standards of behavior, to teach our youngsters the joy and beauty of discipline and order.

"Dinner that evening was worse than lunch. When I told my son and older daughters to wash their hands, Glenda said their hands were clean enough. They mocked me openly, shoved each other, and turned the meal into chaos. I ordered all three to go outside and calm down by arranging bouquets of flowers, a task I've seen accomplish miracles with Japanese children. Glenda contradicted my orders and the youngsters became even more obstreperous.

"Although Glenda may not realize it, she constantly destroys my dignity and undermines my authority with our children. She jeers at my opinions in their presence, screams at me, slams doors, and threatens divorce. This is damaging the kids: Billy is doing badly at school; Janey has a poor appetite and is argumentative and pigheaded; Sue is nervous, bites her nails, and has begun to stutter. Before I proposed to Glenda, she promised that we would share the whole of our lives. She now speaks of my home, my kitchen, my money, and even my children—as though they had no father.

"Unlike me, Glenda is an impulsive buyer. I am willing to take the time to acquire something rare or, with luck, unique. Why choose a sofa with offensive lines or fabric merely to possess a sofa? What's the rush? The daybeds in our living room are honest and unpretentious; the blankets covering them are beautiful.

"I've heard Glenda and her mother discussing all this on the telephone many times. Every morning she hops to the telephone and broadcasts our intimate affairs to everyone in both families. Why can't she see any of this from my point of view?"

THE COUNSELOR'S TURN

"These two artistic people were making an inartistic hash of their marriage," the counselor said. "Both were exceedingly strong-willed, but Arthur was the more obstinate of the two, as well as the more impractical and self-centered.

"Not that Glenda was entirely blameless. She damaged her relationship with Arthur and prejudiced the children when she contradicted him in their presence. It didn't help for her to confide intimate affairs to friends and family and appeal to them for backing.

"Under the circumstances, however, her remarks and behavior were understandable. In the power struggle of their marriage, she was fighting to survive as an individual.

"Arthur was acutely sensitive to color, structure, form, design, and his own reactions and feelings. However he was insensitive to Glenda's feelings, oblivious to her wishes and rights as a wife. He endeavored to rule the entire household. Since he was always on the scene, Glenda and the children were under observation day and night.

"It wasn't until Arthur invaded every corner of Glenda's realm as a wife, a mother, and an artist that she rebelled. When she taunted him with the fact of her financial independence and threatened to pack up the children and move out, she was desperate.

"The real danger to this marriage, and for that matter, the primary flaw in Arthur's personality, was his overwhelming drive for perfection. His expecation of a forever serene household was ridiculous. I told him so. I also told him that his complaints that outside distractions interfered with his inspiration were nonsense. The main obstacle to his work lay in his own personality. Arthur himself wasted time and energy and delayed his labors at the drawing board. He continually dissipated his creativity and interrupted the flow of his talent by thrusting himself into what should have been Glenda's sphere. He did not allow himself the freedom of an uncluttered mind so he could carry out his commissions promptly (he was tardy in nearly all his projects), and he hardly gave Glenda room to breathe.

"It wasn't easy for a man as opinionated and articulate as Arthur to acknowledge that he and Glenda could and should divide the areas of decision-making in their marriage. However, he was extremely anxious to avoid a separation and, eventually, he and Glenda were able to reach a number of compromises.

"They discussed money at great length. Although it seemed impractical at first for the family to live solely on his earnings and bank Glenda's income from her trust fund, she agreed to give this a trial. Arthur realized this would mean Glenda must sacrifice the social value of her service to the P.T.A., her work with charities, her volunteer work in the Head Start program. He then agreed that the value of her contribution to the community outweighed the artificial soothing of his vanity. Glenda now pays the sitters and cleaning women from her income without protest from Arthur, and he tries not to interfere with their efficiency.

"After our first interview, and with Arthur's permission, Glenda went furniture shopping. She selected three sofas in different styles and periods for him to choose from, as well as three sets of dining-room chairs and so on. Within these parameters, he picked out the pieces he liked the most or, perhaps, disliked the least. Within a month, the house was completely furnished.

"It is six months since I have seen Glenda and Arthur, but they send me bulletins from time to time. Arthur is now established in a roomy office in a midtown professional building and his clients—a little to his chagrin—do not seem to miss the charm of his 'at home' atmosphere. Indeed, his clients have multiplied and he has broadened his architectural horizons, entering the field of low-cost housing. He still keeps a drawing board at home, where he may work if inspiration dynamites him in the middle of the night.

"Children mirror the tensions of their parents; so with tensions lessened by the daytime absence of a temperamental father, Billy and his sisters have become less unruly. Arthur is surprised and pleased to have them greet him affectionately when he comes home.

"The marriage of artists is seldom calm, but essentially they pursue the same objectives and have the same goals. Glenda and Arthur belong together—and now they know it."

LIVING WITH A PERFECTIONIST

As far as Arthur is concerned, things are either black or white; there are no shades of gray. Life can be difficult, if not impossible, when you're living with a perfectionist. Not only is it a Herculean task to meet his standards, but decisions and arguments soon fall into an "I'm right/you're wrong" mode. It can help both partners to understand that behind such polarized, all-or-nothing thinking is usually some hidden or unconscious doubt or fear. A person may wonder: Am I really any good? Will others like me? Who will love me? Becoming aware of these fears is the first step. Learning to compromise is the next.

Are you the perfectionist in the house? It can help to shift your frame of reference. Instead of thinking, "I'm right," tell yourself, "I could be wrong." Then ask yourself: "Is there anything I could do differently?" Reframing in this way turns a potential power struggle into a collaborative problem-solving effort.

"I'M NOT THE GIRL HE MARRIED"

Lisa was in love with her new life, but Warren was in love with the old Lisa. What happens when a wife changes—but her husband doesn't?

LISA'S TURN

"My husband's an unbearable male chauvinist," began Lisa, twenty-four, a striking brunette who wore a T-shirt that read 'Women on Top.'

"Warren," Lisa continued, "has always been egotistical. But he's even worse since finishing medical school. He thinks the world revolves around his hospital residency and he could care less about my career writing for a newspaper. He considers journalism frivolous and thinks I should stay at home and wait on him.

"Not too long ago, for example, I rushed home from work to prepare one of his favorite dinners. He didn't lift a finger to help, and when he finished the main course, he pushed back his chair and waited for me to bring dessert. I took one look at the smug expression on his face and said, 'Wait on yourself, Archie Bunker.' Then I left the table in tears.

"Warren didn't try to comfort me or even ask what was wrong. He buried his nose in a magazine, pretending I didn't exist. Later, when he fell asleep—he's tired all the time these days—I packed a few things and went to my girlfriend's apartment for the weekend. Well, when the weekend was over, I couldn't bring myself to go back to him. I found my own apartment and I enjoy being on my own. I love the independence.

"My husband keeps telling me I'm not the girl he married, and he's right. I'm not a twenty-one-year-old girl anymore. I'm an adult, a woman. I've grown up and Warren hasn't. He's still his mother's little boy, expecting to be pampered, petted, and praised.

"Warren's mother is a sweet, devoted homebody who never dared ask anything from Warren's father, an Army colonel, who ordered her around. Warren thinks his mother's perfect, her marriage ideal. He'd like me to be more like her, I'm sure, and he's becoming more like his father—remote, distant, demanding. He finds fault with everything I do. If I'm five minutes late, he says I'm irresponsible.

"Looking back, I think it was probably a mistake to marry Warren. We met at college and I remember telling my roommate that he was not my type. Warren was a big man on campus—class president and an honor student in pre-med. Although he was very good-looking, I thought he was a dud, too serious for my tastes.

"For some reason, however, Warren fell for me right away. I was the only girl he ever introduced to his family. We dated for a year, then he left for medical school. I thought the romance was over, but Warren wouldn't give up. He ran up hundred-dollar-a-month phone bills and insisted we spend every vacation together. He proposed at the end of his first year of medical school and we set a wedding date.

"My parents, who've always had money problems, were impressed as all get-out with Mr. Future Doctor. Mother's something of a martyr, and she kept telling me I was lucky because I'd never have to work as she had to do. My dad was almost as bad. He's a traveling salesman, constantly on the road, so he kept telling me I was lucky because I'd have my husband home every night.

"The only problem was, I didn't feel lucky. I didn't feel ready to settle down. I wanted to finish school. Warren seemed so square, so set in his ways. When I told him about my doubts, he became even more persistent and possessive. My parents needled me, too. I felt surrounded, overwhelmed. I finally gave in, and Warren and I were married when I turned twenty-one.

"The first two years of marriage, I was so busy I didn't have much time to think. I completed my degree and took care of the apartment by myself so Warren would be free to study.

"A friend asked me to join a women's group and as I listened to the other women, I made some discoveries. All my life, I existed simply to please others—my family, the men I dated, my husband. I was raised to be a wife, and that's all I was. Where were my own dreams, my own life?

"I tried to share my discoveries with Warren, to get him to share his feelings with me, but he was totally disinterested. When I suggested marriage counseling, he said, 'Why should I go? There's nothing wrong with me.'

"Warren and I just keep growing further and further apart. Since our separation, two months ago, I've become involved with another man, a colleague at the newspaper. Joe's very easygoing and supportive—totally unlike Warren. But I don't want to marry Joe. I don't want to be married to anyone. I want to concentrate on my career and be a person in my own right. I want Warren to give me a divorce."

WARREN'S TURN

"I really love my wife," said Warren, twenty-six, a soft-spoken physician whose blue eyes were ringed with dark shadows of fatigue. "That is," he continued, "I love the person she once was—warm, supportive, giving. Lisa is now a roaring feminist, as I'm sure you've gathered.

"I was raised to be a gentleman—to pull out chairs and open doors for ladies. My father, an Army colonel, treated my mother with that kind of respect, and she loved it. At first Lisa seemed to enjoy it, but now she calls me a chauvinist.

"Our marriage has gone downhill. I don't know how to handle this new Lisa at all. When she first started her feminist tirades, I'd get so angry that I'd shout back. But then she'd burst into tears, and that made me feel terrible. So the next time she

yelled, I just read a magazine. That infuriated her even more. Reasoning with her was just as bad, perhaps worse. Nothing I did was right.

"She says I'm immature, a mama's boy, which is far from the truth. I was the oldest child in my family and learned about responsibility at an early age. Lisa's being irresponsible and childish—not me. She's always late, for example. And she doesn't take care of things or pay attention to what she's doing. She'll burn the clothes she's ironing or forget about an expensive roast in the oven. Needless to say, when I point out her oversights, she accuses me of trying to control her.

"Here's another way Lisa distorts the truth: She says she resents having been so dependent on her family and then on me. Yet since our separation, she often drops by for food or money. I don't call that independence, and I'd like to point out to her that this career of hers—this career that may cost our marriage—doesn't seem like a gold mine of opportunity. If she's serious about journalism, she should go back to school so she can get a reputable job. Did she tell you her 'paper' is a sleazy, underground tabloid? And she certainly won't take advice from me. In her eyes, I'm the establishment—not to be trusted.

"I don't think there's anything wrong with being dependable, hardworking, and dedicated. I've met her colleagues at the newspaper and they seem lazy and unmotivated. When I told Lisa that, she defended them and said I was narrow and materialistic.

"Her poor opinion of me is really about to destroy me. All through medical school, I tried to keep tight control on my feelings. That was the only way to survive the incredible pressures there. But Lisa's walking out on me is a thousand times harder to deal with. I can't bear to be alone.

"Her affair with another man is also depressing me. The guy is no good, a sponge, but my wife thinks he's wonderful. She says he needs her. She doesn't stop to consider that I need her. I'd do anything to make her happy. If I'm as oppressive as she says I am, I'm willing to change. I just want her to talk rationally about our problems. I want us to work something out.

"I know I probably love Lisa more than she loves me—I always have. I talked her into marriage, now I guess I have to talk her out of a divorce."

THE COUNSELOR'S TURN

"Many couples' expectations of marriage," the counselor said, "are tied to how they related to their mothers and fathers. It's probably not an exaggeration to say that in some ways we all marry our fantasy parents. Women tend to marry the father they wanted to have, not necessarily the one they had, and men tend to marry their fantasy mothers.

"In Warren's eyes, his loving, compliant mother was perfect, and he expected Lisa to behave the same way. Furthermore, he felt that his beneficence and love, his willingness to make all the important decisions—just as his father had done— were all that were required of him as a husband. In the beginning, Lisa, who had no clear idea of her own potential, fell into the role of helpful wife. Warren's constancy, so unlike the behavior of her wandering father, suited her perfectly. A combination of circumstances, however, upset the shaky balance in their marriage.

"When Warren changed from student to professional, Lisa's contributions to the marriage changed. They no longer depended on her income and she felt less valued. She began to see Warren as having all the power, recognition, and prestige, while she had none. Her hurt and disappointment turned into anger—directed, of course, at her husband.

"Much of the scorn she heaped on her partner was a result of how she felt about herself. Since she had never developed her own identity, she felt inferior to the superachieving Warren and was deeply dependent on him. She viewed dependence as a terrible weakness she dared not acknowledge and correct.

Instead, she continually looked for weaknesses in Warren.

"The couple gradually learned that Lisa's desire to establish a separate identity would involve work on both their parts. Warren had to learn to share some of his power, to let Lisa make some major decisions about their life together. She, in turn, learned to be more responsible—to be on time, to take better care of possessions—and in this way she freed Warren to be more relaxed. Lisa further proved that she was responsible when she enrolled in a graduate school of journalism and earned straight A's.

"As they learned to share power, they also found ways to share drudgery. They drew up a list of household chores and divided it right down the middle. Lisa learned how to change the oil in the car; Warren learned how to iron. The arrangement pleases both of them, especially Lisa. Warren's thoughtfulness has earned him new respect in her eyes. She no longer sees her ex-colleague, Joe.

"The last time we spoke with Warren, he had finished his medical training and was in group practice. Lisa, he reported, was happy with her career and much happier with their marriage.

"Warren also said that the changes in his marriage have helped his medical practice as well. He said he's much more attuned to the emotional needs of others, which makes him a more sensitive person and physician."

UNRAVELING THE HIDDEN AGENDA

Although the obvious problem is that Lisa and Warren aren't communicating, the key issue, the one they are unaware of, is the underlying power struggle that precipitates their bickering. Many couples have preconceived notions of their ideal mate and these stereotypes can obscure the expectations each has for marriage. They may not discover until much later that some of their deepest values are in conflict. Could unspoken expectations be at the root of your arguments? To find out, write down five qualities you expect to find in a happy, healthy marriage. Also, jot down five things that you hope will never surface. Be honest. This should be done not only before a couple make a commitment, but also throughout the relationship; it can give you the courage to work on compromises instead of assuming the marriage is over when problems do erupt.

PART 5

LOVE AND MONEY: HOW TO MAKE SENSE OF DOLLARS AND CENTS

—◆—

RARE IS THE COUPLE THAT DOESN'T FIGHT about money. In fact, surveys have singled out money matters as the number-one trigger for everything from the occasional marital skirmish to all-out war. However, while couples are ostensibly fighting over how much to spend on new patio furniture, whether a bonus should go into high-risk stocks or safer mutual funds, or even whether to save or spend at all, they are really fighting about much more than simple dollars and cents. Understanding the hidden meanings inherent in money battles is essential for avoiding irreparable damage to a marriage.

Money is, and always has been, a symbol—for power and control, for love, for security, as well as for self-esteem and accomplishment. A husband may insist on managing the family finances—without consulting his wife and expecting she will not challenge his choices—because that's the only way he feels confident and strong. Or he may believe that he's entitled to sign off on key financial decisions. Then, too, in a culture that judges people by their paychecks, husbands as well as wives who aren't making as much money as they'd like may discover that shaky self-esteem causes ripples of discontent and resentment at various times in their relationship.

Money battles may also mask buried but nonetheless volatile issues—personal values, priorities, as well as each partner's emotional needs for independence or security. Personality and family background play a part: A fiscally cautious wife may prefer to pay bills as soon as they arrive. What happens when she marries a financial juggler who waits until the last minute before writing a check? Similarly, the man from a financially secure family who marries a woman whose parents struggled to make ends meet will most likely have strikingly different attitudes about, and ways of handling, money. Each partner buys or spends according to his or her own values and emotional needs—and when those needs differ from a spouse's, the ensuing arguments can be heated and long-lasting.

In fact, too often, money is a weapon in marital battles, a means of instilling guilt or expressing anger. A shopaholic wife may run up charges on a credit card, because it's a way to retaliate against a domineering or neglectful husband. A husband may balk at supporting a wife's children from a former marriage because he's furious that her ex-husband is reneging on his obligations.

However, *Can This Marriage Be Saved?* shows that, while it's critical to understand the hidden meanings inherent in money arguments, it's equally essential to recognize how these symbolic meanings play themselves out against a shifting backdrop of social and economic change. Today, two-thirds of all wives work full-time—in many cases earning as much as if not more than their spouses. In some of these marriages, the assumptions and expectations about who is entitled to make financial decisions remain as traditionally divided along gender lines as they were a generation ago. In others, they are quite different.

And if both spouses don't agree on the division of financial responsibilities, clashes are inevitable.

What's more, assumptions and expectations about money may change dramatically over the lifetime of a marriage and couples must be flexible enough to accommodate them. A wife, for instance, may work full-time for a few years, stay home while the children are small, then return to work. Divorce, remarriage, and obligations to stepchildren and elderly parents also create new and potentially volatile financial battlegrounds. Each new situation or new role demands new rules for money management, but unfortunately our attitudes and behaviors regarding finances are so deeply ingrained that sorting them out and striking a balance acceptable to both partners can be fraught with tension.

No couple is immune to money conflicts, especially today; as resources barely keep pace with skyrocketing costs, the financial stress on families is enormous. Even couples with two incomes find that while they're working harder than ever, their paychecks buy less and less. Not much is left over for the good times—movies and dinners out, family vacations, or even child-free weekends away. Dreams bear little resemblance to reality—and that puts a strain on even the best relationship. Those couples who navigate best through the churning financial waters have made a conscious effort to chip away the emotional veneer surrounding money issues and, instead, talk openly about finances—what they need, what they want, and how they can best attain these goals. They've learned to brainstorm alternatives until they agree on a decision and, if that's impossible, to negotiate a compromise.

In fact, *Can This Marriage Be Saved?* highlights several characteristics common to couples who are able to keep money matters in perspective:

- Instead of assuming that a spouse's financial goals, habits, or ideas about spending and investing are the same, these couples have taken the time to discuss the following: What role does money play in our lives? What are our attitudes and beliefs about it? Is one of us a risk-taker, another security-conscious? Do we feel money should be spent and enjoyed or squirreled away for emergencies?

- They've hammered out the logistics of budgeting and money management: Does a joint or a separate savings and checking account make sense? Who will actually pay the bills? Will we consult on all purchases or set a ceiling on personal spending? Will we use credit cards or pay cash?

- They've tracked any patterns to their money battles, noticing, for instance, when they are most likely to be triggered—when the bills come in, for instance, or at tax time.

- They've predicted and accounted for any financial changes that may take place at certain transition points in life—after the birth of a baby; when they buy a new house or when the kids go off to college; following the loss of a job. What's more, at each life stage, both partners are aware of and informed about the financial realities.

- When an argument does erupt, they are able to step back from the immediate quarrel and ask themselves: What am I really upset about? The fact that my husband spent money on a new stereo system or new set of golf clubs or the fact that he's not pitching in with childcare?

Indeed, although we are a society that insists money doesn't buy happiness, the reality is that not having enough of it, or arguing over how and where to spend it, seriously disrupts many marriages. Money fights may on the surface be frivolous, but they are well worth attending to.

"My Husband Can't Handle Money"

———

Mary knew that Pete was a spendthrift, but with four children all under five years of age, how could she possibly fend for herself?

MARY'S TURN

"I've reached the end of my rope," said Mary, thirty-six, a slim, pretty woman whose soft voice was flat with emotional exhaustion. When she entered the counselor's office, she was carrying a baby in one arm and leading a toddler along with the other.

"Yesterday morning the bank called to say that another of Pete's checks had bounced. This is the third call I've had like that this week. When I hung up the phone, I was shaking so much I had to sit down. Then I burst into tears and just couldn't stop crying for hours and hours.

"This sort of behavior is unusual for me. So are the physical symptoms I've been experiencing lately. I've never had health problems, but during the past year I've been plagued with skin rashes, indigestion, and insomnia. My doctor says they're all triggered by stress, and I'm sure he's right.

"I'm worried sick about the way my husband handles money. Until I married Pete, it absolutely never occurred to me that people could live the way we do now. I grew up in a home where finances were always in order. My father owned his own business and provided very well for his family, but he didn't believe in going into debt for anything. He never borrowed a nickel or owned a credit card.

"Dad was my favorite parent. He was a kind, gentle man who gave in to my mother on almost everything. Mom was the stronger and more dominant one, and as years passed my father grew more submissive.

"One thing my father remained adamant about, though, was that none of us was ever allowed to purchase anything on credit. Mom could buy whatever she wanted, but she had to be able to pay for it with cash.

"But for Pete, being in debt is simply a way of life. The very first year we were married, our checks started bouncing. We both had good jobs—I was teaching school and he was doing well as a farm-equipment salesman—but Pete kept buying me presents and insisting on expensive holiday vacations, and every month our joint bank account was overdrawn.

"I was terribly upset about being in debt, but Pete kept assuring me he had everything under control. The crazy thing was, he usually did. More often than not, just when I was getting frantic, a commission check would arrive in the mail.

"Pete and I met during our senior year in college and I was attracted to him immediately. He had many of the wonderful traits I admired in my father. Like Dad, he was sensitive and kind, but unlike my father he was a strong man who was not submissive and wouldn't let himself be ordered around by anyone. I was used to running the show in relationships with boyfriends, but with Pete, it was just the opposite—he was the one in charge. I found this quality exciting.

"We graduated, but to my disappointment Pete didn't propose, so I moved back home with my parents and found a job teaching school.

"Pete moved to Detroit, keeping in touch by phone. One night during a storm, a tree fell on our telephone line, pulling the wires down, and the phone was out of order for three whole days. Pete told me afterward that he went crazy not being able to reach me. The first call I got when the phone was working again was from Pete asking me to marry him.

"In the thirteen years we have been married, Pete and I have done a lot of moving around because sales—especially farm-machinery sales—is a line of work that fluctuates with the local economy. Sometimes he received only a low salary plus commission. First, Pete sold equipment to farmers living outside Detroit. Then he received what he said was a much better offer from a company in North Carolina, which was where the first of our four children—now eight, six, two and six months—was born.

"Our second child was born in California, where we moved when the North Carolina market slowed down, and the third when we moved back to North Carolina, where Pete's old company gave him a better offer. Each time we moved, Pete assured me that his new job had much more potential than the one he was leaving. And each time I believed him and told myself, 'Now we're leaving all our money worries behind us.' But each time I've been wrong.

"I quit my teaching job when my first child was born, but since Pete had received a big raise in basic pay at just that point, our financial problems can't be blamed on the loss of a second income.

"The sad truth is, regardless of our current income, Pete spends that much and more. Several times in the course of our marriage I've tried to make him sit down and work out a budget. What a joke! Pete's idea of budgeting is to make a short list of our major expenses, such as house payments, utilities, and food. When I try to get him to add in all the little extra things—shoes, haircuts, movies, disposable diapers, and so on—he says it's ridiculous to get bogged down with details.

"We lived in California for a year and then moved back East again. Pete had a job selling farm machinery in Raleigh, but just at that time the town we lived in was caught in a recession. The farmers could not afford the expensive machinery of Pete's company and for a year he didn't earn a single commission. I thought of going back to teaching, but there were no open-ings at the local school and the only jobs I could find were for part-time remedial reading teachers, which would hardly have covered the cost of a baby-sitter.

"The day Pete told me his job had been terminated, I thought the end had come. Miraculously, though, he was able to land another job, with a large national company, in Dallas.

"But this most recent move was harder for me than all the others. I had made really close friends in North Carolina and it was very painful to leave them. In Dallas, we put most of our belongings into storage and moved into a tiny, cramped apartment. Almost immediately I learned I was pregnant again. Needless to say, it was an accident, but I tried to look on the bright side; Pete and I both love children and Pete assured me his new job would make us rich.

"I love Pete, but I don't know how much longer I can go on living like this. There are days when I don't even have the energy to wash my face or comb my hair. I never go out anymore; Pete does all the grocery shopping and runs all the errands. He seems happy in his job and he tells me he's making good money, but from the way our checks keep bouncing, you would never know it. He won't listen when I try to discuss this ever-worsening problem, and I have given up all hope that we'll ever be free from debt."

"This last pregnancy really seems to have gotten Mary down," said Pete, thirty-seven, a handsome man with an easygoing manner. "It's not like her to sit around the apartment all day, moping and complaining. I don't mind helping out with the grocery shopping and errand running. I know it's hard to drag four little kids around a supermarket, but I'm worried because she has so little energy that she can barely force herself out of bed.

"Mary blames our financial situation for her depression. That makes no sense to me at all. We're a bit overdrawn at the bank, but that's not the end of the world. My next paycheck will come in the mail any day now.

"If it were up to Mary, I think she'd wear rags and go barefoot, which seems strange for a girl who grew up in a well-to-do family and was used to always having nice things.

"My own folks were lower middle class. Dad was a factory worker and Mom was a housewife. I always knew that I wanted to live better than they did. If I ever really wanted something, I found some way to get it. I held part-time jobs all through college, working summers on a pipeline. I had a lot of friends, some of whom were pretty well off, so if my money ran out before the semester ended, I could usually borrow some from them.

"I met Mary while I was at college and I fell for her right away. She was running for campus beauty queen, and when I saw a picture of her in the college newspaper, I asked one of her sorority sisters to introduce us. Even today, as a four-time mother, my wife is still a knockout. Is it any wonder that I'm really proud of her and want to give her nice things?

"I didn't expect to get married right after graduation. My plan was to work for a while before I gave up bachelorhood. Then one night I tried to phone Mary at her folks' house, but I couldn't get through. I called back a half hour later and the line was still out of order. By the time I got through and Mary finally answered the phone, I had worked myself into such a state of anxiety that I asked her to marry me right away.

"Still, I've never once regretted marrying so soon. In the early days, both of us were working, and although neither of us earned all that much money, together we did just fine. By the time we were ready to start a family, I was earning enough so Mary could quit her job and stay home with the children, which was what we both wanted.

"I'm not saying we haven't had our financial ups and downs. That's how it is when you work in sales—feast or famine. You can't let it get you down; you have to learn to roll with the punches. You often have a low base salary, but commissions are the important thing, and they can drop into your lap like coins out of a slot machine.

"The only time I've ever been scared about our finances was that really terrible year right before we moved to Dallas. I was struggling to sell farm equipment to poverty-stricken farmers, and clearly it was a no-win situation. Emotionally I was at rock bottom, but Mary was a trouper.

"That's why I don't understand her terrible depression now. We're at the end of the month right now, so we may be a little short, but by this time next week, we're bound to be back on top."

THE COUNSELOR'S TURN

"During our first two counseling sessions, Pete and Mary brought their two youngest children with them," noted the counselor. "At the end of the second session, I suggested that the next time they leave the babies at home, as their presence in the room was distracting, and Mary in particular couldn't fully focus on what was being discussed.

"At that point Mary informed me that it was always that way. Since there was never any extra cash on hand and baby-sitters could not be paid with credit cards, she and Pete had not spent any time alone since the birth of the new baby.

"With that disclosure, one aspect of her depression became clear to me. Even when Pete was home in the evenings, the needs of the youngsters prevented her from having much in the way of adult companionship.

"The pressures on Mary over the past year had been substantial. Moving from a small town in which she had a support group of other young mothers, she was suddenly confined in a small apartment all day with little children.

"When you added to that her disappointment over losing a home that she had loved and the stress of an unexpected pregnancy, it was easy to see how Mary could have reached a point of such emotional overload that any additional pressure was more than she could handle. The most recent phone call from the bank had been the very last final straw.

"At my insistence, Mary managed to find a neighbor who was willing to keep the children without charge when she and Pete came in for counseling. I then gave Pete and Mary some assignments to do. First, I asked each of them to make a separate list of what they saw as the most important goals for their marriage.

"Their answers presented insights into the diversity of their personalities. Mary listed such long-range goals as working out a budget they could comfortably live within and putting any extra money aside for the children's education. Pete, on the other hand, looked no further ahead than the end of the month.

"The second exercise I gave Pete and Mary was one that Mary herself had tried previously but unsuccessfully to establish; it was to sit down together and itemize all their day-to-day expenditures, everything from the monthly car payment and food to cosmetics and toiletries.

"Making this detailed list of expenses was a painful experience for Mary and a shocking one for happy-go-lucky Pete, who was confronted for the very first time with indisputable evidence that although he was earning good money, he was not in control of the situation as he had thought. He turned to Mary and announced in total horror, 'According to this, every single month we're going in the hole!'

"'He sees it!' Mary told me triumphantly at our next session. 'After all these years, Pete finally sees it!' Once Pete realized that they did indeed have a financial problem, he agreed to set aside all his credit cards (Mary had never used them) and adopt a pay-as-you-go system.

"I then provided them with a set of printed guidelines that had been put together by experts in financial planning. With those as a model, he and Mary drew up a commonsense plan that would allow them not only to live within their means, but also to make regular deposits into a savings account.

"It was important, too, for this couple to reestablish effective communication by spending time alone together, sharing feelings, and truly listening to each other.

"At my suggestion, they included in their monthly budget a specific amount to be used for themselves only, so that one night each week they could hire a baby-sitter and go out to dinner.

"In addition to seeing Pete and Mary together, I also had some sessions alone with Mary, during which we concentrated on the issue of her submissiveness. Mary needed to assume a more adult role in her marriage. She soon realized that she had the right to stand up to—and make reasonable demands of—her husband without having to resort to childish pouting.

"Pete, for his part, had to realize that the college beauty queen he had married was more than a Barbie doll. He needed to start listening to his wife's concerns and treating her as an equal.

"I saw Pete and Mary, either individually or together, a total of eleven times. When they terminated counseling, they were well on the way to forming a healthy, happy, well-balanced partnership, in which Mary had veto power over Pete's impulsive spending habits. Mary's depression had lifted markedly and she was feeling like her former energetic self. When I talked with her one year later, she proudly announced that, despite a few minor setbacks, she and Pete were now routinely operating in the black financially and had invested some of their savings wisely."

MONEY STYLES

Just thinking about money can send some people over the edge. For Mary, caring for so many small children, an unexpected pregnancy, and losing a home she loved had brought her to a point of such emotional overload that any additional pressure—such as that phone call from the bank—was more than she could handle. But a key problem for this couple was that they each looked at money very differently. We all have our own money personalities. Sometimes just understanding that there are different styles can ease a couple's tension.

- **Money hoarders can't bear to part with a penny.**

- **Money spenders can't seem to save anything.**

- **Money obsessors can't stop thinking about money, even if their piggy bank is full. Why are they working so hard? They can't enjoy the fruits of their labor.**

- **Money avoiders can't stand to think or talk about money. Balancing a checkbook brings on an anxiety attack. They prefer not to know about the state of their financial affairs.**

- **Money bingers are part hoarder, part spender. They save and save, then blow it all.**

"MY HUSBAND IS HAVING A MID-LIFE CRISIS"

Jo was frantic when Mark kept postponing his job hunt. But while financial problems precipitated their current crisis, other long-buried issues were also driving a wedge between them.

JO'S TURN

"When you hear what I have to say, you're not going to like me at all," said Jo, forty-four, a beautiful woman with an uncanny resemblance to actress Sigourney Weaver.

"I've been married for almost twenty-five years to the absolutely most wonderful man in the world. I love him very much, but three years ago Mark's parents died, and he quit his job soon after that—now he refuses to look for another. I'm afraid our marriage is not going to survive.

"I met Mark the summer after I graduated from high school. I was working at the five-and-ten-cent store. My best friend was dating Mark's first cousin, so they got us together. Mark is one of the genuinely good, kind people in this world. He makes me feel very loved, very needed; I never felt that way with my parents.

"I was the younger of two girls. My sister, Anna, was very bright and I always felt I had to be as good in school as she was. But school was a struggle for me; I'm dyslexic, though we didn't know it at the time. So while my parents never came right out and said 'You're not as smart as Anna,' I knew they felt that way.

"But Anna was also very depressed—when she was in her teens, she was diagnosed as being schizophrenic. My parents were always so wrapped up in her and her problems that I was ignored.

"My parents were happily married until my father's hardware business went bankrupt, when I was about twelve years old. Then the fighting started between them, the harsh words, always over money.

"When I met Mark, I believed there was no doubt that our marriage was different from my parents. We dated for about a year, got engaged when I was nineteen, married when I was twenty. We went to Florida on our honeymoon. It was a wonderful trip, although we were both inexperienced sexually. In fact, our sex life has always been so-so. But it's not an issue for us. I think we're asexual. We make love maybe once a month.

"So anyway, we moved into a small apartment, and really, our life was perfect. We had two beautiful daughters, Susan and Tricia, three years apart. When our apartment became too small, we moved to a nice split-level on a corner lot in a new subdivision. We lived the typical suburban life. Then the girls grew up, went away to college, got married. They both live nearby. I was starting to get a little bored, so when my friend suggested I work in her store selling tennis and exercise clothes, I said terrific, what a great idea. I've been there for over three years now, and I really love it.

"Like I said, things were going along just fine until Mark's parents died. First his father, and then, a few months later, his mother suffered a stroke. She was ill for about a year before she passed away.

"Then one day, out of the blue, Mark tells me he's decided to quit his job. For years he'd worked in the office-supply business owned by his uncle—his father's brother, for whom Mark's father had also worked. He said he was going to manage his father's so-called investments and look for something—and I quote—'that allows me to be my own man.' And he insisted we move into his parents' house, which is falling down.

"Well, it's been almost two years now and he mostly sits around the house, staring at the TV. He complains that I talk on the phone too much, but what does he do all day? Why, he plays the stock market! I think we should keep our money very safe. This is not the time to take chances. Even though our expenses are much lower these days, my salary is not enough to live on. What about retirement? And although I'd never bring it up, I think it upsets Mark that I'm supporting us now.

"A few months ago, I told him I wanted to sell the house and move to an apartment. The repairs here are astronomical and we really don't need all this space.

"Well, Mark refuses to sell. He won't even discuss it with me. It's always been hard to find out what's on Mark's mind or what he's really thinking about, but now he's more distant than ever.

"What makes me nuts is that Mark acts as if we don't have a care in the world. Here I am, worried sick about money, and we'll go to dinner with friends—and he'll pick up the check! Or he'll go grocery shopping and buy fresh pasta that costs three times as much as the packaged kind.

"We've been fighting a lot, but mostly going round in circles. So ten days ago I walked out. How else was I going to get through to him? I went to live with my daughter Susan.

"Mark went crazy when I did that, so I came back but insisted we get counseling. Is this what they call a mid-life crisis?"

MARK'S TURN

"I just can't sell the house," said Mark, a tall, distinguished-looking man of fifty. "I don't mind doing the repairs. In this house, I feel like a king.

"Of course, that's of no importance to my wife. All she worries about is money. I know her insecurities stem from her father's losing

his money and all. But look, financially speaking, this house is a good investment. Okay, so the real estate market is down right now, but I'm sure it's going to bounce back. You just have to be patient and hang in there.

"I can't seem to convince Jo that there's no reason to panic. We'll never be rich, but we have enough money. We can afford to buy fresh pasta. It really burns me up the way she gets on me for things like that. If I go out for dinner with friends, it makes me feel good to pick up the check once in a while.

"Jo was always hyper—I fell in love with her energy—but now, all that's left is the anxiety. Some days I can't stand to be around her.

"You know, these are the years we looked forward to when the girls were little. Time to enjoy being together, to travel.

"Look, I'm not going to lie to you, I'm not crazy about Jo's working. I was brought up to believe that the man is the provider. So now I'm down on my luck a bit. That'll change. But she's a maniac lately, racing around, always on the phone. She doesn't even acknowledge me when I walk in.

"Jo mentioned our sex life. Well, the simple truth is, I'd like to have sex more often than we do, but Jo's never in the mood. Once she gets going, I know she enjoys it, but I get tired of trying.

"We never used to fight like we

do now. Oh, sure, we'd argue about the usual routine domestic things, but we never had any major problems. Over the years we saw many of our friends get divorced, but I think we always felt like we—and our marriage—were forever.

"Maybe it's me. I've been feeling unhappy for quite a while now. Things got bad when my father died, worse when Mother passed away. My father had taken a lot of, pardon the expression, crap from my uncle, whom he worked for, and I hated the way my uncle patronized my father all those years. He continued to treat me the same way—like dirt. But what was I supposed to do? Quit? With a wife and two kids?

"Still, I inherited a bit of money from my folks, plus this house. It wasn't a fortune by any means, but it was enough that I could stop working, take six months, and figure out what I really wanted to do. What's so bad about that? The girls were done with school and were working on their own.

"Okay, so it's been longer than six months. A lot longer. I've been fooling around a little with the stock market. I've always enjoyed it, and I'm damn good at it if I say so myself. The way Jo talks, of course, you'd think I was into some heavy-duty trading on margin.

"I'm not thrilled with my life, but I don't know what to do with myself. I can't stand the thought of going back to that office grind. I've always wanted to be more of my own man, but . . . I don't know.

"Anyway, I don't need Jo harping on me every second: 'You're lazy . . . you're not motivated.' 'Did you call about this job? Did you look in the paper?'

"Then, last week, Jo walked out and went to stay with Susan. That hurt. I love my daughters and the one thing I can be truly proud of is the relationship I have with them. Now Jo goes there, talking about me, tarnishing it all.

"Maybe we got married too young. People change, grow apart, right? Maybe that's what's happened."

THE COUNSELOR'S TURN

"Yes, Mark is having what has come to be known as a mid-life crisis," said the counselor. "But although Jo and Mark feared their marriage was ending, I felt strongly this was not the case. When I looked at this couple, I saw a long-term caring relationship, and a tremendous amount of love behind the anger.

"I also told them I did not think they would need to be in counseling for a long time. With many couples who have an acute problem—when a husband loses his job, for instance, or when a new baby arrives—I use a form of counseling called crisis intervention. Couples come for a brief period—perhaps eight to ten sessions. We shorten the time spent exploring their individual backgrounds and focus attention on the immediate problem.

"With this form of short-term therapy, I begin by drawing a time line—an actual chart that indicates changes that have taken place over the years. This enabled Jo and Mark to understand more clearly how events in their lives—and the way they reacted to those events—had slowly brought them to a crisis point.

"As far as they were concerned, the immediate problem facing them was whether or not to sell their house. While Jo had no emotional connection to it, for Mark, the house represented not only ties to his parents, but success and achievement, a sense of himself as a man.

"When I first met him, Mark was clearly depressed and phobic about going back to work. An only child, Mark had been a mama's boy, though he also identified with his father, a kind but passive man who had always been beholden to his brother. While Mark had bristled at his uncle's treatment of his father, he nevertheless did what he thought was expected of him and took a job in his uncle's business when it was offered.

"Things went on this way for years. Then, within a short period of time, there were many changes in Mark's life: His parents died . . . he quit his job . . . the children moved out. And finally, his wife, who had always been content to lead the traditional life of the suburban mom, was suddenly working. He felt paralyzed.

"On the other hand, Jo was filled with nervous energy. Her anxiety about money probably started when her father lost his hardware business, but fueling that insecurity was a deep-seated lack of self-confidence.

"As a child, Jo was constantly forced to put her own needs aside; when a person does that, those needs accumulate, often resulting in tension and agitation. Then, too, since she was dyslexic, school was a struggle for her. Though she worked hard, she never felt truly capable.

"Like most women of her generation, Jo looked forward to getting married and having children, and until the girls left home, all this was enough. But for every couple, the empty nest creates an enormous hole in the family, as well as an imbalance in the relationship between husband and wife. Jo and Mark were now forced to relate to each other as individuals. Problems that in the past may have been overlooked rose to the surface.

"What's more, with her daughters on their own, Jo had fewer channels for her energy. Her concern about money grew as she watched her husband whiling away his time day after day, propped up in front of the TV.

"It was to Jo's credit that she, in a sense, instigated the couple's current crisis. She was in effect saying, 'This isn't good enough. We must make some changes.' First, I asked Jo to promise not to involve her daughters in her marital problems. That was unfair to them as well as to Mark. Then I told her that she had to be more sensitive to small things, such as the tone with which she spoke to her husband.

"My next goal was to help Mark find the confidence to embark on a job hunt. (Jo had agreed to postpone any decision about selling the house if Mark would promise to look for a job.) Like many men today who either took early retirement or were forced out of a job due to industry cutbacks, Mark was too young and energetic to sit around doing nothing.

"The fact that I was there to listen to Mark and not judge him helped shore up his confidence and refocus his goals. With Jo's help, he drafted his résumé, set about calling former colleagues and employment agencies, and checked the ads in the newspaper. To his delight, he received several positive responses, and within one week he had scheduled three interviews.

"Mark's self-confidence carried over into his relationship with Jo.

Soft-spoken by nature, he rarely told her when something bothered him. Now, if Jo flew off the handle because he bought an expensive brand of pasta, he pointed out that they could afford it, and besides, it gave him pleasure.

"Jo was thrilled that her husband was finally doing something. But she had a long way to go in learning how to relax. I suggested she buy a small notebook and, throughout the day, jot down all the things she could be happy about—something funny that happened at work, a beautiful garden she saw, anything that gave her pleasure. Although it may sound simple, this exercise helped Jo track the positive things in her life and stop projecting disaster.

"Jo was also suffering from what we refer to as inhibition of sexual desire. She was so tense that she was unable to feel desire. However, once her anxiety lessened, she was more responsive.

"Jo and Mark ended joint counseling after three months, although Mark continued to visit for more career counseling. At his last session, he told me he had been offered a position as a stockbroker trainee at a small, well-regarded firm; he was planning to take the licensing test soon. 'It's a beginner's spot,' he said, 'but I'm my own man. And people trust me. I'll do fine.' There was no doubt in my mind that he would."

WHEN MONEY MATTERS MAGNIFY MARITAL WOES

Mark and Jo needed to understand exactly how outside events can affect a marriage. Recognizing the importance of life stressors—such as losing a job or the death of a parent—is critical in solving marital problems. In this case, the children's growing up and moving out created the first imbalance in the relationship. The death of Mark's parents created another. Problems that may have been overlooked in the past rose to the surface and swamped them both. Instead of facing them together, they blamed each other.

Played out against this backdrop was the immediate problem of Mark's unemployment and Jo's fear that his failure to look for another job would send them careening toward bankruptcy. Marital problems are often magnified when one or both partners are worried about money. And, since money means different things to each of us, we often respond to financial crises in conflicting ways. For Jo, money meant security; without it, she was frantic and lost. For Mark, money meant self-esteem and a sense of himself as a man. Instead of understanding each other's perspective and working together toward a solution, they decided the marriage was over. If similar issues loom large in your marriage:

1. Remember that your spouse is probably just as upset as you are, but he may be dealing with the issues differently (i.e., not talking about it).

2. Acknowledge the strengths your relationship has. Couples whose problems are, in fact, a minor part of their lives sometimes let them overshadow the positive aspects of the marriage. Give yourselves credit for what's good between you.

3. The only person you can change is yourself, so focus on what you can do differently. Jo had to relax and concentrate on those things that gave her pleasure throughout the day instead of dwelling on what her husband was or wasn't doing. Mark needed to have a more positive attitude about his abilities, to shore up his confidence and redirect his goals so he could get back to a job he finds challenging. Looking for a job in the stock market, which had long fascinated him, was his answer. Once he did find a job, Jo felt less anxiety about money and they started enjoying being together.

"He Says I'm a Shopaholic"

—◆—

Linda accused Bob of drinking too much— and he accused her of spending too much. How can a couple ever be close if they each blame the other for their problems?

LINDA'S TURN

"Bob asked me to come here because he thinks I'm the sick one," said Linda, thirty-seven, a petite, soft-spoken brunette, smartly dressed in expensive tailored pants and designer sweater. "He says I'm a shopaholic. Well, I admit I sometimes spend more than I should, but I'm certainly not a compulsive shopper. What does Bob expect from me? I need a little happiness, a little release in my life.

"Besides, Bob only makes matters worse. No, he doesn't abuse me physically, though sometimes the way he degrades me—screaming awful things in public—is just as bad. He seems to get a kick out of belittling me in front of others. Last Sunday, when his brother and sister-in-law came to visit, was the last straw. Hardly a minute went by without Bob making some sort of sarcastic, vulgar remark about how I have no idea about the importance of money. I was utterly humiliated. Just a couple of drinks turns Bob into a maniac; I never know when he's going to turn on me.

"Maybe my mother was right. She predicted from the start that Bob and I would have trouble because we came from such different backgrounds. I'm an only child. My father is a dentist and I grew up in an affluent suburb. My parents made sure I had every possible advantage—piano lessons, nice clothes, trips to the city to see plays and concerts.

"Bob's background is totally different. He's the oldest of six boys, and his father died when he was eighteen. I have to hand it to my mother-in-law, though. She found work here and there and kept her family together. Her life was tough; there was never very much money. But even today I see a real closeness among Bob and his brothers.

"I met Bob at a singles party at a fancy hotel in the city. We hit it off right away. He was so handsome and charming back then; he made me feel beautiful and special. Bob certainly never treated me as horribly then as he does now. We both liked to live well, to go out for dinner and dancing or see a show. And with my job as an executive secretary in a jewelry-design house and his as a builder, we could afford to splurge.

"Ours was a whirlwind courtship—we dated for less than a year. My parents reluctantly agreed to our getting married. We had a small wedding and a reception at a lovely restaurant in town. Through it all, Mother kept calling me a fool. I wish I could ask her advice now, but she died suddenly of a heart attack about a year ago. That's part of my problem. When Mom died, my son, David, was only a few months old. She was to have visited us one afternoon. Well, I waited and waited. I thought she was at the hairdresser, but by midafternoon when she still hadn't arrived and wasn't answering her phone, I called my father at his office. He raced home and found her . . .

"Ironically, this happened when I was truly happy for the first time in a long time. After twelve years of marriage and two miscarriages I had at last given birth to a perfectly healthy child. Bob and I had saved enough money to buy a house; I had decided to quit work to be a full-time mother.

"David was such a terrific baby—for a time he changed things for Bob and me. Almost as soon as we were married, Bob started picking on me, mostly about money. It seems like 'Bank your check for the house' was all I ever heard. Sometimes I'd get so frustrated after having worked hard and not having a penny to spend that I'd just snap and charge a few things. Once we got a little into debt because of that. Of course, Bob never lets me forget it.

"After the baby was born, though, Bob calmed down and focused on his son. He really is a great daddy and that softened my mother. But after she died, I was torn up with grief. My father's sudden decision to retire didn't help. He closed his practice and moved in with us because he couldn't stand being in a house with so many memories. Dad said he didn't want to rent his house, that he'd go back any day. But the weeks turned into months, and he's still with us.

"By this time, Bob had started his own contracting business, which is seasonal, and it wasn't doing well at all. So the men would sit at the dinner table talking about money troubles, or my father would go on about losing Mother. No one realized that perhaps I was hurting, too—that maybe I needed a little stroking. Whenever I dared to cry, Bob would say, 'Snap out of it,' give me a withering look, and leave the room. I was starting to resent him, and our sex life was nonexistent.

"One day after Bob had left for work, I realized I was out of diapers and milk, so I bundled up the baby and headed for the supermarket. On the way, I had to pass an elegant shopping arcade. Before I knew what I was doing, I had parked the car, and the rest is history. I forget how much I spent, but I hit my credit limit. In the back of my mind I knew it was crazy—but I also knew I needed some happiness to hold myself together.

"Anyway, when I got home that afternoon, I hung up all my new clothes without even cutting the tags. Then Bob came home and announced that he'd made reservations for us at a new restaurant in town. I was thrilled—it was just like the old days. I rushed to call a sitter—Dad could never handle the baby alone—and got dressed. I was so excited because we hadn't been out together in ages, but the evening turned into a nightmare.

"Bob ordered one martini, then another. He told me that his brother would be visiting for a few days. I made the most innocent remark—

something like 'Well, I could cook the first few nights, then we could order in Chinese food or eat out,' but Bob went completely berserk. He shouted obscenities at me so loud that the maître d' had to ask him to lower his voice. I was mortified, of course, and could barely eat the food in front of me.

"Somehow we made it through the meal in silence. But when we got home and Bob saw the dresses hanging in the closet, he went nuts again. Why didn't I hide the clothes? I don't know. I felt awful, but I just didn't know what to say.

"One thing I'm sure of, though: Bob is no saint. Maybe if I could get away from him and his drunken tirades, I wouldn't need to cheer myself up with new clothes. I don't want my marriage to end, but I don't know how to make it better either."

BOB'S TURN

"Okay, you've heard Linda's sob story about how I'm a heartless husband who yells at his poor little wife every time she buys a few clothes," said Bob, who looks much younger than his forty years. "Well, I won't pretend I don't blow up now and then, but I can take only so much.

"Linda casually mentioned that she once charged more than our credit limit—but she didn't bother to say that her purchases put us eleven thousand dollars in debt! Eleven thousand dollars! I had to go crawling to her old man and ask for help. How do you think that made me feel? It was as much as admitting I couldn't keep his little girl in the style to which she was accustomed. Well, that's not the way it is, believe me.

"The way Linda spends money is like a disease. She never keeps receipts, charges here and there, never records her checks. Before she realizes it, she's blown a fortune. And everything I say to her falls on deaf ears.

"I make a decent living, and Linda did help out all those years we were saving for the house. But then she had a couple of miscarriages, which were hard on her, although she showed gumption. She reminded me of my mother; I was proud of her. The sprees started after the miscarriages.

"The funny thing is, I love to see Linda all dressed up. Her sense of style is part of what attracted me to her in the first place. She was the prettiest, classiest woman I had ever seen. I could tell she came from the right side of the tracks, not that I lived in the slums or anything. But after my dad died, it wasn't easy. I sort of became the man around the house, and I always worked to help my mother.

"Still, I managed to earn my associate's degree at a community college before striking out on my own. I like to live the good life and it felt great to have a a nice, fat paycheck, to buy some clothes and to be able to take women out. When I met Linda I knew she was the one for me. Her parents wouldn't hear of it; they thought I wasn't good enough. It wasn't until David was born that my mother-in-law started warming up to me. She doted on him and bought him all these silly outfits. Finally, she and I had something in common. We could talk about David.

"It was quite a shock to all of us when she died, but Linda still can't get over it. After a while, I just couldn't take her constant depression. To make matters worse, my father-in-law moved in. When he's not quizzing me on my finances, he's moaning about missing his wife.

"I really can't believe these people. My mother was tough through the worst circumstances, so I find it hard to sympathize with Linda. What kind of a spoiled brat is she, anyway? I'm sorry her mother died, but she's a mother herself now and she should get on with her life.

"So what's her solution? She shops for clothes she doesn't need. I know I shouldn't complain about her spending habits in front of others, but once in a while, if I've had a drink or two, my anger spills out. Linda had the nerve to suggest I have a drinking problem. That's ridiculous. I don't even drink every day. Anyway, if she didn't provoke me with her shopping sprees, I wouldn't lose my temper, booze or no booze.

"Sometimes I've thought about leaving Linda, but it goes against my upbringing. Besides, what would it solve? I have to think about my son. I can just picture sending a child-support check, knowing Linda would blow it in one afternoon. I don't know if we can resolve our problems, but I want to try."

THE COUNSELOR'S TURN

"Bob and Linda's marriage was a classic example of each partner having a serious personal problem but completely refusing to acknowledge it, preferring instead to blame the spouse," said the counselor.

"Linda rejected the label of compulsive shopper, telling herself she deserved nice things to make up for her difficult life. Similarly, Bob insisted he didn't have an alcohol problem. Like many people, he believed only those who 'need' a drink every day can get into trouble with liquor.

"As a result of this double deception, both partners were extremely angry when they first came to my office. Traumatized by her husband's verbal attacks, Linda felt unjustly portrayed as someone with an emotional illness. Bob saw himself as a martyr who not only had to scramble to raise the money to cover his

wife's tracks but then got bawled out for relaxing with a few drinks.

"Before any progress could be made, they both had to face their own shortcomings as well as to recognize how they contributed to each other's problems.

"It took several sessions before Bob admitted he didn't handle liquor well. Many people mistakenly believe that frequent and excessive alcohol consumption are the only symptoms of alcoholism. However, people like Bob, who showed disturbing personality changes after only a few drinks, also have a problem with alcohol.

"Although it was true that Bob drank only once in a while, when he did, he lost control. At these times, Linda couldn't talk to him and she never knew when he would launch another vicious attack.

"To help Bob better understand his problem, I referred him to several publications on alcoholism. Impressed by this information, he promised to work hard at controlling his drinking. Over the next few months, even Linda agreed that he had gotten a grip on his problem and was drinking less.

"It was also crucial for Bob to understand how unreasonable he was to expect Linda to be a carbon copy of his mother. People react differently to stress, I told him, and Linda needed someone to turn to, someone to listen to her expressions of sadness or anxiety. Furthermore, she shouldn't have been made to feel guilty about it.

"Meanwhile, Linda had to admit to her 'addiction' as well as develop her resources and inner strengths. Grieving for her mother and saddled with the needs of her baby and her father, she felt overwhelmed. Bob's outbursts made her even more miserable. She relied on shopping as a way to ease her stress.

"Linda also had to understand, however, that it was inexcusable to spend beyond her means. The obvious band-aid treatment for her compulsive shopping was to cancel all her credit cards. At first, Bob kept his. But when Linda began pleading with him for permission to buy this or that, he cut up his cards too. Now they operate on a cash-only basis. All money is deposited into a joint account; both partners reconcile the checkbook at the end of the month so they have accurate records.

"Although initially upset about this arrangement, Linda was relieved after a while to have such a simple system for controlling her shopping impulses. She now manages the household budget very well. Linda occasionally puts something on layaway, but she no longer runs up huge bills. Once their finances had stabilized and Bob's drinking was under control, general tensions in the household eased.

"Linda, however, still had to find some way to boost her confidence. The answer was a part-time job as an assistant buyer in a local boutique. During counseling, Bob revealed that he resented it that Linda had stopped working when the baby was born, especially because she continued to overspend his hard-earned money. Linda, too, admitted—reluctantly at first—that she was lonely and missed the general camaraderie of an office.

"Their solution was to find a neighborhood play group in which David, not yet two, could spend three mornings a week while Linda worked. Not surprisingly, she's delighted with her job and has developed a deeper sense of personal satisfaction. At my urging, she also encouraged her father to move back to his own house, where a part-time companion helps with the cleaning and cooking. He visits on weekends, so the day-to-day strain of having him around is gone.

"Linda and Bob were in counseling for about a year. In the last few months, they were able to recapture the attraction that brought them together in the first place. Each week, they set aside some money for dinner and dancing as they used to. Their renewed closeness fills a void for Linda, and she no longer feels the need to substitute clothes for love.

"I could tell by the way they exchanged glances and squeezed hands at our last session that their marriage, which had had so many strikes against it, had indeed been saved."

TIT FOR TAT

Linda and Bob each have a serious problem but refuse to acknowledge it completely, what mental health experts call "owning" the problem. Linda, grieving for her mother and saddled with the care of a baby and a despondent father, is understandably overwhelmed. People handle stress in myriad ways and Linda needs somone to listen to her expressions of sadness or anxiety without being made to feel guilty about them. Nevertheless, if she has any hope of saving her marriage, she must admit that she has a habit of overspending.

Similarly, Bob clearly has a problem with alcohol and acknowledging it is the first step in controlling it. The only way these two can end the tit-for-tat cycle is to accept the part each plays in the marital drama.

The following questions can serve as a reality check for any couple if they are answered honestly:

1. Are you spending time and energy trying to support your version of events?

2. When your spouse is upset with you, do you find yourself reacting defensively almost automatically? Do you fling back old accusations and complaints rather than face the current problem?

3. When you argue, are your comments targeted at your husband's character rather than his behavior? Saying "You're such a jerk," or "How could you be so stupid?" won't help you solve your problem but it will cause him to tune you out or become even more convinced that he's right.

If you've answered yes to these questions, you may not be owning up to your part of the problem. In a quiet moment, try arguing your partner's side. Couples often find that they do agree with some of their mate's positions, although they are loath to admit it.

"WE ALWAYS FIGHT ABOUT MONEY"

Mary Beth was proud of the way she handled the family finances in Jerry's absence. But the changes she made infuriated her husband—and set the stage for their current battles.

MARY BETH'S TURN

"Try to imagine how it feels to know your husband is sorry he ever married you," said Mary Beth, thirty, an apple-cheeked brunette with wholesome good looks. "Oh, Jerry doesn't say that flat out, but actions speak louder than words. For one thing, he keeps his money all to himself, just the way he did when he was single, and for another, he won't even talk about us having a baby. Does that sound like a man who has made a commitment?

"I admit I was the one who pushed for us to get married. We had been living together for two years and I was worried that, for all intents and purposes, my kids considered him their father. My daughter, who is eight, and my son, now five, were so little when my ex-husband deserted us, they never knew him. So to them, Jerry was Daddy. For their sake, I felt it was time either to make everything legal or end the relationship.

"Jerry finally gave in. He was pushing thirty, and before he met me he had played the field. When he first asked me and the kids to move into his house, he told me he was surprised how much he wanted to be with me. He had always thought of himself as a confirmed bachelor. Well, the months turned to years, and it was clear that Jerry was a wonderful man. Oh, we had our share of differences—he's a neatnik and I'm something of a clutterbug, and he's got more of a sex drive than I do—but basically we got along great. I wonder if we were both making assumptions and putting up with certain things back then because we hadn't tied the knot.

"I'll give you a for instance. We never pooled our money. We never had any real reason to talk about finances since we're each pretty well set. Jerry has a good job as a mechanic for Boeing. I do all right with my salary as a dental hygienist, plus child support. My ex-husband's employer garnishees his salary, so the checks come right on time. Still, I figured Jerry and I would put our money in one pot when we were husband and wife. One thing we did talk about was having a baby of our own, although the discussions were always kind of vague.

"Jerry finally gave me an engagement ring for Christmas, and we planned a spring wedding. But in January, the Persian Gulf War started, and Jerry, who's in the Marine Corps Reserves, was called to active duty. We sat up all night talking and crying. Jerry said we had to marry before he shipped out. He was afraid to leave me and the kids unless he knew we'd be taken care of.

"We found a justice of the peace who married us. Jerry insisted we open a joint account and arranged for me to have power of attorney. Between Boeing and the Marines, Jerry would continue to get a regular salary, and he arranged to have it deposited directly into our account so I'd have access if I needed it.

"Then he sat me down at the kitchen table and explained all the finances. Until then, I had paid for the kids' clothes and the food and laundry supplies, but Jerry had been handling big-ticket items, like the mortgage and the insurance.

"Three days later he was gone. I don't think I slept a full night the whole time he was overseas. But if I do say so myself, I did a great job of keeping things together. I even improved his bill-paying system and never missed a payment. I was sure he'd be proud of me.

"Now figure this. He gets home, we have this emotional welcome, and the very next day he closes out the joint account and says he's taking over again. He didn't thank me or say one word about how I had managed.

"In fact, he was furious that I had 'splurged,' as he put it, on a pair of recliners for the den. We had always talked about how much we wanted those chairs but that they were too expensive. I had handled the money so carefully I was able to use some of our income-tax refund to buy them. Instead of being thrilled, he accused me of being an impulse shopper.

"He said he'd had a lot of time to think during the war, and he'd changed his mind about our having a child; he couldn't handle the financial responsibility.

"I know Jerry grew up poor. His dad was a logger who made a good living, but with eight kids, there wasn't much to go around. Jerry was the youngest and he's always talking about how he had a paper route from the time he was seven and hasn't stopped working since. Fine, but the past is the past. I know many people were laid off at Boeing, but I don't think Jerry's job is in jeopardy.

"My family was a little better off than Jerry's since my parents owned a stationery store, but we weren't rich. I helped out in the store from the time I was little. It didn't scar me for life. He's frantic about money, as if we were going to starve to death.

"Anyway, at first I was very depressed about Jerry, but then I talked myself into believing he was having trouble adjusting to being back. I'd try to comfort him, but he never responded. Sometimes we'd have sex, but it wasn't lovemaking. Not the way it used to be. He could have been with any woman.

"In the meantime, I had to stop taking the Pill. For a while, we relied on a diaphragm, but that drove us crazy. Jerry didn't want to use a condom. Finally, my doctor suggested I try the new implant. Though it's been in use for about fifteen years in Europe, it's only been available here for a few years. Supposedly it's safe, with a minimum of side effects. Well, maybe it's just me, but I think gaining ten pounds, feeling bloated, and growing a mustache qualify as more than minimal. But I put up with all that

because the doctor assured me the side effects would subside. Secretly, though, I hoped Jerry would agree to have a baby.

"I started to get more and more resentful of the way he was treating me. He's on my back about everything—cleaning the house, doing the laundry—and nothing I do is right anymore. The other day I was late going to a meeting at school and I ran out and forgot to lock the door. I never heard the end of that one.

"I really thought this time I had made the right choice. But our life is a charade. There's no love, no affection, just constant bickering. I'd rather be alone with my kids."

JERRY'S TURN

"Mary Beth has got it into her head that I wish I hadn't married her, but that's not the truth," said Jerry, thirty-one, a handsome man with a full beard. "The war didn't force me into anything; it just made me do it sooner. I loved her too much to leave her a single mother, and I can't understand why she doesn't see that.

"But I suppose the war did get us off to a weird start. As she said, I gave her power of attorney so she could handle everything while I was gone. But I never meant for things to stay that way. Look, she did a fine job, but it was foolish to spend an entire tax refund on two chairs. I don't believe in splurging unless you have the resources to do it. To be blunt, I don't think Mary Beth is responsible enough to make important life decisions. I love her, but she's flighty. She seems to have more than enough on her hands just keeping the house clean and the meals on the table without burdening her with other responsibilities. Besides, I make most of the money and I think I should handle it. It's a man's responsibility to be the provider and I intend to fulfill my obligations.

"That's one reason I stayed single as long as I did. I didn't want to end up like my father, always struggling to feed a huge family. I hated being poor and, Catholic or not, I don't think you should have kids if you can't give them a decent life.

"So I sowed my wild oats in my twenties. But when I hit thirty, I wanted to settle down with someone special. I met Mary Beth at a friend's party, and she was so bubbly and pretty, I let myself fall in love. The fact that she had two little kids scared me a bit, but once we started living together, I fell in love with them, too. They mean as much to me now as if they were my own flesh and blood.

"When Mary Beth saw how good I was with the children, she started lobbying for one of our own. I never said yes, and I never said no. I was pretty sure, though, that in this economy, two is all we could handle.

What about college? I have no idea if her ex-husband will pay for that. What about a wedding for Stacy? Add one of our own . . . forget it. Sure, my job seems secure. But you see these pink slips all around you and read the horror stories in the paper; if you're smart, you don't live beyond your means. Besides, if Mary Beth had a new baby to care for, she'd have to cut back on her hours, and that means even less money.

"This baby thing is ruining our sex life. Mary Beth has this idea that if you're not going to have a child, then you shouldn't make love. I heard all that when I was growing up, too, but I don't agree with it. Besides, I was celibate in that desert for five months and I admit I came home wanting to make love two or three times a day. Of course, I don't want her to be feeling sick because of the birth control, but that means we'll just have to find a method that works for us.

"I know I haven't been myself since I got back. I'm jumpy and I have nightmares. I don't know what to do about it. But I do know she's making a mountain out of a molehill about this money stuff. Before I went away, we did just fine.

"To be perfectly honest, I think I've put up with a lot of things other husbands wouldn't. The lack of sex is one thing; there's also the fact that Mary Beth is a total, well, slob. It's not just that she leaves junk everywhere. She does stuff that is totally irresponsible and sometimes even dangerous. She'll leave her curling iron plugged in all day or the front door unlocked. I've talked to her over and over again about this, but nothing changes. Which is why I'm not thrilled about letting her handle the money. I still think she was rising to the occasion, so to speak, and on a regular basis, I'm not convinced I could trust her.

"You know, now that I'm here saying all this, I really don't know what she's all worked up about. I don't want a divorce, although Mary Beth seems intent on heading us toward one."

THE COUNSELOR'S TURN

"I would have phrased it differently than Jerry did, but this marriage did get off to a bad start," said the counselor. "However, this couple would have had problems even if the war hadn't pushed up their wedding date.

"Although they had lived together in what they honestly believed was a trial marriage, like many couples in a similar position, they had not actually given their relationship a fair test. Assuming that love conquered all, they had failed to discuss the nitty-gritty aspects of their marriage—primarily issues relating to money and children—that are key to a strong relationship.

"For instance, they had never talked about money or how it would

be handled, how much they should save or what kind of budget they needed. If they had, Mary Beth would have realized early on that Jerry's need for financial security, as well as his entrenched belief that a man must be the provider, had to be confronted. They might have realized that Jerry's reluctance to let Mary Beth handle the money had a lot to do with what he saw as her irresponsible behavior—leaving the door unlocked, for instance. They also had never discussed their hopes and dreams for the future, which included how large a family they wanted to have.

"My first job was to get both of them to identify the sources of their conflict and then help them learn to reach a mutually satisfying compromise. To do this, I asked each of them to write down their responses to a set of questions. Among the questions: Who should manage the money in your relationship? How much money should each partner contribute to the family account every month? Do you want to put your savings aside first? The questionnaire also touches on life-choice issues: How often do you want to have sex? How many children would you like to have? What personal habits of your partner do you find annoying? Which habits of yours bother him? The point of the questionnaire is not that you and your spouse should agree on everything, but that you should be aware of your differences.

Mary Beth and Jerry took this assignment very seriously. They not only came to the next session with answers to every question, but they had taken the time to highlight and talk about their disagreements. At this point, I was able to show them that Jerry's need for security was prudent, albeit slightly exaggerated. I suggested that they spend several weeks writing down how much they spent each day so they could see where their money went and then plan a workable budget. Once they did, Jerry was relieved to see that they were actually in better shape than he had imagined. He relaxed his grip on the purse strings and let Mary Beth share in the financial decisions. The one stipulation: She had to make every effort to prove her maturity by being less careless about those things that irked Jerry. Mary Beth agreed, since she now understood that her behavior, which she had always thought to be rather harmless, had seemed to Jerry immature.

"I then began some of the more difficult work: looking into the source of their conflicts. For several weeks we talked about their families, and it became clear that Mary Beth really hadn't felt the pinch of poverty in the same way Jerry had. Nonetheless, she had been convinced their backgrounds were similar. 'Just because you were both raised in large Catholic families doesn't mean your experiences were the same,' I told her. Gradually, she felt more compassion for Jerry and was able to understand why the mere thought of having his money mismanaged could cause him anxiety. She was then able to reassure him that she respected his point of view and would be prudent and honest in her dealings with the finances. This simple assertion brought a visible look of relief to Jerry's face.

"At this point we were able to tackle the subject of having a child. Mary Beth told him that the biggest reason she wanted a baby was that she loved him so much and wished on some level beyond reason that she could bear his child. Jerry, the tough Marine, was moved to tears.

"Jerry was having real adjustment problems related to his service in the Gulf War. It isn't necessary to be engaged in combat to suffer stress from a war. At my suggestion, he joined a group for veterans led by another psychologist, and Jerry has found it comforting to talk to others in similar situations. His nightmares have ceased and he and Mary Beth have once again begun to enjoy a loving sex life.

"This couple ended counseling after a year. The last time I spoke with Mary Beth she told me she'd had the birth control implant removed—with Jerry's blessing—and she was hoping to become pregnant soon."

A CEASE-FIRE IN THE MONEY WARS

Many couples find that finances are a prime source of friction. And, like Mary Beth and Jerry, many couples never really discuss the financial facts of their lives: How do they each feel about money? What's a financial necessity and what's a luxury? How should money be handled and who should handle what? What are their long-range financial goals? If Jerry and Mary Beth had done this, they would have discovered that although they had very different ideas about saving and spending, perhaps they could have resolved these differences before they became too divisive.

If this couple's plight sounds all too familiar, take the time to sit down together with bank statements, pencil, paper, and calculator and draw up a workable budget that you can stick to. You may have to spend a few weeks jotting down what you each spend during the day so you can see where every penny goes. Most of us are aware of the big expenses but it's the smaller ones—dry cleaning or drugstore items—that slip by but add up. Write down your fixed costs: rent, mortgage payments, childcare expenses, insurance. Then include costs that are more flexible: entertainment, clothing, food, and so on. What can you cut out—or cut back? If you've made a realistic budget, you should be able to put aside money for savings every month as well as have money for emergencies. Determine who's going to handle which payments and be sure to put some money into a personal spending account for each of you so you aren't obliged to consult each other on every minor expense. However, always discuss significant purchases or investments. Revise your budget and investment plans if your family or job situation changes.

When discussing money, try to be businesslike, not emotional. Avoid blaming and labeling—calling your spouse a tightwad or saying he spends money like a drunken sailor, for instance, is not conducive to cooperation.

Most important, no matter how tight money is, reserve a small amount for pleasure. Even if you go out once a week to a movie or for pizza—just the two of you—you'll feel better about your relationship in general if you indulge yourselves once in a while.

"FINANCIAL PRESSURES ARE RUINING OUR MARRIAGE"

Martha blamed Hobart for financial mismanagement, while he accused her of being too extravagant. What happens when the economy becomes a scapegoat for a couple's real problems?

"Our financial plight is shattering my dreams of a happy home," said thirty-two-year-old Martha, a plump, five-foot blonde. "My husband, Hobart, and I used to get along beautifully. Now we argue all the time about money.

"Although Hobey and I earn a very good income, we're living from paycheck to paycheck, so meeting monthly bills is a constant juggling act. I once thought I'd be able to stay home with my children—a three-year-old daughter and a nineteen-month-old son—but we just can't afford for me to quit work.

"A few years ago, our income would have seemed like a fortune. These days every penny is swallowed up by taxes, car installments, mortgage payments, and child support for Hobey's first wife. Then there's the cost of childcare, and prescriptions for Hobey's asthma.

"We have no stocks, bonds, or

231

savings of any kind. Our only asset is our home, which is in an okay neighborhood and has two rental units. The property, however, is badly in need of repair. Since we can't afford to hire professional help, Hobey has to do the work in his spare time. I think we should raise the rents to cover the repairs. Hobey agrees, but he says nothing to the tenants, and we stay broke.

"In the last two years, I've worked like a slave and received three salary advances. Considering gas allowances, I probably net more than Hobey, but I'm not sure. We don't track our finances that closely, although I know we should. Hobey just won't do it. He avoids figures like the plague. I have to balance our joint checking account every month, a maddening assignment.

"In my opinion, Hobey is supposed to be the head of the family and should do the household bookkeeping. He admits he took charge of everything in his first marriage. I insisted he pay the bills for at least six months. While looking through his briefcase for a stamp recently, I ran across the unopened bills, every single one. We had to pay late penalties on all our charge accounts. Hobey apologized, saying he had forgotten about it. Consequently, I began paying the bills again, but his casual attitude galled me.

"Hobey seems totally unlike the man I married. When we met, he was supervisor of personnel in a big aeronautics company. I was a lowly, pea-in-the-pod stenographer. He picked me to head the stenographic pool and I was thrilled. He told me I was the brightest, most efficient lady he had ever met—and bing! I fell in love with him.

"At that time, we were both in the process of divorce. His wife, a spoiled rich girl, had grabbed their baby girl and run to her parents, leaving him with a pile of debts. I was ending a two-year struggle to make something of my ex, a mama's boy and pseudo-college student who never cracked a book, while I cooked, cleaned, and supported us. Compared to him, Hobey struck me as the greatest guy on earth.

"For a long while, I regarded Hobey not only as a husband but as a mentor. When he suggested that the aeronautics company didn't offer me sufficient scope, I transferred to my present job with a small public relations firm.

"Hobey, on the other hand, has been stuck in the same personnel slot at the aeronautics company for ten years. He can count on an annual raise, but no bonuses, nothing extra. Even though he knows how badly we've been hit by inflation, he freezes when I urge him to change jobs. I listened to Hobey. Why can't he listen to me?

"I'm beginning to feel that a lot of things are unfair in our relationship. Hobey works a regular nine-to-five shift, while I often put in ten- or twelve-hour days. Nevertheless, the children are considered my job. I bring them to the pediatrician, the dentist, and their sitters every morning. The other night I was busy on the phone with a dissatisfied client, so he gave them their baths. Afterward, I meekly thanked him because he expected it.

"All Hobey ever does is criticize me for being extravagant. I did go overboard at Christmas, but so did he. He gave his father a $300 camera and he bought the kids twice as many toys as I did. Yet he complains that I spend too much on their clothes. I do buy them nice outfits, but they look so darling, and I'm so proud of them I can't resist.

"I really try to be thrifty, but Hobey doesn't appreciate my efforts. Not long ago I drove a few miles out of my way to buy a month's supply of diapers at a considerable discount. Hobey called me 'Mrs. Pennypincher,' spoiling all my pleasure in the saving. Later that evening, he told me I should clip grocery coupons to economize, although that requires hours of time. Well, I got mad. I handed him a pair of scissors and pointed to a pile of newspapers in the basement where he was working. Furious, he threw the scissors on the floor and cursed me.

"I think we're both under too much pressure. We can't afford to do anything that's relaxing or fun. Recently, Hobey made plans for us to weekend in San Francisco. When I

discovered the cheapest hotel accommodations were $100 a night, I canceled the trip. Up until the last minute, I hoped Hobey would talk me into going, but he didn't.

"Nowadays, we don't even have sex. I'm only in the mood when I wake up at dawn. The other morning, I felt so warm and loving, I kissed Hobey awake. He kissed me back and then promptly fell asleep. That evening he was of a different mind, but I was too beat to be responsive. When he put his arms around me, I pushed him off, expecting him to press me the way he usually does. He turned away without a word, and I had a dreadful feeling he was losing interest altogether.

"I'm terrified that our constant bickering over finances is wrecking our relationshp—but I don't know what to do about it."

HOBART'S TURN

"I admit our financial situation isn't ideal, but Martha's worries are ridiculous," said thirty-eight-year-old Hobart, a tall, thin man with curly red hair. "Our marriage is secure. I just wish my wife would stop acting so childishly.

"When I first knew her, Martha seemed so extraordinarily capable, I thought she would be a helpmate. Some of the time she carries more than her share of the load, while other times she shrugs off responsibility like a six-year-old. By insisting that I pay the bills, for example, she's trying to protect herself from the appalling total—specifically, her contributions.

"One time I opened a bill from an exclusive children's shop and discovered my wife had blown $700 in one afternoon. She bought our year-old son a handmade, imported cowboy outfit—a $400 purchase he outgrew in two months. Our three-year-old daughter received six pairs of designer jeans at $50 a crack—six pairs, Martha explained, so she wouldn't waste her time laundering toddler fashion jeans every day.

"Then and there, I quit doing the family bookkeeping. She is just as efficient as I am; indeed, she is more so. Our credit is still A-1, thanks to her expert installment juggling.

"Inflation has forced us, like most other people, to adjust our plans. I doubt, however, that Martha ever seriously intended to stay home with the kids. She loves her job and detests housework. She is considerably more career-oriented than I am and is always at me to get ahead.

"Naturally, I would prefer a fatter paycheck, but my job has advantages that Martha overlooks. I'm out by five o'clock so I can work on the house, and I have job security. Also, I have no wish to get caught in the upper-management rat race and wind up with an ulcer. My asthma is enough of a health problem.

"Although I'm told I came into the world wheezing, I blame my breathing difficulties on the tensions of growing up with my father, a hard-nosed Army colonel. He was constantly pushing me, his only son, to be an athlete. He coached me in football, baseball, wrestling, and track, but I never made the team. To add to my humiliation, the colonel predicted I would fail at everything as an adult. Last Christmas, his eyes popped when I gave him a $300 camera, while his gift to us was a singing tea kettle from the PX.

"Martha and I are doing a lot better than my old man on his Army pension. We have substantial equity in our home, a valuable property that impresses the hell out of my father. When I eventually complete the repairs, the place will be worth double what it cost two years ago.

"I wish we could afford to hire professional help to speed up the renovation. The bathrooms in both rental units are disasters and the tenants are long overdue the showers I promised them. As soon as I can pay a plumber, I'll be able to raise the low rents.

"The messy repair work is hard on Martha, but she should remember that it's not easy on me either. The minute supper dishes are done, she and the kids sack out while my job as handyman is just beginning. She doesn't appreciate the labor and sweat involved.

"I try to be patient with Martha and I think she ought to be understanding toward me. I'm so busy at night painting and plastering that I usually don't get to bed until after midnight. So when Martha wakes up at dawn wanting sex, I'm too exhausted to open an eye. The next evening, I'm myself again, but she's tired and cross and I'm left frustrated.

"Martha and I are going through a tough time now, but tough times pass. I'm confident our marriage will outlast the bad economy."

THE COUNSELOR'S TURN

"Nowadays, financial problems cause many couples to seek marital therapy," said the counselor. "In the case of Martha and Hobey, however, the economy was a scapegoat for their real problem—disappointment in each other.

"Martha and Hobey married, the second time around for both, with false impressions. Freed of the mama's boy who depended on her, Martha wanted a strong man who would take care of her. Since Hobey had babied his first wife, Martha thought, he would lighten her burdens. Hobey was also in search of a change. Soured by the dependence of his rich-girl wife, he fell in love with Martha's competence.

"For several years, they had two good salaries to spend on themselves, and they got along well. When the children were born, the couple faced a big jump in living costs plus double-digit inflation. At that point, the hidden differences in their personalities emerged. They argued over money: where, what, and how to spend. Both felt disillusioned and put down.

"Martha thought her husband should help her with the children as a matter of course, while Hobey, the colonel's son, regarded childrearing as woman's work. He never volunteered to help and she was too proud to ask except in extreme emergencies. With an equal lack of logic, Martha regarded painting, plastering, and carpentry as his domain.

"Early on in counseling, they agreed to strike a balance. If Martha wants help with the children, she now asks Hobey without apologies. When Hobey needs assistance with the renovation, she is pleased to cooperate. Martha has also learned to delegate some of her responsibilities at the office and no longer puts in such long hours. This has helped their out-of-sync sex life—a problem commonly known as the A.M./P.M. syndrome. Martha now has more energy for occasional lovemaking in the evenings and Hobey tries to be more affectionate in the mornings. They also agreed to set aside time for themselves on weekends.

"They both make an effort not to argue over trifling differences. She no longer nags him to seek career advancement and he keeps quiet about her spending habits. Consequently, Martha has become less extravagant.

"Despite these improvements, the couple still needed financial help. I suggested that every evening for three months they make a list of what they spent that day. Three months, we decided, was long enough to cover large expenses and emergencies. Once they knew what their expenses were, they went to a financial adviser at their bank. He assisted them in drawing up a budget tailored to their needs. A major feature of the plan was a small weekly personal allowance. They don't account to each other or even to themselves for that 'free money.'

"The nearly completed renovation of their home has helped ease tensions. To Hobey's relief, Martha struck a bargain with an experienced plumber to install the showers in the rental units. She also asked the tenants for sizable rent increases.

"The added income and the strict budget have improved the couple's finances. Even more important, the two assure me they are in control of the emotional problems so easily stirred up by money problems."

WHEN HE'S NOT THINKING WHAT YOU THINK HE'S THINKING

For years, these two had stuck their heads in the sand and refused to speak honestly to each other. Failure to talk about issues that trouble you, when they trouble you, sets a bad precedent. Before Martha and Hobey can feel close again, let alone begin to solve their financial problems, they have to stop jumping to conclusions about each other's ideas or intentions.

If you suspect this could be happening in your marriage, make a pact to check out unspoken assumptions and expectations. No matter what the disagreement or confusion is, this exercise can help you communicate.

On a sheet of paper, write down any assumptions you think you may be making about what your partner wants, thinks, or needs. Then turn the page over and, on the flip side, write down any assumptions you think he is making about your feelings and needs. Share your lists and set aside half an hour to discuss them. Without judging, blaming, or criticizing, address each point and tell your partner whether or not he was accurate in what he assumed. Be honest but not defensive as you try to clear the confusion, negotiate, and compromise.

"My Husband Is a Penny-Pincher"

Although Andy's desire to save money is admirable, he was doing so at the expense of Beth—and their marriage. Can two people who seem to have little in common work through their differences?

Beth's turn

"I used to carry a sandwich lunch to my office every day just to satisfy Andy," said twenty-four-year-old Beth, a deeply tanned blonde recently separated from her husband. "During our three years together, Andy told me how to dress, where to buy gasoline and groceries—and instructed me in every aspect of my existence. His objective was to save money.

"Andy's insistence on that sandwich lunch had a lot to do with our split-up. I supervise a stenographic pool in my section of a large insurance company. Carrying a package lunch made me feel like a lowly file clerk. My colleagues thought I was a tightwad and laughed at me behind my back.

"But Andy reminded me that he carried a package lunch to college, where he is a part-time engineering student, and got along very nicely with two shirts by washing one every night. This was quite true, but our budget was too restricted for comfort. It eliminated pleasure and the simplest recreation—and his indifference to my humiliation was outrageous.

"Andy's earnings—he held a job in a filling station, a second job in a supermarket—paid for our food, his tuition, books, and college incidentals. He was sinking my salary into payments and improvements on our huge old house. If I dared question him, he flew into a rage.

"From the beginning of our marriage, Andy took charge of all the

237

money and I was too timid to argue. He bought my shoes and stockings and all my clothes, mostly at sleazy discount stores. Frequently I wasn't present. He bought my cosmetics through a wholesaler—brands I detested and often in unbecoming shades.

"Andy and I were also in the process of renovating our barnlike house without professional assistance—a colossal chore. We lived in perpetual chaos, stumbling over boards, wire, and bits of fallen plaster. I never felt I had a home. It seemed that there has been nothing in my life except hard work—no gaiety, no leisure, no freedom.

"I was the oldest of six children, the only girl, and my parents were extremely poor. My mother was terrifically ambitious for me and was determined I go to college. Her wages as a store cashier were badly needed at home, but she put aside ten percent a week for my education. Many times, Father got drunk and beat her to get at that college fund, but she never let him have it. At the age of ten I began washing dishes and vacuuming for neighbors, and every penny of my earnings also went into the education fund. During high school I studied so hard and had so many jobs that I had little time for boys. On Fridays, Mother and I visited the bank and made our deposits. It was the big event of the week.

"I was a college sophomore—a working student who lived off campus and missed the campus fun—when I met Andy. He proposed after one month. I told him no, but he wasn't one bit discouraged. At least once a week for two years he'd telephone. The message was always the same: I was the only wife he would ever want.

"Since he had professed to love me so much for so long, I expected a glamorous honeymoon trip when I finally said yes. It didn't happen. Andy convinced me it was impossible to take a short vacation or draw on his savings account, and he set up an immediate clamor for me to get a job. When I dillydallied—I wanted that one summer of freedom—he called the employment agencies and set up appointments for me. One week after my wedding, I landed a job and began turning over my weekly checks. Andy was so impressed that he decided he, too, should go back to school. He rearranged his schedule—Andy has always worked all the time—and started classes.

"Our only pleasure was sex, and there were times when Andy almost spoiled that for me. Terrified that I might get pregnant, he always checked my supply of birth control pills to make sure there had been no slipup. To me, his lack of trust seemed like a lack of love.

"Another thing I soon discovered about my husband was that he didn't believe in celebrating special occasions—Christmas, birthdays, anniversaries. I turned twenty-one three months after our marriage, but Andy forgot my birthday. Gregory, a man I work with, is the exact opposite of Andy. The day after we had our first office lunch I found on my desk an orchid and a sweet little note. Soon Gregory and I were lunching nearly every business day. He was easy to talk to and a wonderful listener.

"When I told Gregory about Andy's stinginess, he said the situation was ridiculous, that every wife—working or not—was entitled to a personal allowance. He said I ought to make some other living arrangements and he would help any way he could. One Saturday, I ran into him on the street and he took me swimming at his apartment house, which was designed for swinging singles. By coincidence, there was a vacancy in the building, a furnished sublet. Gregory introduced me to the manager and I halfway agreed to rent it. When I got home, Andy was on his knees laying tiles. I spoke to him very quietly before he had a chance to yell at me.

"I told him I was leaving him and I told him about Gregory. To my amazement, Andy didn't bellow or shout. In fact, his voice sounded terribly hurt. I could hardly believe it. We talked all night and in the end we compromised. Next morning Andy helped me move, but he picked the apartment. It was fairly near our house and miles away from Gregory.

"For the last six weeks, ever since the move, I've been totally confused. The first time I collected my own check I bought four new dresses in a single morning, but then I remembered a big payment was due on the house and realized how worried Andy would be. I returned two of the dresses that afternoon and sent the money to him. He came around and thanked me. However, when I suggested we go out to dinner he turned into the same penny-pinching Andy. He said a sandwich was all he wanted.

"I'm still seeing Gregory, though not as much. At the moment, I'm more than satisfied with the joys and freedom of single life."

ANDY'S TURN

"I have loved Beth since the first time I saw her," said Andy, a curly-haired, broad-shouldered young man of twenty-five with fierce blue eyes and a pugnacious jaw.

"Beth has no sense of values—about money or people. She can be conned by anyone. She needs somebody—she needs *me*—to protect and look after her. When she took off six weeks ago, I'm almost sure I could have changed her mind if I'd known the right things to say.

"Beth can easily be talked into

acting against her own principles and her own best interests. To see her influenced by a guy like Gregory, to hear her quote his 'wise' remarks, drives me nuts. I know how his type operates. Regardless of his fast line of chatter, he has no real concern for Beth's welfare.

"Until six weeks ago I thought Beth and I had everything going for us. Beth encouraged me to go to college and I encouraged her to find a job. I took a lot of personal pride and interest in Beth's career. I regarded her income as important in building—for us both—a financial program for the future. On a few occasions I guess she did beef a little, but I was too stupid or too busy to pay much attention. Together we were creating something of value.

"Everything I planned was planned for Beth. I thought she understood that my sole desire was to provide for her security. All that was required of her was a little patience.

"My folks would have made out okay financially—they had only three kids, with me the oldest—except for the extravagance of my mother. My father sold and installed air conditioners, earned good wages, and occasionally even spoke of sending me, the only boy, to college. Mother's wastefulness and silly buying habits drove him into bankruptcy. In disgust, he left her one night and, of course, left me. I was nine.

"Until I met Beth, nobody ever gave a damn for me. At one time she did love me, but now I guess she has changed. I don't know why. I will always love Beth, but I don't know how to tell her so. She means more to me than anybody or anything in this world."

THE COUNSELOR'S TURN

"The appearance of a man like Gregory on the scene of this marriage was inevitable," the counselor said. "Beth quickly realized that although she didn't care for Gregory, he represented a handy exit from an existence that had become intolerable.

"When I first met Beth she had only recently retired from the thankless role of 'the girl who can't say no.' In her formative years, an ambitious and doubtless well-intentioned mother systematically robbed her of initiative and virtually all power of decision. In such circumstances, independence of action later could hardly be expected.

"Andy and Beth were bright young people, but both were very emotionally immature. The lack of communication between them was complete. When Beth married Andy, she expected to enter a world of romance, fun, and freedom. Instead, she had merely exchanged the prison of her girlhood for the prison of marriage.

"Andy had no understanding of Beth's feelings or her increasing bitterness and boredom. After all, with her assistance, he was achieving his dream. Beth was unaware that Andy's concern for her inspired and fired all his actions. She had only the vaguest conception of his financial plans and future projects and she regarded his prudence in money matters as meanness.

"Although Andy deplored the wobbly quality of Beth's disposition, he had been quick to take advantage of it and on occasion bullied his unprotesting young wife unmercifully. Subconsciously, he was reacting to Beth as if she were his free-wheeling, wasteful mother. Once Andy acknowledged that Beth bore no resemblance to his mother, he was on the way to maturity.

"At times, Beth had made half-hearted attempts to speak to him about her unhappiness and very legitimate grievances. Unfortunately, on the occasions she rallied the courage to talk honestly, Andy was either too preoccupied or too overworked to listen. Andy had set himself a work schedule that would have been difficult for six men to follow. Most of the time he was exhausted. In fact, to a certain extent, Beth's complaints that he was a laggard lover were justified. Andy poured such an enormous store of intellectual force, muscular strength, and vitality into his work that his energy and interest in lovemaking were seriously reduced.

"Eventually this marriage was salvaged, but the task took more time than I anticipated. Beth was exhilarated with her newfound freedom and loath to part with it, but Andy was a fighter. From the beginning, he shouldered ninety percent of the blame for the separation; he was dissatisfied with himself and eager to improve.

"He deliberately maintained a curtailed work load, which was tough on a young man of his temperament, and dipped deeply into his savings, which was even tougher, to spend lavishly on the entertainment and recreation Beth fancied. For several months, she was treated to the courtship she had previously missed. Andy did his best to relax and enjoy himself along with her. When he was rested, he and Beth began to rediscover the passion of their lovemaking. Andy has also just about mastered his anxieties of a pregnancy that neither he nor Beth desires at the moment.

"Beth and Andy have now learned to talk freely to each other, to listen, and most important, to try to understand each other's feelings. Beth was urged to talk about what's bothering her instead of retreating into teary silence.

"The big break came, however, when Andy was given a chance to sell their house, which was still unfinished, at a modest profit. When he consulted Beth, she advised him to reject the offer. With considerable indignation, she reminded him of all the time and toil they had invested in the place—and the next day she moved back home.

"Beth and Andy have now completed the remodeling job, and they expect to find a buyer soon. They will invest half their profits in another real-estate venture and spend the other half on a trip to Europe. Both are delighted with their plans and prospects for the future.

"In fact, once Beth and Andy got to know and understand each other more intimately, they discovered they were quite a bit alike."

HOW TO DEAL WITH A CONTROLLING PARTNER

This is a classic example of how money equals power in a marriage. When either partner feels controlled, the result is a backflow of resentment that can destroy love. What's more, the way your parents handled issues of power and control directly affect the way you behave as an adult.

But although these early patterns can be difficult to break, they can be changed. Do you often feel that your partner's wishes and needs come before yours? Do you feel put down and bossed around? It helps to take a look at how decisions were made in your family when you were growing up. By recognizing certain patterns, you can learn to do things differently now.

Below is a list of common family decisions. When you were little, were these decisions made by your father, your mother, or both? Who had the final word?

- **Decisions about how to spend money.**

- **Decisions about whom to socialize with, which relative to visit, etc.**

- **Decisions about childrearing.**

- **Decisions about where to live.**

- **Decisions about how to spend vacations.**

Is your list lopsided? There's a good chance you're bringing an unbalanced view of power and control into your marriage. Go over the questions again and ask yourself: Who makes the decisions on these issues in our home? If that list is also lopsided, find a better balance.

IN THE BEDROOM: UNDERSTANDING INTIMACY

—◆—

A couple's sex life is in one sense a barometer of their marriage. Over the years it will fluctuate, depending on a host of factors: The stress of juggling work and family obligations can be so physically and emotionally exhausting that husbands and wives forget the importance of expressing love and tenderness outside as well as inside the bedroom.

External events and problems—having a baby, losing a job, a death in the family, as well as chronic worries about money, health, or work—also take their toll. In fact, about half of all couples—even those who are happily married—struggle with a sexual problem at some point during their marriage.

As *Can This Marriage Be Saved?* consistently illustrates, however, when husbands and wives complain that the sexual aspect of their marriage is less than satisfying, the impact can usually be felt in other areas of the relationship.

Unexpressed anger and resentment, for instance, can haunt the bedroom like ghosts, inhibiting or extinguishing sexual interest altogether. The mother of young children who feels her husband is not doing his fair share around the house—and who believes she's not entitled to speak up or, when she does, is ignored—may feel less than loving later that evening when her husband, oblivious to her feelings, initiates sex. Or a husband, tired of being the target of his wife's sarcastic, critical remarks may assert, "Lovemaking? Forget it. I can't be in the same room with her, let alone make love." In countless cases, sex is the weapon with which one spouse punishes another.

Sometimes a partner's general unhappiness and dissatisfaction with his or her own life triggers a crisis of intimacy. Although this can happen at any time in the course of a marriage, in *Can This Marriage Be Saved?* we see it frequently in the stories of couples in their late forties and fifties faced with an empty nest. When the focus of a marriage shifts from raising children and being a family back to being a couple, both men and women may feel a painful void. Personal doubts as well as lack of confidence or self-esteem can quickly translate into low sexual desire.

Whatever the trigger for trouble, the results are the same: Routine, mediocre sex replaces the fireworks of the earlier years. As doubts deepen, it's a short leap to questioning the validity of the relationship altogether. Interestingly, when relationship problems spill over into the bedroom, couples are evenly divided between those who say that they are so furious with their partner they can't imagine making love and those whose sex life thrives despite difficulties and animosity in other areas. For the latter couples, sex is the only way they can feel close. Unconsciously they may be hoping that, by reconnecting in bed, they can restore the harmony in the rest of their marriage.

Can This Marriage Be Saved? tackles the spectrum of sexual complaints. We meet physically exhausted and emotionally depleted wives who yearn for tenderness and physical affection—"Why does every kiss have to lead to intercourse?" they want to know. When they are in the mood, many wives wonder if their husbands ever learned the definition of foreplay; "What's the rush?" they gripe.

We also meet men who not only want sex more often, they also want their wives to make the overture—"Why can't she be more spontaneous, more adventurous?" is a common lament. Clearly, women who enjoy sex, who initiate and respond to lovemaking, turn their husbands on.

Chief among sexual complaints throughout the decades has been the inability of couples to reconcile different levels of sexual desire—although the reasons for the differences have changed somewhat. Twenty years ago, therapists focused on psychological factors—problems in the marriage or a strict upbringing—as culprits. Although there is no doubt that these issues heavily influence desire, recent studies in human sexuality have highlighted the key role hormones play in sexual arousal throughout our lives. While many women enjoy sex and are orgasmic, these studies show that men in general have higher levels of testosterone—the hormone responsible for sexual arousal in both sexes. Understanding the effect of hormonal changes on each partner's desire for sex is important in decreasing the arguments about when and how often to engage in lovemaking—and in increasing intimacy in general.

Can This Marriage Be Saved? also reveals that men and women still have a very different take on their sexual relationships. Like the couple in *Annie Hall* discussing with their therapist the frequency of their sexual encounters, he typically says they have sex "Hardly at all," while she insists, "All the time!" Women almost always put sex in the context of a relationship: When a woman feels good about her marriage, she's interested in sex. For women, feeling connected emotionally is an essential prelude to lovemaking. But for men, sex affirms their virility. It may also be the only way they know to be intimate.

Whatever the cause, ignoring the lack of a satisfying sexual life, hoping sexual problems will disappear, or making excuses for the lack of passion in a marriage because a couple is reluctant to deal with their other problems is a prescription for disaster. Couples who have successfully kept their sex lives vital understand that the passionate, romantic love they felt in the beginning of their relationship gives way to a deeper, more enduring, but equally satisfying love.

These couples make their sex life, and their marriage, a priority. That means creating the opportunities to be intimate: romancing—and flirting with—each other, whether it's calling during the day, making lunch dates, or better yet, escaping for a weekend alone, and yes, even scheduling time for sex. It means paying attention to each partner's individual needs, because intimacy cannot flourish when either partner is tense, angry, or resentful.

Making sex a priority also means that, if either partner is dissatisfied, instead of turning complaints into a power struggle, they talk about them candidly. Ironically, talking about sexual problems can actually be a turn-on. When couples resolve the underlying issues that are dividing them and air their differences directly instead of acting them out in the bedroom, they break the sexual stalemate—and, ultimately, discover the right balance between intimacy and autonomy.

"HE WANTS ME TO BE HIS SEX SLAVE"

---

lthough they'd been married for two years, Joan had never told Jeff that she hated the way he made love. Her sudden announcement sent him reeling. How can a couple balance each partner's sexual needs?

JOAN'S TURN

"Jeff only likes sex his way, and he doesn't give a damn about whether I'm enjoying it or not," said Joan, thirty-nine, her dark-blue eyes flashing as she lit a cigarette. "I can count on one hand the number of times we've had intercourse. Practically all Jeff wants is oral sex, with a few other kinky variations mixed in. Sex is about making him feel good.

"It's not that I hate doing it his way—well, at least in the beginning I didn't. I wanted him to love me so much, I'd do anything to please him. I didn't want to let on that I wasn't totally satisfied.

"Jeff has never once asked what I would like. There's no romance, no passionate kissing, no fondling. He's totally uninterested in foreplay of any kind. He doesn't touch my breast—he grabs it. I can't bear it anymore. I feel like a bimbo, like his sex slave.

"I've asked him to be more caring. Just last week I said, 'Foreplay, Jeff. It's in the dictionary; go look it up.' He gave me this blank look. So, until my husband makes love to me, I don't want to have sex at all.

"I fell head over heels in love with Jeff the first moment I saw him. He's gorgeous and witty, in a Cary Grant sort of way. We met at a friend's party that I almost didn't go to; I have a pretty important job—I'm director of personnel for a large transportation company—and I was exhausted that day.

"I'm the older of two kids with a mother I could never, ever, please and a father I adore but who traveled so much on business I hardly ever saw him. He was very poor when he was young and I think he always worried about money. I'm like that now, even though we could live comfortably on my salary.

"Mom is very strong-willed and critical. She's an alcoholic, and I never knew what to expect when I came home from school. Dad used to call her moody, which I suppose was his way of not dealing with the real issue.

"I still have this sadness that Mother never cared about me. She was a beauty, and looks were important to her. I know I disappointed her in that department.

"I was also a mediocre student, and although I was popular, I was always surprised that the kids liked me. Everyone used to tell me I was smart and wonder why I wasn't doing better.

"My sophomore year in college I married the guy who'd been my boyfriend since high school. We stayed together for five years, but the marriage was terrible from the very start. Less than a year after our divorce, I got married for the second time, to a man fifteen years older than I was. We had even less in common.

"During those years, I jumped from job to job. Finally, I was hired at the firm where I work now, and I moved up. After my second marriage ended, I concentrated on work. But I was thirty-seven and I knew I wanted to settle down. Then I met Jeff.

"I was totally flabbergasted that of all the beautiful women at that party, he chose me. I didn't want to come on too strong. So I left all the pursuing to Jeff, but I sensed that he needed someone to take care of him. Jeff is very insecure about the fact that he never did well in school, never graduated from college, and has a dismal track record at work.

"The first business he had when he was in his twenties went bankrupt, and I can see that his current business—he and a friend run their own contracting company—is headed in the same direction. We've been fighting a lot because I see him doing a lot of things that are not productive and he refuses to listen.

"After a year of dating, I pushed to get married, but I do think Jeff was ready, too. Everyone said we were a great couple. We loved going to the movies and trying new restaurants. But lately I'm just disgusted. Jeff constantly stares at other women.

"He never liked to talk much about how he felt, and I wasn't looking for a soulmate either—at first. I also think Jeff feels inadequate because of my success. I'm very organized and in control, which he isn't. Even though he boasts about how tough I am, I think his pride is hurt.

"Well, I'm tired of always being the tough one, of having to direct our lives. Jeff walks in the front door at eight-thirty P.M. and demands, 'What's for dinner?' like some Neanderthal man. Well, excuse me, but I just got home from work myself, and I haven't had a minute to put down my briefcase, let alone prepare a meal. Is there a law that says I have to make dinner every night? Or that I have to do all the banking, pay all the bills, pick up all the dry cleaning? We gave a party last Christmas and I ran myself ragged getting everything ready. Jeff had two jobs to do—get the beer and buy the Christmas tree—and he forgot to do both.

"You're probably thinking, after two failed marriages, how could I be such a dope? I can't explain it, but maybe deep down I thought I could change Jeff and it hasn't happened.

"We haven't slept together in three months. I didn't want to make this the third strike, so I suggested counseling. But I don't see Jeff trying to change."

JEFF'S TURN

"Why do I have to change?" asked Jeff, forty, a tall, suntanned man who sat stone-faced on the couch as his wife spoke. "My wife is refusing to have sex with me. After two years, during which I didn't have the slightest idea that anything was wrong, all of a sudden she's complaining nonstop about everything. And I'm the one that's wrong? I don't get it.

"Sex with Joan used to be fantastic. Believe me, I know. I'm a very sexual guy and I've had a lot of women. If she wasn't happy, why am I only hearing about it now? I'm not embarrassed to say that I like oral sex, and for all I knew, she did, too.

"I wish she'd get off my back. She's a shrew, yelling and putting me down. Joan used to be different. I liked her tough-girl banter. She was funny, a real straight-shooter. I admired her spunk. And when I took her home that first night, the sex was incredible.

"Back then, she didn't complain and criticize me the way she does now. I'm not about to argue with her; I don't like to fight. But she's beginning to sound like all the people in my life who always made me feel stupid.

"I was really unhappy growing up. I could never get along with the other kids; I tried to get them to like me by being funny. I have an older sister who was always the star of the family; she's a doctor now. Compared with her, I've been a failure. All I ever heard was, 'Jeff's not living up to his potential.' I was sharp, I was articulate, but school was impossible. They said I was dyslexic. The kids called me dumbbell because I couldn't read. I still can't spell, and reading is difficult.

"I don't think my parents cared. They had the money, so they sent me to therapists and special schools, but nothing helped. Anyway, most of the time Mother was busy with her social life. And my father, like Joan's, ran his own company, so he was never around.

"For a while, I thought I might want to be an architect, so I took some design courses. I never got a degree, but I'm using some of that background now in my renovation work. I hope to make a better go of it than I did with my last business. You know how it is—a couple of bad bids, I misjudged how long it would take to do a project. I'm lousy with details.

"So maybe I'm not doing as well as I could right now. Who is? But I don't need a wife who makes me feel like a jerk. When we first got married, she put me through basic training for husbands, and I try—I do. I put the toilet seat down and the toilet paper in so it rolls from the bottom the way she likes it. So I forgot to get the tree last Christmas. Is that a felony?

"I'll admit this is not the first time a woman has told me to be more caring. But what does that mean? Who's being selfish? She's refusing to have sex with me! No one's complained the way Joan has. I don't want to brag, but women have always sought me out. Why I can't please my own wife is beyond me.

"Therapy was Joan's idea and I'm not thrilled to be here. But I'm willing to give it a try."

THE COUNSELOR'S TURN

"The first few times I saw Joan and Jeff, we made little progress because Joan kept yelling at her husband," said the counselor. "During her tirades, Jeff rarely said anything. I told Joan that first she has to control her anger. But before she could do that, she had to find out where it was coming from.

"The child of a selfish, critical, alcoholic mother, Joan suffered from very low self-esteem. Like many children of alcoholics, she became the family caretaker, desperately trying to please her mother. Always, she fell short.

"While Joan was very attractive, her low opinion of herself played a key role in her relationship with Jeff. She could not believe that such a handsome man could be interested in her. While they were dating, she was so scared she would lose him that she never spoke up about what she wanted, sexually or otherwise.

"Rarely have I met a man whose self-esteem was as low as Jeff's. I suspected that he suffered from attention deficit hyperactivity disorder (ADHD). When Jeff was growing up, many such children were called hyperactive. Some were put on medication; some were merely labeled behavior problems. Many, like Jeff, had trouble relating to other children. They grew up feeling stupid and unloved.

"A child with learning disabilities as severe as Jeff's requires considerable patience and nurturing. Jeff received neither. Indeed, the only thing that gave him any measure of confidence was his good looks. For him, sex was a way of gratifying his ego, of feeling powerful and manly, and rough sex was manly sex. It never occurred to him to think of his partner's wishes or pleasure.

"In one sense, these two were a perfect match. Jeff needed to be taken care of; Joan was the classic caretaker. Their relationship was based on her attending to his emotional, sexual, and physical needs from the beginning, so Jeff wasn't about to exert himself if he didn't have to. But then Joan changed the rules in the middle of the game.

"Although sex was the biggest problem for this couple, my goal was to encourage a balance—in and out of their bedroom. Our initial sessions focused on helping Joan

control her anger. Her constant complaints made Jeff so resentful he withdrew even more.

"I pointed out that Jeff wasn't sitting around the house doing nothing. He was working hard. Then I suggested that perhaps Joan was focusing on the financial problems when, in truth, she was upset that her husband—like her mother—was not responding to her emotional needs. I told her she had to learn to articulate those needs.

"This rang true for Joan, and she started examining how she was reacting to her husband. At the very next session, she told me she thought I was right. 'When I'm working really late, I just want him to show me that he cares. But he can't read my mind.'

"During these initial sessions, when he saw that I wasn't blaming him, Jeff began to feel more comfortable with me. I suggested he consult a physician and then a learning specialist who could help him figure out ways to improve his job performance. The specialist confirmed my suspicions about ADHD and prescribed an antidepressant, which has helped Jeff concentrate on his work.

"Naming Jeff's problem helped both of them. Once she saw that it wasn't her husband's fault when he miscalculated a project but rather a disability he could learn to work around, Joan became more compassionate. The learning specialist has

251

helped Jeff play up his strengths; a natural salesman, he now takes care of that part of the business while leaving the logistics to his partner. And he bought a computer to help him outline his workday and organize his paperwork.

"About three months into therapy, this couple suffered a major setback. Although they had resumed having sex, Joan discovered that Jeff was having an affair. He insisted that the woman meant nothing to him, but Joan was humiliated and she asked Jeff to leave for two weeks. During that time they both came to see me several times alone. Being on his own made Jeff realize that he loved and needed Joan and had to stop this destructive behavior. I noticed a dramatic shift in his motivation from then on.

"After Joan allowed Jeff to move back in, I asked her a simple question: 'After two years of doing everything Jeff wanted sexually and never telling him you weren't happy, what did you expect? How did you think he would react?' Joan said, naively, that she thought he'd listen to her. This is very much the way Joan related to her mother. Unconsciously she was saying, 'If I do everything you want, then sooner or later you'll love me and want to please me, too.'

"To balance their sexual relationship, Jeff had to change his attitude about what constituted manly sex and Joan had to articulate what she wanted and show her husband how

to please her. Changing Jeff's deep-seated attitude about women and sex was not easy. I assured him that mature men were pleased when their wives were satisfied and said that if he simply tried to follow some of Joan's suggestions, he might find them just as exciting as oral sex. I also gave this couple several professional videos that sex therapists use to demonstrate lovemaking. These videos showed men caressing and stroking their partners in ways that both found arousing.

"Jeff agreed to try. Sensing a renewed commitment, Joan tried to speak up. 'Teach him how to touch you,' I advised. Jeff has learned to slow down, to ask if something is pleasurable to Joan, and to stop if it's not. For the first time they feel they are working as a team.

"Jeff is more affectionate and attentive: He opens doors for Joan and reaches for her hand as they stroll down the street. Also, as Joan stops taking care of everything, Jeff has room to demonstrate that he's capable of being an equal partner. More confident, he's pitching in with household chores. 'Little things,' Joan says, 'but they're what's important.'

"This couple ended counseling after a year and a half, although Joan comes to see me by herself once a month. By developing realistic expectations of each other, they have learned to work together instead of against each other."

THE SEARCH FOR SEXUAL SATISFACTION

It's hard to believe that sex is still such a difficult subject that even high-powered, assertive women such as Joan would feel unable to talk honestly about what pleases them. But in many relationships, that's precisely what happens. Perhaps one partner is too shy or too intimidated to discuss what she likes or dislikes. Or perhaps she's thinking that if her partner really loved her, he would automatically know what she needed. What's more, many think that their sex life will just "happen." But like any aspect of marriage, a satisfying love life takes work. How can you jump-start a stalled sexual relationship? Keep these points in mind:

• **Make your sex life a priority.** If either of you is less than satisfied, do something about it now.

• **Talk about sex.** Don't be a victim of "the mind-reader syndrome": If he (or she) loves me, he (or she) will know what I like. Don't be afraid, either, to express dissatisfaction out of fear of hurting a partner's feelings.

• **Just talk**—period—undistracted by the kids, the telephone, the TV. If you can't have a conversation, you can't be intimate. Create opportunities: Call each other during the day, make a date for lunch, or share a glass of wine after the children are asleep. Make your partner feel safe and loved, and you'll open the door to intimacy.

• **Romance each other.** Don't forget the little gestures—the hugs, kisses, and caresses, the loving pat on the rear. Flirt. Tell him how handsome he looks. Call her that affectionate, silly name you made up years ago. Back up words with loving gestures and surprising or unexpected deeds. Go out of your way to do something or buy something you know your spouse would like, or appreciate.

• **Plan time for sex.** Just because something is scheduled doesn't mean it can't be exciting. When you were dating, you made plans for all sorts of things, right? You made a date, planned what you would wear, where you would go. The passionate sex that ended the evening was the result of all that scheduling and planning. It's no different now.

"WE NO LONGER HAVE A SEX LIFE"

Jon and Cindy were young and head-over-heels in love with each other. So why does a man who seems to have everything lose the ability to make love?

CINDY'S TURN

"I know this sounds ridiculous, but after three years of marriage, my husband and I no longer make love," said Cindy, twenty-four, a pixie-faced woman with curly brown hair. "I don't mean our sex life has diminished; I mean it no longer exists—period. Although we care deeply about each other, Jon has completely lost the ability to make love to me.

"What's so ironic is that sex was wonderful before we were married. Jon and I started dating in high school, and we shared an apartment all through college, which adds up to five full years of healthy, happy, wonderful lovemaking. We were married right after graduation, and six months later, Jon started having problems maintaining an erection.

"I really can't believe this is happening to us—we were the perfect couple, and now I'm afraid my marriage will disintegrate and end just like my parents' did. They fought constantly and kept right on fighting after they finally divorced, when I was five years old. During my teens, everybody in my family seemed to be getting divorced and remarried.

"My father stepped out of my life completely when I was seven, and I was raised by my mother. Mom worked in a local department store and we lived with my grandparents. I had a happy enough childhood; I breezed through school, had many friends, and went out for all the extracurricular activities. I dated a lot in high school, too, but I made it a policy to play the field and not let myself get attached to anyone. I sort of flitted here and there—that is, until I turned sixteen and met Jon.

"We met through friends, and if you asked me what it was that hooked me so quickly, I wouldn't know quite what to say. In many ways, we're opposites. I'm gregarious and outgoing; Jon's quiet and introspective—very solid, thoughtful, and responsible. The moment I saw him, I felt I had known him all my life. I chased him until he caught me. From then on, neither one of us ever looked at anybody else.

"I never thought much about what I wanted to do after high school, but when Jon applied to college, I applied to the same one. We shared an apartment and scheduled our classes so that we could have lots of free time together. That was a happy period for us. I majored in psychology, Jon majored in economics, and we had grants and scholarships to help us along financially.

"During college, our lovemaking was wonderful. We were so much in love, sex just seemed so natural. And since we were virgins when we met, we learned together.

"After our wedding, we settled down to live happily ever after. I found a job doing personnel work and Jon went into the management-training program at the same department store where my mother worked. We both also started taking graduate courses at night—I very much wanted to finish my master's

degree in psychology and Jon was working toward his MBA.

"It seems to me that from that point on, we hardly ever saw each other. My job was a piece of cake, but Jon's was a nightmare. He had a full hour's commute each way, which was time-consuming enough, but on top of that he was always being asked to work overtime and to come in on weekends. When he did have a free night, it was invariably one of the nights I was in class. Jon was also constantly being sent off on buying trips. Sometimes his boss would give him a day's notice, sometimes just a few hours.

"Jon hated his job—he was disgusted by some of the store's unethical business practices—and I knew that the stress was affecting him emotionally. So I never complained. I didn't want our marriage to become a battleground the way my parents' had been, but I couldn't stand the lonely evenings. Since I'm not the type to sit and watch TV for hours, I decided to start a part-time business designing and custom-making clothes—a hobby I had always hoped would lead to something.

"It was during that period that our sex life took its initial nosedive. In college, we made love at least once a day, but on our new schedule, we were lucky to fit sex in twice a week. Then, one night, to our horror, we tried to make love and it just didn't work. We couldn't believe it!

This had never happened before. We kept trying and finally got so frustrated we just gave up.

"Three months later, the very same thing happened. Jon was fine during foreplay, but then, when he was getting ready to enter me, his erection collapsed. From then on, things worsened. I was sure his problem was caused by stress and when Jon lost his job at the department store I was actually relieved.

"Jon found another job that very same day, working for a competing department-store chain, and although it wasn't quite what he would have chosen, at least the hours were decent. Now we did have a lot of time to spend together, but Jon was never able to maintain an erection again.

"We've tried everything, and I do mean everything, to work through this problem. Jon has had physicals by two different doctors and been told by both that he's in perfect health. He takes huge quantities of vitamins every day. I went on a crash diet to make myself more attractive and started wearing lacy black negligees to bed at night. We read a lot of sex books and did all the things they suggested; we took bubble baths together, burned incense in the bedroom, and tried making love by soft candlelight. Jon even bought and mounted mirrored tiles on the ceiling over the bed, but we had to take those down because they kept coming loose and falling on us.

We both dropped out of grad school, thinking we were pressuring ourselves too much. That didn't help either.

"By unspoken agreement, we almost never try to make love anymore. We're too scared. We keep ourselves busy, so on the surface we're still happily married, but the knowledge of what we once had and have now lost has created a barrier between us. I feel I'm losing my husband emotionally as well as physically. I love him so much, I don't think I can bear this much longer."

JON'S TURN

"I don't know what's the matter with me," said Jon, twenty-five, a serious young man with short, neatly cut hair and tortoiseshell glasses. "I'm crazy about my wife, and I'd do anything to be be able to prove it to her physically, but I just can't seem to do it. It's frustrating and embarrassing and scary.

"But to be honest, I'm not very comfortable sitting here talking about sex with a stranger. My family is pretty straitlaced; Dad, who worked as a clerk for an oil company, and Mother, who was a secretary, are serious, quiet types. I certainly never talked with them about sex. I have two sisters. The older one suffers from Down's syndrome, and I think because of that I absorbed a strong sense of responsibility. We were a family that shared a common problem. As a kid I was quiet, inquisitive, interested in different things: the stock market, scientific inventions, nature, and animals. I wasn't particularly social. I had only one girlfriend before Cindy, and I never even kissed her; we were good buddies. Cindy's the only girl I've ever loved.

"Since we're both bright academically, college was a playground. It wasn't until after we graduated and got married that the real world finally caught up with us. My first full-time job was a disillusioning experience. The department store where I was taking retail-management training was part of a major national chain that I had always thought was on the up-and-up. Instead, I discovered they were a total rip-off. At one point, I had a large commission coming and they tried to cheat me out of it. I wouldn't permit that and was never forgiven for having stood up for my rights. From then on, the manager did everything possible to make life miserable for me. One day, on the manager's whim, I was fired. I was never given a reason for my dismissal and the manager's nephew was given my job. I would have initiated a lawsuit except I was afraid they'd take revenge by discharging my mother-in-law who also worked there. I didn't want that to happen.

"It was while I was working at the store that I started having problems performing sexually. The first time, I really wasn't worried. I'd been away on a long buying trip, and although Cindy had never actually said anything, I could tell she was ticked off about my being away. Neither of us was much in the mood for lovemaking that night. But the second time it happened I didn't take it so lightly.

"When I lost my post at the department store, though, it was the end of everything. Of course I went straight out and found another job, but I still felt I'd been kicked in the teeth.

"Counseling was Cindy's idea, but I'm going along with it because it represents our one final chance to save our marriage. Truthfully, I don't have much hope. We've already tried everything. And I have to admit, the whole idea of sex therapy gives me the creeps. But Cindy knows more about this sort of thing than I do. She said you're fully accredited, but even so, if she and I are supposed to get into bed in front of you and, well, do a sort of show-and-tell thing—there's no way I'll go through with it."

THE COUNSELOR'S TURN

"**J**on's apprehension about entering therapy for a sexual problem is very common," said the counselor. "Most of my clients are highly relieved to find out that the only bed they will be using during the course of therapy is their own, and that all sexual activity between them will take place in the privacy of their bedroom.

"Jon and Cindy were as solid a couple as I have ever had as clients. They loved each other very much and were committed to preserving their marriage at all costs, even if that involved the embarrassment of discussing the most intimate part of their relationship with a stranger. As almost always happens in these cases, however, once our initial session was over, the embarrassment vanished.

"During our first counseling session, we reviewed Jon's medical history to make sure there wasn't a physical reason for his impotence. Since he had already been examined by two physicians, this did not seem probable, but I wanted to make sure there was nothing wrong with his diet, that he was getting enough rest, and that he didn't have any serious illnesses, such as diabetes, that could affect his ability to sustain an erection. Certain medications—including the antidepressants commonly prescribed for mild anxiety—can also lower the libido, but Jon was not taking anything.

"As we talked, one point soon became obvious: Jon and Cindy had made their lives so busy that there was little time for sex. Young and energetic, they believed they could juggle everything. Ironically, when

problems developed they piled on still more projects to ward off emotional pain.

"My first goal with this couple was to relieve the pressure they were under by helping them realize how common their problem was. Although most people do not talk about it, periods of sexual dysfunction occur in almost all marriages at one time or another, especially when one or both partners are under unusual stress. These problems generally right themselves automatically once the immediate problem is resolved, but sometimes a couple begin to panic about the situation, which in turn creates a separate but equally disturbing problem. The anticipation of not being able to perform sexually can actually create that situation, causing a man to have erection or ejaculation problems or a woman to be unable to reach orgasm. This frustrating experience increases their fear of failure the next time and soon, like Jon and Cindy, a couple may find themselves locked into a pattern they can't break.

"During our initial sessions we viewed some educational films about impotence that showed how a couple mastered techniques, such as nongenital touching, to help them overcome their problem.

"Once Jon and Cindy became more relaxed about their situation, I described to them various intimacy-enriching experiences they could have at home that would get them more in tune with their sexuality. In the beginning, these activities simply involved touching and closeness so Jon would not be threatened by the challenge of having to perform. Gradually, the exercises were increased to include the caressing of genitals and then actual intercourse. In one exercise, Cindy was instructed that when Jon had an erection she was to wait and allow the penis to become soft again before continuing sex play. Many men are fearful that if an erection is lost once, it won't come back. By having some experiences in which his erection was purposely let go but was then regained, Jon became less threatened.

"Along with actual sex therapy, we also worked on increasing other areas of this couple's intimacy, particularly their verbal communication. Cindy's unhappy memories of her parents' battles made her reluctant to demonstrate any outward signs of anger in her own marriage. As a result, she rarely expressed her negative feelings, allowing them to build up inside her. Jon was sensitive enough to pick up on Cindy's anger, but was frustrated in his efforts to respond appropriately. His family life had been so quiet and so introspective that he had never been encouraged to specifically voice his concerns. By practicing getting their feelings out into the open, they took a second major step in reducing stress.

"Another subject we spoke about at length was the fact that good sex doesn't necessarily have to be spontaneous. Jon had complained during therapy that Cindy was not willing to plan time for sex because she felt that to do so was unnatural and unromantic. When we discussed this, Cindy realized she was being unrealistic; when people's lives are as busy as hers and Jon's, it is not only okay but absolutely necessary to set aside time for sex.

"The more Jon and Cindy shared of themselves, the more relaxed they became—and the less difficulty Jon had maintaining his erections. Because this couple were so highly motivated and committed to working at their relationship, their progress was fast and steady. Inevitably, they hit plateaus, but lost distance was quickly regained, and counseling was terminated after ten weekly sessions. A follow-up session six months later found them still satisfied with all areas of their life together.

"One year later, I contacted Jon and Cindy to ask their permission to propose their case as a possible subject for the *Ladies' Home Journal*'s "Can This Marriage Be Saved" column. During the course of our conversation, Cindy told me that they were 'abstaining from sex these days,' but for a very happy reason— Cindy's doctor had told them to wait six weeks after the birth of their baby daughter before resuming intercourse."

WHEN SEX PROBLEMS ARE RED HERRINGS

As the counselor in this case noted, understanding that impotence is a common problem at every stage of marriage is the first, and highest hurdle most couples have to clear. Talking about the problem can be reassuring and often lessens the anxiety for both partners. In fact, the more both partners worry about the problem, the more intractable it becomes. However, wise couples recognize that impotence can also be a wake-up call, a signal of stress somewhere in the relationship. Instead of banishing feelings of frustration, unhappiness, or emotional overload—at work, at home, with your kids or other family members—ask yourselves if something is bothering one or both of you. Sit down and talk about issues in a nonconfrontational, nonjudgmental, and unhurried way. Although Cindy and Jon shared a deep love and commitment, they unwittingly allowed sexual and other problems to drift along, ignored and unchallenged. Once they found the courage to talk, the episodes of sexual stage fright disappeared.

"MY HUSBAND KEEPS CALLING THOSE SEX HOTLINES"

Terry was devastated to discover that strait-laced Michael was regularly phoning prostitutes. Would she ever be able to trust him again?

TERRY'S TURN

"How could he do it?" asked Terry, thirty-one, her voice rising in anger. "How could Michael call a sex service and talk to some prostitute on the phone, for God's sake? What's wrong with him?

"Never in a million years would I have imagined that my dependable, straight-arrow husband would do something like this. One reason I fell in love with him was that he represented a life so different from the one I had known.

"My childhood was pretty intense. My father was a writer and professor, very dynamic but also moody. There was no question that he was the boss in the family and that he wanted to mold us—I have an older sister—in his image. I always had a sense that I was disappointing him.

"I was shy and insecure as a kid and I stayed by myself a lot. Dad was totally wrapped up in himself and his work, and Mother was always trying to control my rebellious older sister. I was good little Theresa, pretty much forgotten.

"I was nineteen and a sophomore in college when my mother got sick. She came down with viral pneumonia first, but soon we learned she had lung cancer. Until the last few weeks, when she entered the hospital, I fed her, bathed her, held her hand, read to her. When she died, I flipped out.

"Just before Mother died, my father started an affair with one of his grad students. I never forgave him. Four years later, when he had a heart attack and died, I flipped out again. I was alone.

"After college, I didn't know what I wanted to do, so I took this secretarial job with a large corporation. It's drone-type work and I hate it; I come home from work with my stomach all tied up in knots. Anyway, Michael is in charge of ordering supplies for another division of the same company. He works downtown and he called me one day to check on a shipment.

"It turned out I had to be in his office the following week for a meeting. I walked in the door and I fell madly in love. He asked me to lunch and from that day on we dated steadily.

"Michael is a diabetic and at first I didn't understand the seriousness of that. Sometimes he'd say, out of the blue, 'I'm really hungry, I gotta eat now.' I'd think, 'Fine, I'm hungry, too.' But the truth is, Michael has to eat regularly throughout the day. He has to test his blood-sugar level two or three times a day. And if he's not careful, he can die.

"Once in the very beginning he casually mentioned, 'Oh, I'm diabetic.' I remember asking, 'What does that mean?' and he said,

'Nothing, really. I take insulin.' End of discussion. Michael appeared perfectly healthy, so I never thought anything more about it. Not once did he say, 'I am seriously ill and if I start to have an attack get me some orange juice or something else with sugar.'

"Anyway, we'd been dating about six months when we flew to Chicago for a friend's wedding. We had some time to kill, so we went to the Museum of Contemporary Art. All of a sudden, Michael got very quiet. It was about one o'clock and we hadn't eaten since breakfast, but back then I didn't know to pay attention to that.

"We walked outside and Michael started weaving and bobbing and looking as if he were going to pass out. I thought, God, he's a lunatic. Then it hit me: He's got to eat! I raced to a phone and called the emergency medical squad. I told them where I was and they told me to get him some orange juice. So I ran to this snack bar, but Michael was so far gone he couldn't even get the juice down. Finally the EMS guys arrived and gave him an injection. After an eternity he started to come out of it—fine, but embarrassed.

"That was the beginning of our problems. You see, Michael refuses to take his disease seriously. In fact, he refuses even to talk about it. Each time he has an attack, he promises it will never happen again—as if it were a question of willpower.

"Meanwhile, we'd become engaged and I'd moved into his apartment. We had a beautiful wedding at a small hotel in the city—we paid for it ourselves—and then went to Spain for a three-week honeymoon.

"But the honeymoon was over before a week was up. One night, after a long day of sight-seeing, we fell asleep early. Around two in the morning I woke up and realized Michael was having a severe reaction. It was horrifying, trying to communicate with the emergency medical people in my high school Spanish, thinking my husband was going to die right there.

"He came out of it, but I was devastated. I felt as if my whole future was crashing down around me. How could Michael do this? How would he be able to take care of me and the children we dreamed of having if he wouldn't take care of himself?

"We came back from our honeymoon early. That was four years ago and things between us have just gotten worse. Our marriage is a sham.

"When we come home from work, I rush around and get dinner ready and we usually eat in silence. Then Michael goes into the living room to watch TV and I go into the bedroom to unwind. I'm so angry at him now that there are nights I

can't even stand to be in the same room with him. I certainly don't want to have sex.

"I'm tired of pleading with him to take care of himself. Lately we've been fighting about everything. I'll buy a new sweater and he'll hit the ceiling. Look, I'm not frivolous. I don't buy four-hundred-dollar shoes. We both make very decent money, but Michael is an incredible penny-pincher, yelling at me to hurry up and close the refrigerator door so I don't use up electricity. He is so overly meticulous that he even gets upset if I don't put something back in the refrigerator in the exact same place it was before. His stinginess even extends to the baby we've talked about having—he's so hung up on how we'll be able to afford it that even that discussion goes nowhere.

"When Michael gets angry, he does things like refuse to take me to the grocery store. I hate to drive. The first year we were married I had an accident—nothing serious, but it left me terrified to get behind the wheel. And now when he's mad he uses this driving thing to get back at me.

"But as I said, our problems don't stop there. Last Sunday I was sleeping late. I woke up because I heard Michael talking to somebody on the phone in the hall. I peeked out the door and heard him say, 'So when was the last time you had sex?' and other things. I could see he had an erection. Something clicked in my brain; I remembered that the husband of one of my dear friends had been calling these sex services and seeing prostitutes—my friend found the charges on their credit-card bills.

"Later that day, while he was watching the football game, I went on a search-and-destroy mission. I pulled out all the credit-card receipts, and sure enough, there were hundreds of dollars' worth of calls going back for over a year and a half to things like Entre-Nous and Dial Desiree. I stormed into the living room. Michael didn't know what to say.

"I insisted we get help. I won't give up without a good fight, but I don't know what to do anymore."

MICHAEL'S TURN

"I'm glad Terry finally found out, I really am," said Michael, thirty-four, in a voice barely above a whisper. "It's a relief to have it out in the open. I know I have a problem. I'm very embarrassed. But at least I didn't go out and have an affair.

"Terry is wonderful; I don't want to lose her, but she's pushing me away. She won't let me be close. I can tell she's angry with me, but she won't tell me why. At least now we're here talking.

"Our problem is very simple: Terry doesn't want to make love. She says no so often I've stopped trying. You should see her when we get home from work. She's a maniac, whirling around the kitchen, throwing things into pots—you'd think she was trying to set a world record in dinner preparation. At the end of the day I like to relax. I know she thinks I don't help her enough, but if she took a half hour to unwind first, I'd help.

"Then, after dinner, instead of sitting and talking like normal people, maybe watching a little TV, Terry disappears into the bedroom. Or she'll rant and rave at the top of her lungs.

"She thinks I try to get back at her by not driving her all over the place. That's ridiculous. I'm not that kind of guy. I know she was very shook up after her car accident, and I was sympathetic. But that was three years ago. It's time she got over this hang-up.

"The only time we talk is when we argue over how much money she spends. I cannot understand why she has to buy a sweater a week. Both of us have good jobs, but we also have a lot of expenses. And if she wants to have kids in the future, we have to start saving today. I'm not saying she shouldn't buy any clothes—I'm saying she should be realistic. Buy what you need.

"Maybe my money worries are left over from my childhood. Dad was in the dry-cleaning business; he made a decent living, but we never really had much.

"I guess you could say it was a fairly traditional home: Mom stayed home and took care of my younger brother and me, while Dad was the boss, very strict, with lots of rules. My parents were so overprotective it made me crazy. I know they were very concerned about my health, but they never let me make any decisions on my own. I fought with them a lot. They didn't think I was studying hard enough, they didn't like the colleges I was applying to, they thought my decision to major in psychology was dumb.

"I was first diagnosed with diabetes when I was seventeen. I'd started to lose weight; I'd get very tired, hungry, and thirsty, and I'd urinate a lot. I had to go to the hospital for tests. When I got out, my parents said I shouldn't tell anyone about my diabetes. What did I know? I was a kid; I did what they told me to do.

"But I guess I was angry. I didn't want to be sick, and for a long time I relied on my mother to give me the injections. Terry's right. I don't know why I don't take better care of myself.

"Look, I don't know what else to say. I don't know why I started calling phone-sex services. I got the number from the back of a porno magazine. And yes, at first I denied it. I was scared. I'd never seen Terry so angry. But something drastic had to happen."

"Although this couple first came to see me about a sexual problem, that issue quickly became framed in the broader context of Terry's anger and resentment over Michael's refusal to own up to his illness, as well as their inability to resolve issues of control in their marriage," said the counselor.

"Michael had never made peace with the fact that he has diabetes. Like many people with a chronic illness, he hated to think of himself as anything less than a whole, well person. Sadly, his parents had made him feel ashamed of his illness. Michael grew up in a home suffused with what we call a Depression-era mentality, the belief that the world is a dangerous, terrible place, and as a result, safety and security must be your paramount concerns. Michael was convinced that Terry would reject him if she knew how sick he was. Because he had functioned in this pattern of denial for so many years, Michael was truly unable to see that his frequent attacks were directly linked to his unwillingness to deal responsibly with his disease.

"At the same time that his parents encouraged his denial, however, they also pampered him—his mother took on the responsibility of managing his illness and, later on, Michael expected his wife to do the same. His parents tried to control his life in other ways, too, issuing edicts on everything from where to go to school to what profession he should choose. Although Michael thought he was rebelling against such strictures, with few exceptions he did what they told him to do.

"Not surprisingly, as an adult, Michael had a compulsive need to control all areas of his life, no matter how minute. Even his arguments about having a child broke down into dollars-and-cents issues.

"In the beginning, Terry willingly played the role of rescuer—just as she had nursed her dying mother—because it made her feel needed. But those good feelings soon gave way to a simmering rage, and just as she couldn't express that anger to her autocratic father, so, too, did she have trouble telling her husband.

"When Michael refused to take care of himself and Terry was forced to witness his attacks again and again, she grew terrified of losing him just as she had lost her parents. Her anger was further fueled by his nit-picking control over her life: 'How can he bug me about closing the refrigerator door,' she demanded, 'when he refuses to take care of his health?'

"Terry was similarly conflicted at work. A bright, creative woman, she was stifled by a routine job but was afraid to ask for more responsibility. By the end of the day, she was wound so tight she couldn't relax.

"The first step in counseling was to insist that Michael take responsibility for his illness. When he finally realized that their success hinged on this issue, he began to change. He started to watch his diet, monitor his blood sugar, and take his insulin. Terry pulled back and stopped reminding him to eat properly. At one point, his doctor advised him to check into the hospital for a three-day evaluation. This was difficult for Michael to do, because it meant that his disease might be getting more serious and could involve a whole new set of instructions. But he went ahead with the tests, and as a show of support, Terry—who had signed up for a refresher course in driving—drove him there.

"Once the issue of Michael's illness was out in the open, this couple made progress very quickly. By talking about the connection between her childhood and her fear of losing Michael, Terry was able to label her anger for what it was and no longer had to act it out sexually. As she became more loving and responsive to him, Michael stopped calling the sex hotlines.

"We encouraged Terry to speak up in other ways. When Michael questioned her about a pair of shoes, she learned to say, 'I'm a responsible adult. I know whether I can afford these shoes. I resent the way you interrogate me.' She spoke up at the office, too, and when she did, her supervisors were impressed with her ideas and broadened her duties.

Happier at work, she arrives home calmer and more available to her husband.

"Terry and Michael ended therapy after a year. 'I get anxious about Michael's illness,' Terry told me at her last session, 'but I can trust him to stay on top of it now. And we've found that old closeness. I can't ask for anything more.'"

WORKING THROUGH THE TOUGHEST SEX PROBLEMS

It's understandable that Terry would be shocked at such a disclosure—and not surprising that she would immediately begin to doubt herself, her sexuality, and her marriage. Any wife in a similar circumstance would wonder: What does he get from these calls that he doesn't get from me? Is he sick?

While such behavior need not signal the end of a marriage, it does indicate a serious problem that must be resolved. Sexual problems left unspoken can ruin a relationship. Women like Terry need answers: What's behind such secret calls? The proliferation of sex hotlines clearly indicates that many couples are not able to talk honestly about sexual concerns and desires. Indeed, most men who resort to phone sex are afraid to express their deepest sexual fantasies to their wives, out of fear of being ridiculed or rejected. Simply bringing these concerns into the open, however, can enrich your sex life in general. Perhaps there are things you can do differently in bed that will please your husband as well as yourself. On the other hand, if he confides sexual fears or desires with which you are uncomfortable, you might consult a sex therapist for guidance. In either case, seek professional counseling to shore up your own self-esteem and feelings of confidence so you don't wallow in what's-wrong-with-me feelings.

"My Husband Doesn't Want to Make Love Anymore"

Liza tried absolutely everything she could think of to woo her husband—even greeting him at the front door in a skimpy negligee—but David still pulled away. Is a marriage without intimacy worth saving?

LIZA'S TURN

"I could meet David at the door wrapped in plastic wrap and he wouldn't notice," said Liza, thirty-two, a stunning redhead who managed to laugh in spite of the seriousness of her statement. "That's how bad things have gotten in the five years of our marriage.

"Not that they were ever great. I think I always sensed that David didn't really like me: Even when we were dating and I'd spend the weekend at his place, by Sunday I felt that he couldn't wait for me to disappear and leave him alone with the newspapers.

"You see, I could be in the same room with David while he's reading or working on one of his endless renovation projects, and he won't even see me, let alone hear when I talk to him. It makes me feel like a big zero, like I used to feel around my parents.

"My folks were wealthy and they gave me and my siblings—I have two older sisters and two younger brothers—a privileged life. We had riding and tennis lessons, live-in governesses, new wardrobes every season, the whole bit. But my parents were emotionally uninvolved. To this day I don't feel as if I know them as people. Mother was—still is—totally caught up in her own life.

"After high school, I enrolled in a state school and got odd jobs to pay for everything myself. I managed that way for two years, but I didn't think I could possibly keep it up. So I switched to an undergraduate nursing program.

"I met David when I was twenty-five. He'd just gotten his master's degree in architecture and was working for a large firm in the city. He was best friends with Rob, this guy I had been going with and planned to marry.

"Anyway, David moved in with Rob so we saw a lot of each other. But Rob became involved with drugs and the relationship was much too painful, so I ended it. That's when I sought out David. Coincidentally, he'd also just broken off with a girl who had broken his heart.

"One night, toward the end of one of our marathon phone conversations—we used to talk for hours about the kind of person we dreamed of meeting—David got very quiet and said, 'Liza, I think I'm looking for you.'

"That was a turning point. Soon we were seeing each other on a regular basis. But even then David was so remote. I'd want to talk to him or read him a passage from a book I was looking at, and he'd abruptly say, 'Read to yourself. Can't you see I'm busy?'

"Our sex life was pretty bad, too, and I used to wonder if we should go for therapy. David was simply not—is still not for that matter—interested in sex. My idea of romance is to climb into bed with a cold bottle of champagne and stay there for a week; David doesn't understand that.

"Still, after about a year or so of mostly seeing each other on weekends, I wanted to get married. David, of course, never mentioned the subject. So I gave him an ultimatum—marry me or call it quits. I guess that made him nervous. Anyway, we had a small, very romantic wedding at a country inn.

"But getting married didn't help as I thought it might. David was still very cold. He's not a handholder, not a toucher. What makes it all the more difficult is that I know he can be very loving. He's the most affectionate and devoted father to Jessie, our two-year-old son. So why can't he be a devoted husband to me, too?

"Tell me, is it too much to expect my husband to talk to me in the evening when he comes home from work, maybe give me a kiss and want to make love? I can't tell you the last time we had sex. It's clear David doesn't enjoy it when we do. Is he bored? Is he having an affair? I feel so rejected and unattractive. I try to tell him what's on my mind, but David does everything to avoid a fight.

"Look, I'm tired, too, at the end of the day. I love my job, and the more hours I work, the more money I make. David's the same way. He wants to earn more money and become a partner in the firm. We both wanted to buy and renovate this house, to have fine things, to go on nice vacations. But when I'm home, I'm home.

"What really astonishes me is that David will tell you he's perfectly content and happy. He always makes me feel as if I'm crazy to feel the way I do. Do you know how I got him to come here? I told him, 'Look, you've got to change. Either you figure it out, or I'm leaving. Period.'"

DAVID'S TURN

"It's amazing. Liza has absolutely no idea that she's a bitch on wheels," said David, thirty-four, a handsome six-footer with sun-streaked brown hair. "She constantly criticizes everything I do—from how I fix the bathroom tiles to how I make love.

"I know I'm not perfect, but this person Liza is talking about, this guy who is never there and doesn't care, well, it's just not me. And frankly, yes, I'd much rather spend my time with Jessie. It's a lot more pleasant than being with Liza.

"God forbid I forget the smallest detail of something we discussed earlier in the week, Liza attacks.

"But you know, if Liza was really as mad at me as she's saying she is now, how come she never tells me? I never have any idea that she's unhappy about something until several days later, when she suddenly blows up. And when she gets going, you can forget any kind of civilized discussion. I don't stand a chance. She is vicious.

"Liza keeps bringing up all this stuff about hugging and hand-holding. I don't even know what she's talking about. I love her, I've told her that—what does she want from me?

"Unlike Liza, I was pretty happy growing up, although my parents were very strict. You didn't talk to Dad; he ran his dry-cleaning business and he was The Boss. Mother worked full-time as a dental hygienist, so I could understand that at the end of the day they wouldn't want my younger sister and me hanging around. They'd feed us in the kitchen, then take their plates to the dining room and close the door. They needed some time to themselves.

"We didn't talk a lot in my house, but then again, I don't remember having any real problems that I needed to talk to my folks about. I did well in school and had lots of friends. If I ever did anything my parents didn't approve of, they wouldn't yell or scream, but you always knew how they felt.

"Liza says that even at the very beginning of our relationship, I was always remote. That's not fair. Liza was my best friend's girlfriend, and although I was really flattered that she was attracted to me, I felt damned uncomfortable with the whole situation. In my mind, she was off-limits.

"When I finally discovered that Rob didn't care about his relationship with Liza continuing, I loosened up. But she's right that I wanted her to go home at the end of the weekend. Liza smothered me; she still does.

"She says I ignore her when we're home together, but what she doesn't realize is that I get totally immersed in anything that I do—whether I'm at the office working or home fixing the bathroom—to the point that I simply don't notice what's going on around me. It doesn't mean I don't love her.

"Same with our sex life. It's not that I don't like sex or don't want to make love, but Liza's timing is lousy. When I get home from work, I need to slip into neutral for a while. So if she greets me in a flimsy robe and has candles lit all over the place, that's very nice, but it's just not going to generate the kind of romantic response she wants right then and there. I'm not bored, and I am not having an affair, but I'm not a wind-up toy.

"I'll tell you one thing: It's not easy making love to someone who finds fault with absolutely everything I do. I know I'm never going to please her, in or out of bed, so why try?

"Clearly she thinks I'm a failure when it comes to my work. She keeps pushing me to ask for more money, to go for that big promotion. Liza has much higher expectations than I do about the kind of lifestyle she wants to lead. I'm not saying I don't want these creature comforts. But she has visions of grandeur that go far beyond anything I think we ever need.

"Look, I don't want to split up. I know something's wrong, though I have no idea what to do about it. But all these problems are not solely my fault. I resent Liza blaming me for everything."

THE COUNSELOR'S TURN

"This is really a story of intimacy and anger," said the counselor. "Liza, ignored by her unhappy, uninterested mother and workaholic father, lost in the middle of five siblings, was largely on her own as a child.

"An earthy, physical woman with a high capacity for intimacy, Liza desperately needed to feel important, to be loved and nurtured. But she fell in love with David, a man who had never learned to get in touch with his own feelings and emotions and who, in fact, was afraid to get too close to anyone. Liza's hurt and disappointment that David could not respond to her in the way she expected turned to anger and bitchiness, which further pushed her husband away.

"Although Liza clearly felt a lack of love and intimacy in her relationship and thought she'd told David how she felt, until they began counseling, she had never specifically expressed her wishes and needs to him. Instead, she would focus on material goods because these were things she felt more comfortable asking for. (In spite of the fact that Liza came from a wealthy background, she had never really had much money of her own to spend; now she often found herself going overboard, mistakenly thinking she had to own something in order to be happy.)

"As a result, David was always afraid he'd never meet any of Liza's expectations or that his response would never be on target. Rather than fail, he chose not to respond at all—in as well as out of bed. And so the cycle continued: Liza tried everything to get David's attention, including coming to the door in sexy lingerie.

"When they first came for counseling, Liza was furious, David quiet but tense. I sensed he was terrified that she was going to leave him.

"Although I legitimized Liza's feelings—she did have a right to expect her husband to be affectionate and loving—I told her point-blank that the way she went about achieving her goals was totally inappropriate.

"For weeks Liza failed to see that her bitchiness was perpetuating David's withdrawal. During one session, when David was trying very hard to express how badly he felt when Liza screamed at him, she turned to face him on the couch and practically jumped on him and started shouting. David involuntarily pulled back. At that point I stopped the conversation: Did she realize, I asked, the terrible effect her words and her physical pushiness had on her husband? That session was a turning point for Liza. She finally started to understand that you can't demand love, that you have to be loving to get love.

"Liza had to learn, too, that David might at times be upset about work or something unrelated to her, and if he appeared distant, she should not automatically assume he didn't love her.

"It took David a long time to admit that his past family life was anything less than perfect. But as he spoke, I recognized right away that he had grown up in a household devoid of intimacy on two levels: a symbolic one in which the parents would never include the children in any daily activities (having them eat dinner by themselves in the kitchen, for instance) as well as a real one—David acknowledged that he never once recalled seeing his parents hold hands or kiss each other. He also didn't remember being picked up and hugged as a child. 'Dad wanted me to be tough, to be a man,' he recalled ruefully.

"David first had to learn how to recognize his feelings and then how to speak up and challenge Liza when he felt she was wrong. This was difficult for him: 'I'm scared she'll leave me,' he admitted at one point. 'I feel as if I'm hanging by a thread.'

"But as Liza learned to curb her outbursts, David felt much more comfortable opening up, and although he sometimes falls back into his old silent ways and tunes her out, he, too, has started to catch himself in the act.

"To help him maintain a better balance between office and home, I suggested he build transition time into his schedule. 'On the train coming home', David said, 'I try not to think about the problems of work. Now I just sit and stare out the window and sort of vegetate, so when I walk in the door I'm really there.'

"As the overall tension eased and as David and Liza became more naturally affectionate, their sex life improved, too. I suggested at this point that they make an intimacy pact: If Liza initiated sex one time, then David had to initiate it the next time. And if they went for more than eight days without having sex, they had to sit down together and discuss why. 'That worked great,' Liza reported. 'Now David doesn't have to worry. He just knows it's his turn!'

"Finally, we talked about the importance of building small moments of intimacy into their daily lives, something many long-married couples, especially those with two jobs and small children, often forget. Holding hands when they walk around the mall on a shopping trip or at the movies, and doing errands together instead of running off in opposite directions can make a difference.

"Liza and David ended counseling after a year and a half, but they call periodically to touch base. 'We both realized something else,' David said the last time we spoke: 'No job, no fancy clothes or boat is worth not being close with your family. I'm in the midst of this huge project at work and I'm going to see it through. But we've both agreed we're going to scale back. Now we know what's really important in life.'"

PLEDGING INTIMACY

Many couples, like David and Liza, have forgotten how to be intimate. The stress of balancing work and family obligations can be physically and emotionally exhausting, and a couple's sex life often reflects this strain. One partner may be in the mood, the other isn't. The rejected partner feels hurt and angry and unloved. In fact, it's quite common for partners to generalize a mate's sexual rejection at a given moment into a blanket "He doesn't love me or want me at all." Resentment brews. The result: stalemate.

The "intimacy pledge" below was written by Evelyn and Paul Moschetta, a husband and wife counseling team. Many couples in their practice have found it to be a catalyst for closeness. See if it works for you. On a piece of paper, write out the following pledge, sign it, and put it safely in a drawer.

We both agree that greater sexual closeness is a joint responsibility and we pledge that:

1. Each of us will be an active initiator of sex.

2. Each of us is free to decline, and the other will not be angry or resentful.

3. If more than a week goes by without sex, we will examine all the reasons why this has happened. In doing so we will speak honestly and openly, without criticizing or judging each other.

4. The partner who refuses an invitation will make the next overture within one week.

"MY HUSBAND IS IMPOTENT"

For twenty-six years, Janet and Ken had a wonderful sex life. But now something was very wrong and their search for an answer was driving them farther and farther apart.

JANET'S TURN

"It's very hard for me to talk about my sex life with a stranger," said Janet, forty-four, a striking woman who sat forward in her chair as she spoke. "It's such a private thing. But I love my husband very much . . . and I want our marriage to be the way it was. I hope you can help.

"Counseling was my idea. Ken would never have called you if I hadn't insisted. That's the way he is . . . Ken brushes problems under the rug. Even now, he'll probably tell you things aren't so bad.

"But there's no question this is tearing us apart. We are fighting more than we have in our entire marriage because Ken can't sustain an erection. And I have to say it isn't a once-in-a-while thing. This has been going on for nearly two years. I'm at my wit's end.

"You see, we've been married for twenty-six years and sex has always been a very important part of our lives. I met Ken when I was only fifteen; he was seventeen. We were both doing volunteer work at the community center. We started dating, and as soon as Ken graduated from college, we were married and he began teaching English at the local high school. Two years later I finished my college degree and became pregnant with our first child.

"Over the years, we've raised three terrific kids—of course, there have been rough times along the way. Our youngest, Greg, who's eighteen, was born with a clubfoot. He's fine now, but you can imagine how hard it was dealing with one specialist after another. The point I'm trying to make is that through all the years of bringing up kids, when you read about people not having time for sex and their love life fizzling, ours was fine. That's why it's so difficult to figure out what's wrong now.

"Of course, with a man like Ken it's always difficult to know what he's feeling, and hard as I try, I can never get him to tell me outright what's bothering him. This problem he's had recently with the school board is typical.

"Ken is a wonderful teacher and he's been acting as assistant principal for several years. About two years ago, the principal retired. Now, Ken was the ideal candidate for the job. In fact, they pretty much promised he'd get the position. But the school system is so political and people on the board threw a monkey wrench into the process. It was really awful and Ken had to fight for himself. After months of wrangling, they ended up giving the the job to someone else.

"Ken didn't even tell me right away. I found out from one of the other teachers. And when I asked him about it, he just shrugged and said, 'Janet, it doesn't really matter. We'll manage.'

"I know he was torn up by it. He'd worked hard his whole life— Ken's family was very poor. He put himself through school, getting

honors all the way. As usual, though, he pretended everything was fine. And when he does that, I always feel so closed off. Doesn't he want to share things with me?

"We're such opposites in that respect. I worry a lot and it helps me to talk things out. But whether it's a problem one of our kids is having in school or an argument I've had with my mother, I often feel Ken just doesn't want to hear about it. I start to talk and he tunes me out. The best I ever get is, 'Janet, I'm sure you'll work it out.' I get so angry that before I know it, I'm yelling my head off.

"You know, I've always had a sense that Ken's there for everyone except me. He's a very generous man, very involved in the community. You name a committee or board and he's on it—probably as chairman. Everyone knows they can count on Ken to help out if they have a problem.

"So why has it taken him so long to get around to doing something about his own problem? Ken just makes up excuses instead of seeking help. He'll bring up our vacation in Vermont last summer and the trip we took to Mexico last Christmas to prove that there isn't really anything the matter. Yes, sex was great on both those trips, but as soon as we got back home…

"In fact, lately, sex has become a major ordeal for me. I've started to dread it. It's frustrating, not being able to let myself go and enjoy it, but how can I? I never know if Ken will be able to make love or not. And when he can't, I feel so unsatisfied, so alone, I want to cry.

"I guess after all these years Ken isn't attracted to me anymore. I don't think he's having an affair or anything like that, and I know I'm not as young or as thin or as pretty as I used to be. Last Valentine's Day, Ken bought me these flimsy nightgowns and teddies; I knew he thought it might give our love life a boost, but to tell the truth, I feel very silly wearing them. And none of that stuff ever mattered before, so what difference can it make now?

"You know, we've been through a great deal together. I guess we'll manage to get through this, too. But we're at this impasse. Everything is so confusing, I don't know what to expect."

KEN'S TURN

"I'm tired of having sex be the sword of Damocles hanging over my head," said Ken, forty-six, a handsome man who spoke in a soft, deliberate way.

"I'm perfectly aware that I have a problem. And I'm also sure I'm a lot more uncomfortable being here discussing all this than she is.

"Look, I may not talk about it, but I think about sex plenty. I'm not used to having a problem and not being able to solve it. But Laura is exaggerating. When we're on vacation, when we get away, sex is super. Last year in Mexico we had night after night of terrific sex. I don't get it. Same plumbing.

"But what's this business about my not being there for her or talking to her about problems? Janet is a very bright, capable woman. She knows exactly how to handle any situation, always has. It's not that I don't care; she simply doesn't need my help.

"Look, I've never said this before, but sometimes Janet carries on so much, discussing every minute angle and detail of whatever it is that's bothering her, that I just can't take it. If I didn't tune her out, frankly, I think I'd go out of my mind. I wish she wouldn't yell so much, too, but that's just the way she is.

"And how can she say I'm more involved with other people than I am with my own family? For years I've worked hard, sometimes at two jobs, so we could have a nice home, raise three kids, send them to camp. When Greg had to go to the doctor because of his foot, I always took off from school to go. What does Janet want?

"This constant arguing is wearing me down, too. My parents fought a lot, and though it was mostly about money, I swore that in my own house we would never have such conflict.

"Besides, lately I've had to deal with more than my share of fighting. As Janet mentioned, I've been having some difficulties at school. I was up for a principalship, which I thought I deserved, but I didn't get it. Unfortunately, the whole process dragged on for a long time and there was nothing I could do about it. It wasn't that I didn't want it or wasn't upset that I didn't get it, but what good would it do to lose my temper after the fact?

"Right now, I'm not sure what I'm going to do. Should I keep on working at my same old job? Should I look for another one? I guess I could do some consulting; several people have approached me about working for them, but I don't know if I'll be able to make enough money doing that. I hate this feeling of being in limbo. But look, we'll work it out, we always have.

"I'd like to think we can work out this sex thing, too. I feel terrible that Janet is so unhappy with me. She's a wonderful wife and she deserves better. But sometimes when I start to kiss her, she pulls away. Wouldn't that get any guy upset? Other times I can tell she's just not into it. If the phone rings, she'll even get up and answer it, and by the time she's finished talking, well, forget it. My desire is gone and it's impossible to continue. So I figure it's best to just get up and focus my mind on something else.

"But it's gotten to the point that every time I touch her, I'm terrified I won't get an erection. I find myself thinking about it all day long. I tell myself, 'Tonight, it'll be different. Tonight, we'll try something new and different.' I even bought Janet some sexy nightgowns, but that didn't do any good.

"Still, all I want is for Janet to be happy. I don't want to let her down, and I hate it when she's this mad at me. So I'm hoping you can help."

THE COUNSELOR'S TURN

"**K**en and Janet knew intellectually that fighting about sex could only make things worse, but they were still unable to stop," said the counselor. "I wasn't surprised. No matter how well-read a couple is on sexual matters, impotence is such a volatile issue—reaching, as it does, to the core of a person's self-image and self-esteem—that many couples find it extremely difficult to deal with it on their own.

"Impotence is usually psychological in origin, but it's important to rule out any physical causes. Structural or hormonal abnormalities may be responsible. So I suggested that Ken see his doctor for a complete physical.

"Once Ken received a clean bill of health, we discussed some facts about impotence in general. First, I explained that certain changes in sexual responsiveness as one ages are perfectly normal. A man in his forties may need more stimulation to achieve and maintain an erection than he did in his twenties. Medication, such as the kind many men take to lower their blood pressure, can also adversely affect sexual responsiveness.

"But by far the single most common cause of temporary impotence is stress, such as Ken had on his job. Sometimes, simply recognizing that fact can go a long way toward reducing anxiety. But unfortunately, one episode of impotence often shakes a man's confidence so much that it becomes a self-perpetuating condition.

"That's precisely what was happening to Ken: Unable to find a solution on his own, he felt ashamed and he dwelled constantly on his failure. 'I didn't link my problems in bed to my problems at school,' Ken admitted during one of our sessions, 'but that's probably why things were better when we were away on vacation.'

"Interestingly, the fact that Ken and Janet were finally talking about their problem in a nonjudgmental atmosphere was an enormous relief to both of them. As often happens, this initial recognition was followed by a honeymoon period of several weeks in which their sex life was mutually exciting. Some couples stop therapy at this point. However, I reminded Ken and Janet that there had been other times during their marriage when sex had been fine for a period of time, only to have the impotence resurface, and I suggested they remain in counseling to determine what factors might be contributing to their difficulties. They agreed.

"Since Ken and Janet had been married such a long time, their life together had a much greater impact on their current problem than their early background did. So we concentrated on how they had developed a pattern of relating to each other that discouraged honest communication.

"For instance, Ken tended to avoid conflict of any kind—if Janet had problems at home or if he had them at work, he kept his own counsel. This greatly upset Janet, who dealt with her own anxieties by analyzing everything.

"What's more, Ken so keenly felt the need to be a good husband and provider that over the years he had completely lost his ability to assert himself. Since he truly believed he didn't deserve much happiness, Ken had to learn what I call healthy selfishness—that it was okay to express his own needs and desires, in bed or on the job. At the same time, however, he had to heed Janet's concern that he wasn't there for her emotionally. By expecting her to read his mind about problems in their relationship, he was actually pushing her away.

"Quick to anger, Janet had to

realize that you can't force someone to communicate. As she learned to control her temper and to talk calmly about something that bothered her, Ken started to speak up more. He finally admitted how unhappy he was at work, and after some discussion he decided to take an early retirement from his teaching post to accept a more lucrative consulting job at an educational research foundation.

"This decision was a turning point for Ken and Janet. Now that Ken was no longer burdened by concerns about his future, the tension at home eased considerably. This allowed them to start talking honestly about their sexual feelings for the first time.

"As Janet described how abandoned she felt when he couldn't make love, Ken finally understood how frustrating sex had become for his wife. Because he was so upset by his impotence, Ken had gotten into the habit of abruptly ending their lovemaking sessions, leaving Janet hurt and unfulfilled. With only harsh words and very little discussion between them, it was not surprising that Janet started to withdraw sexually as well as to doubt her own physical attractiveness. My next step was to give them homework assignments designed to make sex a truly communicative experience for them both.

"First, I instructed them to set aside time at least twice a week to shower together, to massage each other with lotion or oil, to fantasize together if they wished. They had to abstain from intercourse for the first week. I urged them instead to talk to each other about what pleased them as well as to focus on their own sensations and the joy of being together without worrying about performance.

"During the second week, I told them they could have intercourse only if they both wanted to, but they were to incorporate their massage and shower techniques into their lovemaking.

"These exercises proved very successful; Ken and Janet realized that if Ken lost his erection one night, it was not the end of the world nor did it signal a major problem. This gave them the confidence to vary their lovemaking; Janet learned how pleasurable it could be to try new sexual techniques or to wear a sexy nightgown if her husband asked her to. Ken learned that instead of leaping out of bed if he was unable to have an erection, he could satisfy Laura in other ways.

"After thirteen months, Ken and Janet ended counseling, thrilled with their success and confident that they can solve any future problems."

IMPOTENCE: WHAT TO DO, HOW TO HELP

Nearly every married couple, especially if they've been together as long as Janet and Ken, endure periods of sexual dysfunction. However, it is such a volatile issue that couples often find it difficult to resolve on their own.

While impotence is usually psychological in origin, it's vital to see a physician for a complete physical checkup to rule out any medical conditions—cardiovascular disease, diabetes, or prostatitis—that may be triggering the problem.

By far the most common trigger for the kind of temporary impotence that Ken is experiencing is stress. Stress can block the body's response to stimulation and cause a decrease of blood flow to the penis. The disappointments he recently had at work could certainly have contributed to his problem. Sometimes, simply recognizing that fact can go a long way toward reducing anxieties.

Couples struggling with impotence problems need to relearn how to be intimate so performance anxiety doesn't permeate every close moment. This playful exercise can do that: On separate sheets of paper, make a list of the physical things you would like to do together—everything from holding hands and taking showers to making love. Studies have shown that touch is very important in triggering emotional closeness, and when a couple is physically close it's often easier to recapture the exuberance and spontaneity they used to share. Compare lists and come up with a third master list composed of ideas from each. Select at least one activity from the list to do each week. At first, this exercise may sound silly. You may think: We have serious problems and you're telling us to take a shower together! Although it certainly won't make problems go away, it does make them seem less monumental—and you will be more willing to press for resolutions. At the same time, it can help you focus on what gives each of you pleasure without worrying about performance.

THE TIES THAT BIND: HOW OTHER PEOPLE CAN WRECK A MARRIAGE

PROTECTING A MARRIAGE FROM THE BATTLES triggered by others is the final area of conflict that can prove fatal to a marriage. Parents, in-laws, friends, siblings, ex-spouses, children, and step-children all affect a couple's relationship in many ways. In fact, over the years, the *Ladies' Home Journal's* column "Can This Marriage Be Saved?" has often focused on the friction, anger, and ultimate havoc that other people can wreak on a marriage. And the high divorce rate and the ensuing interlocking family relationships only complicate the matter.

Mothers-in-law, of course, have long been the butt of comedians' jokes, but no less divisive is the parent who can't stop criticizing or undermining a spouse; the rude stepdaughter who "borrows" her stepmother's clothes without asking or saying thank you; the ex-wife who still makes suggestive comments to a husband when she picks up the kids; or the in-laws who insist that, since they paid for a young couple's first new car, that automatically means they'll visit every Sunday.

Then there are the can't-be-ignored needs and demands of growing children. In couple after couple, marital problems surface once children enter the picture. Some couples enter counseling because they simply can't decide whether, or when, to have children in the first place or, if infertility is an issue, whether to adopt. Others find that once a child arrives, battles over who does what around the house, how financial resources will be allocated—not to mention why they never make love any more—drive a wedge between them. What's more, the dilemmas of raising young children often pale before the clashes and conflicts parents endure during a child's teenage years. What may have appeared to be insignificant differences between husband and wife become, through the prism of parenthood, magnified—and seemingly unmanageable.

While particular outside intrusions may change from case to case, the impact on a marriage is the same: less harmonious time for a couple to be together; feelings of guilt, frustration, and anger that trigger repetitive arguments; and a gradual drifting apart. Many couples are at first genuinely surprised that these "outside" relationships can become so highly charged and damaging to a marriage. *Can This Marriage Be Saved?* shows that understanding the potential for problems complex relationships hold is the first step in preventing those problems. The next step is for couples to figure out ways to deal with conflicts triggered by outsiders before the issues become so heated that all lines of communication are severed.

Of course, it's not merely the specific things outsiders do that can upset the balance in a marriage. It's the fact that, at times, they also become a lightning rod for marital tensions in general. A wife may be furious and hurt that her husband rarely has time for her. But, afraid to speak up, she may rail instead against her impossible mother-in-law, setting up an emotional triangle that obscures the couple's real problems. In the short run, it's easier to blame someone else for problems than to face the pain and disappointment her husband is causing. When this happens, it can be difficult for a couple to figure out what's really wrong, let alone resolve the problem.

In-law and other outsider problems are exacerbated when husband and wife don't see eye-to-eye on a situation. Perhaps a husband doesn't agree (or even realize) that his parents are causing problems for his wife—they've always been busybodies, he may insist, so why can't his wife let their comments roll off her back? Perhaps his hesitation to admit a problem stems from a fear of upsetting his parents or a reluctance to break with family traditions. Whatever the case, ignoring one partner's feelings or pretending a problem doesn't exist only makes it worse.

Can This Marriage Be Saved? shows that although it may seem like a Herculean task, partners can learn to deal diplomatically with others and still keep the marriage in sharp focus. But to accomplish this delicate balance—be it with in-laws, children, stepchildren, or others—certain points are worth remembering:

- Couples must acknowledge that one partner may have a problem; they can then draw upon a host of communication skills to calmly and candidly discuss each partner's view on the situation and negotiate differences. The man whose wife complains that her mother-in-law is constantly dropping over without calling, or offering unsolicited advice and comments on her childrearing, has a responsibility to tell his mother to stop.

- Couples must set limits, and they must present a united front when they do. Setting limits can mean many different things— limits on time, limits on behavior, limits on the kinds of information that are shared and discussed, and, if in-laws or other relatives live under one roof, limits on everything from who does the grocery shopping and cooking to how late at night it's acceptable to receive phone calls.

- Setting limits also means learning to say no, but not in a hurtful way. For instance, "I'm afraid we can't make dinner every Sunday, but we'd love to come in two weeks. Could we bring dessert?" sends an intrusive in-law the message that a couple want to maintain a relationship, but on terms that are comfortable for them, too.

- Couples must strike a balance between themselves and their children. While kids need reassurance that they are loved and cared for, parents still need to establish rules—especially for privacy and time for themselves—that they both enforce. Differences of opinion should always be discussed privately, not in front of the children.

- The problems of stepfamilies must be always acknowledged and respected. The Brady Bunch notwithstanding, it's not easy to combine two families, each with its own values, traditions, and expectations. Since it often takes years to work through all the resentments and conflicts, couples should not berate themselves for failing to make the process seamless or painless. Nor should they expect to love stepchildren the way they love their own. However, they must treat them, and expect to be treated, with courtesy. What's more, couples who have weathered the upheavals of stepparenthood have learned to leave disciplinary issues to the natural parent rather than march in like gangbusters and assert their power.

Also essential is the need for new stepparents to forge their own relationship with stepchildren, apart from a spouse. It can be hard for a new stepparent to enter the circle of a family. It helps when he or she makes a conscious effort to spend time with each child, listening to his or her feelings, sharing dreams.

As the following case histories reveal, couples can indeed work together to prevent outsiders from playing one spouse against the other. And in doing so, couples learn to appreciate that other people in their lives can add to, not just subtract from, a marriage.

"MY IN-LAWS ARE DRIVING ME CRAZY"

Ever since Don's parents moved in, Leslie insists, their marriage has disintegrated. How can she make him understand she feels like a stranger in her own home?

"I want a divorce," said Leslie, thirty, a petite blonde. "Our five-year marriage is hopeless and I don't want Don to talk me out of ending it.

"The thought of going it alone with an infant daughter is pretty scary, but I feel so alone already, it can't be much different. Since Don's parents moved in with us, he's turned into a different person. We never talk anymore. We just scream.

"Actually, it was my idea to move my in-laws here. They had retired and moved to California, but they were very unhappy there. They had health problems, too, so I thought that if they lived with us, we'd be in a better position to help them if they needed it. Pooling our financial assets to buy a nice house made sense, too.

"Don had reservations about my idea, but I convinced him. Actually, I had never met his parents—they couldn't come to our wedding because his mom had been hospitalized with heart problems and didn't want to make the long trip. But we had talked on the phone and got along great. I was so naive!

"An only child, I grew up in a very small town—there were six people in my high school graduating class. My dad came from a wealthy family, but when I was ten, he was cheated out of his hardware business by a dishonest partner. We lost everything. My parents sued the man, and the only thing that kept my parents going was the hope that justice would prevail. We ultimately lost the court case, however. After the decision, my parents were devastated, and they divorced a short time later.

I never see my father and speak to my mother only rarely.

"When I was nineteen, I moved to San Antonio, the nearest big city, and found a job as a clerk in a department store. You can't imagine what a culture shock that was. But after five years I had settled into a quiet life. I think I fell in love with Don the first moment I saw him. I had gone to a club with my girlfriend, something I had never done before, and there he was in his Army uniform. We danced a few times and then he asked me out. Part of me was terrified; he was from Boston and my small-town up-bringing made me wary of big-city types.

"Don was wearing a suit and tie when he picked me up for our first date and he brought me yellow roses, too. We went to an elegant restau-rant, another first for me.

"Don had been married and had two small children. His wife had left him for another man—his best friend, no less—and my heart went out to him. But everything seemed to be per-fect between us. Don was making plans for a wedding as well as for the rest of our lives, which was fine with me. He had everything under control.

"I suppose I was so blinded by love I didn't realize how wrapped up Don was in his military career. This man lives and breathes his job. Don is a medical lab technician and he signs on for every committee at work; to him, that's part of being a 'good soldier.' So, even though we were married, I wasn't seeing very much of him at all.

"On top of that, his children—Caitlin was five at the time, and Jere-my was three—came to visit every other weekend. After an hour of token fatherhood, he'd inevitably have to go to work. I'd be left to en-tertain his kids.

"But I never said anything. I just didn't know how to bring it up and thought I would sound selfish if I did. Instead, I decided to surprise Don by joining the military myself shortly after we married. My clerk's job had no future and I wanted to share Tom's life more. I hoped it would bring us closer.

"Don was furious; he resents any decision that's not his. But he came around after he went with me to the recruiter and helped set me up in the computer training program.

"His parents arrived just before I came back home after my basic train-ing. I walked in the door of our tiny apartment to find the whole thing re-arranged. There was even a sign hanging on the refrigerator saying 'Alice's Kitchen'—that's Don's mother's name. She did ask if I mind-ed and, of course, I said no, but it re-ally broke my heart.

"I'll never forget our first Thanks-giving morning together. Don's mother and I were getting dinner ready. In my mind, I had imagined it would be wonderful, the two of us in the kitchen talking and cooking. That morning, I was peeling potatoes and left a little skin on one. Don's mother didn't want to ruffle my feathers, so instead, she told Don to tell me. He came in and whispered in my ear, 'Be sure to get all the skin off.' I could have died.

"But that's now typical of our family life. My mother-in-law complains to Don about everything I do. She puts me down when he's not around. Don will say things like, 'Mom, you'll have to teach Leslie how to make a pot roast like this.' He doesn't realize that every time I try to help her with anything, she informs me that her son has never eaten anything like that and never will.

"On top of this, Don and his mother argue all the time, yelling and swearing at each other. I'm not used to that. Don's father pretends he doesn't even hear them, hiding behind his newspaper. Whenever I try to talk to Don about how I feel, he tells me I'm being too sensitive.

"I soon realized I'd become the outsider in my own home. All the spontaneity had gone out of our marriage. No more romantic things, like tossing a blanket in the back seat of the car and heading to the woods for an impromptu picnic.

"Despite the distance between us, Don and I were determined to have a baby. At the time Lindsey was born, she was the only bright spot in my life. We had been married almost four years. I put Lindsey in day care—my mother-in-law couldn't handle the responsibility of a baby—

and returned to work when she was six weeks old. Don was working crazy hours and I was left to deal with his mother. Don and I were hardly speaking. I know I shouldn't have, but I began bringing the baby into our bed to sleep. I admit it was my way of telling Don it was hands off. I was so mad.

"When Lindsey was two months old, we found a house we all agreed on. I was so relieved, thinking, again naively, that once we had a bigger place, my mother-in-law and I would stop getting on each other's nerves. But things got worse.

"I've had it. I have to face the fact that Don and I are strangers. The worst part is that Don has become compulsive just like his mother. The other day he had a fit because I had the coasters for drinks on the coffee table instead of the table where they used to be.

"I love Don, but our marriage is in a shambles and the only way I can survive is to get out. You've got to help me convince him that divorce is best for everyone concerned."

DON'S TURN

"This is just like Leslie," said Don, thirty-seven, a tall, serious man with a precise, disciplined manner. "She wants a divorce, and I'm the last one to know about it.

"Leslie operates entirely on emotion and impulse. Like when she joined the military. Without one word to me, she quit her job and enlisted. Most wives would discuss a career change with their husbands, but Leslie had to 'surprise' me. I found out from a message on the answering machine. I don't enjoy surprises. My first wife surprised me by running off with my best friend.

"I love Leslie and I love our daughter. I won't deny we've had major problems, but I did try to warn her about having my parents move in with us. She was determined we'd be this big happy family, and now that the reality doesn't match her fantasy, she's ready to pack her bags and quit.

"There's also no doubt that I come from a vocal family. Yelling and swearing were commonplace when I was growing up. It doesn't mean anything, and I can't understand why Leslie goes into such a tailspin. My father was always, well, complacent, so I guess I expected Leslie to tune it out like he did.

"I should tell you that my father is a recovered alcoholic, but before he joined Alcoholics Anonymous, it was sort of Mom and me against the world—my two sisters are seven and ten years older than I am. We never knew from one day to the next what he would be like when he got home from work. I think yelling allowed us to let off steam over the frustration and anger we were feeling about Dad. We always knew there was love underneath.

"I moved out when I went to college, which went over like a lead balloon with my mother; she had depended on me for so long. I loved my independence, but I wasn't especially excited about college. Some Vietnam veterans in my classes got me interested in the military, though, so I decided to drop out and enlist in the Army.

"Except for a couple of low moments, I even loved basic training. I'd had twelve years of parochial schooling, so the discipline wasn't anything new to me. The rest of the guys were in shock from being yelled at all the time, but again, that wasn't new for me either. Once I got over the shock of Leslie's enlistment, I was proud that she wanted to serve in the Army, too.

"Leslie was so easy to love, so sincere and refreshing. When I met her, I had just gotten divorced and I felt shy and awkward dating again. I didn't think she'd go out with me; she didn't know I was just as excited and nervous as she was. I think I fell in love with her that night, too.

"Then, immediately after we married, Leslie started campaigning to have my parents move in with us. I tried to tell her that my mother is the kind of person who is happy being unhappy, but she wouldn't listen. I loved Leslie's compassion. Besides, splitting the cost with them was the only way we could afford a house, which we both wanted.

"Right away, I felt the pressure. I

was working long hours in the lab; the research we were involved with at the time was critical. I was stressed to the breaking point, and suddenly I had to deal with a new bride, my parents, and disputes over potato peelings.

"You know, Leslie never told me how much it bothered her that my mother rearranged the furniture. And she never told me that my mother criticized her cooking. I thought Leslie was relieved that Mother was there to cook and clean since she had a new full-time job.

"Look, I know my mother can be difficult. But it's easier to placate her than to fight her. I've been doing that all my life. Why can't Leslie? Her remark about token fatherhood hurts. She was the one who wanted to be close to my kids. I thought she wanted the time to develop her own relationship with them.

"Lately, I feel my world is closing in on me. I've got a stressful job, a crushing mortgage, a new baby, an ex-wife, and two kids. On top of that, I feel guilty because I can't make peace between my wife and my parents.

"Leslie says I've changed. Well, I think she's the one who's changed. She is no longer interested in being close and makes it clear she doesn't want to have sex, since she has been bringing Lindsey into bed with us.

"No, I don't want a divorce. I'm as sad as my wife that our family is torn apart."

THE COUNSELOR'S TURN

"These two were struggling with so many pressures that even a couple who communicated well would be under stress," said the counselor. "Leslie and Don had such serious communication problems, I wasn't surprised that they were in turmoil. Although it was clear that the arrangement with Don's parents was not working, both Leslie and Don continued to feel guilty about it. Neither was able to discuss the subject without exploding.

"Don and Leslie are sincere, likable people, and both of them had known considerable pain. They also shared a genuine compassion for the needs of others. Unfortunately, from the beginning of their relationship, they had put everything and everyone ahead of themselves. And they never had the chance to establish themselves as a couple before Don's parents moved in.

"Like many children of alcoholics, Don yearned for stability and order. His idealized vision of military life and responsibility gave him a convenient excuse to ignore the problems in his marriage. Leslie had also been raised in an unpredictable, emotionally barren home. On a lifelong quest for the happy family life she had lost at an early age, she desperately hoped her in-laws would fill the void.

"When they met, Leslie and Don

each perceived the other as having the missing piece they needed to make their life complete. Leslie was attracted by Don's big-city background; he was the sophisticated man who would be decisive and educate her in the ways of the world. However, Leslie gave him far more credit in this department than he deserved. Having attended an all-male high school, Don's experience with the opposite sex was limited: Shy, demure Leslie seemed ideal compared to his wayward first wife and domineering mother.

"Don's assessment of their basic personalities was correct. He operated on logic; Leslie operated on emotion. This combination of 'feeler' and 'thinker' can be very effective in a marriage when they complement each other. Unfortunately, by the time I saw these two, the qualities that had attracted them to each other had become intimidating and irritating. My goal was to build on their genuine love and concern for each other's welfare.

"During our first few sessions, Don and Leslie tended to talk more to me than to each other. But in time, and with my guidance, they grew more comfortable expressing their feelings to each other. During one session, they discovered that they both yearned for time alone together but had never made it a priority. Now they've agreed to hire a baby-sitter every other Saturday night so they can go out alone.

They'll reserve every other Sunday for a family outing with all three children. They've also promised to discuss any new plans or extra projects with each other before committing to do them. Leslie also realized that bringing their daughter into bed was a childish way of getting back at her husband and she's agreed not to do it.

"Because of their poor communication skills, this couple ran into problems whenever conflict arose. I pointed out that Leslie's stoic refusal to vent her anger and frustration was just as damaging to the peaceful home they both wanted as Don's yelling was. Don was honestly baffled at his wife's unhappiness, because she had never expressed her feelings to him. Once he was aware of how hurt she had been, he was much more conscious of making comments about his mother's cooking—and less willing to play middleman between them. Instead of placating Mom, he tried hard to support his wife. Instead of tuning out when his mother spoke to Leslie, he came to his wife's defense whenever his mother made a cutting remark.

"At this point, I outlined some fair-fighting strategies for them: Whenever tempers started to flare, I told them, they had to agree to stick to one subject at a time. What's more, they had to give each other a chance to say everything they had to say, without criticizing, judging, or interrupting. If they couldn't resolve a dispute, they learned to set a time limit of no more than one-half hour for discussion, at which point they would table the discussion but set another time and place to resume the conversation.

"This structured form of discussion enabled Don and Leslie to finally face some hard decisions about his parents. They decided to put their house on the market and look for a smaller one so that their mortgage payments would be more manageable. They were lucky and got back what they paid for the house. They've asked Don's parents to move to an apartment complex for senior citizens a few miles away, where they will be safe and cared for.

"As the tension eased at home, as Leslie saw her husband stand up to his mother and support her, these two began to feel much closer. Don was also more relaxed at home. Although he will probably always be more conscious of neatness and order than Leslie is, they have both learned to laugh at his idiosyncrasy rather than argue about it.

" 'We've had our own basic training in marriage,' Don said at one of our last sessions. Leslie agreed: 'I think we feel much more capable of handling problems.' "

HOW TO MAKE PEACE WITH YOUR IN-LAWS

As Don and Leslie are finding, it's not easy to live under one roof with another generation. As more young couples move back home to live with parents, and as elderly parents move in with adult children, these fairly predictable problems often result. Whether the new living arrangement is for one month, one year, or longer, it's essential to establish rules as well as methods for compromising when those rules must be bent. The following two suggestions can ease the tension:

1. When problems with in-laws loom, take immediate steps to talk openly and candidly about each partner's feelings and perspective on the issues.

2. Set limits that are clear to everyone. Setting limits has a dual purpose: It protects a couple from outside intrusions and allows them to form a more intimate bond. Limits should be set not only on the amount of time you spend with others, but also on the kind of information about your personal life you will share, as well as the help and advice you will seek. And if that help extends to financial aid, be specific about unspoken expectations. For example: Does borrowing money to remodel your home mean you are expected to add a guest room so relatives can visit?

"My Stepdaughters Are Destroying Our Marriage"

—

Rona expected her step-daughters to resent her initially, but she thought that in time they'd all get along. How can a marriage flourish when others seem hell-bent on destroying it.

RONA'S TURN

"I try so hard to be a good stepmother, but I always feel like a failure," said Rona, thirty-eight, as she slowly twisted the strap of her shoulder bag. "The girls are at best distant; we fight all the time, and I'm afraid I'm losing Patrick, too.

"I grew up in a rural community in Pennsylvania. My father was a fireman, my mother was a home-maker, but ever since I can remember she was very sick. She had a stroke when I was twelve and was totally disabled after that. I took on all the household chores.

"My father was very strict. Although he never hit us, my sister and I were absolutely terrified of his temper. I was a lonely kid, and most of the time I felt so angry that all I wanted to do was get out of there. I had to pay for college myself, so I worked during summers and vacations to save money. I also won a few scholarships, which of course helped.

"One of my jobs had been with a large marketing company, and when I graduated from college, they offered me a position in the personnel department. I liked the company, so I stayed, and now I head the department. The company agreed to pay for me to get my master's in management training. Patrick was in the same program.

"Ours was a two-year program; you went one weekend a month, plus two full weeks spliced in there somewhere. It was pretty intense and we all got very close. I'd had a series of relationships that never worked out—mostly with married men, and I'm not very proud of that. When I met Patrick, I wasn't thinking marriage; I was happy being single.

"But slowly the relationship changed; we fell deeply in love and got married two years ago.

"Patrick had always told me about his first marriage and his two daughters—Beth, who's now sixteen, and Hilary, twelve. He and his ex-wife, Cheryl, have joint custody. Although Patrick and Cheryl had been divorced for five years, the girls were wary of me from the start. That didn't surprise me—but I wasn't prepared for the continued hostility.

"It's hard to know where to begin. The girls don't treat me with any respect. From what I can determine, they had few rules when they were growing up. Even now, when they're at their mother's house—the girls spend one week at our house, one week at hers—they never make their beds or do any chores. I've always worked and feel it's important for everyone to be a full participant in family life. But they don't even set the table or put their own dishes in the dishwasher.

"The girls don't respect my things, either. They think nothing of borrowing my shampoo or of shuffling through my drawers for a sweater or a piece of jewelry without asking. They just assume it's okay, and although I ask them not to do it, they still do.

"What makes me angry is that Patrick never comes to my defense. He promises he'll speak to the girls, but he never follows through.

"I can tell they think I'm a real bitch. I lose my temper, but sometimes they do very hurtful things. Last month I organized a sweet-sixteen party for Beth. I cooked an enormous amount of food for all her friends—and I didn't even get a simple thank you. Last Mother's Day was probably the saddest day of my life. Neither one even gave me a card or wished me Happy Mother's Day.

"Patrick lets his kids do whatever they want. Oh, he'll tell Beth she has an eleven o'clock curfew, but if she waltzes in at midnight, he leaves it to me to punish her.

"This past year has been particularly bad with Beth. She recently announced that she wanted to live with her mother full-time—she hates switching houses. Patrick doesn't know whether to let her go, and we're all fighting about it constantly.

"But most of the time, Patrick is in a state of blissful oblivion about all this. We talk about what the rules should be concerning home-work or having boys over and agree on something, and then Patrick just doesn't follow through.

"And as I said, I'm afraid that soon I won't even have a marriage. Oh, our sex life is fine, but I just feel Patrick isn't there for me anymore. I try to discuss problems at work, but he doesn't listen. He cuts the con-versation short by saying, 'Rona, you can do this and you can do this.'

"I love these girls, but some-times I feel that maybe I don't love them enough. I resent the fact that I do all those things a mother does yet they don't feel close to me. I don't want children of my own, and I know that Patrick doesn't want to start over either, so that's not the issue. Having a close relationship with my stepdaughters means the world to me. Why can't I do any-thing right?"

PATRICK'S TURN

"Why is everyone on my case?" asked Patrick, forty-nine, a lanky, bearded man with bright red hair. "I know it's not easy for Rona, but to tell you the truth, I don't see what the fuss is all about. Beth and Hilary are good kids. Okay, maybe if we're going by Emily Post's book of etiquette, my daughters should ask permission to borrow a sweater. But, hey, that's what teenage girls do. They rum-mage through their parents' closets. I don't mind; what's mine is my kids', too.

"Look, I raised my kids a certain way. Maybe my ex-wife and I were too laid-back, I don't know. I think Rona is too strict and expects too much. Right now, the girls are very upset. From their point of view, the rules are changing in the middle of the game. Rona also makes a big deal about presents and cards. I know she is upset about last Moth-er's Day and birthdays and such, but I just can't get worked up about things like that.

"Rona talks a lot about what the girls should do to change. Well, I think she should make some changes, too. I want Rona to be more tolerant. I want her to share the responsibility and discipline with me. If the girls take stuff she doesn't want them to take, then she should tell them right away, and not expect me to handle it for her later.

"Rona's right, though: I do say I'll talk to them and then I don't. I guess I just don't want any trouble. I want us all to be happy.

"You know, I was so unhappy growing up, I wanted life for my kids to be different. I grew up the oldest of four in a middle-class sub-urb of Boston. My dad was a manag-er in a steamship company. He was very cold and unaffectionate. I knew he wanted me to excel academically and become a model child, and I did. He went to work, came home, had dinner, and read a newspaper. I desperately wanted to know him, but I never knew him at all.

"My mother was an alcoholic. I'd come home from school and find her still in bed. I tried to take care of her, but she got worse, and when I was in high school, she died of a heart attack.

"I started dating my first wife in high school, went to college nearby, got a degree in marketing, got married, and had two kids. Pretty standard stuff. But after fifteen years, we had grown apart.

"After the divorce, Cheryl and I did everything to make our daughters' lives as stable as possible. I had hoped the week-to-week arrangement would work; I'm very upset that Beth wants to move out.

"Rona and I used to have an extraordinary relationship. How can she say I'm not there for her? Has she told you that when she gets upset she won't talk to me for days? She plays the silent martyr. I ask what's wrong and she says, 'I don't know.' That's why I walk away. I tell myself, 'If and when she figures it out, she'll tell me.'

"I love Rona very much. She's tremendously capable and her new boss does expect a lot of her. So when she becomes agitated, I help her figure out exactly how she can manage her time—after all, I make my living as a strategic planner! Why, when I'm trying to help her, does she see me as uncaring?"

THE COUNSELOR'S TURN

"The problems Rona and Patrick were having are typical of stepfamilies. Although they also needed help dealing with such marital issues as communication and lack of intimacy, Rona's problems with her stepdaughters proved so divisive that it was vital to tackle those first.

"Rona's childhood in a home devoid of love, warmth, and emotional closeness did not prepare her well for her new role. She grew up feeling alone, unloved, and insecure—but with a steely determination to make her own way in life.

"Underneath that strong exterior, however, there was a frightened little girl who yearned to be loved. Her history of affairs with married men reflected her lack of self-worth; she didn't feel she deserved to have a full, rich relationship of her own.

"When I first met him, Patrick was sad and confused. He had no idea how to handle the conflicts between his wife and his children, and after some feeble attempts and many broken promises, he chose not to deal with the problems at all.

"Like his wife, Patrick grew up in an emotionally empty household. With no one to talk to, this quiet, sensitive little boy would simply retreat to his own room. Patrick learned to turn inward and deny his emotions; he was totally divorced from his feelings.

"Interestingly, Patrick unconsciously became the same kind of absentee parent to his daughters that his own parents had been to him. He and his first wife had a laissez-faire attitude toward disciplining children, which proved to be a serious obstacle in his marriage to Rona.

"The problems began when Patrick started to date Rona and escalated when they married. I explained that when children reach their teens, many stepfamily problems, especially those involving joint custody, intensify. Teens are very concerned with their social lives; they want their friends to know where they are. And their emotional state is so chaotic that they often need the structure and stability of one home. There is also a desire at this age to live with the same-sex parent.

"As a family therapist, I felt it was important to meet Beth and Hilary. I saw the girls in separate as well as joint sessions with Patrick and Rona, and this gave me the perspective I needed.

"The girls were clearly angry at seeing Rona take over their father. They told me Rona was snarling, stiff, and formal, which was all true. In fact, Beth felt that the only way she could find herself was to leave. She didn't have enough of a history with Rona to be able to yell and fight, then come back loving, as you could do with a natural parent.

"I told Rona that she was expecting too much of herself and of the girls. In most cases, a stepmother will never love her stepchildren the way she would love biological children, and they will never love her in the same way they love their biological mother. She should stop berating herself and feeling guilty for something that is a fact of life. I also told her that she should not expect to change her stepdaughters' behavior. That was the job of the biological parent.

"Then I turned to Patrick and told him that it was *his* job to discipline his daughters, not Rona's. Any stepparent who disciplines a stepchild without a long history with them is doomed to failure. If Hilary doesn't do her homework, Patrick, not Rona, must say something to her. If Beth misses curfew, Patrick must speak up. However, if Hilary refuses to help clean up the dishes after dinner, it's Rona's responsibility to make her feelings known. She should say, 'I don't like it when I ask you to do something and you don't do it.' The first situation involves discipline in general; the second relates directly to Rona and Hilary's relationship.

"Many stepfamily problems simply take time to work out, but at the very least, Patrick had to ensure that the girls would treat Rona with respect. He also had to tell the girls that if they wanted to borrow something, all they had to do was ask—

but that asking was very important. And they were required to pitch in with the housework.

"I told Rona that some of her problems with her stepdaughters would ease if she could learn to be more flexible. She had lived alone for many years and she was not used to compromising. When Hilary used her shampoo or borrowed a sweater, she had to try not to feel threatened. Once Patrick made it clear to the girls how important it was to Rona that they ask before borrowing something, and once they started to clean up their rooms and help with the dishes, Rona's anger subsided—as did the family fights and tears.

"Then, in meetings with Patrick and Rona, we discussed the pros and cons of honoring Beth's wishes. Finally, Rona and Patrick decided it would be best for everyone not to fight her desire to move out of the house. At the end of the school year, Beth will move in with her mother; Hilary will stay with Rona and Patrick.

"It was time, then, to focus on the marriage. Rona and Patrick wanted a more intimate relationship but were at a loss as to how to build one. This was a couple that didn't know how to have fun together. So, although it may sound silly, we tried scheduling some fun. Patrick and Rona took turns planning evenings out, finding a restaurant or getting tickets for a show. They've started to make friends as a couple and travel.

"When Rona was upset, she'd refuse to talk. I suggested that Patrick follow her and insist she tell him what was bothering her. In time, Rona stopped walking away. Or, if she felt she needed some space, she learned to say, 'I need time to pull myself together. I'll be back in half an hour.' By working together, a disappointment or hurt was settled in a matter of hours instead of dragging on for a week.

"I also tried to help Patrick learn to listen when Rona was upset instead of leaping in with a solution. Like many men, Patrick was oriented toward solving problems and saw her many comments about work as mere complaining.

"'Rona doesn't need help in solving her problems, at least not right now,' I told Patrick. 'Right now, she needs nurturing and reassurance.' And in one session, when Rona was extremely anxious about work, Patrick leaned over, put his arm around her shoulder and said, 'Rona, everything is going to be all right. And you know why? Because I love you.' No one had ever said anything like that to Rona before. I could see her whole body instantly begin to relax.

"This couple was in counseling for two years. They worked hard, and they've learned it takes a long time to forge new bonds as a family. And they have far exceeded my—as well as their own—expectations."

WHEN PARENTS REMARRY: SMOOTHING THE WAY FOR THE KIDS

It's not unusual for children, even those who are adults themselves, to be suspicious, if not undermining, of a parent's remarriage. They may wonder: What will my relationship with this new person be like? How will my relationship with my parents change? How will holidays and other special occasions be celebrated? Which rituals will be continued, and which forgotten? The first task in dealing with such issues is for both partners to acknowledge that they are real and *will* happen. Keep these pointers in mind:

1. **Give peace a chance.** Change may take a long time. Experts in stepfamily problems often remind us that a stepfamily, by definition, is born of a loss. It can take years—the Stepfamily Association cites seven as average—to resolve conflicts, so don't be too hard on yourselves. Remember, too, that all families, even intact ones, fight. The Stepfamily Foundation, Inc. is located at 333 West End Avenue, New York, NY 10023, 212-877-3244. Their 24-hour information line is 212-799-STEP.

2. **Remind yourselves** that you have the power to change the way you act and react to others. Acknowledge your stepchildren's feelings. While you can certainly hope that they will feel close to you in time, you can't legislate love. You can insist, however, that they treat you and your belongings with care.

3. **Expect children,** especially teens, to be rebellious and at times undermining. It's not easy to figure out who you are, as well as what your role and place are in the new family—all at the same time.

Don't be surprised, either, if a stepfamily situation that seemed to work when the youngsters were grade-school age suddenly goes awry when they enter the teenage years. It may be time to rethink family rules and procedures, even custody arrangements.

4. **Don't force love or affection.** Make it clear to stepchildren that you have no intention of supplanting their biological parent. Meanwhile, give them time and space to develop their own relationship with you. Be a friend or mentor first. Spend time with each child, one-on-one if possible, so you can learn to enjoy each other and share interests. Keep promises and confidences. Once they know they can trust you, the rest will follow.

5. **Make sure children** know the rules and acceptable boundaries, and when they have gone too far, leave discipline to the biological parent. While stepparents should never swallow their anger when a child misbehaves, trying to be the major rule enforcer, especially with a defiant teenager, will likely backfire.

"HIS EX-WIFE IS RUINING OUR MARRIAGE"

evon doesn't understand why Luke can't tell his ex-wife to leave them alone. But although her husband tries to explain, they remain trapped in a cycle of arguments that prevent them from being civil.

DEVON'S TURN

"If my husband really loves me, why doesn't he tell his ex-wife to leave us alone? She's destroying our family," sobbed Devon, a ruddy-cheeked thirty-five-year-old with more than a trace of an accent left from her British girlhood. "I can't believe I'm crying like this. I'm sorry. This is so unusual for me. I never break down, not even during major tragedies. I mean, my little sister Amy died of spinal meningitis when she was four and I was seven, and I kept my composure even then.

"You know, I haven't thought about that for years, but now I see how much my stepdaughter Cassie reminds me of Amy. Amy was the sweetest child ever born. Never contrary, not even when she should have been a terrible two. We always had a wonderful time together.

"It's eerie, actually, how much Cassie looks and behaves like Amy, although I must admit, Cassie hasn't been herself lately. She's nine now, and her mother is really trying to turn her against me. This woman—her name is Ronnie—is seriously disturbed and an alcoholic, but she does have joint custody of Cassie with Luke, my husband. Cassie goes to visit Ronnie every weekend and some holidays. Those visits are traumatic for all of us. Ronnie gets hysterical about minutiae, like Cassie's clothes or the way she wears her hair. Cassie can wear the usual jeans and a T-shirt one time and we hear nothing, and then next week it's a huge issue, with Ronnie throwing a tantrum right in front of the poor child. She's totally unpredictable. My heart breaks; how could it not affect her child?

"Still, it pains me to see Cassie changing and becoming sharp-tongued and cantankerous. When I first met her she was three. Luke was trying to teach her to ice skate. Afterward, we all went for hot chocolate, and I remember thinking, this is the man I will marry. Seriously, I was already thirty and I knew what I wanted. Luke was soft-spoken, earnest, and obviously a wonderful father. I sensed without even asking that he was religious, and sure enough, he's a minister.

"Actually he's not the type I thought I was going to fall for when I came to America. I went to the university in England, and every year, there was a group of exchange students from Boulder. I was fascinated by this crowd of vivacious, outgoing people in their down jackets and hiking boots, and I was determined to go to Colorado after graduation to see if everyone was like that. When I got to Denver, I took a job in an organic-food store— I've worked up to manager—and I

did meet a lot of lively people. But in the end, it was this quiet, good-hearted man with the soul of a poet who won my heart. He had grown up in Ohio with what I've learned are Midwestern values, and he's never changed. I felt blessed. I never thought I would ever get so lucky.

"The first several years of our marriage were wonderful. Fairly quickly, we had a child of our own, Geoffrey, who's now four, and so we were the perfect little family. At the beginning, Ronnie hardly ever exercised her visitation rights and Cassie was with us much of the time, which was fine with me. I adored her. And I love being the minister's wife. I enjoyed working with all the women in the parish, getting involved in community affairs. My work there really gives me great pleasure.

"Then, when Cassie was about seven, Ronnie started intruding more and more. I imagine she had felt unable to cope with the baby, but once Cassie reached the age of reason, she wanted her back. So she'd appear unannounced on our doorstep, demanding to take the child for the weekend and then failing to bring her back in time for school the following Monday.

"Around the same time, Ronnie stopped sending her child support checks. You see, she has a great deal of family money and, in fact, she lives once again with her parents. The courts decreed that she had to pay fifty percent of Cassie's extracurricular education—music lessons, things like that—as well as for summer camp. Goodness knows, on a minister's salary we're hard pressed to give two kids everything they need, particularly since I was working only part-time until Geoffrey was three.

"But frankly, I'd forget about the money if we could just get her to leave us alone. She is like a tornado ripping through our family. And the language she uses in front of the children! I'm at a loss for what to say.

"What infuriates me most, though, is that Luke refuses to stand up to her. Ronnie will call at any hour of the day or night to rant and rave and Luke lets her go on and on. Why can't he just hang up? Who is she that she has the power to wedge herself between my husband and me? What he ever saw in such a person and why he stayed with her for seven years is beyond me. And he still coddles her and lets her get away with impossible behavior, mostly at my expense. I've had just about all I can take.

"I have a perfect right to be angry with Luke, especially since he is now taking Cassie's side and not mine whenever there's something between us. When she forgets to do one of her chores and I reprimand her, he'll say—right in front of her—that I was too harsh. This completely undermines my authority, and since I'm not even her real

mother, I've got little enough clout as it is. Of course, she's learned to play this to the hilt, saying, 'If you really loved me, you wouldn't make me do such and such.' Or she'll threaten to go and live with her mother. I try so hard and this is the thanks I get? I feel like the wicked stepmother much of the time. But I just don't know how to handle her.

"I'll be honest. I'm drained. I feel as though no one is there for me anymore. I try to talk to my husband about this and he walks out of the room. I'm exhausted. I work, I'm trying to bring up two children, trying to maintain my position as the minister's wife, and it seems as though everyone is berating me for one thing or another. I can't take it. Even Geoffrey is starting to talk disrespectfully, since he hears everyone else talk to me that way.

"I love Luke and the last thing I want is a divorce, but I'm having a hard time now. In England, people don't go for marriage counseling, but I simply can't cope anymore."

LUKE'S TURN

"Devon is wonderful, but she has a blind spot when it comes to my ex-wife," said Luke, a tall, bespectacled man who chooses his words carefully. "Granted, Ronnie is difficult, but I still feel I have to help her. My mother always used to say that compassion was both my vice and virtue. She probably had a point. I do feel a deep need to reach out to others, but sometimes nothing you do really helps. Ronnie is bright and pretty and has the potential to be a wonderful person. But she resists therapy, she won't attend Alcoholics Anonymous, and she won't work. Thank goodness her family is well off enough to support her. She'd be on the streets, I imagine, if she had to fend for herself. I just can't write her out of my life and forget her.

"In any case, I divorced her when Cassie was two. As you can imagine, this was not easy, but I believed it was in Cassie's best interest. It certainly wasn't a healthy environment in which to raise a child.

"Being a single father wasn't easy, but Cassie was always a delightful child and we managed with day care and baby-sitters. Then one afternoon I met Devon at the skating rink. I was captivated by this bubbly, witty Englishwoman. I was also pleased to see how well she got along with Cassie. To make a long story short, we were married six months later, with Cassie as the flower girl. My whole family flew in from Ohio and they all loved Devon.

"Before our second anniversary, we had a son of our own. Cassie experienced a bit of sibling rivalry, but basically, she loved the idea of having a baby brother. Ronnie really wasn't in the picture very much then. Our lives ran fairly smoothly.

"Then two years ago, Ronnie decided she wanted to see more of Cassie. Cassie seemed fine about it all, since her mother gave her presents and took her out to eat and never made her do any chores or finish her homework. What child wouldn't be happy? I think she actually looked forward to the days when she wasn't with someone who was always making her mind her p's and q's. Although I could see that this irritated Devon, what was I supposed to do? Ronnie is Cassie's natural mother. I can't keep them apart.

"I know the woman is impossible, but I would feel responsible if anything happened to Ronnie.

"The problem is, Devon really resents my having anything to do with Ronnie and she's taken to shouting at me, demanding that I take a stand and keep my ex at arm's length. So now I have two women yelling at me and I can't think straight. I've even gotten confrontational myself, in self-defense, and I hear myself criticizing Devon in front of the children. I'm amazed at some of the things I say. I know that's wrong, but I get so flustered, it just comes out. It's hard to get a word in edgewise with Devon. She never gives me a chance to speak. Sometimes I wonder if she even hears me.

"Look, I think that Devon and I are very right for each other. But we've gotten into a bizarre pattern of behavior that we can't break. I fervently hope you have some suggestions. I truly love my wife and don't want this marriage to end."

THE COUNSELOR'S TURN

"These lovely, articulate people were clearly in love and did not want a divorce," said the counselor. "Their problems weren't intrinsic to their relationship, but were precipitated by an external maelstrom: Luke's emotionally disturbed ex-wife. Even so, I could see immediately that Luke and Devon had two completely different communication styles, and I realized that while this was not a problem during 'peace time,' it could in fact become a serious issue when they were in conflict.

"My first goal was to instruct them on how to speak and listen effectively to one another. That way, we could all be able to talk intelligently about the Ronnie situation.

"I explained to Luke and Devon what I had observed about the way they communicate: Luke speaks slowly and thoughtfully, pausing to find just the right word, while Devon is glib and tends to speak at an impressive clip. When they talk to each other, she jumps in to fill the pauses in his sentences, supplying the word she thinks he's looking for. Usually, she's close, but not always on target. Nevertheless, this habit annoys Luke and it was time she learned to change.

"To help them better understand what I was talking about, I asked them to tape record one of their discussions at home. In the beginning, I suggested they start off discussing a nonvolatile issue. The following conversation is about the menu for an upcoming dinner party:

Luke: Not everybody on the guest list is into organic foods. Maybe we should have...

Devon: Two menus. We could do couscous and vegetables and also have a heartier dish, something with meat.

Luke: Well, yes. That's not a bad idea. But I was thinking we could have...

Devon: A buffet. That way everyone could pick what suits them. Good idea.

Luke: Yes, well, no. I mean, that is a good idea. But I was going to suggest one menu with...oh, never mind. Whatever you want.

Devon: Look, it's your party, too. I want you to have a say in this. Luke? Luke, don't leave. Fine. Okay. Fine.

"I asked them to bring the tape with them to their next session, and when we played it back, they both burst out laughing. Although recognizing a pattern is a first step in understanding it, simple recognition isn't always enough to break the pattern. I had them record a series of conversations in my office to see if they could begin to catch themselves before the conversation escalated into a heated argument. I instructed Luke to try to speak more quickly and not worry about his phrasing. And I told Devon to take a deep breath before she gave in to her desire to complete her husband's sentences.

"Once they were able to alter the way they conversed, I directed the conversation toward some of the areas of conflict. First, I had a session alone with Devon in which I asked her to think of Ronnie as a dust devil, which is a Colorado sandstorm. In this arid climate, dust devils seem to come from nowhere. You can be standing at a bus stop on a bright, clear day, when all of a sudden the sky is dark and the sand is swirling around you. But if you keep your mouth and eyes shut, the sand won't hurt you. Within minutes, the dust devil will have been spent and the sun will again shine.

"Devon loved this metaphor. At our next session, she reported that she had been able to withstand a typical Ronnie scene, simply by keeping her mouth and eyes shut and not jumping into the fray. 'She is basically harmless and temporary, if I don't make things worse,' admitted Devon. She also reported that, for the first time, she had a sense that even Cassie thought her mother's reaction was out of line. 'Later that same evening, Cassie actually came and asked me what I thought of an English assignment she had written,' Devon said. 'She'd never done that before.'

"As Devon told me the story, the subject of her sister Amy surfaced again and we were able to relate the loss of Amy to the loss, years later, of the little girl Cassie had been when Devon first started mothering her. This was a painful reminder of a childhood event that Devon had never fully worked through, largely because of her parents' extremely reserved emotional style. Once she was able to discuss this openly, Devon was also able to accept Cassie as a child who was torn by the divorce of her parents. I also pointed out that it was perfectly normal for nine-year-old girls on the verge of adolescence to have mini outbursts, especially with their mothers or a mother figure. 'She is probably dealing with her own feelings of separation and growing up,' I told Devon and Luke. 'She has to rebel against you in order to figure out who she is, so try to pick your battles.'

"I also saw Luke for several sessions alone, during which I helped him confront the fact that his upbringing as well as his personal convictions and his calling as a minister were causing him to invest too much in his relationship with his ex-wife. He conceded that he needed to let go of Ronnie and to give himself fully to his children and his new wife. I also told him that he had to take a stronger role in disciplining Cassie, since Devon, as a stepparent, was often in a difficult position. He agreed.

"In time, Luke was ready to set guidelines for Ronnie: She had to give advance notice if she wanted to arrange unscheduled time to see Cassie; she was not to call after nine P.M. nor prior to eight A.M.; and she was to send the support checks or risk being taken back to court.

"Interestingly, Ronnie was very easily cowed and seemed only to need to have the rules laid down before she began to behave somewhat more reasonably.

"Devon was thrilled that Luke had finally taken a stand and that their lives had returned to a much more peaceful state—although Cassie is obviously going to have a turbulent adolescence. Still, both Devon and Luke realize that this could have been the case regardless of the family constellation, and at least they are now able to talk about the situation constructively."

PACING CONVERSATIONS SO YOUR PARTNER KNOWS YOU'RE LISTENING

Devon and Luke's problems were precipitated by an external maelstrom: Luke's ex-wife Ronnie. However, because they had two completely different communication styles, they were unable to resolve the kinds of conflicts that inevitably crop up in every marriage.

Like many husbands, Luke is not as articulate as his wife. He speaks slowly and thoughtfully and pauses to find just the right word. Devon is glib and chatters at an impressive clip. When her husband pauses, she jumps right in with the word she thinks he's searching for. Sometimes she's on target; sometimes she's not. But the habit is annoying and destroys open, honest communication.

If you and your mate fit the stereotype of talkative wife/silent husband, this exercise will help you, as it helped Devon and Luke. If a particular issue has been bothering you, jot down the points you want to make before you bring up the subject. At an appropriate time—not when you're both stressed out or about to fall asleep—state your case as concisely as possible. Then, take a deep breath and wait a few minutes to allow your spouse to think about what you've just said. You may be surprised to find that he has some valid points to make that you had never thought of—and that he might never have voiced them if you hadn't paused to give him a chance to speak up.

"MY MOTHER-IN-LAW IS THE OTHER WOMAN"

Betsy was jealous of Sam's intrusive mother. How does a wife handle a mother-in-law who won't let go?

BETSY'S TURN

"When Sam advised his mother to buy the condominium only two miles from where we live, I was so hurt I wanted to die," began thirty-one-year-old Betsy, a dental hygienist. "Deedee, as my mother-in-law insists I call her, used to live fifty miles away. Even at that distance Sam spent practically every weekend at his mother's place, struggling to solve her endless problems.

"If he isn't in the office, he's in a huddle with Deedee at the condo or on the telephone listening to her tale of woe. The other night, for example, Deedee called while we were having dinner and she and Sam yakked and yakked like a pair of teenagers going steady. Then, instead of finishing his dinner, he said he had to rush over to her condo for a very immediate consultation. Deedee's drapery samples arrived that afternoon and she needed him to come over and help her decide what color and pattern would go best with the carpeting.

"At that I blew my stack. In spite of all my good intentions, I staged a dreadful scene and he walked out the door. At the last minute he came back inside the door and invited me to come with him and vote on the drapery matter. His suggestion only made me angrier and angrier.

"Deedee treats Sam like a boyfriend instead of like a grown man with a wife and children of his own. Everybody notices the way she clings to him in public. I can't help being jealous of the influence she wields over Sam, the way he puts her first in everything, regardless of my feelings.

"Anyway, when he marched out the door, I screamed that I didn't ever want him to come home again, which I didn't really mean, of course. It was after midnight when he did return, pale and tense from our emotional scene earlier. I was so glad he was home I longed to open my arms to him. I couldn't do it, though. I was still too deeply wounded by his rejection of me.

"Indeed, when he made a somewhat timid sexual approach, no doubt meant as an apology, my pent-up hurt and frustration exploded into rage. I shoved him out of our bed. Then I screamed at him to run over to the condo, climb into his mother's bed, and stay out of mine forever and ever.

"Sam and I haven't made love since that night, six months ago. He sleeps in the den, stays late at his office, and, although he hasn't said so and I haven't inquired, I imagine he stays over at his mother's condo sometimes.

"Frankly, I'm afraid to bring the subject up. I'm just not a sane person when it comes to any discussion of my mother-in-law. Just thinking of her hold on Sam drives me up the wall. It scares the children, and Sam and I get absolutely nowhere. He walks away without a word. Needless to say, we weren't always this way.

"When I met Sam, eight years ago, I knew he was right for me. My mother had always told me I was too ugly to catch a man, but at the same time she'd tell me that I ought to get married like other girls my age. Her criticism made me miserable, but Sam made me feel good about myself.

"We dated just three months before our marriage. To my secret relief, the honeymoon went just fine. Both of us were sexually inexperienced—but Sam had done a lot of reading on the subject.

"Anyway, I was satisfied and so, I think, was Sam. Sex really isn't a big thing in our marriage. Actually, since Sam has been sleeping elsewhere, I haven't missed lovemaking a bit. I have, however, desperately missed the companionship and affection he's now showering on Deedee.

"In the beginning of our marriage, I wasn't particularly upset or disturbed by Sam's mother, although I couldn't understand for the life of me why she and his sister Ann were forever hugging and kissing him—my family doesn't hug and kiss except on special occasions. Perhaps I was too busy putting Sam through school to be worried about Deedee.

"Everything changed, however, when Sam's father ran off with his secretary. It's my opinion that Deedee tried to replace her husband with mine. Until then I was unaware of her helplessness (she can't even write a check), her inappropriate clothes, her coyness with her own son. Nowadays, I can think of nothing else.

"I consider Deedee, my mother-in-law; my rival—the other woman in my life. I feel that she has stolen Sam's love from me and robbed my children of their father. Because of her, I have turned into the very kind of woman I can't stand—suspicious, nasty, hysterical, and filled with hatred. I hate Deedee. I hate Sam. I hate myself. Unless he breaks away from his mother, puts her out of his life, and shares my life again, I think divorce is the only answer."

SAM'S TURN

"I don't want a divorce, but I won't oppose Betsy if she insists upon one," began thirty-two-year-old Sam, a tall, thin man, wearing horn-rimmed glasses.

"Our kids would probably be better off if we were permanently separated. Our home is a battleground. The tension affects each and every one of us. Our two-year-old whines all the time and six-year-old Tommy has eczema, which the pediatrician says is emotionally triggered. Of course, Betsy blames our unhappiness, our fights—even the family's health—on my poor mother. It's become an obsession with her. She hurls insults at Mom and at me that I'm ashamed to repeat—irrational, unbelievable stuff.

"She screams that Mom, who's sixty-five years old, is a common tramp, out to seduce me. Then she yells that I love Mom more than I love her and the kids.

"I've tried to dispel her lunatic fantasies and to explain that there are different kinds of love. I love my mother one way. I love my children another way. And at one time I loved Betsy more than anyone in the world.

"Without Betsy's encouragement and hard work during our first year of marriage, I would never have become an engineer. She made me believe in myself, something I desperately needed.

"My father was a successful inventor, a near genius, and he was convinced that I was an idiot son. No school marks I earned were ever high enough, no award of mine ever impressed him. My mother, sister, and I lived in terror of him. He heaped sarcasm and contempt on us all.

"When he took off six years ago, I expected Mom to be relieved. Instead, she fell apart as though her meager supply of strength had disappeared with my father and his secretary.

"Sammy had arrived by this time and Betsy and I were completely absorbed with the new and wonderful joys of parenthood. For a while, I hoped little Sammy would draw us all together as one big happy family. Mom was delighted at being a grandmother and buried Sammy in all kinds gifts. That's when the trouble started.

"Betsy's mother sent nothing for Sammy, not even a card. I think the contrast between the two mothers hurt Betsy, so she took it out on Mom. To soothe things, I told Mom to restrain her generosity, which naturally upset her. From that day on, I've been torn between my mother and my wife.

"Since Betsy never sees her own family and couldn't care less about them, she thinks I should feel the same way about mine. She has no compassion for a lonely old lady who has only one person in the world to love.

"I admit the idea of the condominium was mine. I thought Betsy might soften and help Mom find new friends and interests in this new environment. But I can't even call my mother without Betsy making an ugly scene. Mom knows how she feels—it's pretty obvious to everyone—and is as scared of Betsy as she used to be of my father.

"Betsy insists she loves me, but that's hard to believe. In fact, I sometimes wonder whether she ever loved me. Not once in our eight years together has she ever initiated lovemaking.

"Betsy forced me from her bed six months ago and I'm not about to force my way back. Nor am I going to abandon my responsibility to my mother. Either Betsy and I agree on a compromise or we agree on terms of a divorce."

THE COUNSELOR'S TURN

"Betsy and Sam held such contrasting views of his mother," the counselor said, "that it was impossible to discover the objective truth. At one session of group counseling they attended, their descriptions of Deedee were so contradictory that members of the group thought they were discussing two different women!

"Rather than waste energy on arguments about Deedee, I strongly urged Betsy and Sam to concentrate on understanding each other. After all, they couldn't change the older woman but they could try to change themselves and their marriage.

"Both Betsy and Sam had been

scarred by very unhappy childhoods. Years of strife with her ungiving, unloving mother, whom she resembled in many respects, left Betsy with a poor self-image, no self-esteem. Attractive to everyone except herself, she didn't feel self-confident or secure, and reassurances from Sam didn't help.

"She regarded her marriage as a stroke of miraculous luck and was ever fearful of losing her prize. As soon as she sensed a threat—imagined or real—from Sam's mother, she reacted as she had reacted long ago to her critical mother. She threw a tantrum.

"Sam was appalled. Instead of fighting back, he withdrew in silence—a childhood maneuver he had used to deal with his formidable father. His passivity fed the fires of Betsy's jealousy and rage.

"Betsy was engaged in a no-win contest and she knew it. Nevertheless, she seemed unable to stop herself from destroying herself and her marriage.

"Loath to talk about sex, Betsy mistakenly believed that she behaved like the average wife. I told her in plain words that Sam needed proof of her expressed love—sexual proof. Since he refused to approach her and risk a rebuff as in the past, it was up to her to make amends. For the first time, Betsy took the initiative in lovemaking. She tiptoed to Sam's den and quietly and tenderly embraced him.

The result was predictable.

"With the resumption of their sexual relationship, the marriage improved—but not nearly enough. Although Betsy tried very hard to control her angry outbursts, or so she said, she made little progress. The habit was too deeply entrenched. And, as I pointed out to Sam, his retreats from the domestic battlefield weren't helping Betsy gain self-control.

"It was time to take a firm stand. The next time Betsy threw a tantrum, Sam followed my directions, tailored for this particular case. He grabbed his screaming, kicking, foot-stamping wife, shoved her out the door—no easy task, he told me later—and locked it. She raged on for a while, but he wouldn't let her back in until she was quiet.

"This sharp change in response to unreasonable behavior was eventually effective. After several episodes, Betsy learned to manage her temper and hysterics. In time, her obsessive hatred of her mother-in-law faded too.

"Sam now sees his mother perhaps once a week, and Betsy occasionally accompanies him. They often take the children along, and sometimes—at Betsy's request—Deedee baby-sits. Recently she entertained her grandchildren over a long weekend. Sam and Betsy were at a ski resort, treating themselves to a second honeymoon."

TAMING THE FURIES: HOW TO BLOCK INTERFERENCE FROM OTHERS

Everyone has a mother-in-law story, and while Betsy's reaction to Sam's mother was certainly extreme, it's one that many can identify with. Many of us carry ancient animosities that drive a wedge between ourselves, our spouses, and other family members. It may never be possible to develop love and affection for our in-laws, but we can, in time, learn to tolerate their attitudes and behavior.

If in-laws are manipulating or interfering in your relationship, it's critical that both spouses recognize the divisive influence of others. Refuse to be used as weapons in someone else's war and learn to work as a team. This advice can also help you attain a more harmonious relationship with your spouse's parents:

1. Try to maintain personal and direct contact with in-laws if possible, instead of relying on a spouse as a go-between. Don't expect instant love and affection; expect, instead, to build a relationship as you would with any person you meet. Also, by establishing an open, honest, and direct relationship in the beginning, you may well avoid common divide-and-conquer in-law problems, in which one spouse is played against another—and everyone loses.

2. Think of your in-laws as people— separate from the role they play in your lives. What are their interests and strengths? Get them to talk about them and share their enthusiasm.

3. Ask for their advice and opinions once in a while. Everyone needs to feel needed. While you should make it clear that you're confident you can make your own decisions, consider their opinion as you would a friend's or other advisor's.

4. Don't blame an in-law for problems you're having with your spouse. In this case, Betsy and Sam had many other issues to resolve that had nothing to do with Deedee. She was, however, an easy target for her daughter-in-law's rage.

"HE'S A SUPER DAD, BUT AN AWFUL HUSBAND"

Jeannie yearned for Joe's attention, but her daughters were getting it all. What happens when the kids always come first?

JEANNIE'S TURN

"I have friends who complain that their husbands don't spend enough time with their kids," said Jeannie, thirty-nine, a small, fine-featured woman with long honey-colored hair. "But with us, it's just the opposite. Kim, fifteen, and Sally, fourteen, monopolize Joe's attention. It's as if I don't even exist. Lately, we're either fighting all the time about the girls or we're simply not speaking to each other.

"Joe was always the most loving, giving person. We met on a ski slope seventeen years ago—I had careened off course, landed in a snowbank, and badly twisted my ankle. Joe, who had been skiing right behind me, raced over to help. We started dating soon after that, and before long, I had fallen madly and deeply in love.

"Joe is nine years older than I, a professional singer whose voice you hear on many radio and TV commercials. I had never met anyone so fascinating; he introduced me to music, books, poetry, foreign films—being with him was always so stimulating, I was miserable when we were apart.

"Even though I was very busy with classes—I had almost completed my M.B.A. in accounting—Joe and I still managed to see each other often. One night, after he picked me up at the library where I was studying, we stopped for a snack at a McDonald's close to campus. When I opened my Big Mac container, I found a beautiful diamond ring inside!

"We were married the following summer. From my side only my parents and grandmother attended the wedding, but Joe had dozens of sisters and brothers, cousins and nieces, all joking around with him and having a great time. Joe's parents had been poor and his father was often away searching for work. But obviously, those kids had formed their own close-knit family.

"My own father was a lawyer—a true workaholic who used to stay at his office well past seven o'clock every night. And my mother, always in the kitchen or busy with something around the house, never seemed to welcome my help or even my company. Usually she'd tell me brusquely, 'Go study.'

"So I did; I worked hard throughout school, and Joe was one of the first men I had dated who seemed to understand my commitment to my work.

"After we were married, we moved into a small apartment near campus, and for the first few months, our life was just as I had hoped and envisioned. The only sore point was that I never really felt a part of Joe's family, and I suppose I resented the fact that they all felt free to call on him at any time

for just about everything. Being second place in Joe's life hurt a lot, but whenever I felt bad, I simply buried myself in my work.

"We had been married just a little more than two years when I discovered I was pregnant. Joe was absolutely thrilled, and although I was a bit nervous, I felt very grown-up and important as a mother-to-be.

"I wanted so much to be a good mother, a perfect mother, but I have to admit that when the baby arrived, it was Joe, not I, who turned into Super Parent. In fact, I felt inadequate. I adored Kim, but by that time I had completed my master's degree and started my career as an associate at one of the Big Eight accounting firms in the city—a dream job. When I got home from the office each day—usually around seven o'clock—I was often so tired I could barely see straight.

"When Sally was born about a year later, though, the pressure at work really escalated. I was all the more grateful that Joe was such a terrific father. In fact, over the years, Joe was always there to fill in the blanks, introducing the girls to all sorts of exciting activities and interests just as he had done for me the years before.

"The problem is, it's gone too far. Now that I've reached a level of achievement at work that allows me to take a breather, I see Joe is too indulgent—to the point of not disciplining the girls at all. And quite frankly, when I look at my two girls—trying to dress like Madonna with teased hair, barely-there midriff tops, and tight skirts—I'm terrified they're turning into wild tramps.

"Even their fascination with music, which initially pleased me very much, has gotten way out of hand. They are positively addicted to MTV—they do their homework in front of the television and venture downstairs only to eat. When I tell Joe I'm afraid the girls' grades will start slipping, he either dismisses my comments quickly or tells me that they're just going through a harmless stage so I should quit worrying.

"Last year, Kim and Sally kept hounding us for their own television. Without consulting me, Joe went and bought them their own set for Christmas, and even hooked up the cable in their room! I was livid and demanded that the girls at least assume more chores around the house to earn their new privilege. Joe finally agreed to that—but of course, my efforts turned out to be a farce.

"The Prince concert last year was the final straw for me. The girls had begged to attend, but I had heard plenty of reports that it was going to be a very wild scene.

"Instead of taking my no as their final answer, they called Joe at the recording studio and asked him.

You'd think he'd have backed me up on something as important as this, but no, Joe actually stopped off at the box office on his way home from work, found out the concert was sold out, and paid scalpers $100 each for three tickets, volunteering to take the girls to the concert himself.

"I don't want to have to compete with the girls for Joe's attention. Last week, when I suggested we go for a drive after dinner—just the two of us—he said 'Great idea.' But, when we told the girls we were going out and Sally asked if she could go, too, Joe said yes. Doesn't he enjoy being alone with me at all anymore?

"Right now, I don't know what to do. I don't want my children to think I'm an ogre, but I also don't want them to grow up to be self-centered and spoiled.

"I've actually thought of packing up and moving out with the girls—my work load is much more manageable now, and perhaps that's the only way to get my daughters back on track."

JOE'S TURN

"With Jeannie, I always feel as if I'm between a rock and a hard place," said Joe, forty-eight, a tall, rugged-looking man with warm blue eyes. "I've loved Jeannie since the day I yanked her out of that snowbank, but I can't seem to get that through her head. And just because I want to give my kids the best of everything, she thinks my feelings for her have changed.

"Jeannie is right about one thing, though—lately I really don't enjoy being with her. Her constant complaining about Kim and Sally and her insisting that I'm a bad parent because I don't discipline the kids enough are driving me nuts. I know we must come to some agreement about the girls, but as far as I'm concerned, she is much too harsh on them.

"One day Jeannie will go on a rampage because the girls haven't cleaned up their room as they had promised they would; the next day she'll complain about the way the girls dress. For Pete's sake, has she opened her eyes lately? All the kids dress like that—and besides, before you know it, they'll be into something else, some other fad. Has it been so long since Jeannie was young herself?

"Jeannie has been getting so uptight. I often feel I have to protect the kids from her martial law. I just don't think our kids are that irresponsible. But Jeannie can't let up on this discipline bit.

"She still complains—constantly, I might add—about the television I bought Kim and Sally last year for Christmas. What more can I say about that darned TV set? Kim and Sally are two smart kids, and they continue to bring home good report cards.

"Jeannie thinks they spend all their time glued to the TV—I know they don't. She's not home as much as I am. What's more, she insisted that the girls practically scrub floors like Cinderella to earn their television. Jeannie told me that her mother and father were never very warm or giving when she was growing up. If that's true, you'd think she'd bend over backward to be just the opposite with her own daughters.

"My dad disappointed me so many times, I swore I would never be that way to my own kids. I want to be there for my children in every way possible. Isn't that how a mature, loving parent should be? Parents have got to give of themselves. So what if Sally comes for a ride with us; after all, Jeannie and I can talk anytime.

"I think Jeannie's the one who's been acting self-centered lately. In fact, she has always had a tendency to want things her own way.

"When we first met, she was very perky and charming—but only for as long as she had my full, undivided attention. If a niece or cousin called, for example, and asked me to do something, Jeannie would immediately become clingy and wistful.

"I think that's what's happening now, too. Of course, we have wonderful times together, and if we lived on some desert island, we could spend every second being alone. But we don't and I can't understand her resentment. I love my wife and I want to be a good husband. But does that mean I can't be a good parent, too?"

THE COUNSELOR'S TURN

"Joe and Jeannie were caught in a vicious circle," the counselor said. "The more Jeannie said no to Kim and Sally, the more Joe said yes—and the girls were taking full advantage of the situation.

"This was happening in part because Jeannie was jealous of her own children—a common feeling for a woman with very low self-esteem—but there were other factors aggravating the situation, among them, Joe's failure to recognize that he was not giving his wife the emotional support she needed and unquestionably deserved.

"Our first task in counseling was to help Jeannie and Joe come to some agreement about the raising of their children. During one of our first sessions, I pointed out to Joe that, although it was normal for mother-daughter conflicts to arise when a daughter reaches puberty, he was actually intensifying the battles each time he stepped in the middle. By doing so, he reduced Jeannie's status from being parent to being one of the girls. I stressed the need for Jeannie and Joe to discuss all potential conflicts in pri-

vate and to agree to back each other up in front of the children.

"Joe insisted that any tendency he had to overindulge the girls was in response to Jeannie's rigidity, but I asked him to take a look at the factors in his background that might also account for his attitudes and behavior.

"For example, Joe had come from a large and affectionate family, but while there were lots of children to play with, he had always felt a keen and secret sense of deprivation because his father was never there for him.

"Joe vowed to treat his children differently, a plan that made it difficult for him to see Jeannie, or himself, for that matter, as having any legitimate emotional or psychological needs. It took him a while to truly understand that adults, like children, have emotional needs too . . . that both he and Jeannie had a right to set some priorities that had nothing to do with their daughters.

"When Joe finally realized this, he was ready to work with Jeannie to create some rules that would make both of them feel comfortable as parents. First, when a problem arose with one of the girls, I suggested to Jeannie that she say, 'Why don't you ask your father?' instead of automatically saying no to them. That way, Joe would see first hand just how often, and to what extent, the girls were making demands, and he would then have to use his judgment about setting rules. What's more, Jeannie wouldn't always be the bad guy.

"Much to Jeannie's surprise and relief, Joe agreed to set some limits on the amount of television the girls could watch. Together, they decided to allow one and a half hours of television—either MTV or some other program—each weekday night, but only after the girls had completed their homework assignments.

"They both informed Kim and Sally of the new rules for watching television and predictably there was a fuss. However, once the girls realized that both Joe and Jeannie were standing firm on the matter, their rebellion became more muted and, sooner than Joe and Jeannie would have imagined, ceased entirely.

"Our next step was to take a closer look at Jeannie's problems. For an adult, Jeannie was a very emotionally needy person. Her parents had been so cold and rejecting that she had grown up with an almost insatiable longing to be loved. She married Joe, an older man who seemed like a wonderful caretaker—and he was, but not to her. As a result, Jeannie panicked when her daughters, in adolescence, began to fight her on many fronts.

"I told Jeannie that it was absolutely essential for her to start sharing time with Kim and Sally, to juggle her work schedule so she could spend time and plan special activities with them. Even if the planned activity didn't seem to be going well, Jeannie was not to retreat into work.

"I also thought it would be helpful to see Kim and Sally, and the four sessions we had were indeed productive. I invited them to look at their mother not as a parent but as a person—one who had not been treated very lovingly herself as a child but who loved her daughters greatly and wanted them to love her, too.

"The results of these simple steps were very positive. Within several weeks, Jeannie told me she and the girls actually looked forward to being together. Jeannie was also pleased that Kim and Sally seemed more willing to listen to her and not so quick to run to Joe for everything. Though she is still not delighted with their current style of dress, Jeannie finds it easier to relax about it because she is happier with herself and more confident in her relationship with Joe as well as the girls.

"Joe and Jeannie stopped coming to counseling sessions about four months ago, but we still speak occasionally by phone. Jeannie recently called to tell me that she and Joe had planned a week's vacation out West to go skiing: 'And this time, I know I'm on course,' she said with a laugh."

PARENTING—EVEN TEENAGERS— AS PARTNERS

As this case illustrates, disciplining the kids can trigger battles as fierce as money fights. Jeannie and Joe are making things worse: Instead of talking reasonably about their differences they're arguing, loudly, about them. And they're doing so in front of their children who, like all kids, are savvy enough to manipulate the situation to their own advantage.

Also, although she's expressing it the wrong way, Jeannie has a point: Parents have every right to have their emotional needs met, and if that means setting priorities that have nothing to do with the children, so be it. To make up for his own emotionally barren childhood, Joe is giving to his daughters at the expense of his wife. Jeannie deserves more.

Of course, this couple's immediate problem—disciplining teenagers—can bring out the worst in any parent. These guidelines can make it a little easier:

1. Expect a teen to be moody, sulky, and short-tempered and remind yourself that this behavior often has nothing to do with you. Although you may be the target of their unhappiness, you're not the cause. And you're not responsible for making their world rosier, either. Give them time to work things out themselves. Despite their grousing, even teens want to know that there are guidelines and that you're there for them when they need you.

2. Listen, but don't lecture or judge, if teens come to you with a problem. That doesn't mean you have to condone rude or disrespectful behavior. Explain what you will tolerate and accept, listen while they express their feelings, then compromise until you reach an agreement you can still live with.

3. If punishment is in order, make sure both parents agree to it and that it fits the crime. Consequences for missing a curfew or failing to do a homework assignment should be logical. Grounding or taking away the car keys for a week makes sense; doing so for six months doesn't.

"My Terrible Past Is Destroying Our Future"

Richard yearned to help Jill, but first she had to tell him the dark secret she couldn't face or forget. What happens when a couple can't talk about a serious problem?

RICHARD'S TURN

"Personally, I don't feel there's anything all that wrong with our marriage," began Richard, thirty-six, an attractive, curly-haired man with an easygoing manner. "I'm just here to humor Jill.

"Jill's a great pal, but she expects too much of everybody, especially herself. She's so uptight that she can't relax enough to enjoy either our sex life or our kids. Now she says she's under so much pressure we may have to end our marriage. That's ridiculous! I know she needs me more than she realizes. She may be the super-achieving career woman, but I'm the shoulder she leans on when the workday's over.

"I grew up in a warm, affectionate family where there was always a lot of horseplay and kidding around. Both my parents were professionals, and my sister and I had just about anything we wanted. My parents always took it for granted that I'd go to college, but at nineteen I got my girlfriend pregnant and had to marry her. Then, like a couple of idiots, we slipped up all over again and had a second baby. We were just kids ourselves, and for six years we bumbled along, playing at being married. Finally, my wife and I decided to call it quits.

"I didn't really plan to marry again, but when I met Jill, I fell head over heels. She was divorced and had a baby daughter, and I must say that the thought of all that responsibility scared me. She'd had a bad first marriage, too, and was also nervous about trying it again.

"Jill's family has always been a mystery to me. Her mother writes occasionally, but we never see her. Jill says she and her half-brother, Steven, were good buddies when they were younger, but you'd never guess it now. They act like total strangers. And her dad and younger brother seem to have disowned her completely—I've never even met them. I gather there was some big family blow-up—Jill won't discuss it—and that she was hurt pretty badly. The thing is, it's way behind her now and I think she could forget it. She has a new family—me and our son, Mark, who's six, and the kids from our previous marriages.

"My kids stay with us in the summers. Jill says we can't afford such long visits, but for me they're the high point of the year. So what if we're a little crowded—it's worth it! Jill's the wage earner in our family, with drive and ambition like you wouldn't believe. Jill's doing so great that I don't have to worry about the future. Besides, she worries enough for both of us.

"The place Jill's tension shows up most is in our love life. I think sex is fun, and I'd like my wife to think so,

too. It'll never happen. She's got a cute figure, but let me make one playful remark about it and she gets so upset you'd think I'd told her she was ugly. In bed at night she's never ready for love, even if I let her know way ahead of time that I'm feeling romantic. She lies there, all huddled up and about as responsive as a stick, making apologies about how she is tired of worrying about whether Mark's going to come walking in on us. Despite ten years of marriage to me and three to her first husband, she's still scared of sex.

"I can't see why a woman with as much going for her as Jill has so many hang-ups. I love her, but I don't understand her at all. I sometimes feel as if I'm trying to put together a puzzle with an important piece missing. I want Jill to be happy in our marriage, but I don't know what to do to make her that way."

JILL'S TURN

"I've tried, but I can't bring myself to tell my husband the truth about my terrible past," began Jill, a pretty, smartly dressed woman of thirty-three, who was vice president of a public relations firm. "I had a love affair at a very young age and it was the most intense, all-consuming relationship of my life. I don't think I'll ever forget it.

"The man—or perhaps I should say 'boy' although he seemed a man to me—was my half-brother, Steven, my mother's son by a former marriage. Steven lived with his father until he was sixteen and then came to live with us. I was twelve at the time, a lonely child with few close friends and I knew nothing at all about boys. At first I was very awkward and stiff when I was around him. But his kindness, which was a total contrast to my father's angry ways, eventually dissolved my shyness. Our intimacy grew and when I was fourteen we became secret lovers.

"Our relationship was close, and very special. Steven made me feel attractive and didn't poke fun at me like my father did. I knew I could count on him. It was as if the two of us were united against the world. I used to write him love notes every day and leave them under his pillow. When I was nineteen and a sophomore in college, my younger brother discovered one of those notes and showed it to my parents. All hell broke loose and my dream world exploded in my face. My father threw Steven out of the house and I was made to feel like the filthiest creature on the face of the earth. My mother, a gentle, loving woman, was heartsick for both of us, but she was never able to stand up to my father when he was in a rage. I kept my sanity by clinging to a shred of hope that Steven would come back for me, but that was shattered a few

months later when he married someone else.

"I had never dated during high school—all my emotions were invested in Steven—but now, desperately hurt and miserable in my home situation, I grabbed at the first man who showed an interest in me. But I felt no joy when we were married. Standing there in the church after the ceremony, I asked myself, 'What in God's name have you done!' I thought I was going to be sick to my stomach.

"The marriage was a disaster. The only good thing that came out of it was the birth of my daughter. Soon after that, we were divorced, and I threw myself wholeheartedly into a new role—career woman.

"I never thought I'd remarry, but then I never expected to meet a man like Richard. Now I wonder if my second marriage may not have been as much of a mistake as my first.

"Richard and I don't seem to be able to live up to each other's expectations. I thought I was getting a life partner, not another dependent. I enjoy my job and I work hard at it, and I'm moving up in the world professionally, but our marriage isn't keeping pace. Richard's a charming, adorable man, but he has no ambition, no desire to grow and achieve. He comes from a well-to-do family and he never learned to take on responsibility. Nothing rattles him and how we live doesn't matter to him at all. Until my last raise, we were living—all six of us when his kids were here—in a tiny, two-bedroom apartment. Richard is an absolutely wonderful father, the kids worship him, but I'm the one who has to earn the money to put food in their mouths.

"On the other hand, I know that I'm letting Richard down when it comes to sex. He needs a woman who can open up and give him everything. I did that once—with Steven. I just can't seem to be able to do that again. I'm self-conscious about my body. He's always teasing me and telling me to loosen up. How can you make yourself loosen up when your body doesn't want to? It's especially impossible when the living quarters are so cramped and there are children coming out of the woodwork. Some mornings when I'm leaving for work, Richard gives me a kiss and says, take it easy today, honey. We're going to have a big date tonight. The rest of the day I'm a nervous wreck. I know he's giving me the whole day to get ready for the idea of sex, but what if I'm not ready? What if I can't have an orgasm? I feel as if I'm on trial. Richard puts too much pressure on me, and it makes me feel like a failure as a woman.

"Some women may not be meant for marriage. I'm afraid I may be one of them. If so, it's not fair to either of us to keep on living together and making each other more and more unhappy."

324

"Richard sensed that Jill was hiding something from him," the counselor said. "And what he called 'the missing piece of the puzzle' was, of course, Jill's long-term, incestuous relationship with her half-brother. Steven had come into Jill's life just as she reached puberty, a time when she was terribly vulnerable and just beginning to become aware of herself as a woman. Because they had not grown up together, Jill did not think of Steven as a brother and even managed to convince herself that someday they would be married. Their affair, shrouded as it was in secrecy and made even more exciting by the constant threat of discovery, became the foundation for Jill's feelings about sex in general—that it was something shameful, illicit, and only enjoyable if it was kept hidden.

"The exposure of the relationship, her mother's distress, her father's disgust, and what she saw as Steven's subsequent desertion and betrayal were very traumatic for Jill. Steven's rejection was internalized as 'If I were worth loving, he wouldn't have gone off and married somebody else.' Her first marriage, made on the rebound, did nothing to raise her poor opinion of herself. It was little wonder that she entered her marriage to Richard with misconceptions of what a wife's role should entail and anxiety about her ability to live up to what was expected of her.

"Richard unintentionally perpetuated her fears with his own behavior. It was one thing to have a strong, efficient, and successful wife in the work world, but in the bedroom he wanted to be the one in control. His teasing, though affectionate, reminded Jill of her father's taunts and made her unsure of herself. When Jill told him the whole story behind her feelings of sexual inadequacy, he was eager to help. He was also extremely sympathetic about her relationship with Steven, and his attitude did much to relieve Jill's guilt.

"Part of my counseling with this couple involved basic instruction on the female anatomy and lovemaking. Most women who are anxious about their sexuality know little about their own bodies, and that proved to be the case with Jill. Richard also had a great deal to learn and he had to drop the notion that a woman could prepare herself for lovemaking simply by being told it was going to occur. He also was unaware of how a woman like Jill could be affected by overcrowded home conditions and the distraction of children playing and chattering on the far side of a thin bedroom wall. The fact that the two of them were working on the problem together helped Jill relax and find more pleasure in the physical side of their relationship.

"Despite her complaints about Richard's lack of ambition, Jill, like many other strong women, had been attracted to him in the first place because of his easygoing temperament. Richard had felt no real guilt about letting his wife assume the role of principal bread winner. Examining the situation in counseling, he agreed that a more equal partnership was needed and that it was time for him to take steps toward becoming financially responsible for his family. He enrolled at the local university and is now an education major, aiming toward a career as a high school mathematics teacher.

"One thing I was able to offer Jill, during her long and painful struggle toward self-understanding, was the assurance that she was not alone with her problems. Of the women who have come to me for counseling over the years, a very high percent have been traumatized by incestuous experiences. In Jill's case, there was no abuse involved. She was a willing partner—but this is not the norm. In the majority of instances, the child is an unwilling victim, threatened with severe punishment if she reveals what has occurred.

"Jill finished her counseling six months ago. She appeared happy with herself and with her marriage. She came for help—and fortunately she's among the lucky ones."

SURVIVING THE TRAUMA

Are the victims of incest or other childhood traumas doomed to a lifetime of suffering? Studies show that the answer is no—however, physical and psychological problems may be longlasting. That's why it's critical for victims to get the help they need. Victims must be allowed to recognize and grieve for the past violence and/or trauma—as well as encouraged to release justifiable anger. Such a journey is difficult, often painful.Many find solace not only through counseling with a professional experienced in treating cases of abuse, but also in self-help groups such as Survivors of Incest Anonymous, P.O. Box 26870, Baltimore, MD 21212 (410-433-2365).

"WE CAN'T HAVE A BABY"

Cathy and Wayne dreamed of a large family, but their five-year struggle with infertility not only dashed their hopes for a child, it threatened the very existence of their marriage.

CATHY'S TURN

"Ever since I was three years old, I've wanted to be a mother," said Cathy, twenty-nine, a tall, thin woman with shoulder-length blond hair. "It's not that I didn't think anything else was important—I went to college, got my degree in accounting, and found a wonderful job in the city. I've been there seven years now and I still enjoy the work. But to me, being a mother is the most important thing in the world.

"It's kind of ironic, I suppose, because I had a terrible relationship with my own mother. She devoted herself to my father and us kids—I have three younger sisters—and used to tell me proudly how she and my father never took a vacation alone because she didn't want to leave us with a baby-sitter. She was always reminding me of the sacrifices she'd made for me, but I found her very distant, very critical. My father was just the opposite; he was an administrator with the local school district until his death two years ago, and I had a great relationship with him.

"Of course, he had certain ideas of how I should lead my life. He'd often tell me that women should stay home and raise their kids. I feel every woman has to make that choice for herself, but I know my father's message sank in.

"My parents' marriage was happy, though, and I had a typical suburban upbringing. I was the good kid who studied hard and never dreamed of rebelling. I was twelve when my youngest sister was born and I practically raised her.

"I met Wayne at work. My desk was right behind his, and we became pretty close. Wayne is five years older than I am; he'd been in the Army for several years, stationed in Europe, and was trying to earn enough to get his own place.

"Well, the friendship blossomed into romance. Our first date was New Year's Eve. A bunch of us went for a drink after work; neither Wayne nor I had plans that night and, well, the rest is history.

"Wayne was everything I had always hoped for in a man—he was smart and ambitious, yet kind. He also wanted to have a lot of children and a wife who would put aside her career and raise them. In March, on my birthday, he proposed, and we were married in June. We went to the Caribbean for two weeks and a few months later we moved into a beautiful seventy-year-old three-bedroom colonial on a small lake about an hour north of the city. We didn't know anyone there, but it was a picture-perfect town, a wonderful place to raise kids.

"We started trying to have a baby the day we got married. Having children was the focus of our married life—at least it was for me. But I just couldn't get pregnant.

"I'd read in a magazine that if you've been trying for six months and you still aren't pregnant, you should speak to your doctor. I was anxious; my gynecologist told me not to worry, but I made her promise to give me a fertility drug if in a few months I still hadn't conceived.

"Although I had no adverse reactions to the drug, I didn't get pregnant either. My gynecologist referred me to a fertility specialist. The doctors did the basic workup—they tested Wayne, too—but nothing yielded a clue. I started taking my temperature every morning and keeping a detailed chart.

"Now I feel like a laboratory specimen. My whole life revolves around my menstrual cycle. The first two weeks of the month I'm nervous but still hopeful. Then I'll get my period and sink into despair. Every time I see a baby on the street or in a commercial, my heart aches.

"I thought Wayne would be bothered by the sperm tests, but he's taken the whole thing in stride. Maybe that's why I get so upset; I want him to be more involved on an emotional level, but he's an automaton. Sex isn't fun anymore, it's business, and even that doesn't faze him.

"Meanwhile, about a year after we were married, Wayne found a better job at a small company closer to our home, and he's moving up fast. But the more involved he gets, the more oblivious he seems to what I'm going through. Wayne's sister-in-law, Kelly, said something to me at her baby shower last year that I will never forget. 'Cathy, you come stand by me,' she said. 'Maybe some of my fertility will rub off on you.' It took everything in me not to burst into tears.

"Wayne doesn't understand why I was upset. He insists I'm too sensitive and implies that I'm crazy to feel the way I do. That's why I'm so happy I joined Resolve—it's a nationwide organization of couples who can't get pregnant. We talk and share information on fertility treatments. Wayne comes with me occasionally, but he never says anything.

"I'm afraid our marriage is falling apart. Wayne is working night and day, often seven days a week. If he's working late, he rarely calls. Or he calls, says he'll be home in a hour, and then he shows up three hours later.

"When Wayne spends so little time at home, it makes me feel worthless. It would be nice if once he did something that made me feel special. He never brings me flowers or gives me a little hug. Not that he ever did, but I'm feeling particularly needy now.

"I'm also tired of spending all my evenings—and most weekends—alone. When we moved here, it didn't bother me that it was far from my friends—I knew it was the ideal place to raise kids. But now I have no babies, no friends, and no husband. I sit in front of the TV and eat.

"I know I should go out and make new friends, but how? Most of our neighbors are older and the women my age are busy with their families. All my friends at work live close to the city and it would take me an hour just to get to their homes.

"The worst is that Wayne and I hardly talk anymore. We went for a rare dinner out last week and I tried to tell him about a new fertility technique I'd read about, but he tuned me out. That happens all the time. Lately, he thinks nothing of criticizing me—my cooking is terrible, the house isn't neat enough.

"It's been five years now. I feel as if there's no purpose to my life. I've started thinking about adoption, but Wayne won't even discuss it.

"I dread getting up in the morning because the first thing I have to look forward to is that thermometer."

WAYNE'S TURN

"I'll do anything to make my wife happy," said Wayne, thirty-four, a muscular man with a neatly trimmed beard. "But this baby business has taken over our lives. I'm sick of it.

"So maybe we won't have a child—that's not the end of the world. Cathy says I don't care, that I'm not involved. That's not true. But I see myself as just a player in this game; she's the boss, the one who sets the rules. If she says tonight's the night, well then, we make love. I go to the doctors' appointments with her; I listen. If they tell me I have to ejaculate into a little plastic jar, I do it. Maybe it's my strict upbringing, or being in the Army and learning to follow orders. I just don't understand what I'm doing that's so terrible.

"I will tell you one thing: I don't feel like spending every waking moment talking about having a baby. Cathy's incapable of having a conversation about anything else. That's why I tuned out in the restaurant. I know Cathy also loves going to these Resolve meetings, but I'm not thrilled to talk about my sex life with total strangers.

"And we never do anything as a couple anymore. We used to go out to dinner or to catch a hockey game. But now Cathy refuses to do anything in the evening because it might conflict with some test she has to have, or maybe we have to make love that night because it's her fertile time. She won't even go away on a vacation—she can't bear to miss a doctor's appointment.

"Let's talk about this not-calling business. I used to call—but every time I did we'd get into a twenty-minute argument about why I had to stay late. Everyone in the office would hear me fighting with my wife. And when I do walk in the door, no matter what time it is, she starts screaming.

"What can I tell you? I love my work. I love the pressure, the challenge. It's very demanding, but it stretches me as a person every single day. How many guys these days can

honestly say that they love their job?

"I guess I got this strong work ethic from my parents. My father was a commercial fisherman and my mother was a housewife, and they instilled in me and my four brothers the importance of hard work. We had a strict Catholic upbringing: blue collar, old values. Dinner was at five on the dot every night and we ate huge Sunday dinners with all our aunts and uncles. We were close, even though no one talked very much—especially about feelings.

"If I had a problem when I was a kid, I'd never go to my father. It would embarrass him to talk about personal things. But I tell you this: I never saw my parents fight. That's why it's so hard for me now. Cathy and I fight constantly, but we never get anywhere.

"I didn't have a lot of friends when I was young. The neighbors used to call me Lone Ranger because I'd hang out by myself. I got decent grades in school and I went on to a local college, but then joined the Army. During my tour of duty, I worked in the accounting department at military headquarters and caught the accounting bug.

"After the Army, I moved back home while I looked for a job. By the time I met Cathy, I was ready to settle down. I wanted a big family, too, but if it's not meant to be, it's not meant to be. Now Cathy's on my back about adopting, but I'm not sure it's right for me.

"Look, I know how hard this is for my wife, but living with someone who is hysterical and anxious most of the time is not easy either. She's way too sensitive, takes offense too easily, and overreacts. She needs to see you more than I do. That business with my brother's wife is a perfect example. I don't know why Kelly said what she did, but I don't believe she said it to be hurtful.

"Also, if I make the slightest comment—like maybe the chicken was a little dry—my wife slams the plate down in front of me, marches upstairs, slams the door, and broods for hours. Cathy is not Susie Homemaker. My mother used to get up at five A.M. to cook my father a hot breakfast, and then she'd spend the rest of her day thinking about dinner, and never complain. Do I resent the fact that Cathy's not more like that? Yeah, sometimes, and if we're having one of our fights, I will say something to that effect.

"I know I'm not the perfect husband, but I love my wife very much. It's getting harder and harder to live with her, though. Maybe you can calm her down."

THE COUNSELOR'S TURN

"Like many couples, Cathy and Wayne placed a tremendous strain on their marriage," said the counselor. "Every problem they had was magnified by the infertility issue.

"Cathy and Wayne's inability to conceive was a blow to their egos, to their sense of themselves as a complete woman and a complete man, but they handled their disappointment in different ways. Wayne put his pain in a little compartment and insisted the whole business never really bothered him. To admit that he was having difficulty dealing with his problems would mean talking about them—something Wayne had never been able to do. His frustration and anger were manifested in other ways: He threw himself into his work, criticized his wife, and was insensitive to her feelings.

"The favorite son, Wayne had been babied by his mother most of his life. Although he maintained it didn't bother him that much that Cathy was not an ideal homemaker, his disappointment was evident, and when they fought, he hurled little insults at her. This further weakened Cathy's self-esteem. Although Wayne insisted his family was close, in reality they adhered to the trappings of closeness but not the substance.

"Cathy's struggle with infertility was more obvious than her husband's: To be a mother was her main goal in life, and her inability to reach it was devastating. Her frustration was compounded by the physical stress of having to monitor her temperature and blood counts, the surgeries and procedures she had to endure, as well as feeling

331

that her husband was unsympathetic to her unhappiness.

"Although she had never felt fully wanted or accepted by her critical mother, Cathy felt loved by her father, and she expected her husband to cherish her the way Daddy had. To some extent, her sense of self was also defined by her father's views about women's place in the home. Instead, Wayne was a closed-down guy, more like her mother than her father. Furious and disappointed at his lack of sensitivity, she bottled up her emotions.

"The biggest problem for both of them was learning to recognize and deal with their anger. We spent many sessions simply talking about this, and in time, they both learned to recognize that some of the things they did and said could be handled in less destructive ways.

"For instance, I told Wayne he had to learn to stop scapegoating Cathy, to pay attention to her feelings and respect them even if they didn't seem logical to him. 'Just because you don't feel the way she does,' I said, 'doesn't mean she's crazy.' In time, Wayne learned to listen when Cathy talked rather than immediately dismiss her as hysterical. Once she felt her husband was really listening to her, Cathy didn't feel the need to constantly repeat herself.

"Next I told Cathy she had to stop defining herself as wife or mother and start forging her own identity. Although we agreed that it's very hard to refocus the way you think about yourself, and particularly hard to meet people and find new interests when you feel so down, I insisted she push herself. She signed up for a ten-week aerobics class at the local YMCA and has started to lose the pounds she gained by overeating. She's also met other neighborhood women there, and next month she will start pottery classes on Saturdays. Over the past few months, she has become less lonely and happier with herself. As a result, she has interesting things to talk about, so their conversations are no longer one-note monologues.

"Wayne also began to realize that part of the reason he and Cathy never did things together was because he was always unavailable. I told him he had to stop putting work ahead of his marriage. Now he's making an effort to give priority to Cathy. If he does have to work late, he is more diligent about calling. I also pointed out to Cathy that Wayne can't possibly say to the minute when he is coming home, and she has tried to be reasonable. They've also agreed to reserve every Wednesday for dinner out.

"Once the hostility and tension between them eased, Cathy and Wayne were able to confront more calmly their inability to have a child. We spent several sessions discussing their feelings and fears about adoption. Finally, I said to them: 'What is more important: to be pregnant or to be a parent?' Once the issue was phrased like that, they both agreed that as much as they longed for a child of their own, it was more important to be a mother and a father. They began to face the problem more realistically and decided to pursue adoption.

"Cathy and Wayne stopped coming to see me after ten months, although Cathy visits every once in a while to touch base. Last week she told us with joy that she and Wayne hope to fly to Texas at the end of the month to adopt a baby. I'm confident that in spite of other pressures, they have finally learned to put their marriage first."

RECOGNIZING THE INFLUENCE OF OUTSIDE PRESSURES

This couple's inability to conceive is a piercing blow to their egos and is placing an enormous strain on their marriage. Cathy is dealing with the stress by obsessing about it. Wayne is withdrawing and numbing himself with work. In any marriage, outside pressures—problems at work, the illness of a friend or family member, the relationship we have with parents or siblings or, as in this case, the emotional upheavals of infertility—can strain a person's self-esteem and place extraordinary demands on a relationship. Any problems a couple may have will be magnified. It's important to first identify these stressors and then separate yourself emotionally from them. Cathy and Wayne used this technique to short-circuit their emotional response to issues and to ease the tension between them:

At a quiet moment, think about an argument you had with your spouse recently. Ask yourself: What was I really feeling when we were fighting? Was I really uncared for? Guilty? Unworthy? Can you remember having that feeling before? When? Try to isolate the events or comments that triggered your emotion and think about how it might be similar to the way you're reacting to a comment or action on your spouse's part now. Share these discoveries with your partner. The important part of this exercise is to learn how to put the brakes on your emotions before events sweep you along. Once Cathy and Wayne were able to do this, they could more calmly discuss their inability to have a child and refocus their energies on adoption.

"HE'S NOT THE MAN HE USED TO BE"

Following a freak construction accident, Ben and Kate had to come to terms with changes in their lives. Could their marriage survive this added burden?

KATE'S TURN

"I just don't know if Ben can survive this," said Kate, forty, a pale woman with dark circles under her eyes. In a voice barely above a whisper, she continued: "I mean, I know he will survive physically, but will he be just a shell of the man I used to know?

"In December 1989, Ben had a terrible accident. He was working as a pile driver, helping to reconstruct the freeway after the San Francisco earthquake. He was excited and proud to be a part of that team. We're not sure why or how it happened, but one of those huge pilings fell out of a crane and landed on top of him.

"I was at home alone doing the housework when I got the call. The nurse from the hospital said Ben was all right, but I could tell from the tone in her voice that it had to be very bad. I started shaking so hard I knew I wouldn't be able to drive, so I called Ben's mother, who lives nearby. Somehow she managed to drive me to the hospital.

"Ben's right leg and foot were crushed so badly that at first the doctors didn't think they could save them. Several vertebrae in his back were crushed, he had internal injuries, and for the first five days after the accident, he slipped in and out of consciousness. He was on morphine for the pain and even now must take a lot of medication.

"It's hard to remember what came next. Ben hated it in the hospital. So, after a month, once he was no longer in life-threatening danger, he demanded to be moved back home. The doctors reluctantly agreed to release him and he was driven home in an ambulance. We set up a hospital bed in the living room and the nurses and physical therapists were wonderful. They came regularly and taught me what I needed to know, but basically I became a full-time nurse—feeding him, washing him, changing the sheets with him still in the bed, changing his dressings, helping him go to the bathroom.

"Not only did I find myself taking care of all the household tasks, but I also had to find the strength to help the children cope with their father's injury. Ben has one son from a previous marriage who lives with us, and I have a daughter, Kristy, whom I raised on my own until I met Ben.

"To say that our lives were turned inside out is an understatement. Ben has already undergone five surgeries and the doctors anticipate more. He's two inches shorter because of the damage to his legs. He now gets around in a wheelchair and, when he's feeling better, with a cane, but he will never be the same.

"Although we'd been married only three years before the accident, our lives were full. It was as if we were still on our honeymoon. It wasn't easy blending two families, that's for sure. Ben's boy was seventeen when we were married, but my daughter was only twelve. She went through some hard times and is at the age of rebelling and acting out. Like every mother of a teenager, I'm often at my wit's end with her. Ben's accident meant even less time for Kristy.

"But, like I said, until that day, our lives were blessed and full. I met Ben through my baby brother— they'd been friends growing up, but I had never really known him back then. One night when I was feeling blue, I went over to my brother's house. Ben had just come back from a fishing trip to Idaho and he was regaling everyone with wild stories. I'd resigned myself to the fact that I'd never meet anyone to spend my life with. I was lonely, and it was a struggle to raise my daughter on a waitress's wages, but I had a history of falling in love with losers. It was easier to be on my own.

"Ben was like a breath of fresh air. We were always doing things— bowling was one of our hobbies, but mostly we loved being outdoors. We'd pile everything into the wagon and go for camping trips to the mountains. I'd always loved sports and Ben taught me how to fish and hunt. We had lots of friends who were always dropping over.

"Now I feel as if I'm telling you about someone else's life. Three months ago, we moved here to be closer to Ben's physical-rehabilitation clinic. It's much more rural than our old neighborhood and we don't know anyone. In fact, we're nearly two hours away from friends and family.

"While we seemed to pull together right after the accident, in the last few weeks we've started bickering and fighting. Ben says things I know he doesn't mean, but I'm so worn out that I can't help bursting into tears. I know he feels trapped, but I resent some of his comments. Believe me, I'm no angel and I'm not so proud of the way I've been feeling lately.

"I don't think Ben wants me to talk about this, but I have to. We've always had a very good sex life. But when he was first injured, Ben couldn't do it. And the fact that he couldn't was killing him and me, too. One of his doctors, a urologist, prescribed some shots of a medication called Prostin that Ben gives himself so he can have an erection. Once he gets the injection, everything is normal; it usually lasts about twenty minutes. But there's no spontaneity. We have to plan it.

"You know, I've always managed. My parents divorced when I was about nine; I was never very close to either of them. I never graduated from high school but I've been able to find work and support myself. I don't like feeling sorry for myself. That's not me. And I don't want to lose Ben. But I feel helpless. I'm not sleeping and I'm drinking more than I'm happy about.

"Yes. I am grateful that my husband is alive, but I'm angry too. That doesn't do anyone any good. The man I love is in unimaginable pain, and I think he's very de-

pressed, although he certainly won't admit it. One of the nurses suggested we see a counselor a few months ago and Ben got very defensive. He said we don't need it—but I think we desperately do."

BEN'S TURN

"I'm scared to death that Kate is going to leave me," said Ben, forty, a muscular, bearded man who was in obvious pain. "We had a damn good marriage. But now, I'm not much of a man. I can't even make love to my wife unless I give myself a shot. The doctors say that the nerves will regenerate and I won't be like this my whole life, but who knows? What woman would put up with that?

"I resisted this counseling for a long time, but I guess Kate is right. I hate that I'm taking so many pain pills. I'm not one to sit around and moan about my problems, but I don't know what I'm going to do with my life. I can't go back to construction work, but I'm used to hard work and making my way.

"I was born in Arizona and moved to California with my mother and younger sister after my parents divorced; I was in the fifth grade. I didn't see my dad much, but we managed. I'm still pretty close to my mother. After high school, I got a job in a food-processing plant and held a variety of positions until I moved into construction. My dream, though, had always been to be a pilot. When I was a kid, my dad had his own plane and I did a little flying with him. I guess I'll never fulfill that dream now. My medical bills are all paid through worker's compensation and each month we get something from Social Security and the union—but it's tough. We have a court case pending, which might mean a little more money. I'd feel better knowing I could support my family on my own.

"I was living the single life when I met Kate. I had dated a lot of women, but I wasn't in any hurry to settle down. I had made a big mistake the first time by getting married when I was too young to know any better. But I fell in love with Kate that night at her brother's house. She had such a strong, independent spirit. I admired a woman who could handle life on her own. Besides, she laughed at my jokes!

"I don't remember much about the accident except that when I came to, I told the doctors that I couldn't move my legs at all. That scared me to death, but in the beginning, the only thing I thought about was getting well.

"Since we moved here, it seems like everything's just gone downhill. There are some days when I break down and cry. I'm not sleeping well and I've been snapping at everyone. The kids and the dog are afraid of me. Kristy has been acting up a lot, giving her mom a real hard

time, not going to school and all. I'm sure this is affecting her too, but we can't seem to get through to her.

"I don't know what else to say. It's not easy for me to talk to a stranger about personal stuff. But I'm terrified that Kate is going to leave me. She should. I'll just be a burden her whole life."

THE COUNSELOR'S TURN

"This couple was referred to me by Ben's rehabilitation nurse, who was very concerned about the depression she was witnessing in both of them," said the counselor. "In my practice, I work with many couples who are facing one kind of trauma or another. Whether a partner has a heart attack, a debilitating disease, or a severe accident, there are some reactions and responses that others can learn from.

"I was not surprised, for example, to discover that both Kate and Ben had virtually shut down emotionally. While each admitted to crying on occasion, for the most part they buried their emotions and operated on automatic pilot. This is a common initial reaction to a crisis, when all energies must be focused simply on surviving. But the accident occurred a year and a half ago. It was time for Ben and Kate to get on with their lives.

"Despite the catastrophe, this couple had much in common and I was optimistic about their progress. They were both strong, self-reliant, take-charge people who had already weathered many storms: Each was a child of divorce; each had functioned as a single parent. It was also clear that they loved each other very much and, until the accident, had had a strong marriage.

"Kate was actually far more shut down emotionally than Ben. In order to cope with the trauma, she had shifted her role in the relationship from wife and lover to caretaker and nurse. She repressed her own emotional needs, and instead of confronting her pain in a healthy way, she was turning to alcohol.

"Ben's approach to life had always been that he could conquer whatever obstacle was thrown in his path. For the first year after his accident, he poured all his energies into his physical rehabilitation. But now, the reality and the permanence of his injuries had finally sunk in.

"Simply having an impartial third person to talk to and to sympathize and cry with was essential for them, as it is for any couple in the aftermath of a trauma. However, it took several occasions before they were able to focus their thoughts and trust me enough to reveal what they were feeling. Once they could share their feelings with me, my next goal was to encourage them to share with each other.

"Although Kate and Ben conversed on an intellectual level about

the accident, they never discussed how they felt about what happened. Neither wanted to hurt the other, as if the admission of weakness, fear, or despair would somehow impede the healing process. Kate, especially, could talk intelligently with any medical professional about her husband's surgeries, medications, and treatments. But she never allowed herself to question or feel how these treatments affected her.

"Since their sex life was an important part of their marriage, the prospect of Ben's continued impotence was devastating to them. Again, this was a topic that they both feared, and that both had talked over with me, but not with each other. I believed it was important for them to assert their commitment to each other and the relationship before we could heal wounds in the other areas. It was very moving to see Kate tell Ben, 'You're the only man I'll ever love.' Ben was truly able to hear and believe her.

"We also talked about how, for various reasons, many couples could forsake spontaneity in their sex lives, and how that lack of spontaneity didn't have to render their lovemaking less satisfying as long as the commitment was there.

"I also told them it was important to bring other people into their lives again: 'You can't do this alone and there's no reason why you should.' Kate finally agreed to look for work and has since found a part-time job working as a salesclerk in a stationery store. A sociable person, she not only gets out of the house, but she's had a chance to meet other people in the community. Like many 'survivors' of a trauma, Kate had often blamed herself and felt guilty when she allowed herself, even for a second, to think of her own needs. After several months in counseling, however, she has finally given herself permission to be angry and upset. Now, since Ben is able to care for himself more, when she begins to feel trapped and irritable, she drives to San Francisco to visit with her old friends for a few days. 'I come back refreshed,' she told me.

"Ben's sense of himself as a man was closely linked to his physical condition. He had a difficult time adjusting to the fact that he would have to make a real lifestyle change. The rehabilitation specialists assigned to his case were advising that he take some sort of desk job. This was unacceptable to Ben. I referred him to a career counselor, who administered a series of aptitude tests. Together with the counselor, Ben discussed the results of the tests and the fields that might combine his experience and his interests. Recently, he began a two-year program at a state college, studying gunsmithing —one of a handful of such programs in the country. When he graduates he will be able to work at one of the large munitions companies in the manufacture and maintenance of guns for police and sheriff departments. This is a job that blends his old love of hunting and his need to feel useful in the community.

"Kristy, Kate's daughter, had indeed gotten lost in the shuffle when the family was forced to focus on Ben's survival. The natural rebelliousness of adolescence was further fueled by her struggle to find her place in the newly blended family. She had started skipping classes and staying out past curfew with friends. I suggested that Kristy talk with a colleague of mine, a specialist in dealing with adolescents. By forging her own private relationship with this woman, as well as joining our sessions on occasion, Kristy no longer felt ignored and was better able to understand what her parents were going through. Her self-esteem and self-confidence have been bolstered, and she no longer needs to act out her feelings.

"I saw this couple regularly for a year and a half, at which point we cut back to once-a-month visits. Physically, Ben continues to improve. Just last month he underwent another operation to replace the metal rod in his leg, since it was beginning to protrude from his hip. Doctors are hopeful that this surgery will relieve the pressure on the nerves and dramatically reduce his pain. If not, he will be referred to a pain clinic in San Francisco, where specialists will help him and Kate cope with the chronic pain.

"I also suggested that Kate and Ben talk to other couples recovering from catastrophic accidents. While there are support groups for the injured, society in general tends to forget the spouses and family members of the injured, whose lives are also dramatically changed and who are often under terrible stress. Kate and Ben are not sure they're ready to take this step yet, but they've agreed to consider it later on. I'm confident they're all on the road to recovery."

GETTING BETTER ALL THE TIME: HOW COUPLES COPE WITH TRAUMA

Ben and Kate are both suffering from depression, a common reaction to a crisis. Whether a partner has a heart attack, a debilitating disease or, like Ben, a serious accident, there are some reactions and responses from which others can learn.

With all their energies focused simply on surviving, many people in crisis bury their emotions and operate on automatic pilot. Since recovery from either a trauma or severe injury can take a long time, couples just find ways to maintain hope in the face of daily frustrations. The absence of hope, doctors note, can not only lead to depression, it can actually delay the healing process. If your family has endured a crisis, keep these points in mind.

1. **Don't ignore the needs of the healthy while you're attending to the needs of the ill.** As the counselor noted, Kathy was actually more closed off emotionally than Ben. It's essential for her, and anyone else in a similar situation, to reconnect with friends and family as well as the activities that bring joy. There's no reason to go through this crisis alone. What's more, totally denying your own needs won't help your loved one get better any faster. Don't hesitate to seek professional counseling for children as well as adolescents who need help in sorting through their feelings.

2. **Set aside time to reminisce about your good times and pleasant memories:** the first time you met, your honeymoon, the births of your children. Music often helps rekindle happy memories, so play a tape you both enjoy. If possible, revisit places where good experiences occurred—a favorite restaurant, a theater, or a park. If traveling is impossible, bring in dishes from a favorite restaurant.

3. **This exercise can help you tap into residual emotional pain.** First, find a quiet place. On a sheet of paper, each of you should complete the following sentences: The most painful part of the experience for me was . . . What I needed most and was unable to receive was . . . Discuss what you've written and begin to sort through those feelings.